13TH AGE

SHARDS
OF THE
BROKEN SKY

by ASH LAW & Rob Heinsoo

DESIGNERS
ASH LAW, Rob Heinsoo

DEVELOPERS
Rob Heinsoo, Paul Fanning

EDITOR
Trisha DeFoggi

COVER
Pascal Quidault

ARTWORK
Gislaine Avila, Wagner Chrissante, Rich Longmore, Dagmara Matuszak, Jeremy McHugh, Ernanda Souza

CARTOGRAPHERS
Gill Pearce, Christina Trani, ASH LAW

ART DIRECTORS
Cat Tobin, Rob Heinsoo

PRIMEVAL INKLINGS
Greg Stolze

LAYOUT
Jen McCleary

PUBLISHERS
Cathriona Tobin, Simon Rogers

MONSTER DESIGNERS
To populate this sandbox adventure, we've drawn in monsters from many of our previously published books. If you worked on a *13th Age* book, your monster may be here!

PLAYTESTERS
Tim Baker, Caleb Shoemaker, Dave Ledvora, Marty Lund, Durkon, Kevin Robertson, and other good souls we didn't track

SPECIAL THANKS
Tim Baker, J-M DeFoggi

SYMBOLS IN DUNGEON MAPS
We use many symbols obtained via Creative Commons at: http://game-icons.net Full license at: https:// creativecommons.org /licenses/by/3.0/legalcode Full list of symbols on next page.

13TH AGE IS A FANTASY ROLEPLAYING GAME BY
Rob Heinsoo, Jonathan Tweet, Lee Moyer, & Aaron McConnell

Pelgrane Press

FIRE OPAL GAMES

www.pelgranepress.com

Creative Commons symbols from game-icons.net

Icons created by Delapouite: *bank, observatory, trumpet flag, Arabic door, rolled cloth, perspective dice six faces random, invisible, throne king, weight lifting up, pillow, 3d-stairs, cube, castle ruins.*

Icons created by Delapouite that we modified: *barricade, stone bust & 3d stairs* (combined), *amphora, lightning-dome & glass ball* (combined), *viking longhouse & viking church & congress & coliseum and great pyramid* (combined).

Icons created by Lorc: *boomerang sun, splurt, orb direction, eclipse, pointy hat, raven, dripping star, portal, anvil impact, fire zone, world, uncertainty, brain, microscope lens, scroll unfurled, mirror mirror, spyglass, circle sparks cogsplosion, lightning electron, cubes, stone block, bubbles, tower fall, castle.*

Icons created by Lorc that we modified: *mirror mirror & cracked glass* (combined), *book cover & water splash* (combined), *black hole bolas & dead eye* (combined).

Icons created by Delapouite and Lorc that we merged into one: *bed & white cat* (combined), *g-clef & lyre* (combined), *glass ball & gold shell* (combined).

Icon created by faithtoken: *minerals.*

Icon created by sbed: *falling.*

TABLE OF
CONTENTS

Introduction

When I got the chance to write this adventure I jumped at it. It is an adventure that takes the old trope of rocks-fall-everyone-dies and asks: *". . . so, what happens next?"*

Shards of the Broken Sky is a sandbox adventure. It has many unique locations and there is no "right" order in which player characters must visit them, though most have level guidelines that suggest rough sequences. The adventure's dramatic pivot-point involves a flying island dropping out of the sky, causing a multitude of magical wards to fail, and unleashing ancient evils.

A sandbox adventure is one where adventurers can go where they please, do what they want, and interact with whatever they find interesting. However, as the GM, you may want to set or discover one of the following themes for the campaign:

Investigation. *Shards of the Broken Sky* is a detective story, if you want it to be. Who caused the flying island of Vantage to fall, and why, and how? Can they be brought to justice? Should they be brought to justice?

Heroic. *Shards of the Broken Sky* is a story about rescue and heroism, if you so desire. Two villages existed under the flying island, and both have suffered. Whom do the adventurers choose to rescue? What sacrifices are they willing to make? What hard choices could they be forced into?

Survival horror. *Shards of the Broken Sky* is about survival against all odds, if you want it to be. The adventurers are—without warning or preparation—thrust into a world of danger. Will they survive? Can they survive? What dangers must they overcome so they may live another day?

Treasure. *Shards of the Broken Sky* is about personal glory and plunder, if you decide to take it in that direction. Danger, heroism, and lost treasure await—the adventure is the crucible for the player characters' legends.

Exploration. *Shards of the Broken Sky* is about ancient mystery; lost tombs, hidden treasure, and arcane knowledge—all awaiting the adventurer brave enough to raid those tombs, find the treasure, and unearth the arcana.

We present the adventure assuming you'll have the players visit the villages of Appleton and Crownhill before beginning an adventure in Vakevale; then, as you wrap up that adventure, Vantage falls from the sky. Dropping a flying death trap onto everything is more meaningful if the adventurers have completed quests in the area and gotten to know a few NPCs and a village or two. It also gives them people and places to save and protect.

However, this doesn't have to be the order of events. You could bring Vantage down in the very first act, dropping a dungeon onto the party with no warning.

Of course, any of the adventures in this book can be split off and used as stand-alone pieces for your home campaign. Feel free to take things apart and remix them.

Above all, *Shards of the Broken Sky* is meant to be uniquely yours. Use what you want from this sandbox, adapt what you will, and discard what doesn't fit *your* campaign. We've supplied you with everything you need to tune the adventure to the icon relationships and backgrounds of your group's adventurers.

So, round up your players, warm up your dice, and watch out for falling cities!

ASH LAW, 2018

GETTING STARTED

Shards of the Broken Sky contains adventure material for every character level, 1st through 10th. There's only one epic dungeon and quite a bit more material for the adventurer and champion tiers. In fact, there's more than enough serious content for adventurer and champion tiers to run this campaign a couple of times for groups with different icon relationships and adventuring obsessions and avoid duplicating dungeoneering targets.

Depending on how quickly you level up characters in your campaign, it's possible that you could use *Shards of the Broken Sky* as the only adventure-source for an entire champion-tier campaign. It's been done! You'll likely want to add sessions of your own creation into the mix or borrow adventures from the battle scenes books (*High Magic & Low Cunning, The Crown Commands,* and *Fire & Faith*), or *Eyes of the Stone Thief*.

As Written

The adventurers turn up in Redfield Valley and remain there from 1st to 7th level, dealing with the apocalyptic happenings and ever-rising stakes. In this campaign, it is best that adventurers have strong ties to the valley (see *PC Ties to Redfield Valley* later in this section).

Adventurers might want to leave Redfield Valley to resupply in larger cities and then swiftly return, especially if they find a lot of treasure and want to convert it into healing potions and runes. If their return is less than swift, you can remind the players that their characters know of urgent situations in Redfield Valley that can only get worse the longer they go unresolved.

As a Starting Point

The party starts in Redfield Valley, but at some point they leave to deal with the implications of or fallout from one of their adventures: perhaps to raise an army to fight against the risen serpent archons, or maybe to evacuate a city in the path of a stampede of unleashed great beasts, or even to prevent the taint of the Orcwell from spreading.

If you decide after the characters leave Redfield Valley that you'd like them to come back, unfinished business from the fall of Vantage can haunt the party in such a way that they must return, or an icon can hire them to go back and complete a mission on the icon's behalf (rescue mission, retrieve an artifact, open or seal a ward, lead others into the valley, etc.).

As Inspiration

Maybe you like one of the dungeons here but have your own idea for a campaign structure or are mid-way through another campaign. In this case, simply use parts of this adventure in your own adventure.

CHAPTERS IN SHARDS OF THE BROKEN SKY

CHAPTER 1: REDFIELD VALLEY introduces Redfield Valley as a friendly village and sets the scene for your adventurers, giving them a sense of the place and perhaps something to strive to save later in the adventure. It also contains a very short introductory encounter (saving an NPC from goblins) and introduces a few icon-related NPCs you may find useful while playing through the rest of the adventures in this book.

CHAPTER 2: ADVENTURES IN THE VAKEVALE contains details of an adjoining valley, the Vakevale. If the PCs came to Redfield Valley following rumors of secret treasures, this is where they'll want to head. Until Vantage falls, the Vakevale appears to be where the action is buried. The chapter starts with a couple adventurer-tier adventures set there. Since your sandbox campaign may not be starting at 1st or 2nd level, this chapter also contains another couple of adventures for higher-level PCs. The PCs might return to the Vakevale several times, even after the fall of Vantage.

CHAPTER 3: THE FALL OF VANTAGE deals with the catastrophic destruction of Vantage, the flying island/castle/city that hovers invisibly over Redfield Valley and maintains the wards in the valley below.

The fall of Vantage is the pivotal moment in the campaign, the point at which everything changes and the story switches into high gear. This chapter ends with a variety of possible icon reactions, as well as notes about iconic missions and messengers.

CHAPTER 4: THE GLITTERFALL details the ongoing consequences of the destruction of a city-sized magical flying island. Vantage doesn't fall all at once; pieces of the flying realm rain down for weeks. The *glitterfall* is an environmental hazard and an ever-changing open-air dungeon that adventurers must navigate several times during *Shards of the Broken Sky*.

CHAPTER 5: SHATTERED SECRETS contains two dungeon-style adventures for 1st and 2nd level characters. *The Shattered Spine* is an exploration of a fallen part of Vantage; *The Lost Tomb* is a forgotten tomb uncovered by the collapsed wards.

CHAPTER 6: THUNDER & LIGHTNING consists of four adventures for 3rd and 4th level characters. *The Lightening Spires* deals with further ruins of fallen Vantage, while *The Great Beasts* introduces dinosaur-like creatures released from an ancient, time-locked area of Redfield Valley. *Redfield Rising* concerns the reappearance of an ancient, magically frozen battlefield. *The Orcwell* pivots on a dangerous, secret source of power linked to the Orc Lord.

THE SKY ROADS, an interlude between chapters, introduces the Sky Roads—invisible paths that led up to Vantage until the fall. The Sky Roads are both a decent way to get around the valley without having to deal with the worst of the *glitterfall* and a bad place to get ambushed by flying monkeys.

CHAPTER 7: LOST & FOUND contains four adventures for 5th and 6th level characters. *The Great Prism* deals with a strange artifact from Vantage that fell to earth. *Old Tusk & Magaheim* introduces a lost city—still inhabited but cut off from the outside world for several ages. *The Winding Gyre* further explores Vantage's ruins—this time, part of the flying magical city that still hangs in the sky. And *Rynth* is a lost dungeon inhabited by oozefolk—a sentient race created by a past Archmage.

CHAPTER 8: PAST & FUTURE contains two adventures for 6th and 7th level characters. *The Grand Spike* is a quest into a dangerous magical-science pyramid that fell off Vantage. *Tomb of the Serpent Archons* digs into a long-sealed tomb, a lost race, and the living demigods that now stir within the tomb.

CHAPTER 9: CROWNING SPELL contains a final, epic-level adventure: *The Tomb of the First Emperor*, which involves a dangerous descent into the First Emperor's tomb.

CHAPTER 10: NEWCOMERS introduces three new playable races. If you intend to allow players to create characters from Redfield Valley after the fall of Vantage, consider allowing them to play these "lost" races.

APPENDICES

Magical Treasures includes a couple of new magic item types unique (or at least connected) to the fall of Vantage: fading and crystal items.

Adversary Groups contains rosters of creatures and monsters devoted to enemy icons who will contest the PCs' exploration of Redfield Valley. Several pre-built battles for each group and tier make your life easier, though you'll probably want to branch out with your monsters eventually.

The *Monster Index* is a guide to the new creatures scattered throughout the book to make it easier to pull creatures for use outside Redfield Valley.

PC TIES TO REDFIELD VALLEY

If you are starting this adventure with new characters or bringing in a new character mid-way, you may want to suggest to players that they create characters from Redfield Valley or ones who have a connection to it. Here are some ideas:

This is your home.

You are the youngest child of a farming family, returning after serving a tour in the Imperial Army.

You inherited land near the village of Appleton. None of your family live here, and you need to take a census to find out who owes you rent and what your land is worth.

You fled Redfield Valley after discovering something unnatural in the Vakevale. Now you are returning with your friends to investigate and lay old fears to rest.

You left home to learn magic and are now returning from university having completed your studies. You look forward to "catching up" with some childhood bullies.

You married somebody from Crownhill and are now returning with your spouse to visit the in-laws. The rest of the adventuring party are tagging along for emotional support.

You were accused of a crime in Crownhill and fled. Your accuser died (of natural causes?) and it is now safe to return home.

You won big while gambling, and the other person couldn't pay up. . . but did own the deed to a house in Appleton. Now, you own the deed.

A relative you never knew you had left you property in a will. You have vague memories of visiting the property during your childhood.

A good friend of yours died, and you are honoring their last wish by taking their remains home to Crownhill. It is a solemn duty.

You ended up, through a series of (clever/unwise/shady) business deals, being part-owner of a bakery in the town of Appleton.

You have heard tales of lost treasure and a hidden secret somewhere near Redfield Valley, possibly in the Vakevale. You intend to make your fortune.

You once served at Vakefort and became friends with somebody from Redfield Valley.

You have a treasure map tattooed on your body, which identifies locations in or near Redfield Valley. Oddly, the map doesn't make much sense, referring to places that no one has heard of . . . at least until Vantage falls!

REFERENCES TO OTHER BOOKS

We often refer to other *13th Age* books in what follows. When we don't spell out the full name of the reference, here are some common abbreviations:

13A: *13th Age* core rulebook
13B: *13th Age Bestiary*
13B2: *13th Age Bestiary 2*
13TW: *13 True Ways*
13G: *13th Age Glorantha*
CC: *The Crown Commands*
F&F: *Fire and Faith*
HM&LC: *High Magic & Low Cunning*
SBS: *Shards of the Broken Sky*

CHAPTER I:

REDFIELD VALLEY

This chapter focuses on establishing Redfield Valley and environs as the background for low-level adventuring. Players may know that there are dramatic explosions on the way, but the players' characters don't, so their introduction to Redfield Valley happens via social interactions with its villagers, tavern-goers, and somewhat lackadaisical imperial garrison. Besides introducing Redfield Valley's villages, taverns, and fort, this chapter includes an assortment of champion-tier NPCs and agents of the icons. The PCs may encounter some of them early on in their adventures and meet others later, after Vantage falls.

The Valley: Redfield Valley is a bucolic slice of farmland, a quiet place far away from danger. This is a place where adventurers might retire because it is so supremely boring. No, boring is not the right word; it's *idyllic*.

Two towns: On the east side of the valley lies Crownhill, a village of about 500 people. Crownhill is home to sheep farmers; whose white flocks move around on the hillsides like reflections of the clouds in the sky above. Most inhabitants of Redfield Valley live outside Crownhill, in scattered crofts and freehold farms. The farmers raise a variety of crops from the rich, red clay—you'll find barley, vetches, beets, beans, flax, hemp, and hops available in the market—and almost everybody has a vegetable garden to supplement whatever they farm.

On the opposite side of the valley lies Appleton, a sheep-herding community also known for its orchards. Appleton is slightly smaller than Crownhill, but it is closer to a trade road and the buildings here are made from stone, unlike the timber buildings of Crownhill. The Red River runs through Appleton, providing power to its mill.

The fort: At the head of the valley is an old, undermanned imperial garrison: Vakefort. What the commoners find idyllic, soldiers find boring; young soldiers consider a posting to Vakefort a punishment, while veterans see it as a blessing.

Vakefort guards the narrow pass into the Vakevale, a mazelike series of narrow valleys that local tales say were once home to a monster. In truth, the guards' work at this assignment is minimal; any locals who wish to hunt in the overgrown Vakevale Wood can easily scale the long wall upon which Vakefort sits. Instead of patrolling, the guards spend their time drilling, drinking Appleton's hard cider, and marrying the locals.

Inhabitants: Most villagers in Redfield Valley are human, though there is a strong half-orc tendency. Long ago, there was a battle here; legend says an Emperor fought here, then died in another battle a couple of valleys over. The villagers believe the lingering influence of that ancient battle explains the occasional half-orc born in the valley today. Many of Vakefort's soldiers are half-orcs, and some of them marry into local families.

Almost everybody living in or near Redfield Valley remains blissfully unaware of the invisible flying island that hovers miles above the valley.

TRAVEL MONTAGE

Ask a player to describe a problem that the group encounters on the way to Redfield Valley, but not how it's solved or who solved it. Turn to the next player and tell them that their character successfully solved the problem and ask them to describe how they did so (no d20 rolls required, this is a storytelling montage). Go around the group, player by player, and build a travel montage.

Montages are a quick way to build a shared group history. Who pulled the cart out of quicksand that one time? Who prefers to bribe guards rather than pay their taxes? Who starts tavern fights? Who likes using magic to solve their problems? Who has a constant craving for gooseberry pies? A montage can build an adventuring group's history rapidly and organically.

Montages are also a good way to give the group a sense of time passing (such as being on watch, or training) or distance covered (walking cross-country, sailing in a boat, climbing a mountain), without having to make penny ante dice rolls.

THE VILLAGE OF APPLETON

The village of Appleton is built along the western ridge of Redfield Valley, where the Red River begins its rush into the valley below. It is a quarter-day's walk up a dirt path following the river to get to any road of note, and a sign at the road directs travelers to the village. The sign also states that the first drink in the Lucky Grape Tavern is free.

The village is arranged around a common green, a square plot of land where any may graze their sheep. Situated around the square are the low stone houses of the town's richest people: the tannery owner, the blacksmith, the potter, and the lens grinder. (As the PCs might or might not learn, Redfield Valley's clay becomes almost glass-like when baked at high temperatures—indeed, an unusual property—and the resultant red lenses are in high enough demand that the village can support both a potter and a lens grinder.)

The tavern is on the river side of the square. A temple, where a local priest holds services once a day, stands at the square's high point. The remaining side of the square boasts a covered market—a series of brick pillars that hold up a slate roof. Traders come to the market from outlying farms once a week to sell their

THE VAKEFORT

THE RED RIVER

APPLETON

CROWNHILL

REDFIELD VALLEY

OLD TUSK

N
W E
S

wares. The rest of the village follows the pattern of the square, with streets running parallel to the larger stone houses around the common green.

IF VANTAGE HAS FALLEN

Most of the larger houses have cellars, and if the villagers received at least some warning, they likely survived the initial fall. However, hundreds do die in the crash.

THE LUCKY GRAPE TAVERN

The Lucky Grape sits on the edge of Appleton's communal green, near the wide lazy river. If the sun is up, various cooking smells waft from the Lucky Grape's kitchen. Outside the tavern are the archery butts—straw men lined up against the tavern's side wall, most of them peppered with arrows.

The building itself is an old rambling stone structure, the remains of a fortified mill. The water wheel no longer turns, and the massive grindstone sits in the middle of the tavern floor as its central table. The locals say the mill exploded and caught fire long ago (grain dust is explosively flammable under the right conditions) and the owner, Old Mother Applyred, took to selling scrumpy (a type of very hard cider) to make ends meet. When Applyred earned enough to rebuild the mill, she chose instead to open a new mill downstream and turned the old mill into the Lucky Grape.

TAVERN STAFF

The tavern staff are well-intentioned villagers, NPCs who will likely be kind to the PCs.

Jolly Jobry—"Jolly" Jobry Applyred, a short florid man in his 50s, now owns the tavern. Though stern looking, his face splits into a wide grin whenever he sees adventurers. He knows adventurers have more gold than sense and is keen to make them happy.

Dagfried—Jolly Jobry's daughter, Dagfried Applyred, is the brains of the operation. She manages the massive brewing vats and casks in the cellars, purchases the fruit that goes into the cider, and runs the mill downstream. She has a keen sense for when a cask is about to go from cider to vinegar and throws a party whenever that happens; she figures it is better to give away cider and keep everybody happy than let the drink go bad. She uses the remnants to make a vinegar and honey drink to trade with dwarves who pass through the valley, as it keeps a long time and they seem to enjoy it.

Donny—Donny Applyred is Dagfried's son, and he works in the tavern as the cook. He keeps a stew bubbling all day and always has porridge available for hungry farmers. His mutton pie is the best within a ten day walk in any direction.

Jenny—Jenny Hosbons does odd jobs around the place: serving, sweeping, and anything else that needs doing. When not working, she can be found curled up with a book. She has a touch of magic to her and wants to learn more, but nobody in town is willing to teach her.

TAVERN PATRONS

The Lucky Grape's patrons are a somewhat shadier group, though none are what a PC would call threatening.

Hackney Mascall—A traveling priest, Hackney moves in a circuit around the countryside, casting spells and leading worship ceremonies for various Gods of Light. He always stops in to see Dagfried when traveling nearby; he was sweet on her during his youth.

Doak and Bester Lillywhite—Young brothers whose mother always gives them a few pennies to spend when they visit town from the farm to run an errand or two. Their eyes have an almost elven look to them, though their mother is human.

Tarley Akkerman, Finnik Delacot, and Tenner Fifoot—A trio of farmers who come to the Lucky Grape to engage in friendly contests and drink away their wages. All three are sweet on Jenny Hosbons, which is a point of contention between them.

Fourthman—A forgeborn who has lived in the town of Appleton for longer than anybody can remember, Fourthman takes on odd jobs, mostly hauling loads and building walls, to earn money. Fourthman refuses to kill animals, reap crops, or discuss his past before he arrived in Appleton. The massive living construct spends money frugally, preferring to give away most of what he earns to good causes. Scars and dents all over Fourthman's metal body indicate that the forgeborn's life before coming to Appleton was not peaceful.

Gurta Sitwaller—The elected magistrate of Appleton, Gurta administers taxes in the town, hauls trouble-makers to the stocks, and decides minor disputes. Her "office" is a back room in the tavern.

IF VANTAGE HAS FALLEN

The Lucky Grape has thick walls and serves as a refuge and meeting place in times of danger. Most of the NPCs listed here are likely in the tavern's large cellar, cowering among the casks of cider (many of which split and flooded the area with sticky juices). If Gurta Sitwaller survives, she'll work with Fourthman the forgeborn to rescue villagers and bring them to safety. Beman Wortt, Elspeth Woecaster, and Hackney Maskell are trying to heal those they can and give comfort to those they cannot save.

Beman Wortt—A hedge-wizard, Beman deals mostly in signs above doors to ward off evil, healing poultices, herbal restoratives, and the most minor of magics. If a chicken stops laying or the vegetables refuse to grow, he may be able to help.

Elspeth Woecaster—An elderly half-elf who settled down in Appleton, Elspeth has a loud cackle, eyes like gimlets, and no teeth. Some say that long ago in her youth she was exiled from her service in the Court of Stars. Others say she was a widely renowned warcaster who lost her magic to a dragon. Elspeth tells any tale you like if you buy her a gooseberry pie.

APPLETON MONTAGE

Ask a player to describe and name a new, minor NPC villager (a farmer, shepherd, swineherd, etc.), but not how they met the character. Turn to the next player and tell them that their character met this NPC and found them helpful; then, ask them to describe the ways in which the NPC was friendly and helpful (*no rolling needed*, this is a montage). Go around the group and build a montage for their visit to the village of Appleton.

If players get stuck, remind them that there are no wrong answers. If they decide that they met an enchanter, then the town has a local small-time enchanter. If they say he gave them a magic item, give them a one shot +1 magic whatever (in exchange for money). Don't outright crush any ideas, but do guide them away from such ideas as, "The Great Gold Worm shows up and personally gives me a +100 sword," by suggesting they may instead bump into a retired paladin who lets them train with him for a bit. The point of a montage is not to get cool stuff, but to tell a cool story and allow the players to build some of the flavor of the world.

Of course, the point of *this* montage is also to create characters the PCs want to protect... or mourn.

THE VILLAGE OF CROWNHILL

Crownhill is primarily a rural community. The village itself is a simple cluster of thatched houses on a flat-topped hill that is surrounded by an ancient, square wall. The wall is in poor repair, and a wooden fence fills a gap in it. Though the wall is now quite low (much of the stone was carted off to make other walls around fields and paddocks), it is still as wide as a house. The villagers of Crownhill do not consider the wall a defensive structure, but rather a barrier to keep sheep in and wolves out at night. They don't know who originally built the wall; in fact, they never really talk about it. Strangers who pay careful attention might find that odd.

IF VANTAGE HAS FALLEN

The village is likely destroyed entirely. The wooden houses are smashed to flinders, and the hill (an ancient barrow) has caved in here and there, pulling the ruins of houses deep into the soil and crushing any inhabitants. If anybody is next to the wall, they might survive; as the ancient stones prevent them from being flattened.

THE QUACKING GOBLIN TAVERN

At the crest of the hill sits the Quacking Goblin Tavern, a central meeting point for farmers from the surrounding countryside.

Nestled under a huge dolmen (a collection of standing stones), the Quacking Goblin Tavern is a squat wooden structure that spills out into a series of interconnected tents and cloth-roofed chambers kept warm with stoves. The tavern closes for one day each month to rearrange the tents and display new pieces of local artwork throughout them. The locals look forward to exploring the "new" tavern when it reopens.

The tavern got its name from a pickled goblin head in a jar, which the previous tavern owner purchased and displayed behind the bar for some time (the goblin had especially large lips, resembling a duck's bill). The goblin head in a jar has since become a trophy that Appleton and Crownhill compete for in their annual post-harvest, town-versus-town game of kick-ball.

Ask a player to describe and name a new, minor NPC villager (a farmer, shepherd, swineherd, etc.) the party encounters in the Quacking Goblin. Turn to the next player and tell them that their character met this NPC and caroused with them (or whatever is appropriate for the character). Then ask them to describe *how* they caroused with the NPC (*no rolling needed*, this is a montage). Go around the group and build a montage of their visit to the Quacking Goblin.

Listen carefully to what players say during montages. Use story elements they introduce later in the adventure. Take cues from what they say to help you set the tone for what they want from their gaming experience.

TAVERN PATRONS

Flay Cadbeak—The handsome Flay Cadbeak is, in fact, a fugitive from Axis named Zeller Maple who is wanted for the murder of an Axis official. He ran away after committing his crime and re-invented himself as Flay Cadbeak, a wanderer looking for work. He settled down in Crownhill and now has a family.

Wipvard Glen—The elderly Wipvard used to make intricate mechanisms, including children's toys and music boxes. His family is from Redfield Valley and he had enough wealth to retire to a small, stone cottage (with a large stone wine-cellar) just outside Crownhill.

Hislene Treis—Hislene's husbands and sons have all died or disappeared while working the land in Redfield Valley. Some whisper that she is cursed. She obeys the commands of the Gods of Light, even when it costs her to do so.

Haftrad Hardfold—Haftrad is a traveling singer, who was formerly part of a group. When his fellow musicians began robbing travelers on the road, he took a stand against them. They beat him and left him for dead, but Wipvard Glen found him and nursed him back to health.

Kitred Gload—Kitred smells like an unwashed orc, no matter what he does. The loveable oaf knows this and prefers to sit in areas of the tents with good airflow to avoid stinking up the place.

Cilla Moonwater—Cilla was in love with an adventurer who met his end near the Repository.

Sidney Bishopsgate—A tough from the slums of Axis, Sidney used his dubiously-gotten gains to retire to a nice cottage in the country.

FLAMEWEED

The tents are usually thick with flameweed smoke. Flameweed is a red-flowered weed—smoked for non-medicinal purposes—that affects the smoker's voice, causing them to cough in such a way that their voice sounds like a crackling fire. Flameweed smokers find the sound hilarious. Besides the voice alteration, the flameweed smoker also receives a rush of strength and invincibility (take a 1d8 penalty to your next skill check but gain 2d4 temporary hp that last until you lose them or until the next rest). The rush is accompanied by a desire to use this newfound "strength." Often, flameweed smokers pull muscles as they overexert themselves, and fights between flameweed smokers are quite common.

TAVERN STAFF

Gar Brisby—A half-orc who decided to settle down in Redfield Valley, Gar owns the Quacking Goblin. Gar used to be a sergeant in the Imperial Army and served at Vakefort.

Gar's children—Gar runs the tavern with the help of his adopted children—Marrie, Yenna, and Anim Brisby—whom he rescued from the edge of a far-off battlefield.

Simon Tanner—Simon and his friends manage hospitality in the tents (Simon is pledged to be married to Anim next spring).

Villager Stats

We hope these stats are unnecessary and that player characters and villagers live in harmony, never to wave pitchforks at each other.

Villager

0 level mook [HUMANOID]
Initiative: +4

Knife +4 vs. AC—4 damage

Nastier Specials

Pitchforks and torches: +2 damage, and +1 to hit if there is another villager engaged with the target.

Shortbow: The villager may make a ranged attack…
   R: Shortbow +5 vs. AC (1 nearby or faraway
    1. **target)—4 damage**

AC 16	
PD 10	**HP 6 (mook)**
MD 14	

Mook: Kill one villager mook for every 6 damage dealt to the mob.

Tough Villager/ Vakefort Soldier

2nd level mook [HUMANOID]
Initiative: +5

Axe or Sword +7 vs. AC— 5 damage

Home-team advantage: Once per fight, all villagers (or soldiers) may use the escalation die for one round, provided the GM describes some home-team advantage such as knowing the terrain better than the adventurers.

AC 18	
PD 16	**HP 9 (mook)**
MD 12	

Mook: Kill one tough villager (Vakefort soldier) mook for every 9 damage dealt to the mob.

If Vantage Has Fallen

The dolmen collapses onto the wooden shack underneath, flattening anybody inside. The network of tents that makes up the extended tavern is not only flattened, it catches fire. It is possible to find survivors here and there, pinned beneath wreckage or freed as wreckage phases in and out of reality, but the Quacking Goblin's tents are no refuge when the sky falls.

VAKEFORT

Vakefort is an imperial outpost that sits across the northern end of the valley. To the north lies the Vakevale, a mazelike collection of wooded valleys full of wild animals. To the east and west lies a pass over the Ryde mountains. The pass is the easiest way to travel through the mountains, unless you are planning to slog up and down every podunk valley along the way.

Vakefort is home to about 100 soldiers, mostly older and close to retirement. However, there are a few younger soldiers, some of whom were posted to the quiet fort as a punishment or because they were judged unsuitable for more active duty. The younger soldiers' duty is patrolling the walled entrance to the Vakevale, at which they are expert derelicts in favor of hunting or heading into Redfield Valley for a drink.

The fort was built to guard something in Vakevale; more on *that* in the *Adventures in Vakevale* chapter (page 16). The truth is, Vantage's existence makes Vakefort mostly superfluous, which may explain the lax standards at the fort. Only the commander and a couple of the older soldiers know something of Vantage and the fact that it guards other secrets in Redfield Valley.

Stats and plot ideas for Vakefort's commander, a half-orc named Merry Hosard, appear in the next section: *Icon-Related NPCs.*

If Vantage Has Fallen

The soldiers of the fort were called up to Vantage through a magic circle in the commander's chambers. It doesn't go well: they either die in the fighting that led to the fall of Vantage or during the fall itself. The only soldiers remaining are those troops who were supposed to be guarding the pass and went hunting in the Vakevale. When they return, they are surprised to see runes glowing in the watchtower—warnings of the failing wards. They are even more surprised to see the wreckage of the flying island. They have a lot of history to figure out in a hurry, and the civilians in the valley below (some of whom are the soldiers' loved ones) need rescuing.

Icon-Related NPCs

Each NPC that follows has potential connections to several icons. As agents of the icons who are more-or-less on the player characters' side, these NPCs can be useful when setting up initial campaign storylines or delivering complications associated with icon relationship advantages! If these NPCs aren't useful immediately, keep them in mind for later adventures after Vantage has fallen.

As you'll see, most of these NPCs are champion-tier characters. You can adjust the stats up or down to suit your campaign or avoid them if you have a good use for icon-related

NPCs other than combat. Obviously, if you start your campaign at 1st or 2nd level and use one of these NPCs as a villain early-on, they're likely to become a recurring villain!

At the start of each NPC entry, we list two or three possible icon-connections. Most NPCs aren't seriously related to more than one icon, but hey, PCs often have multiple icon connections, so why shouldn't NPCs?

MERRY HOSARD, HALF-ORC VAKEFORT COMMANDER

Commander Merry Hosard has been a soldier for most of his life and was born close to Redfield, so his posting at Vakefort is a semi-retirement. He's one of the few soldiers at the fort that knows about Vantage, and some of the other things Redfield Valley and the Vakevale hide, and he is responsible for ensuring such things stay hidden. He spends most of his days doing paperwork and trying to come up with new ways to keep his soldiers occupied.

However, Commander Hosard might know more than he lets on. Perhaps he works for the Archmage, sending and receiving regular high-level reports through the magic circle hidden under a rug in his chamber. A lot of the make-work Hosard assigns his troops could be cleverly disguised ward testing. He may send a squad to march the length of Redfield Valley to time how long it takes them, which provides data on distortion fields the soldiers aren't equipped to notice, just go around. Or, he might ask a squad to go count all the rocks in a field in what sounds like a punishment, but if the soldiers can find the field in the first place, then he knows the ward near that field has weakened.

Perhaps the Archmage appointed Commander Hosard to this post so the half-orc could personally watch over the old imperial tomb, making him one of the few mortals trusted with the knowledge of its exact location.

Alternatively, Hosard could be a traitor who opened the path to Vantage's destruction. Perhaps his survival, while the rest of his troops perish, is a very bad sign.

Until Vantage falls, the player characters are most likely to find Commander Hosard in his chambers at Vakefort. After Vantage falls, assuming Hosard doesn't perish with his troops, they might find him nearly anywhere duty or ambition call.

COMMANDER HOSARD

Double-strength 4th level troop [HUMANOID]
Initiative: +8

Well-used shortsword +10 vs. AC—28 damage
Miss: 10 damage.

Disciplined: Commander Hosard rolls twice for each saving roll and uses the best result.

AC	21	
PD	18	**HP 108**
MD	15	

LIENTS RECHARCHE, HIGH ELF BARD

Lients Recharche of the Opals is a high elf bard, though she doesn't carry an instrument. Instead, she "plays" a scimitar she calls Warchime that collects and plays back sounds. When she unsheathes her weapon, she can sing a duet with herself, or copy and play back sounds such as a hammer hitting an anvil.

The player characters can find Lients almost anywhere, sitting cross-legged with Warchime on her lap. The scars on her face and arms show that she has seen many battles.

The high elf is keen to engage the adventurers in conversation. Have they heard any unusual sounds? Can they bang their weapons against their shields for her? Could Warchime "listen" while they cast a spell? She seems slightly crazed, and more than a little obsessed with the ideas of battle and death (especially large-scale disasters).

She claims that she followed the Crusader's army into battle so her sword could hear their sounds, spent time in Santa Cora attempting to capture the last gasp of a dying bishop, and attended many duels in the Court of Stars.

There might be more to Lients than meets the eye. She could be a spy for the Priestess, a servant of the Elf Queen, or a crazed follower of the Crusader, whose mind has finally snapped. She could even be working for the Diabolist, attempting to bring about disasters so she can sing about them!

LIENTS RECHARCHE

Double-strength 4th level spoiler [HUMANOID]
Initiative: +10

Warchime, the acoustic scimitar +9 vs. AC (2 attacks)—12 damage, and 4 thunder damage to a different, random nearby enemy
Miss: 4 thunder damage.

C: Singing blade +9 vs. PD (1 or 2 nearby enemies)—10 psychic damage and the target is hampered (save ends)
Limited use: Only when escalation die is odd.

Kill song: Lients gains a +1 attack bonus for each nearby hampered enemy.

Highblood teleport: Once per battle, as a quick action, Lients can teleport to a nearby location she can see.

AC	19	
PD	17	**HP 110**
MD	16	

Why are there no magic item stats for Warchime? Because I like to play as though Warchime isn't all that magical. Lients' bardic magic uses Warchime as a focus. Instead of talking to herself, Lients talks with—and through—her sword. Or maybe Warchime is magical enough that it chose a single person to which it would attune, and a player character is not Lients. Alternatively, I'm obnoxiously withholding treasure from your PCs and you should present Warchime as a very basic magic sword at first, while it's sulking over saying goodbye to Lients, then ramp up its sound magic level-by-level.

IRKMA, HALF-ORC BOUNTY HUNTER

Irkma is a half-orc who was born in the valley. Unlike most of her kind, the unstable alchemy of her lineage makes her unusually attractive to humans and elves. She dresses to impress, making the most of her exotic appearance, but her fierce intelligence and dry wit are her real assets. She clearly studied as a sorceress, but also knows how to fight with a sword.

Irkma was born on a farm in Redfield Valley, though she only came into her own after leaving the valley. She has returned home after making her fortune, intending to buy either the Lucky Grape or the Quacking Goblin and settle down as a respectable member of the community. Most of her family moved away or died, but there are some who remember her as a child.

She claims she worked for the Dwarf King as a bounty hunter and in the Court of Stars as a dancer, and she owns battered dwarven armor and exotic elven gowns that might or might not prove her claims. But she's mum about where she learned magic. Because she's coming back to town to put down roots, she is very careful not to offend anybody and is quite friendly and helpful to the adventurers.

Like all the NPCs presented here, Irkma is more than she seems. Perhaps she learned her magic at the feet of the Diabolist herself, and now returns home to sacrifice the whole valley beneath a crashing flying island. . . or, she could have genuinely decided to retire from her past life. Her tale about working for the Dwarf King could be a double-bluff—perhaps she is an elite treasure-hunter still in his employ. . . after all, who would suspect that a half-orc who looks like an elf is working for the Dwarf King? She might be a spy for the Court of Stars, here to suppress information that leaks once Vantage falls. She could even be a favorite of the Orc Lord, though his affection might not be returned.

The player characters might encounter Irkma as she returns to the valley, her pack-donkey drinking from a trough in Crownhill or Appleton as she decides her next move. Or, perhaps she's already been back for some time and has set herself up in a farmhouse that once belonged to her family.

IRKMA

Double-strength 5th level wrecker [HUMANOID]

Initiative: +12

Longsword +10 vs. AC—30 damage
 Miss: 15 damage

R: Chain lightning +10 vs. PD (1 nearby or faraway enemy)
 —25 lightning damage
 Natural even hit or miss: Roll the attack again against a nearby enemy that has not already been targeted by *chain lightning* this attack.
 Limited use: Only when escalation die is 0 or even.

Dance of clubs: When Irkma hits with a melee attack she may choose to pop free OR give each enemy engaged with her a cumulative −2 attack penalty against her (lasts until the target is no longer engaged with her).

Tracker: Irkma eventually tracks down anybody she's looking for, unless it's a player character who can successfully avoid her with a DC 25 skill check!

AC	**21**	
PD	**19**	**HP 140**
MD	**17**	

GWYDDION, HALF-ELF ACTOR AND SPY

Gwyddion is a short, half-elf with a fair complexion and slight features. He's often mistaken for a young, human woman, which aids him in both his profession and his secret mission.

He is employed by a traveling troupe called the Moonflower Players, whose leading man is too obnoxious for skilled human actresses to tolerate for long. Gwyddion says he's not bothered, and perhaps he's not. He's capable of memorizing lines quickly and plays several female roles in most of the troupe's productions.

The Moonflower Players are currently camped about a half-day's walk outside the valley, fixing a broken axle on one of their wagons. They sent Gwyddion ahead to buy supplies and see if it is worth the troupe's time to stop in one of the villages.

Unless you're happy to introduce an actor whose face mirrors his soul, Gwyddion is also a spy for the icons. They recruited him long before he joined the Moonflower Players. He travels from place to place, memorizing names, faces, routes, defenses, and anything else of note and reporting back to his hidden controllers in the city of Axis. The Moonflower Players are simply the most convenient way for him to get around the empire, providing a band of misfits he can hide among.

Doubling his financial return, Gwyddion recently started taking coin from the Lich King in exchange for other reports. It is up to you to decide whether Gwyddion is a true double-agent, was corrupted by the Lich King's promises of power, or reports only carefully screened and approved disinformation crafted by his imperial controllers to the Lich King.

The player characters are most likely to meet Gwyddion on the road, walking toward either Appleton or Crownhill. Alternatively, schedule a Moonflower Players' performance for the Quacking Goblin the night everything goes down!

Gwyddion

Double-strength 4th level troop [HUMANOID]
Initiative: +8

Rapier +11 vs. AC—22 damage
Miss: 11 damage.

Sly feint: When Gwyddion misses, he gains a cumulative +1 to his next attack roll, the bonus accumulates until Gwyddion hits.

Slip into shadows: Once per battle, as a move action when the escalation die is 2+, Gwyddion can remove himself from the battle, returning at the start of his next turn in a nearby spot of his choice and dealing double damage with his first attack roll.

AC	20	
PD	14	**HP 110**
MD	18	

Rezlorkis, Dragonic Wizard

Rezlorkis is a dragonic—a humanoid dragon or a draconic humanoid, depending on your perspective. If dragonics are not a common race in your game, then Rezlorkis is even more suspicious for being highly unusual!

He dresses like a wizard, in richly embroidered robes that show he is from the city of Horizon. The party can find Rezlorkis in the first smithy they pass; he is attempting to get his walking staff re-shod, as he lost the tip of it in Redfield Valley's rich, red mud.

The dragonic wizard claims to be on a pilgrimage to his master's tower, which lies in the Vakevale. He isn't surprised that the villagers haven't heard of it, his master Grandon Halfelven keeps his tower cloaked in illusion to guard his library from jealous rivals. It is up to you how honest Rezlorkis is, and whether a Grandon Halfelven really exists in the woods of the Vakevale. Rezlorkis carries a wicked-big knife under his cloak; if he were a normal-sized person, it would be considered a sword. He also wears leather armor under his robe. Is he even a wizard? Or does multiclassing also apply to NPCs?

Rezlorkis

Double-strength 4th level caster [HUMANOID]
Initiative: +8

Shortsword +9 vs. AC—28 damage

C: Frost breath +9 vs. PD (1d3 nearby enemies)—22 cold damage
Quick use: 1/battle, as a quick action.

R: Magic missile (2 attacks, automatic hits)—7 force damage.

Shield: Once per battle when an attack hits Rezlorkis' AC or PD, the attack misses Rezlorkis, instead.

AC	20	
PD	18	**HP 108**
MD	14	

Bykki Gritsour, Burly Dwarf and Possible Thief

Bykki Gritsour is a thick-bodied dwarf, tanned and freckled from working in the sun. Her large, calloused hands reveal that she's a physical laborer. Bykki travels around the empire, trying to see all that there is to see. She'll stay in one place just long enough to earn her way to her next destination, and then she is off. Perhaps, that is all there is to Bykki. If you are using one of the other NPCs in this section as your go-to devious NPC, then it's fine to have an NPC who isn't up to special tricks.

However, she may be working for thieves associated with the Prince of Shadows—going from town to town, figuring out what is worth stealing, and scratching small thieves-signs on the corners of buildings. A week later, her accomplices come through town and steal everything that is not nailed down in one single night of burglary. Nobody would ever pin the crime on good old salt-of-the-earth Bykki Gritsour, and nobody sees the actual thieves as they rush in and out with their ill-gotten goods.

Of course, smart cookies like Gwyddion or Irkma who travel a bit themselves may have met Bykki before and may put two and two together. Rezlorkis is certainly smart enough to recognize the signs she's scratching on buildings.

Or maybe the story is even more odd. Perhaps Bykki Gritsour is a druidic saboteur. The signs that she scratches slowly change the terrain, causing weeds to reclaim fields and houses to collapse, nudging settlements back to nature. Dreams and visions led her here, but it's unlikely her druidic connections would bring Vantage down *so quickly*.

BYKKI GRITSOUR

Double-strength 3rd level blocker [HUMANOID]
Initiative: +6

Dwarven hammer +8 vs. AC—18 damage
  Miss: 6 damage.

Lucky break: Once per battle when an odd natural attack roll hits
  Bykki's PD or MD, the attack hits a nearby enemy, instead.

AC	19	
PD	16	**HP 120**
MD	16	

ELDER BECK RASHMAN, HUMAN CLERIC

Elder Beck Rashman is a priest who recently took up residency in
Appleton. He serves both Appleton and Crownhill, speaking the
words of the Gods of Light and tending to the many small shrines
that dot the landscape.

Few know that his real job is to keep an eye on the wards and
unobtrusively check their strength. His ward-related activities are
clandestine and easily explained (such as leaning sticks upright in
the middle of a field and watching them out of the corner of his
eye as he walks away, keeping careful logs of certain birds' flight
patterns, and checking rocks along a certain path to see on which
side the moss grows).

For whom he checks the wards is up to you. He could be a
priest in the Priestess' employ, carefully tending to an ancient
battlefield and preventing anything unwholesome from rising.
Or perhaps Elder Rashman works for the Emperor and reports
back to Commander Hosard at Vakefort.

The party may find Elder Rashman in the small temple in
Appleton, or in the house attached to the back of the temple, but
he has reason to be most anywhere.

ELDER BECK RASHMAN

Double-strength 5th level leader [HUMANOID]
Initiative: +9

Spear +10 vs. AC—30 damage
  Miss: 10 damage.

R: Spark of faith +10 vs. PD (1 nearby or faraway enemy)—30
  holy damage
  Natural even miss: 10 holy damage, and Elder Rashman uses
    his holy fire ability as a free action, even if it was already
    expended or used this turn!

Cure wounds: Once per battle, all Elder Rashman's mook allies do
  not follow mook mob rules when one mook dies.

Inspirational leader: Each of Elder Rashman's mook allies adds
  the number on the escalation die to their total hit points.

Holy fire: Once per battle; until the end of their next turn, all
  Elder Rashman's allies do an extra 1d8 holy damage when they
  hit with an attack.

AC	22	
PD	15	**HP 130**
MD	19	

GOBLIN KIDNAPPERS

If you're playing with 1st and 2nd level PCs, at some point during
the first few sessions the villagers of Crownhill or Appleton
come to the adventurers for help. Goblins captured a villager—
or an icon-related NPC—and are holding them for ransom. The
Vakefort soldiers are unable to locate the goblin camp in the
Vakevale, but perhaps the adventurers can?

Secretly happy to have someone competent-looking handle
the problem, the soldiers tell the villagers it's "too dangerous" to
go into the Vakevale, but they'll let the adventurers in "this one
time."

If your group is already rolling and making connections with
NPCs, you may not need to bother with this clichéd approach;
still, it can give less proactive groups a quick introduction to
combat and some easy skill rolls. If the hostage isn't an icon-
related NPC, you could use this as an opportunity to introduce
one if the PCs end up needing help against the goblins.

GOBLIN CAMP

The camp is located next to a waterfall in a forested valley, and
can only be found by following an overgrown road that seemingly
leads nowhere (this could also provide a lead-in to an adventure
in the Vakevale). It takes a DC 15 skill check to find the goblin
camp; a DC 20 check to creep up and ambush the goblins; gaining
surprise (*13th Age* core rulebook, page 164). Even if the PCs don't
gain surprise, this isn't an especially hard fight.

Treasure: It's curious that the goblins demanded ransom.
Choose a number of gold pieces that sounds crazy to villagers
and incredibly low to adventurers! Clearly, the kidnapping game
hasn't worked out for the goblins before, since they have no
treasure. An icon-related NPC, however, might be able to provide
a suitable gift to rescuers.

GOBLIN WRETCH

1st level mook [HUMANOID]

Initiative: +3

Club +5 vs. AC—5 damage

R: Shortbow +7 vs. AC—4 damage

Shifty bugger: Goblins gain a +5 bonus to disengage checks.

AC 16	
PD 14	**HP 8 (mook)**
MD 11	

Mook: Kill one goblin wretch mook for every 8 damage dealt to the mob.

GOBLIN SHAMAN

2nd level caster [HUMANOID]

Initiative: +6

Pointy spear +6 vs. AC—5 damage

R: Shaking curse, +6 vs. PD—8 damage, and until the end of the shaman's next turn, the target takes 2 damage whenever an enemy engages it or disengages from it
Natural even hit or miss: Choose another nearby enemy; it also takes the *shaking curse* engage/disengage damage until the end of the shaman's next turn.

Shifty bugger: Goblins gain a +5 bonus to disengage checks.

AC 17	
PD 12	**HP 34**
MD 16	

GOBLIN WOLFRIDER

2nd level troop [BEAST & HUMANOID]

Initiative: +5

Spear and fangs +7 vs. AC—7 damage
Natural even hit: +2 damage if at least one ally is engaged with the target.
Natural odd hit or miss: The goblin wolfrider gains a +5 bonus to disengage checks until the start of their next turn.

R: Shortbow +7 vs. AC—5 damage

AC 18	
PD 15	**HP 34**
MD 13	

GOBLIN PACKMASTER

4th level leader [BEAST & HUMANOID]

Initiative: +6

Sword and worg +10 vs. AC—7 damage
Natural even hit: + 5 damage.

Tactics: +1 to hit and +1 damage for each ally engaged with the target (maximum +4).

Packmaster: An ally can take a move action that ends with engaging an enemy
Quick use: 1/round, as a quick action.

Shifty bugger: Goblins gain a +5 bonus to disengage checks.

AC 19	
PD 16	**HP 50**
MD 16	

#/Level of PCs	Wretch	Wolfrider	Packmaster
3 x 1st level	2	2	0
4 x 1st level	3	2	0
5 x 1st level	2	3	0
6 x 1st level	4	1	1
7 x 1st level	3	2	1
3 x 2nd level	4	3	0
4 x 2nd level	3	2	1
5 x 2nd level	4	3	1
6 x 2nd level	6	4	1
7 x 2nd level	4	6	1
3 x 3rd level	3	2	1
4 x 3rd level	3	4	1
5 x 3rd level	6	5	1
6 x 3rd level	6	4	2
7 x 3rd level	6	6	2

CHAPTER 2:

ADVENTURES IN THE VAKEVALE

The Vakevale adventure "thru-line" is that the adventurers should already know, or at least strongly suspect, the Archmage is hiding *something* near Redfield Valley. Of course, suspicious minds have plenty to focus on, since Vakevale has several hidden secrets! You should drop Vantage from the sky once the PCs' adventures in the Vakevale are complete and they head back to Appleton or Crownhill to rest.

PAST ICONS' HIDDEN SECRETS

Vakefort was built to guard anything the empire wanted to hide; before Vantage took over the job, the empire hid all its secrets in the Vakevale. This is the real reason the Vakefort soldiers' orders are to stop people from going in the Vakevale. Still, Vantage's many wards allowed Vakefort's guardians to grow lax. The young soldiers who guard the entrance to the network of twisting valleys and wooded gullies don't know its true history. They believe guard-duty is make-work, and they frequently let Redfield Valley residents into the Vakevale to hunt. As often as not, guard duty amounts to hunting-in-uniform.

Here, we describe four areas hidden in the Vakevale that the PCs might encounter before or after Vantage falls. As the GM, you don't have to limit yourself to these adventure zones; you're free to cram as many interesting locations into the Vakevale as you like. Vantage's wards keep many things hidden, but the flying realm's imminent fall proves the wards are failing. The adventurers could encounter centuries-long secrets in a brief window before the fall.

We designed the first two adventure zones as potential introductory experiences—they involve skill challenges, some minor peril, and a fight. The fact that they're short and don't necessarily have full storyline implications means you can easily add encounters and complications if you like, especially if they fit the player characters' backgrounds and *uniques*. The final two adventures zones are much more dangerous and are best avoided by adventurer-tier characters.

THE LOST CITY OF DUSKVAKKE

This lost city was once home to a former icon. Now, Duskvakke is time-locked and hidden away by the Archmage's power. This area is fine for low-level PCs to explore.

THE FOREST OF THE DREAM PRINCESS

Also aimed at low-level PCs, with encounters suitable for the end of the heroic-tier. This remnant of the Dream Princess' realm hides the reality of her demise. There are several areas for adventurers to explore here.

THE REPOSITORY

A storehouse for artifacts too dangerous to leave in the hands of mortals, yet too intriguing to destroy. Over the eons, the Repository fell into disrepair and was largely forgotten. It is half warehouse of the forbidden and half contaminated dump. It's also substantially more dangerous than the first two Vakevale adventure zones, particularly if the PCs venture down to the Repository's lower levels. Groups with 2nd and 3rd level characters can enter the Repository, but its inner sections are quite obviously champion-tier environments. Other areas are dangerous no matter how high a PC's level!

THE CORPSE OF KROON

A living god, frozen in its final moment as it was about to explode. The god's corpse was stored here long ago, wrapped in illusions and wards to prevent its followers from trying to save it. Its followers are probably long dead, for what that's worth, unless you're in the mood for a strange *One Unique Thing* for one of your PCs! Appropriate for 6th-9th level PCs, though low-level PCs might manage to climb Kroon's legs.

THE LOST CITY OF DUSKVAKKE

Level range: Adventurer-tier, aimed at 1st and 2nd level, but could also work for 3rd and 4th

The Dark Jester was the masked trickster icon of a previous age. His city, Duskvakke, was a vibrant center of civilization; and his plots stretched the length and breadth of the old empire, playing both prince and pauper as puppets. When it suited him, he ruled from Harlequin Palace on the city's highest hill.

Who might have overthrown him: The Prince of Shadows, who stole his position and fame and slew him in battle. The battle was the culmination of a shadowy war that shaped an age, yet few ever knew of it.

What Vantage's wards are hiding: The city of Duskvakke, held out-of-phase with the rest of reality by the Archmage's wards. The Dark Jester's palace is in the center of the city, and its citizens are trapped in magical ice crystals. If Duskvakke ever returns, it won't be as the vibrant metropolis it once was, but a gloomy city of the dead.

Why adventurers might go looking for Duskvakke: A lost city, hidden treasure, and adventure! If that's not enough, perhaps your group includes a trickster PC from *13th Age Glorantha*—the Dark Jester would ring all a trickster's bells.

THE CITY OF DUSKVAKKE

The city of Duskvakke is stuck in time, trapped by an icon's magics and hidden away by the Archmage's power. Almost all memory of the city was suppressed, though, if it suited your campaign's icon relationship advantages, some traces may escape as the wards begin to fail.

IF VANTAGE HAS FALLEN

Duskvakke gets hit by its fair share of rubble and the *glitterfall* occurs here too, but the unused sewers and some of the sturdier buildings (like the palace) survive. Any time-frozen citizens probably unfreeze when Vantage falls, only to have Vantage fall on them!

CITY WALL

The city's outer wall is only partially frozen in time. Accordingly, it suffers the ravages of the passing centuries more than the rest of the time-locked city. The wall is overgrown with vines and the guards on the walls perished ages ago, though they are partially preserved as skeletons, slumped over their spears among the vines.

The walkway on top of the high stone wall has huge gaps in it and looks quite unstable. Anybody who walks along the wall to get a better view of the city risks their safety with uncertain footing. Each character must make a DC 15 skill check to pass safely without slipping and falling; failure causes 2d6 damage.

The lead character might notice that the vines growing over the wall are not just passively waiting for somebody to trample them. It is a DC 15 skill check to detect the animated thornyvines before they attack.

Animated thornyvines +5 vs. AC (everyone in area if lead character fails to notice them)—2d6 damage.

Treasure: Most of the guards' belongings have rusted or rotted, but one of the skeletons might have a valuable necklace around its neck.

MARKETPLACE

The once-bustling marketplace is fully under the time-lock. The people are frozen in supernaturally unbreakable blocks of ice. Most of the market goods are also sealed away, but some of the food appears to have escaped this fate; it's still fresh and unspoiled. The smells of fresh pies waft on the breeze. Baked goods, weapons, bolts of cloth, pears, bread—all are frozen in ice in the market traders' stalls.

Pie problems: If the adventurers come close to the market, it soon becomes obvious that some of the "fresh" pies are truly rotten! Inspecting the delicious-smelling pies, or even commenting on them or looking in their direction, results in an ambush attempt by pie mimics (DC 15 to avoid being *surprised*)! Pie mimics, you ask? Well, a jester created this city, remember?

A few of the goblins hiding out in the Vakevale show up during the second round of battle, attracted by the fighting and the smell of pie. If the PCs already fought goblin hostage-takers earlier in the adventure, it's your call whether there's any relationship between those kidnappers and these hungry opportunists.

Treasure: The market traders have plenty of coins lying around for the taking; the party can easily scoop up 10 gp each in loose change, maybe even up to 50 gp extra for the party if they really go looking. Otherwise, it looks like somebody already smashed open many of the market trader's boxes searching for coins. Probably more goblins....

#/Level of PCs	Pie Mimic	Prize-winning Pie Mimic	Best-In-Show Pie Mimics	Hungry Goblin Grunt
3 x 1st level	3	1	0	1
4 x 1st level	6	1	0	1
5 x 1st level	6	2	0	2
6 x 1st level	6	2	0	2
7 x 1st level	6	3	0	2
3 x 2nd level	4	1	0	2
4 x 2nd level	6	2	0	2
5 x 2nd level	4	3	1	1
6 x 2nd level	4	2	2	1
7 x 2nd level	6	3	2	1
3 x 3rd level	5	3	1	1
4 x 3rd level	5	4	1	2
5 x 3rd level	10	3	2	1
6 x 3rd level	5	4	2	3
7 x 3rd level	5	6	2	4
3 x 4th level	0	0	3	1
4 x 4th level	0	0	4	1
5 x 4th level	0	0	5	1
6 x 4th level	0	0	6	2
7 x 4th level	0	0	7	3

Pie Mimic

In Duskvakke, pie eats you.

1st level mook [CONSTRUCT]
Initiative: +2

Toothsome nip +6 vs. AC—4 damage

Magically delicious filling: When a pie mimic is reduced to 0 hp, each enemy engaged with it is vulnerable to the attacks of beasts, humanoids, and other pie mimics until taking a critical hit.

AC 17
PD 11   **HP 7 (mook)**
MD 15

Mook: Kill one pie mimic for every 7 damage dealt to the mob.

Prize-Winning Pie Mimic

This pie is larger and even more delicioust. Not that we'd recommend eating it...

1st level spoiler [CONSTRUCT]
Initiative: +2

Toothsome bite +6 vs. AC—5 damage

Ridiculously delicious filling: When a prize-winning pie mimic is hit by an attack, each enemy engaged with it is vulnerable to the attacks of beasts, humanoids, and other pie mimics until taking a critical hit.

AC 17
PD 11   **HP 25**
MD 15

BEST-IN-SHOW PIE MIMIC

This pie is larger, more delicious, and deadlier. Treat it with the respect it deserves, and it'll still try to eat you.

4th level spoiler [CONSTRUCT]
Initiative: +5

Toothsome bite +9 vs. AC—15 damage

Outrageously delicious filling: When a best-in-show pie mimic is hit by an attack, each enemy engaged with it is vulnerable to the attacks of beasts, humanoids, and other pie mimics until the end of the battle.

AC 20	
PD 14	**HP 54**
MD 18	

HUNGRY GOBLIN GRUNT

1st level troop [HUMANOID]
Initiative: +3

Club +6 vs. AC—6 damage, if the goblins and pie mimics outnumber the PCs; 4 damage if they don't.

R: Shortbow +7 vs. AC—4 damage

Shifty bugger: Goblins gain a +5 bonus to disengage checks.

AC 16	
PD 13	**HP 22**
MD 12	

THE PALACE

The Dark Jester's palace is twisted out of true—no line is completely straight, no angle exactly right. The whole thing is covered in black and white tile, though use of false perspective and confusing *trompe l'oeil*s mean actual distances and spatial relationships are hard to judge. Smoke rises from one of the chimneys.

Servants and courtiers are frozen in magical ice crystals mid-action throughout the palace. There are also signs of recent habitation: a fire burns unattended in a fireplace, and some of the furniture is broken up for firewood. It takes a DC 15 skill check to deduce that goblins were here—unless the PCs fought goblins here already, in which case it is immediately obvious.

Apart from the headache you'll get from looking at the internal décor, there isn't much of interest. The magic used to shut down the Dark Jester's power worked extremely well, and unless your player characters are fascinated by an ancient jester icon, there's not much else going on here.

However, there are more goblins sneaking up through the deceptive sightlines!

Perspective problems: First, the bad news: the first time a PC attacks an enemy that is not already engaged with them or moves to engage an enemy with whom they are not already engaged, they must roll an easy save (6+). If they fail the save, the goblin enemy wasn't where they thought; their attack misses, and they deal no damage (not even miss damage) or their move action is canceled.

Now, the good news: even though the goblin bat-riders are technically flyers, flying here in the Dark Jester's palace works just well enough to keep the bats and goblins from running into all the stuck-in-time courtiers. Thanks to weird ceilings and unpredictable physics, the flying bats are just as vulnerable to melee attacks from ground-bound PCs as their wretched companions.

Treasure: There are several goblin knick-knacks and one leftover trinket from the Dark Jester's days: a magical top that spins while someone nearby is asleep. If the PCs enjoy this battle, bring back the goblin bat cavalry later in the campaign, wound up and desperate to regain their magical top.

#/Level of PCs	Goblin Wretch	Bat Cavalry	Goblin Bat-Mage
3 x 1st level	4	1	0
4 x 1st level	8	1	0
5 x 1st level	4	1	1
6 x 1st level	3	1	2
7 x 1st level	4	2	2
3 x 2nd level	4	1	1
4 x 2nd level	8	1	1
5 x 2nd level	6	1	2
6 x 2nd level	4	2	2
7 x 2nd level	4	3	2
3 x 3rd level	10	1	1
4 x 3rd level	8	2	1
5 x 3rd level	8	2	2
6 x 3rd level	6	3	2
7 x 3rd level	8	3	3
3 x 4th level	4	2	2
4 x 4th level	4	3	2
5 x 4th level	4	4	2
6 x 4th level	4	4	4
7 x 4th level	4	5	4

GOBLIN WRETCH

1st level mook [HUMANOID]
Initiative: +3

Club +5 vs. AC—5 damage

R: Shortbow +7 vs. AC—4 damage

Shifty bugger: Goblins gain a +5 bonus to disengage checks.

AC 16
PD 14　　　　**HP 8 (mook)**
MD 11

Mook: Kill one goblin wretch mook for every 8 damage dealt to the mob.

BAT CAVALRY

One goblin warrior, one dire bat. Two bad little creatures that go great together.

Large 2nd level wrecker [BEAST & HUMANOID]
Initiative: +6
Vulnerability: thunder

Fangs, wings, and sword +8 vs. AC—Damage and effect depends on the natural roll
　Natural even hit: The target takes 10 damage from a sword strike, and the bat cavalry pops free from the target and can move as a free action.
　Natural odd hit: The target takes 8 damage, and 5 ongoing damage from bat fangs.
　Natural even miss against a target taking ongoing damage: The target takes 6 damage from clawing wings.
　Natural 2–5: In addition to any other effects, the bat cavalry pops free from the target, and can move to another nearby enemy and make a *fangs, wings, and sword* attack against them as a free action.

R: Thrown javelin +5 vs. AC—8 damage

Resist ranged damage 16+: When a ranged attack targets this creature while it's flying, the attacker must roll a natural 16+ on the attack roll or they only deal half damage. (Shifty spinning bats are hard to hit unless they're grounded or stuck.)

Skittish: After attacking, a bat cavalry engaged with a conscious enemy attempts to disengage and fly into the air if it has a move action remaining that turn.

<u>Nastier Specials</u>

Blood drinker: When the bat cavalry drops an enemy to 0 hp or below, it continues to attack that enemy until that enemy dies, instead of attacking other enemies.

AC	19	
PD	17	**HP 70**
MD	14	

GOBLIN BAT-MAGE

Learning to ride a flying bat left this runty goblin just enough time to learn one nasty little spell.

3rd level spoiler [BEAST & HUMANOID]
Initiative: +7
Vulnerability: thunder

Bloody fangs +7 vs. AC—6 damage, and 6 ongoing damage
Natural 2–5: The goblin bat-mage pops free from the target and can move as a free action.

R: Blood bolt spell +7 vs. PD—8 negative energy damage
Natural even hit: If target is staggered after taking the damage, it's also hampered until the end of its next turn.
Natural odd hit: One of the target's random nearby allies takes 2d6 negative energy damage.

Resist ranged damage 16+: When a ranged attack targets this creature while it's flying, the attacker must roll a natural 16+ on the attack roll or they only deal half damage. (Shifty spinning bats are hard to hit unless they're grounded or stuck.)

Skittish: After attacking, a goblin bat-mage engaged with a conscious enemy attempts to disengage and fly into the air if it has a move action remaining that turn.

Unwieldy flyer: When the goblin bat-mage is staggered, it must roll an immediate save. If it fails, it loses its ability to fly until the end of its next turn. If flying near the ground, it lands immediately. If flying far from the ground, it lands badly and takes 15 damage.

AC	19	
PD	16	**HP 44**
MD	16	

INTERLUDE: RANDOM HOMUNCULI

If you find yourself wanting another random battle during low-level adventures in Duskvakke, or even during the upcoming *glitterfall*, consider adapting the following encounter with magical constructs who somehow broke free from Vantage's system.

If the PCs encounter them in *The Lost City of Duskvakke*, it's possible the homunculi were sucked into the leftover magic of the Dark Jester's tricks, and they attempt to tell jokes while fighting. If the PCs encounter them in *The Forest of the Dream Princess*, the homunculi may have attempted to "go fey," dressing like sprites and sticking twigs through their heads to mimic hair.

#/Level of PCs	Lesser Homunculus	Homunculus	Greater Homunculus
3 x 1st level	4	1	1
4 x 1st level	5	0	2
5 x 1st level	6	1	2
6 x 1st level	4	1	3
7 x 1st level	6	2	3
3 x 2nd level	3	1	2
4 x 2nd level	3	1	3
5 x 2nd level	3	1	4
6 x 2nd level	6	2	4
7 x 2nd level	6	4	4

LESSER HOMUNCULUS

One of the near-mindless servitors on Vantage, the homunculus may now have a mind of its own, but it's not a sane mind.

0 level mook [CONSTRUCT]
Initiative: +3

Tiny sharp claws +5 vs. AC—3 damage

R: Alchemical blurp +4 vs. PD (1d3 nearby or far away enemies in a group)—2 acid damage
First natural 16+: The next ally to attack the target gains +2 to hit.

AC 16
PD 14   HP 5 (mook)
MD 10

Mook: Kill one homunculus mook for every 5 damage dealt to the mob.

HOMUNCULUS

"Have you heard the one about the [unintelligible muttering]?"

0 level troop [CONSTRUCT]
Initiative: +3

Small sharp claws +5 vs. AC—4 damage

R: Alchemical blurp +5 vs. PD (1d3 nearby or far away enemies in a group)—3 acid damage
First natural 16+: The next ally to attack the target gains +2 to hit.

AC 16
PD 14   HP 20
MD 10

GREATER HOMUNCULUS

"Go away. Farther! Farther!"

2nd level troop [CONSTRUCT]
Initiative: +5

Sharp claws +5 vs. AC—7 damage

R: Alchemical blurp +7 vs. PD (1d3 nearby or far away enemies in a group)—6 acid damage
First natural 16+: The next ally to attack the target gains +2 to hit.

AC 18
PD 16   HP 36
MD 12

THE FOREST OF THE DREAM PRINCESS

Level range: Adventurer-tier, best at 3rd or 4th level

The *Book of Ages* introduced many possible ancient icons, some of whose histories were tangled with that of the Elf Queen. The Dream Princess is another forgotten icon from a previous age whose story could complicate matters for the current Elf Queen, provided you or your campaign have interest in the shocking-revelation school of ancient iconography. We'll continue as though you're interested in such secrets. If you're not, simply treat the Dream Princess as another icon who got lost in the shuffle.

Possible revelations: One version of history is that the Dream Princess was the ultimate power when it came to the magics of the mind—the world's psychic-supreme. She ruled from a palace in the middle of the Opals, and the elves were her children. There were more than just three races of elves in her age, though the High Elves, Wood Elves, and Dark Elves were still the most populous.

Who might have overthrown her: If you listen to enemies of the Court of Stars, the Elf Queen overthrew the Dream Princess, shattering her crown and her people. This version of history holds that the Elf Queen still possesses a piece of the Dream Princess' crown, through which she maintains a psychic connection to all other elves.

What Vantage's wards are hiding: The memory of the Dream Princess herself. If the wards fail, the elves may remember that another once led them. A series of crystals scattered throughout the dragon empire hold their memories, though most are located near Vantage.

As you'll see, the main threats in the slice of the Dream Princess' realm that exists here in the Vakevale don't come from the Princess—they come from her ancient enemy: The Nightmare Prince.

Why adventurers might go looking for the crystals: The crystals can reveal the elves' hidden history; plus, the crystals themselves may be valuable.

Bringing back memories of the Dream Princess could unlock chaotic magic powers in many people (and monsters), and it might cause a civil war in the elven lands.

INTO THE FOREST

This remnant of the Dream Princess' realm has several areas for adventurers to explore and encounters suitable for the end of the heroic-tier. For a wide variety of other creatures that would be right at home in this forest, see the fey, naiads, and nymphs in the *13th Age Bestiary 2*.

THE FOREST OF DREAMS

The Forest of Dreams was the fairy-tale domain of the Dream Princess, an icon whose power came from the magic of imagination. Legions of chaos mages and dream-creatures served her and fought against her rival icon, known as the Nightmare Prince. It was a time of wonder and terror unlike any before or since.

Over time, the forest grew wild and tangled; it is now impassable on horseback. The adventurers see strange creatures out of the corners of their eyes; and songs from birds they can't see float on the flower-scented breeze.

IF VANTAGE HAS FALLEN

The Forest of Dreams remains clear of the *glitterfall*. This might be a good place to lead refugees—depending on how the PCs feel about leaving civilians in a place called the Forest of Dreams.

THE STREAM OF CONSCIOUSNESS

A bubbling brook runs through the forest, its banks mossy and soft. Vines climb over the trees, their deep purple flowers filling the air with a heady perfume. Among the trees, around an extinguished campfire, the PCs find another group of adventurers. They are motionless, slumped over in death. It appears they were poisoned several days ago; though flowers are already growing on the corpses.

The flowers on the vines are deadly and poison the air. Each adventurer must make a DC 20 skill check to recognize the threat; failure means they get sleepy and want to relax on the soft moss.

Poison flowers +10 vs. MD—1d12 ongoing poison damage

Looting the corpses provides 50 + 5d20 gp and an adventurer-tier magic weapon or implement; but it also allows the flowers another chance to attack the adventurers.

THE LAKE

An island sits in the middle of a placid, glass-smooth lake deep within in the forest. A ruined temple built of pillars with no surviving roof stands on this island. At the edge of the lake is a small, swan-shaped boat with no oars. A dozen young women wearing flowers in their hair are frozen in place mid-dance on the shore.

If the adventurers board the boat, it automatically moves toward the island. As it does so, the adventurers see many people frozen beneath the lake, as though they tried to flee in terror.

Terrible remnants of the Princess' great enemy—the Nightmare Prince—lurk on the island. He is long gone, but his creatures still haunt this place.

Treasure: There are several large crystals at the very center of the island. They're certainly visible from the shore, if the PCs need a reason to bother trying to cross over. If they look into the crystals, the crystals reveal images from the age of the Dream Princess. If the PCs sell the crystals, they might fetch about 200 gp—more if they sell them to somebody dangerous, which inevitably leads to trouble with one or more icon's agents.

Alternatively, if you really want the PCs to cross over to the island, your best bet might be to use an icon relationship advantage to inform them that the island contains magical treasure related to the Elf Queen.

#/Level of PCs	Knightmare	Living Spell
3 x 3rd level	3	0
4 x 3rd level	2	1
5 x 3rd level	3	1
6 x 3rd level	2	2
7 x 3rd level	3	2
3 x 4th level	2	1
4 x 4th level	1	2
5 x 4th level	3	2
6 x 4th level	2	3
7 x 4th level	3	4

KNIGHTMARE

Apparently, the Nightmare Prince was also devoted to terrible puns. Figures.

3rd level blocker [SPIRIT]
Initiative: +8

Spectral sword +8 vs. PD—7 negative energy damage
 Miss: 3 damage.

C: Figments of horror +8 vs. MD (one nearby enemy)—Target is dazed (−4 to attack) until it hits the knightmare with an attack
 Quick use: 1/round, as a quick action.

Immaterial: The knightmare can drift through walls, phase through floors, and otherwise defy solidity, though it can't end its turn in solid objects.

AC	16	
PD	12	HP 55
MD	14	

LIVING SPELL

This roiling ball of energy is intelligent and eager to defend the Nightmare Prince, entirely unaware that he is long gone.

5th level archer [SPIRIT]
Initiative: +10

Magefire +10 vs. AC (1d3 attacks)—8 force and fire damage
Natural odd miss: The target pops free.

R: Spell burn +10 vs. AC (2 nearby or far away enemies in a group)—14 force damage
Natural odd hit: The target becomes vulnerable to force damage.

Mana burn: When a magical attack or a weapon attack with a magic weapon targets the living spell, the attacker takes force damage equal to their level.

Flight: The living spell floats about, paying no mind to minor things like gravity.

Immaterial: The living spell can drift through walls, phase through floors, and otherwise defy solidity, though it can't end its turn in solid objects.

AC	18	
PD	21	HP 72
MD	21	

THE DREAMING STONES

The tangled forest opens out into a flowering meadow with a slight rise in the center where standing stones rest in a circle. The magic of the standing stones has long faded away; their only mysterious property now is that they are uncountable (there are either 11 or 13 of them, depending in which direction you count). Anyone standing at the center of the circle feels uneasy, as though they are being watched.

Fight or no fight?: Several pucks circle lazily through the stones. This need not be a fight, especially if the group isn't up for a fight with dozens of mooks. The pucks might just want to talk or may be feeling mischievous.

If the PCs treat the pucks kindly (requires a DC 20 skill check to discover what they want, unless you'd rather roleplay it), they deposit a small number of gemstones in the adventurers' pockets. If they treat the pucks badly (or attack them) some of the pucks hunt the adventurers down and play tricks on them: the adventurers take a −1 penalty to attack rolls for the entirety of one fight during the next level (the pucks turn up and tie bootlaces together, undo the buckles on armor, and so on).

If the adventurers managed to avoid the swan lake, a discussion with the pucks might point them back toward the island and true magical treasure.

If the PCs do end up fighting the pucks, it won't be a battle to the death—the pucks fly away as soon as they start to lose the fight.

PUCK

This pixie-like creature enjoys pelting bigger creatures with thorn-like arrows. Happily, everyone is bigger!

3rd level mook [HUMANOID]
Initiative: +9

Sharp teeth +8 vs. AC—5 damage

R: Tiny green bow +8 vs. AC (1 nearby enemy)—6 damage

Flight: Pucks can fly, and though they prefer to fight on foot, they always fly when they disengage.

AC	18	
PD	17	HP 10 (mook)
MD	13	

Mook: Kill one puck mook for every 10 damage dealt to the mob.

#/Level of PCs	Puck
3 x 3rd level	12
4 x 3rd level	16
5 x 3rd level	20
6 x 3rd level	24
7 x 3rd level	28
3 x 4th level	17
4 x 4th level	23
5 x 4th level	29
6 x 4th level	34
7 x 4th level	40

THE REPOSITORY

Level range: 2nd and 3rd level characters can enter the Repository and explore its outer layers, but penetrating the lower levels is a mission for champion-tier characters

Sometimes, a bad idea can seem like a good idea—and when those in charge have access to magic, they can turn what seems like a good idea into a disastrous reality. This Repository holds objects a past Archmage thought too disruptive or dangerous to be allowed loose in the world, but too interesting or expensive to destroy.

The Repository might be a good way to introduce your treasure-oriented adventuring group to the Redfield Valley. Start them off on the road to the Repository to rob the place. Have them stop off at Crownhill or Appleton to rest, pick up supplies, and get local rumors. Then, run a small adventure inside the Repository before Vantage comes crashing out of the sky. The party might even believe something they do in the Repository causes the crash.

Many areas, three tiers: Unlike most adventure locations, the Repository starts out as an adventurer-tier area and grows progressively more dangerous the deeper you go (yes, that's how dungeons worked in the good old days). Adventurer-tier characters might be able to handle traveling through the outer corridors and the storage cubes; however, the lower levels are a champion-tier environment, and the lowest vaults—where everything went wrong—are a challenging champion-tier or low epic-tier environment. Further, they're not places anyone can stay for long!

It's not our intent for you to ambush the players with the shift in environments. Adventurer-tier characters should have a clear sense that the lower levels are spooky and dangerous before they begin their descent.

If the PCs don't visit the Repository until they're champion-tier, choose between waving off the adventurer-tier battles or pumping them up.

THE REPOSITORY'S VALLEY

The Repository is a squat stone building, a mile long on each side, built right across a valley. The building is mostly underground, so only a few walls peek out from the rolling mossy ground. Water pours over the Repository's front wall.

Only one entrance to the Repository is visible from the valley; it has no windows or other features. It was probably dauntingly monolithic in its heyday, but it has been an age or four since then. The valley behind the Repository is flooded, and the front of the building is a mile-long waterfall. Simply knowing the building is there is not enough—it takes a DC 20 check to find the 100-foot tall door behind the water. If the party can't find the Repository (or the door), they should come back when they are more experienced.

Introduce adventurers who spend too much time futzing around under the clear valley sky to a hunting flight from the *Raptors* adversary group (page 217), who once called the Repository home.

INTO THE REPOSITORY

Once the PCs enter the Repository, they find that the interior is a lightless maze of stairways, corridors, and small rooms. Most of the rooms are identical 10-foot cubes, each corridor measures exactly 10 feet x 10 feet, and the featureless 5-foot thick walls and floors resist any attempts to mark them.

The doors to the rooms are made of 2-inch thick oak, banded with iron; they also have heavy locks, some of which are magical, that require a DC 20 skill check to get through the door (a DC 30 check to do so without attracting the attention of guardian golems). If the PCs fail these checks, introduce an appropriate battle from the *Golems* adversary group (page 207 or page 58).

Golems, programmed to perform maintenance on the structure and dispose of intruders, patrol the corridors. It's possible that icon relationship advantages could help the PCs avoid trouble with one or more golems, particularly Archmage advantages, but the fun way to handle such stories is to explain how the icon-connected PC doesn't register as a golem target, while the other PCs do!

The Repository's interior is maze-like and may even magically shift between visits. Feel free to add a golem battle whenever you like if rolling on the *Random Interior Creator* table doesn't provide enough!

RANDOM INTERIOR CREATOR TABLE

The corridor is (roll a d6):

1. A featureless corridor with no rooms.

2-5. A corridor with empty rooms.

6. A corridor with locked rooms that contain log books.

The corridor ends at (roll a d12):

1. A cross-junction with another corridor.

2. A T-junction with another corridor.

3. A short flight of stairs going down, and the corridor continues.

4. A short flight of stairs going up, and the corridor continues.

5. Stairs going up.

6. Stairs going down.

7-8. A dead-end with a Special Area (see below).

9-12. A Special Area (see below), with a door to another corridor behind it.

SPECIAL AREAS TABLE (D12)

1. A cupboard full of cleaning supplies (mops, buckets, brooms).

2. An unresponsive "dead" golem in an alcove.

3. An empty golem alcove.

4-5. An aware and aggressive golem(s): it's battle time.

6. A workshop (roll a d6):

   1-3. Carpentry workshop for repairing doors, making new brooms, etc.

   4-5. Masonry workshop for repairing stonework.

   6. Golem-repair workshop.

7-8. A deep shaft, with water and treasure worth 100-200 gp at the bottom.

9-12. A deep shaft with a wooden lid, into which the golems dump trash (and dead adventurers). A gelatinous cubahedron is lurking at the bottom. Treasure worth 200-300 gp and possibly a true magic item or two are suspended in the cube. It takes a DC 20 to notice the cube instead of the treasure. (If you roll this result subsequent times, cue another golem attack instead of a second trash shaft.)

ADVENTURER-TIER BATTLES

These are the main battles you'll run while the PCs move through the Repository's outer layers. Use the *Golems* adversary group on page 207 for the golem battles. If you or the players tire of repeated golem battles, consider letting them advance swiftly to the champion-tier section of the Repository!

FIGHT IN THE DEEP SHAFT

A roll of 9-12 on the *Special Areas* table may result in a fight with a single gelatinous cubahedron. If this happens, compare the monster's level to that of your group to determine whether the battle should count as a normal or double-strength battle (see **13A: 186**).

GELATINOUS CUBAHEDRON, AKA CUBE

There's a simplicity of design to the gelatinous cubahedron, a unity of form and function that is truly appreciated only by monstrous overlords.

Huge 5th level blocker [OOZE]
Initiative: +4

Shlup'n'schlorp +10 vs. PD—30 acid damage, and the cube engulfs the target (functions like a grab; see below) if the target is smaller than the cube
Miss: The cube can make a *spasms* attack as a free action.

[Special trigger] **C: Spasms +10 vs. AC (up to 2 attacks, each against a different nearby enemy)**—15 damage

Engulf and dissolve: Targets engulfed/grabbed by the cube take 30 acid damage at the start of the cube's turn but are not viable targets for additional attacks by the cube. The cube can hold multiple targets within itself simultaneously. Any engulfed creature that is also staggered must begin making last gasp saves or become paralyzed as the cube's toxins overwhelm it.

Instinctive actions: A gelatinous creature has no brain, so sometimes, it just *does things*. When the escalation die is odd, instead of attacking or moving, roll a d6 to see what the cubahedron does. If you roll an option that is not viable (such as rolling a 5 when there is no engulfed enemy), re-roll until you get a valid option.

1. The cubahedron jiggles in place. Each nearby enemy takes 5 acid damage. Each creature engulfed by the cube takes a −4 penalty to its saves until the end of its next turn.

2. The cubahedron moves as a quick action. If the cube ends its movement engaged with enemies, each of those enemies must roll a save; on a failure, the cubahedron grabs them (but they're not engulfed).

3. The cubahedron spits an engulfed creature into the air above it and makes a *shlup'n'schlorp* attack against that creature with a +5 attack bonus. Then, the cube engulfs the creature again.

4. The cubahedron flattens itself slightly and crawls up the wall or across the ceiling. The cube falls at the end of its turn. Each creature engulfed by the cube takes 30 damage, and it makes a *gel drop attack* against enemies below it. **Gel drop +10 vs. PD (1d3 nearby enemies)**—15 damage, and the cube engulfs the target if the target is smaller than the cube.

5. The cubahedron moves one engulfed creature to the surface. The target gains a +4 bonus to any attempt to escape the cube, but each time the cube is targeted by an attack, the engulfed creature must roll a save; on a failure, it becomes the target of the attack instead.

6. The cubahedron spits out each engulfed enemy in different directions with great force; each of them takes 50 damage.

Flows where it likes: The ooze is immune to opportunity attacks.

Ooze: The ooze is immune to effects. When an attack applies a condition to an ooze (dazed, hampered, weakened, ongoing damage, etc.), that condition doesn't affect it.

AC	20	
PD	18	**HP 200**
MD	15	

THE INTERIOR

Play the interior of the Repository as a high adventurer-tier or low champion-tier environment, even if the PCs have not yet reached that level. Build battles from the *Golems* adversary group (page 208) for 5th and 6th level PCs, using griffon golems and bronze golems, among others. If your adventuring party's level isn't that high, they need to get the message to turn back or flee!

Yes, a group with epic-tier characters should be able to quickly cut through this section of the Repository. Still, with so many interesting things to investigate, they may not want to move quickly.

DUBIOUS TREASURES

If the PCs go deep into the Repository, they'll uncover some of its dubious treasures. Each interior room has a book on a chain by the door. The front of the book details what treasure the room contains and why it was put here. The remaining pages contain a log of official visitors who came to check on the item (most logs are blank).

Here are samples of the items, as listed in their log books:

10206—Coin that causes the owner to tell the absolute truth. Creation commissioned by D.E. as joke. Absolute truth determined to be more than mortals can bear, coin eventually kills owner.

11198—Crystal that increases in brightness the more it is exposed to light. Must be kept in a velvet bag, in an iron box, in a bucket of water. Room must always be kept free of light (log indicates that the water is regularly topped off). When charged and exposed, the crystal causes all nearby creatures and objects to be treated as invisible.

12830—Unraveled flying carpet, stored in glass sphere. When triggered, it attacks without mercy (**single target, +10 vs. PD**— *2d8 ongoing damage). Was investigated as a weapon of war but found to have the ability to infect clothing. All other samples burned.*

13521—Pair of statues of a dead god that swap the appearances of those who touch them. A party gift to the Emperor. One statue now broken—in storage while replacement is sought.

13591—A gold coin that causes other gold coins placed near it to tarnish. Recovered from imperial treasury. To be stored until it is determined safe to destroy.

14872—A rusted helmet of ancient design. Causes items held by the wearer to rust, crack, or dissolve. Held in storage until it becomes useful. (The room contains only a pile of inert rust on a stand).

15682—A grey metal that causes all thought to cease in most who touch it, while they are touching it (**↓10 vs. MD**—*stunned until the end of your next turn). Developed by the alchemist Peer Mortrach for use in shackles. Very hard for jailors to apply or use the shackles, and the metal keeps growing.*

16556—Greenish sludge, sickens those who view it. (Looking into the room and seeing the sludge does indeed cause nausea, **+10 vs. MD**—*1d12 ongoing psychic damage, hard save ends).*

16630—127 pairs of magical dancing shoes in various sizes and styles, and 82 lone, unpaired dancing shoes. To be stored until the dances they know come back into style.

17093—Club, double handed. Swaps the wielder's sense of smell with that of the one struck. Held in storage until a way can be found to swap more than the sense of smell.

18419—Small, clay water basin. Any water placed into it becomes vinegar. Potential use as a siege weapon to foul water supplies, to be held in storage until its creator can be deduced and the magic applied to arrows or other useful items.

19964—A book that erases its contents from the reader's mind. As it is unknowable what the book contains, it is to be stored until a method of reading it is discovered.

Very few of the artifacts are weapons, most are destructive "toys" that are only deadly to the foolish and unwary.

TREASURE & ODDITIES

Avoid putting too many useful items in the Repository. It's a place to store dangerous and hard to control objects, or curiosities the Archmage never got around to studying. If you want to hand out actual treasure the adventurers can take with them, use one or two true magic items and maybe throw in a cursed item, too!

It is possible that clever adventurers could come up with some unstable combination of deadly oddities that could benefit them somehow. Reward their cleverness by letting it work—one time. Afterward, the objects' magical fields start to intermingle and produce unwelcome effects.

Ghosts & Golems: If you want to run a second battle in the interior, consider the following encounter with former tomb robbers' ghosts (for the full ghost writeup, see **13B2**: 105). For a challenge vs. higher-level PCs (and let's just treat everyone as 8th level, since we may as well start broadcasting that this place is dangerous!), add the golems that killed the tomb robbers to the battle, and play up that the ghosts are trying to acquire company.

If you don't use this fight in the Repository, consider adding it to a latter battle the adventurers fight against golems or magical defenders.

#/Level of PCs	Petulant Never-Was	Disgraced Legionnaire	Major Haunting Mook	Stone Golem
3 x 5th level	1	1	3	0
4 x 5th level	1	1	8	0
5 x 5th level	1	2	3	0
6 x 5th level	2	2	3	0
7 x 5th level	3	2	2	0
3 x 6th level	1	2	2	0
4 x 6th level	2	2	2	0
5 x 6th level	2	2	8	0
6 x 6th level	1	2	2	1
7 x 6th level	2	2	4	1
3 x 7th level	2	2	6	0
4 x 7th level	1	2	6	1
5 x7th level	2	2	8	1
6 x 7th level	3	3	2	1
7 x 7th level	4	4	2	1

PETULANT NEVER-WAS

A failure as a wizard, a failure as a high elf, a failure as a husband and provider.

Double-strength 5th level caster [UNDEAD]
Initiative: +9
Vulnerability: holy

Ghostly staff +10 vs. PD—26 negative energy damage
Natural even hit: The petulant never-was can make a *disparaging rummage* attack as a free action.

R: Flashy zaps +10 vs. PD (1 or 2 nearby targets)—28 energy damage (damage is either force OR a type of energy most recently used by an enemy spellcaster, as the petulant never-was demonstrates that they also control that energy type).
Natural odd miss: Petulant never-was takes 3d6 damage that ignores its ghostly resistance.

C: Disparaging rummage +10 vs. MD (nearby enemy) 10 ongoing psychic damage and hampered (save ends both); hampered only affects spellcasters!
Quick use: 1/round, as a quick action

Ghostly: This creature has *Resist cold and fire 16+* to all damage except holy damage AND force damage. A ghost can move through solid objects but can't end its turn inside them.

Iconic sadsack: Each enemy that has one or more icon relationship points with the Archmage and misses an attack with a natural odd roll takes a −2 penalty to all their defenses until the end of the battle.

AC	19	
PD	15	**HP 123**
MD	18	

DISGRACED LEGIONNAIRE

The real disgrace is that this ghost is still trying to drag everyone else down.

Double-strength 6th level wrecker [UNDEAD]
Initiative: +12
Vulnerability: holy

Ghostly sword +13 vs. PD—40 negative energy damage
Natural even hit or miss: The disgraced legionnaire can make a *confusing orders* attack as a free action.

C: Confusing orders +11 vs. MD (nearby enemy)—5 ongoing psychic damage and target's weapon attacks do not add the escalation die (save ends both)
Critical hit: Target is also confused (same save ends).
Quick use: 1/round, as a quick action.

Ghostly: This creature has *resist damage 12+* to all damage except holy damage. A ghost can move through solid objects but can't end its turn inside them.

Iconic sadsack: Each enemy that has one or more icon relationship points with the Emperor and misses an attack with a natural odd roll takes a −2 penalty to all their defenses until the end of the battle.

AC	22	
PD	19	**HP 140**
MD	16	

Major Haunting

Who's scared of mooks?

6th level mook [undead]
Initiative: +9

Terrible touch +10 vs. PD—8 negative energy damage

Mob-based: For every separate mob of major haunting mooks in the battle (mobs start with at least four mooks), add a +1 bonus to the major haunting's attacks and +2 to its damage.

Ghostly: This creature has *resist damage 14+* to all damage except holy damage. A haunting can move through solid objects, but it can't end its movement inside them.

Fear-boosters: While there are three or more lesser or major haunting mooks in a battle, their allies' fear abilities affect enemies with half again as many hit points as usual.

AC 21		
PD 19	**HP 18 (mook)**	
MD 16		

Mook: Kill one major haunting mook for every 18 damage dealt to the mob.

Stone Golem Ghost Rock

Centuries of anchoring the ghosts of would-be Repository tomb robbers has made this golem… strange.

Large 8th level blocker [construct]
Initiative: +11

Massive stone fists +12 vs. AC (2 attacks)—35 damage
  Miss: 15 damage.

Finishing smash +14 vs. AC (one staggered enemy)—80 damage, and the target pops free and moves a short distance away (the golem chooses where)
  Natural even hit: +20 damage, and the target is hampered (save ends).
  Natural even miss: The target is hampered (save ends)
  Natural odd miss: 20 damage, and the target is dazed (save ends).

Golem immunity: Non-organic golems are immune to effects. They can't be dazed, weakened, confused, made vulnerable, or touched by ongoing damage. You can damage a golem, but that's about it.

Ghost rock: If the PCs drop this creature's hp to 0, it collects a spirit from every battle they fight this level and returns—once—to fight them, accompanied by the ghostly spirits, sometime after they have gained a level and ideally when they are not prepared to fight. Don't explain the threat; simply mention that "something was not right" about that golem, and begin to narrate a spirit being snatched away from the dead in each battle.

AC 25	
PD 23	**HP 280**
MD 18	

The Lower Levels: Champion-Tier Terror

The real trouble is in the basement, where the Archmage stored centuries-worth of magical reagents and materials. Whenever he finished a project, the Archmage would invariably have something left over—a spoonful of ground unicorn hoof here, an offcut of magical wood there. Shelves upon shelves containing pinches of this and pounds of that stretch across the basement, all waiting for a day they might become relevant. The person responsible for storing all these precious items was quite careless. Perhaps they left the stopper off a bottle or two, didn't bother to right an item that got knocked over, or even ignored a mote of rogue magic that flared up. Whatever happened, at least one corner in the basement is now "odd". And not whimsically odd. Deadly-odd.

The metal shelves sprouted whipping tentacles. Acidic fumes hover over a cracked vial, remaining stationary in the air. Even the ground itself is untrustworthy, moving like the skin of a living being. A vortex to another plain grows larger when observed, and there are unwholesome things moving about beyond the veil.

Adventurers who proceed into the basement must each pass a DC 25 skill check to avoid being targeted by one of the following attacks:

Corrosive vortex +10 vs. PD—2d12 acid damage

OR

Noxious fumes +10 vs. PD—4d6 poison damage

OR

Whipping tentacles +10 vs. AC—5d6+3 damage.

Whatever accident occurred here, it's getting worse—growing, even. It is obvious someone just stacked up the most recent deliveries to the basement at the foot of the stairs. And, lest we forget, there are oozes and more oozes. In fact, whenever a PC fumbles (rolls a natural 1 on an attack), add another gray ooze to the fight. Yeah!

Options: Some of the level and player character combinations have multiple options for building battles, in case you want to run a battle like this more than once.

#/Level of PCs	Gray Ooze	Lesser Black Pudding
3 x 4th level	0	1
4 x 4th level	2	0
5 x 4th level	1	1
6 x 4th level	3	0
7 x 4th level	0	2
3 x 4th level	2	1
3 x 5th level	3	0
4 x 5th level	4	0
5 x 5th level	2	2
6 x 5th level	3	2
6 x 5th level	0	4
6 x 5th level	6	0
7 x 5th level	4	2
7 x 5th level	1	4
7 x 5th level	7	0
3 x 6th level	0	3
3 x 6th level	3	1
4 x 6th level	3	4
4 x 6th level	3	2
5 x 6th level	0	5
5 x 6th level	3	3
6 x 6th level	0	6
6 x 6th level	3	4
7 x 6th level	0	7
7 x 6th level	3	4

GRAY OOZE

These oozes look like slick, flowing stones. You can find them in volcanic dungeons, wizard's towers on mountain peaks, quiet swamps, and sadistic death traps.

6th level blocker [OOZE]
Initiative: +5

Hungry mass +11 v AC—20 damage
Natural even hit: The target is grabbed.

Acidic constriction (one creature the ooze has grabbed) + 12 vs. PD—10 acid damage
Miss: 5 damage.
Limited use: 1/round as a quick action, only against a creature the ooze has grabbed.

Resist cold and fire 16+: When a cold or fire attack targets this creature, the attacker must roll a natural 16+ on the attack roll or it only deals half damage.

Flows where it likes: The ooze is immune to opportunity attacks.

Ooze: The ooze is immune to effects. When an attack applies a condition to an ooze (dazed, hampered, weakened, ongoing damage, etc.), that condition doesn't affect it.

AC 21	
PD 19	**HP 80**
MD 15	

LESSER BLACK PUDDING

These blobs demonstrate an uncanny penchant for getting into places they're not supposed to be.

7th level wrecker [OOZE]
Initiative: +6

Acid-drenched pseudopod +12 v PD (1 or 2 attacks, each against a different nearby enemy)—20 acid damage, and 5 ongoing acid damage.

Climber: A black pudding sticks to ceilings and walls when it wishes, sliding along as easily as on the floor.

Slippery: The pudding has *resist weapons 12+*.

Flows where it likes: The ooze is immune to opportunity attacks.

Ooze: The ooze is immune to effects. When an attack applies a condition to an ooze (dazed, hampered, weakened, ongoing damage, etc.), that condition doesn't affect it.

AC 21	
PD 18	**HP 94**
MD 17	

EPIC-TIER: THE VAULT

The vault—where the ridiculously dangerous things are kept—lies on the other side of the basement. The vault door, which looks like a living acid puddle has eaten through it, is barely visible through areas of warped reality in the distance.

Behind the door is an area where the Archmage stored spells that came alive and had to be contained. Left unattended in the vault for centuries, they cross-bred and cannibalized each other until anything remaining is much worse than any "living spell." Who knows what lurks down there today?

We have some suggestions, of course. Grab some extremely powerful creatures like the 13th level hagunemnon (**13B**: 69) or a fomori torturer (**13B2**: 86) to use here. Use enough of these creatures that the PCs soon understand they must flee or die.

IF VANTAGE HAS FALLEN

The ward keeping the living spells contained fails when Vantage falls. This means the adventurers can get into the vault; however, it also means the spells can get out into the Repository.

We did not detail the inside of the vault—we imagine it is much like the inside of a nuclear reactor, only consisting of jars and scrolls instead of fuel rods and such. Adventurers take 1d20 of a random damage type each round they spend in the vault, and 1d10 force damage per round from being near the unwarded vault.

THE CORPSE OF KROON

Level range: 6th through 9th, with foot lice problems for lower level PCs

A giant that styled itself as a living god, Kroon implanted magical items and powerful relics of the gods throughout its body, gaining power as it mutated and grew mad. When Kroon was finally defeated, all the magic stored within it began to go wild.

When at last someone dealt the killing blow to Kroon, time around the giant slowed. It is not technically dead (yet), but it has been falling backward for centuries from the fatal stroke's force. Its body was stored in the Vakevale to keep it from anybody who might try to feed it healing magic during its final heartbeat.

The giant's body is still accessible—if you know where to look and, more importantly, *how* to look. Those who know the trick to it can glimpse the giant, brightly illuminated from the inside by the centuries-slow explosion ripping its body apart.

The crows that feast upon the almost-dead giant's flesh are the key to finding it. They can see through the illusion and land on its scalp, picking at the meat. The time behind the illusion is slowed, though it is not as slowed for the crows as it is for the giant. Observers who watch the crows carefully (a DC 20 skill check) can teach themselves to pierce the aura of illusion around the giant.

Kroon's body contains many magical items. Unlike the crows, adventurers can't simply fly up to Kroon—the time-dilating effects disrupt flight attempts so badly, it takes years of practice to fly anywhere near the corpse. Still, if adventurers manage to prop a ladder against the frozen creature's heel, they can climb to where an item is and cut it free. Of course, centuries-worth of slowed time and free food did strange things to the Vakevale crows, so the party must face some unusual "monsters" on this corpse-looting climb.

Lower level attempts: If you want your PCs to encounter Kroon as adventurer-tier characters, they might find the giant and manage to climb its lower limbs. Attempts to loot the body get dicey fast, though, unless you adjust the monsters downward by several levels.

KROON'S BODY

Once the adventurers find Kroon and climb up its body, what they encounter isn't pretty.

LIMBS

Adventurers must make a DC 20 skill check to climb the giant's limbs; failure inflicts 2d12 falling damage. Kroon's tattooed skin flaps from its arms in the wind, torn to strips by the many unwholesome creatures that feast upon it as it dies in slow-motion.

If the PCs are daring to attempt this at adventurer-tier, hit them with a slightly difficult battle against two mobs of Kroon's foot-lice (one mob per foot, naturally) for 3rd or 4th level heroes. Reward them with a single, disgustingly toe-jammed true magical item should they emerge victorious (you can wave off this battle and treasure if the PCs are champion-tier; or use it to make them feel good about themselves).

Show no mercy if lower-level PCs decide to climb higher; at the very least they should encounter a battle meant for several 6th level heroes.

#/Level of PCs	Left Foot Lice	Right Foot Lice	Kroon's Maggots
3 x 1st level	3	2	0
4 x 1st level	3	3	0
5 x 1st level	4	3	0
6 x 1st level	5	4	0
7 x 1st level	6	5	0
3 x 2nd level	3	3	0
4 x 2nd level	4	4	0
5 x 2nd level	5	5	0
6 x 2nd level	6	5	0
7 x 2nd level	7	6	0
3 x 3rd level	4	5	0
4 x 3rd level	6	6	0
5 x 3rd level	8	7	0
6 x 3rd level	8	8	1
7 x 3rd level	8	8	2
3 x 4th level	5	6	1
4 x 4th level	6	7	2
5 x 4th level	8	8	2
6 x 4th level	9	8	3
7 x 4th level	9	9	5

KROON'S FOOT LICE

An enterprising gourmet might recognize these creatures as a once-in-a-lifetime opportunity. They certainly feel that way about you.

5th level mook [ABERRATION]
Initiative: +8

Chew right through +7 vs. PD—10 damage
 Natural even hit: The target makes a DC 15 skill check to maintain their grip on Kroon's body. Failure means the target falls and takes 2d6 falling damage; further, the target is out of the fight for at least one full round until they can climb back up.

AC	22	
PD	17	**HP 16 (mook)**
MD	16	

Mook: Kill one foot louse of Kroon mook for every 16 damage dealt to the mob.

KROON'S MAGGOTS

These hairy white maggots swim through Kroon's flesh like lion seals in a pond.

7th level mook [BEAST]
Initiative: +9

Chew +12 vs. AC—24 damage

R: Silken strand +13 vs. AC (one nearby or far away enemy)—18 damage, and the target is pulled into engagement with the maggot
 Natural 18+: The attack is a critical hit.

AC	24	
PD	20	**HP 26 (mook)**
MD	20	

Mook: Kill one maggot of Kroon mook for every 26 damage dealt to the mob.

TORSO

Kroon's giant breastplate has pitted and rusted over the centuries, and carrion birds pecked at its ribcage, which is now their home. It takes a DC 22 skill check for the adventurers to climb onto the torso; failure deals 3d12 falling damage.

The adventurers can see a champion-tier magic item deep within the giant's chest cavity (make it an epic-tier item if the PCs are epic tier.) Retrieving the item involves fighting Kroon's maggots and birds. Build this battle as though the PCs are a minimum of 6th level. If that's too tough for them, they may need to flee—treat the campaign loss from fleeing as a victory over its wards for Kroon or as a general failing of wards near the Vakevale.

#/Level of PCs	Kroon's Maggots	Kroon's Birds
3 x 6th level	5	1
4 x 6th level	0	2
5 x 6th level	5	2
6 x 6th level	0	3
7 x 6th level	5	3
3 x 7th level	0	2
4 x 7th level	7	2
5 x 7th level	3	3
6 x 7th level	0	4
7 x 7th level	7	4
3 x 8th level	10	3
4 x 8th level	10	4
5 x 8th level	10	5
6 x 8th level	10	6
7 x 8th level	10	7

KROON'S BIRDS

These oversized "crows" have feasted on Kroon for centuries.

9th level troop [ABERRATION]
Initiative: +14

Raking claws +13 vs. AC—50 damage
Natural even hit or miss: The bird may pop free.
Natural 16+ (eye peck): The target is dazed (save ends).

Flight: The bird of Kroon flies swiftly, flocking in search of meat.

Nastier Special
Eye pluck: When a target that is dazed by *eye peck* would be dazed again by *eye peck*, they are instead dazed until they receive magical healing (through a spell or other supernatural power, a potion, a magic item, etc.). If this happens again to the same creature before they are magically healed, they are instead blinded (treat all creatures and objects as *invisible*) until they receive magical healing.

AC	23	
PD	22	**HP 180**
MD	22	

BLINDING?

Use the *eye pluck* nastier special sparingly. Only peck out both an adventurers' eyes if the party has a way to restore sight to the now-blind adventurer quickly, perhaps within the same session. The game isn't fun for players if you cripple their characters too early. Of course, letting your players *fear* the *possibility* that the crows might peck out both their eyes is fine.

HEAD

There are two champion-tier (or epic-tier, if the PCs are epic-tier) magic items glowing just beneath Kroon's neck flesh. The giant's bearded head has a maggot-infested wound on its brow, and smoke from where the killing spell struck still rises in slow-motion. Carrion crows ate the soft parts of its face long ago (DC 30 to climb onto the giant's head; failure deals 4d12 falling damage).

The battle on Kroon's head assumes the PCs are at least 8th level. The PCs should feel in their bones that climbing beyond Kroon's dangling guts will lead them into an epic-tier situation. It turns out the ghosts of great enemies Kroon slew surround the giant. They may hate Kroon, but the giant is beyond their touch, and people who climb Kroon's body are usually worshipers trying to bring it back. The ghosts won't suffer the PCs' presence here.

Healing? Not so much: In addition, the magic that prevents Kroon from healing is in full force here at its head. PCs receive only half the amount of healing from all healing effects (don't warn them ahead of time, this should come as a surprise). Perhaps an icon relationship advantage can turn this around... but, that may also come at the cost of enlivening Kroon!

So far as we know, Kroon is a "god" you loot and run from, not a dungeon you beat. But perhaps your PCs may surprise us.

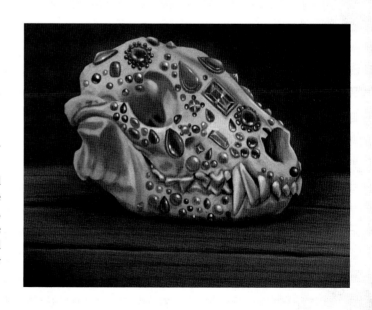

#/Level of PCs	Kroon's Birds	Ghost of the Slain
3 x 8th level	2	2
4 x 8th level	2	3
5 x 8th level	4	3
6 x 8th level	5	4
7 x 8th level	6	5
3 x 9th level	3	2
4 x 9th level	4	4
5 x 9th level	5	5
6 x 9th level	6	6
7 x 9th level	8	7
3 x 10th level	4	5
4 x 10th level	5	7
5 x 10th level	8	8
6 x 10th level	10	9
7 x 10th level	10	11

GHOST OF THE SLAIN

Maybe this was one of Kroon's enemies and you're all on the same side. Sure... if that side is DEATH!

11th level spoiler [UNDEAD]
Initiative: +18
Vulnerability: holy

Ghostly weapon +17 vs. PD—60 negative energy damage
Natural even hit or miss: A ghost of the slain can make a *disorient* attack as a free action.

[Special trigger] C: Disorient +17 vs. MD (nearby enemy)—At the end of the target's next turn, it must roll a save. The save is easy if the target took one action on its turn, normal if it took two actions, and hard if it took three or more actions. If the save fails, the target falls off Kroon's head, taking 4d12 falling damage. It takes a bit of time to get back to the fight, though a ghost of the slain might follow an enemy down to finish them on the ground.

Ghostly: This creature has *resist damage 12+* to all damage except holy damage. A ghost can move through solid objects, but it can't end its movement inside them.

Flight: Flies like a drifting spirit. Not as quick as some.

AC 27
PD 21   **HP 220**
MD 25

IF VANTAGE HAS FALLEN

Vantage falling doesn't automatically mean that Kroon falls entirely out of its stasis field. The illusion surrounding Kroon gradually disappears—meaning the giant is eventually easier to find—but that doesn't necessarily end the giant's life; the stasis effect ends, but it does so in magic-geological time, not player character action time! Plenty of frozen moments remain—enough to allow low-level PCs to find Kroon, even after Vantage falls.

Epic endgames: If the PCs climb the giant (at least partway) early in their careers, consider holding on to Kroon like a final horror-movie villain. Just when the PCs think they finally have Redfield Valley's menaces under control, the stasis field surrounding Kroon finally fizzles and an enraged, epic-tier giant spends the last dozen rounds of its life trying to get its hands on whatever it can to destroy.

Here's one way to portray Kroon in its dying rampage.

DYING KROON

Problems don't have to be permanent to end your world.

Huge 14th level wrecker [GIANT]
Initiative: +25

Vulnerability: Attacks by PCs attuned to magic items acquired from Kroon's body

Giant weapon +20 vs. AC (3 attacks)—120 damage
Miss against a target carrying one or more true magic items acquired from Kroon: 60 damage.

R: Negation wave +20 vs. PD (1d8 nearby enemies)—100 negative energy damage and target is stunned
Limited use: Only when the escalation die is odd.

Resist damage 14+: When an attack targets dying Kroon, the attacker must roll a natural 14+ on the attack roll or they only deal half damage.

Impending death: When the escalation die hits 4, Kroon must attempt a normal save at the end of each of its turns. If the save fails, Kroon dies. Better yet, for GMs to who don't wish to award more Kroon-scented treasure, Kroon explodes! What happens then? Perhaps a wave of magical energy washes out across the land, uprooting trees, hurling boulders, and flattening walls. Or maybe a great weight of pain and sadness lifts from every heart. It's up to you.

Almost immune to conditions: PCs attuned to magic items they stole or acquired from Kroon can place conditions on Kroon. It is otherwise immune to conditions.

AC 28
PD 26   **HP 1600**
MD 22

CHAPTER 3:

THE FALL OF VANTAGE

IT'S THE END OF THE WORLD AS WE KNOW IT

Vantage is ordinarily invisible; a floating citadel of power that hovers above Redfield Valley, serene and inviolate. At some point in this adventure, you need to destroy it. When you do so, go nuts.

The flying island is an artifact of rare beauty and ineffable power. When it falls, it falls with a bang.

Here is ASH's write-up of the fall.

PRE-SHOCKS

Start with small pre-shocks....

- The birds all fly up and out of sight, and there is no more bird song.
- A group of children playing kick-ball watch in puzzlement as the ground buckles and their ball hits a suddenly up-thrust stone. They run to tell somebody standing near the adventurers, but nobody pays them any heed.
- All the dogs in town begin to bark at the sky, but everything looks clear with no storm on the horizon.
- Horses break out of their stables and run pell-mell up the street.

VANTAGE APPEARS

Give the PCs a few moments to puzzle over these events, then...

- The sky darkens, though nobody can see any cause for the light dimming.
- Clouds begin to whip around in a circular pattern in an area of empty sky.
- The PCs feel more than hear a rumble—a low, bass sound that seems to come up from the ground.

By this time, the villagers realize something is happening, and everybody comes outdoors to look at the sky. Smart adventurers try to get everybody to take cover in their cellars or under something solid and follow suit themselves; but, most are not smart and probably stand around gawking. Then...

- There's a flash of light and a shimmering road appears in the eastern sky; it seems to be moving toward the disturbance in the sky.
- Lightning crackles. . . and suddenly Vantage is fully visible overhead.

VANTAGE FALLS

- The ground around the adventurers (and everybody else) begins to explode as falling debris strike.
- Arcs of rainbow-hued lightning strike the ground, trees catch fire, and a hay cart explodes.
- If the adventurers decide to run toward something for cover, it either explodes or falling debris impacts and blocks their path before shimmering into invisibility.
- The world turns into a hellscape of explosions and screams.

It seems everything and everyone is on fire, frozen solid in a block of ice, or in a building that just collapsed. There is no opportunity to pause and try to get a bigger picture—adventurers are living heartbeat-to-heartbeat just trying to survive.

Everybody must make a skill check (it's a DC 20 check to *run, duck,* or *run toward the tavern;* a DC 30 check for *I see if I can...* or *I look around for a . . . .* The adventurers take 3d4 points of damage if they succeed; 12 points of damage if they fail. Sorry! There is no time to do much of anything other than react).

The pyrotechnic cacophony also temporarily deafens and blinds everybody.

This is where you decide how harsh you want to be as a GM. You can require just one round of survival rolls, or you can keep going until the first PC hits 0 hp. If you want to be really harsh, you can decide that critically failing the skill check instantly reduces a character to 1 hp. Personally, I'm not that harsh; but it depends on how "old-school" your group likes to play.

Then, there is a period of silence as the dirt and dust settle. You hear occasional screams and flames crackling, then there is an agonizingly loud shredding sound, like the world tearing itself apart. Vantage begins to slide sideways out of the sky; it falls quickly, though it appears to move glacially slow due to its gigantic mass. It hits one side of the valley, gouging new geography into the landscape, and then impossibly lifts off again. A magical energy storm discharges around Vantage as the last functioning spell-engine flickers and dies, and then the world goes dark—the previous explosions put to shame by the world-ending ferocity of Vantage's last moments.

*Rob runs this a bit differently, with the fight highly visible to the adventurers, giant shadowy monsters clashing high above, and epic magical battles causing rainbow lightning to crack across the sky.*

Personally, I prefer to throw Vantage at the adventurers with little explanation, keeping the action with them, front and center. Focusing on the adventurers huddled under a stone bridge or in a building's basement as the dust engulfs them and they hear the villagers' screams before the apocalyptic thunder drowns them out seems more visceral and personal.

However, I can see Rob's reasoning and if I were to run this Rob's way, I'd follow his lead and do it at night so the fireworks are more spectacular and the adventurers can see thrilling dog-fights on dragon-back, flaming bodies raining from the sky, lightning and explosions, and the whole nine yards.

Still, I prefer to drop Vantage on the adventurers during the day because I think the sky going dark is a great way to signal the campaign's shift in tone.

AFTER THE FALL

While the bulk of Vantage is a twisted, burning ruin that fills the valley, parts of it remain adrift in the sky. Some chunks spin madly in mid-air, while others ride aloft on columns of purple fire. The adventurers' primary concern at this point should be to dodge the pieces that continue to fall.

At this point in the adventure, it's likely the PCs have completely lost their bearings. The landscape is shrouded in dust and smoke, and there is fire everywhere. They either hear loud sounds and explosions, or a deathly hush—and sometimes all that lies between the two are a few yards. Large shapes in the sky are mostly indistinct, except when coruscating light covers them or they make loud noises

There is no real structure to this part of the adventure. Shocked survivors search for loved-ones or desperately try to find safety. The injured stumble about or lie dying. The adventurers, being slightly more accustomed to such conditions than ordinary farmers, might have a plan. Listen to what your players suggest. If they want to search for NPCs, this becomes a rescue mission as they move through the rubble to get to where they think those NPCs might be. If you want a vital NPC to show up later, treat them differently than you would a regular NPC the party met in passing.

APOCALYPSE MONTAGE

Ask a player to describe a scene of destruction that the party can see from whatever place of shelter they find. Turn to the next player and ask them how their character reacts to what they see. Turn to a third player and ask them how the reaction of the second player's adventurer impacts their character. Continue to go around the group and help them narrate an apocalypse.

Hopefully, your group has gotten the hang of montages by now. Montages are perfect for winding down a session (players narrate what their characters do once they get back to town with the loot), generating story ideas at the start of a session, re-introducing characters after a group has not played together for a while, or introducing new characters to a group of adventurers. We find they are best used at the beginning of a session to start things off with a bang.

You won't find additional montages in this book because we assume that as a GM, you also have gotten the hang of this narrative tool. Like all tools, use montages wisely. They can slow play down if you overuse them mid-session, so try to limit them to natural lulls in play. Like a video-game cut scene (or a movie montage), they are ideal for dealing with travel and the passage of time, or skipping past the less interesting bits to get to the parts where amazing adventures happen.

IMMEDIATE HAZARDS

Here are four common hazards the adventurers must face as they move through the immediate aftermath of Vantage's fall. Like the rest of this chapter, these hazards assume the campaign starts at adventurer-tier; however, some of these hazards are powerful and are better suited for higher-level adventurers (or for instilling real fear in low-level PCs).

A **fire roars out of control**, spreading toward the adventurers and eventually enveloping the area. Each must make a DC 15 check to dodge before being overrun by flames; **roaring fire +5 vs. PD**—2d6 fire damage.

A **wall collapses**, crushing those beneath it and sending out a spray of rocks. Each adventurer must make a DC 20 check to notice the problem or dodge it; **spray of rocks +10 vs. AC**—2d10 damage.

Sudden subsidence opens the ground itself, trapping the adventurers' feet and crushing their legs. Each must make a DC 25 check to dodge or avoid the area; **crushing ground +15 vs. PD**—2d12 damage.

An **explosion of random debris** creates a pulverizing shockwave. Each adventurer must make a DC 25 check to dodge the explosion; **shockwave +15 vs. AC**—3d8 thunder damage.

UNCOMMON HAZARDS

Here are six uncommon hazards the adventurers might occasionally come across as they move through the immediate aftermath of the fall. These are likely to be one-time occurrences.

A **flickering magical field** springs to life, inflicting pain on anybody caught in it. Each adventurer must make a DC 15 check to detect or dodge; **mana surge +5 vs. MD**—2d6 force damage.

Acid drips from the corpse of a dragon impaled on a piece of Vantage, pooling at its base. Each adventurer must make a DC 15 check to dodge; **dragon marrow +5 vs. PD**—2d4 + 4 acid damage.

A **chunk of debris** has a still-functioning mechanism that whirls to life, whipping a chain this way and that. Each adventurer must make a DC 20 check to dodge; **chain whip +10 vs. PD**—3d6 damage.

Lightning arcs between two twisted spires of metal. Each adventurer must make a DC 20 check to dodge; **lightning arc +10 vs. PD**—2d6 + 4 lightning damage.

A **section of debris phases in and out of reality**, crushing and blasting anything caught within it. Each adventurer must make a DC 25 check to dodge; **unstable reality +15 vs. PD**—2d6 + 8 force damage.

Psychic screams emanate from the wreckage, as somewhere within it, a wizard dies. Each adventurer must make a DC 25 check to guard their minds; **dying wizard's mind-link +15 vs. MD**—4d6 psychic damage.

RESCUE OPERATIONS

The adventurers may wish to rescue NPCs who managed to find immediate shelter. They'll find most survivors scattered in pockets of relative safety (basements and cellars) or trapped alone or in small groups beneath rubble. If the adventurers are heroic, they'll probably want to do some good here.

I both played in and ran this campaign on alternate days of the week. In one campaign, the players didn't care at all about the NPCs and left them to live or die as fate determined, while the party set out to loot the ruins of Vantage. In the other campaign, the players arranged search parties, found places of shelter for the surviving NPCs, and led a trek to the still-intact Vakefort where they hoped to find shelter, food, and water for themselves and the refugees. I'll leave it a mystery as to which game I played in and which I ran.

If the adventurers decide to rescue NPCs, here are a variety of options to help you set up each rescue moment. Roll a d6 for each.

A named NPC that you want to use later in the campaign:

1. Slight injuries but on their feet and moving.
2-3. Injured and trapped under wreckage (DC 15 check to free them; failure means the adventurer takes 2d4 damage from sharp/hot edges).
4-6. Trapped in a building cellar, but otherwise unharmed.

A named NPC for whom the adventurers are specifically looking:

1. Injured, slumped somewhere. Needs magical healing or similar before they can move on their own, but otherwise safe.
2-3. Severely injured and in danger (DC 20 check to rescue them; failure means the NPC takes 2d6 damage from exploding debris, two failures mean the NPC dies unless they receive immediate magical healing).
4-6. Missing, presumed (but not necessarily) dead.

A named NPC the adventurers met in passing who is not essential to the campaign:

1. Conscious, but trapped, and calling for help (DC 20 check to free them; failure means they remain trapped until more rescuers can help).
2-3. Conscious and calling for help, but they'll die if the adventurers do not intervene (DC 20 check to help; failure means the NPC dies).
4-6. Dead (joined the choir invisible; is now an ex-NPC).

Previously unmet and nameless NPC:

1. Unconscious. They'll die if the adventurers do not intervene (DC 25 check to help; failure means the NPC dies).
2-3. Injured but... oh, wait, no. Dead. Gruesomely expired, in fact. Cleft in twain.
4-6. Not merely dead, but really, most sincerely dead.

Rescue locations: Where and how the adventurers search for survivors depends a lot on their experience of Redfield Valley before Vantage fell from the sky.

They're in luck if they were staying in the Lucky Grape—though their rooms are partially destroyed, the cellar and many NPCs huddled in it are safe. If they were staying in the Quacking Goblin they are out of luck—everything is either flattened or on fire, or both.

Appleton, with its stone buildings and position on a slope, generally fares better than Crownhill and its mostly wooden buildings with no cellars clustered atop a hill. However, as the GM, you may choose to spare certain locations (especially if doing so adds to the drama because they are now endangered, and the adventurers can intervene). Include pockets of shelter where the villagers and adventurers can flee and find protection.

This is also a prime opportunity to drop random battles and treasures in the group's lap. Whoever caused Vantage to fall could still be around in some capacity or other, and likely plans to attack the adventurers, next. Whoever did this might also be carrying treasure. More on this in *Chapter 4: The Glitterfall.*

A Note About Pacing

You could run several grim sessions dealing with the immediate aftermath of the fall: performing triage for the wounded, finding shelter for the survivors come nightfall, searching for clean water, etc.

Run this section for as long as it remains *fun*; as soon as the players grab a plot hook, downplay the rescue operations and run with the hook instead. Spend just enough time on the immediate aftermath to get a taste of the action, then move on to other stuff.

Contested rescues: If monsters or villains involved in Vantage's fall are doing more damage while the PCs attempt rescues, use battle stats from the *Adversary Groups* beginning on page 191. You'll be using them a lot in chapters to come, and there's no harm in revealing antagonists early on!

Treasure: It's likely that some of the things falling from the sky are useful. Choose something interesting from the *Magical Treasures* appendix (page 189) to drop near the party. Or, maybe place a magic item on a corpse.

ICONIC ANGLES

Why did Vantage fall? The notes below suggest motives and means for many of the icons, including those who are not the usual suspects. We don't provide adversary groups for all the icons, instead we focus on the main suspects. However, especially if you're running *Shards of the Broken Sky* for a second time, you may decide to use icons who wouldn't ordinarily initiate such attacks.

As the campaign develops, the PCs may find the bodies of creatures that appear to have attacked Vantage. See *Detective Stories* on the *Glitterfall Plot Point* table (page 51) for advice on running stories in which the PCs care a great deal about uncovering the truth.

Next steps: Whatever the cause of Vantage's fall, no icon can afford to ignore this transformation of the landscape. Each section includes notes on possible iconic agendas.

ICON MESSENGERS

The icons themselves may wish to communicate directly with the adventurers during the campaign, especially once the wards start to fail and fall. We list ideas for each icon to get you started in those moments you'd like communication between an icon and the party, but we leave the specifics up to you. You can also make use of the *Icon-Related NPCs* at the end of Chapter 1 (page 9).

ARCHMAGE

The Archmage might have poured energy into Vantage when it was attacked, trying valiantly to keep it aloft. Alternatively, he might have withdrawn his mystic power from the flying realm when he realized defending it was a lost cause.

The Archmage might even have caused the fall, in a sense, if his vast (yet waning) magical power was needed elsewhere and he could simply no longer support Vantage or prevent enemy icons from attacking. Was the fall of Vantage a sign of his weakness, or the result of terrifying enemy action?

Whatever the truth, the Archmage must restore the wards. Exactly what restoring the wards involves is up to you as a GM—maybe he needs artifacts from the wreckage, maybe it requires some monumental rituals, or perhaps restoration even has a potentially dark cost. Restoring the wards in Redfield Valley could spark a whole campaign.

MESSENGERS

Sprite. Magical mouth. Talking familiar. Arcane image.

CRUSADER

Old Tusk, a nearby mountain, is in fact a demon-filled volcano. The Archmage managed to keep the volcano under control for so long that everybody forgot it was anything more than a big pile of uninteresting rocks. Knowledge about how the Archmage controlled the volcano could help the Crusader battle the Diabolist. Maybe that's why the Crusader attacked Vantage.

The Crusader wants to jump right in and contain the situation in Redfield Valley, and may not care who gets hurt in the process. Perhaps this is the beginning of a new crusade to contain and slay the many monsters and demons unleashed by the failing wards.

MESSENGERS

Imp with its mouth sewn closed and a scroll attached to its leg. Sealed letter delivered by a soldier. A bat that screeches a message.

DIABOLIST

Unleashing demons, uncorking a hellhole, and sticking it to the so-called forces of "good" and "law"... the Diabolist is a woman of simple tastes, and bringing down Vantage would be just her cup of demonic tea. Even if she isn't directly responsible for the fall, she'll be quick to send agents to recover artifacts and free trapped demons. A Diabolist-focused campaign could see the adventurers racing to stop cultists from causing more damage; or it could focus on service to the Diabolist—freeing demons and recovering unholy artifacts.

MESSENGERS

Nightmares. Fresh scars that burn like fire. Messages divined in a sacrifice's entrails.

DWARF KING

Ancient treasure! The fall of Vantage and breaking of the wards allow the dwarven leader to send agents to scoop up mundane items—among which there are bound to be weapons he can use to eventually reclaim the dwarves' lost Underhome. Though the Dwarf King probably had no hand in the fall, it does present fascinating opportunities for the dwarves.

The Dwarf King must protect his people from anything that comes out of Redfield Valley, so it's possible he'll send agents to stem the tide of evil at its source. Of course, if he had foreknowledge of the fall, his agents are already nearby.

MESSENGERS

Mind-to-mind communication through a magical treasure thought long lost. A book of dwarven prophecies the adventurers received prior to the adventure, with cryptic sayings that only make sense at the right time. Tiny dwarven-forged construct.

ELF QUEEN

Who can say why the absolute ruler of the Court of Stars has an interest in the happenings here? The Court of Stars has more secrets than most would guess—and they work hard to keep them secret. What ancient power bound here long ago would the elves wish to keep safe? What old evil must the elves defeat now that it is free? What treasure must the elves recover, at any cost? We leave the answers up to you.

It's possible one elven faction (*drow, we're looking at you*) caused the crash without their queen's permission—a power-play that means Redfield Valley is about to become a pivotal piece in the elven nobles' immortal games.

MESSENGERS

Direct, soul-to-soul whispers scented with the cool breeze of the Queen's Wood. Spiders or leaves spelling out messages on the night wind. Magical messenger arrows.

EMPEROR

The Emperor has the most to lose from the fall of Vantage— the failing wards unleash many half-vanquished foes on the Dragon Empire, and ancient embarrassments come to light. The Emperor might send heroes to defeat the evil and prevent it from spreading, or he might send agents to evacuate the innocent and recover treasures before the Archmage seals the valley away forever. In a Machiavellian campaign, the Emperor—or elements of his staff—might opt to silence all witnesses, instead....

Is it possible the Emperor sabotaged Vantage to wrest control of the First Emperor's Tomb from the Archmage? Certainly, in some campaigns!

MESSENGERS

Letter and "care package" of healing potions air-dropped by an imperial dragon rider. Messenger orb. Legionnaire's emblem magically pressed into a message before melting under mystic pressure.

GREAT GOLD WYRM

The golden paladins were responsible for defeating many of the ancient evils trapped behind the failing wards. They dragged demons, unearthly monsters, and evil artifacts here from across the world to imprison them. Now that the prison doors are springing open, the Great Gold Wyrm wants heroes on hand to contain the unleashed tide of darkness.

Who can know the mind of an icon, though? If the Great Gold Wyrm was behind Vantage's fall, reality is more complicated than the *13th Age* core rulebook expected!

MESSENGERS

A dream within a dream, incepted into the minds of the party. The fighter's magic shield sheds its usual quirk and speaks with the voice of a far-off dragon.

HIGH DRUID

Vantage was a stain upon the world, a mystic dam in the flow of nature, a canker that ate away... well, you get the idea. The High Druid might have caused the fall of Vantage—she certainly isn't sad that it's gone.

Of course, she may not be too happy at what the fall unleashed and no doubt wishes to contain any unnatural things, while letting natural beasts (no matter how destructive they may be) go free. If the High Druid bought down Vantage (or worked with another icon to do so), she likely sent agents into the valley ahead of time to stop unnatural forces from escaping the failing wards.

MESSENGERS

An owl, squirrel, etc. with the ability to speak. Psychic communion with a stag. Whispering winds. A voice in a storm. Singing stones.

LICH KING

Perhaps the Lich King built Vantage when he was the Wizard King, and still regards it as *his* floating palace. That the empire parked it in one place instead of using it as a flying fortress of terror only attests to the Emperor's crass stupidity. The empire deserves to fall, and Vantage might be the Lich King's opening gambit to unfold the plan he crafted over thousands of years.

Then again, maybe the Lich King had no idea that Vantage was about to fall. Either way, he contributed to many of its secrets; so, he's sure to send his creatures to gain the greatest possible benefit from his enemy's misfortune.

MESSENGERS

An undead crow drops an eyeball to an adventurer—the last thing the eyeball saw was a letter addressed to the adventurer—a vision shared if the adventurer follows protocol and looks through the eyeball (or eats it!). A skeletal hand thrusts out of a grave and writes a message in the dirt or is clutching a scroll. A corpse speaks directly to the adventurers.

ORC LORD

The Orc Lord probably didn't bring down Vantage, as aerial attacks are not his *forte*. Then again, it's possible an orc army marched up one of the invisible sky bridges to lay siege to the flying fortress, in which case, there's a lot of evidence—if one knows where to look. Perhaps thousands of dead orcs are still orbiting high above and begin to rain down on the valley once Vantage's lingering broken magic wears off. Or, maybe orc corpses litter one of the sky bridges.

Regardless of who bought Vantage down, the Orc Lord is certainly interested in looting the ruins. He also has a keen interest in collapsing the wards around the Orcwell.

MESSENGERS

A terrified goblin. Visions in the flames. Carved bone delivered by a dire wolf.

PRIESTESS

The Priestess is the least likely icon to have any involvement in the fall of Vantage.

. . . though the Archmage did help her build her Cathedral, and with Vantage gone he has more time and magical energy to devote to her projects and the Gods of Light. Or maybe she is trying to weaken her "allies" and cause the people of the empire to rely on her clerics and paladins for protection and safety.

Still, this seems like a stretch for most campaigns. If she *is* involved, it's much more likely her agents accidentally brought down the wards while attempting to free a trapped deity or find a lost holy book.

The Priestess sends divinely favored heroes to aid in the fight against the darkness, as she wants to stop the flow of evil from spreading outward. She may even have had prior warnings in the form of visions and signs from above.

MESSENGERS

Prophetic visions in the flames of a campfire. A message delivered by miracle (spelled out in the seeds of a fruit, the clouds form letters, etc.). A small ball of light that flares once and leaves an afterimage for hours.

PRINCE OF SHADOWS

The hidden master of Shadow Port is an expert at *Xanatos Roulette*—setting complex plans into motion that ultimately benefit him no matter how they are opposed. Even if the Prince of Shadows wasn't directly responsible for attacking Vantage, he could easily have arranged affairs so one of the other icons did the dirty work for him.

Whether he was or was not behind the attack, the Prince almost certainly has agents in the area looking for specific treasures; he might even send somebody in to plant treasures for another power's agents to find, either to stir up the Dragon Empire's politics or to lay the groundwork for a deeper plan.

MESSENGERS

A letter just kind of shows up, as though somebody just slipped it to you. A living shadow slips into camp to whisper secrets to you. The tattoo you've always had on your wrist temporarily rearranges itself to deliver a message, then returns to normal before anyone else sees it.

THE THREE

If anybody had the ability to attack the flying invisible magical island it was the Three. Their draconic followers can fly, and they have access to sorcery and good reasons to work against other icons. While Drakkenhall's official imperial ruler is the Blue, that doesn't mean the Three are angels.

Indeed, any number of the Blue's sorcerers, the Black's shadow warrior monks, or the Red's fire-cultists could be involved, separately or jointly. If they did bring down Vantage, they could be rebelling—their agents openly combing the ruins for treasure and killing survivors. Or, they might quietly send in assassins to kill any witnesses and remove evidence of their involvement.

MESSENGERS

Lightning that burns a message into the soil. Thunder that speaks your name. A hot wind that roars commands.

CHAPTER 4:

THE GLITTERFALL

Most adventure locations in this book list suggested PC level ranges. This chapter covers any level you choose for Vantage's fall, and the aftermath; the *glitterfall* lasts awhile and the PCs are likely to progress while some *glitterfall* aspects are still a problem. Therefore, some of the suggested battles here are outlines of creatures you can use at various levels, rather than fully-built battles.

THE POST-FALL ENVIRONMENT

At this point in the adventure, the PCs should have found some sort of refuge from the initial fall and rescued any NPCs in immediate danger. Perhaps they found a safe place to regroup. Maybe they are hip-deep in a stream, hiding under a bridge that offers shelter from falling objects. Or, they might be huddled in the one corner of a root cellar that has not collapsed. It's even possible they are cowering in the unlit furnace of a village smith. Occasionally, falling rocks pelt their temporary shelter; but, for now, they are safe.

Eventually, the adventurers are going to want to (or be forced to) move. When they do, the valley is almost unrecognizable—the whole landscape has changed. Gouges in the red clay are filling with water. Metal and stone spires flicker with threatening magical fields, obviously dangerous to approach. Rubble is everywhere, and rocks hover in the sky or fall at great speeds. Fires burn, uncontrolled. Twisted spires and ridges of wreckage dot the landscape; and in the sky, a ring of smoke and fire has replaced the sun.

GLITTER IN THE AIR

Pieces of the flying island, most of which are tiny metal flakes, steadily drift down from the sky—a rain of glitter. Many of these particles falling from the sky are sharp or hot; adventurers take a −2 penalty to their d20 rolls until they find some way to keep these particles out of their eyes and lungs.

FALLING MASONRY

There are, of course, much larger pieces of falling wreckage—chunks of masonry held aloft by shreds of magic. When such a piece falls, it is generally preceded by a flash of light or a screaming whine as the magic holding it finally fails.

These large chunks are dangerous to anyone who ventures out in the open. It requires a DC 15 skill check to avoid a falling chunk, whether that means avoiding the area or seeking cover once the masonry tumbles from the sky; failure means the falling masonry hits you.

Vantage masonry chunk +5 vs. AC—2d6 damage

SMALL CRATERS, TWISTED RUINS, AND RUBBLE

More dangerous still are those pieces of Vantage that embedded themselves deep into the ground or are hidden from view under the rubble of a house. Such hidden wreckage may have magical wards that flicker to life, defenses misfiring and attacking anybody nearby. Avoiding the misfiring defenses requires a DC 25 skill check; failure means the defenses make one of the following attacks:

Mind stab +15 vs. MD—4d6 psychic damage

OR

Lightning arc +10 vs. PD (two attacks)—2d8 + 2 lightning damage

OR

Life drain +5 vs. PD (three attacks)—5 ongoing negative energy damage

No Map
Early drafts of Shards of the Broken Sky *called for a new map of Redfield Valley after the fall of Vantage; but each campaign uses a different set of secrets. Some campaigns focus on Old Tusk and the Orcwell, others* have more than enough plotlines and deadly enemies without even mentioning those locations. So, there's no single map of Redfield, though villagers and adventurers alike are starting to grasp the bloody origins of the valley's name. Take the map of Redfield Valley on page 5 and complicate it as you choose.

GLITTERFALL ADVERSARY GROUPS

We'll get to the mechanics of moving around the new landscape with the *glitterfall* shortly. However, before we dig into what makes the *glitterfall* entirely different, we want to touch on the more standard complications the environment may throw against the PCs: fights with enemies!

The PCs are not the only combat-ready warriors exploring the new landscape. Choose one or more of these adversary groups to complicate each expedition in the *glitterfall*. Maybe the adversary group is working with those responsible for the crash, maybe they had advance knowledge of the crash, or maybe they are opportunists.

Sandboxing it: The dungeons that appear in later chapters provide level guidelines for PCs and tables for building specific battles. The *glitterfall* is more of a sandbox environment. All PC groups experience the *glitterfall* in their own way, so we don't provide specific battle tables for multiple possible wandering-monster style encounters at all levels.

Instead, each of the many possible adversary groups that appear in the Appendix (starting on page 191) list groups of associated creatures and battles that use those creatures at different levels. Some of these creatures are reprinted or slightly revised from other *13th Age* books, while others make their debut here. If you feel these groups need more competent leadership, consider an icon-related NPC from Chapter 1 (page 9).

Many adversary groups could eventually get involved in the campaign. Here, we mention the villainous groups we think are most likely to be active soon after Vantage's fall.

Demons of the Prism

The *Great Prism* is a plotline we present in detail on page 116. Roving demons that break out of warded areas or containment areas housed on Vantage feel like an excellent "looter" variant, especially if the demons try to destroy the areas in which they were imprisoned before the Diabolist can recapture or control them.

You don't have to use the plot to use this assortment of demons as recurring villains—you could run this as a more straightforward Diabolist-inspired plotline.

You'll find adventurer-tier *Demons of the Prism* on page 200 and champion-tier versions of these adversaries on page 204.

Dragonic Agents of the Three

Agents of the Three make for extremely effective rapid responders—but they're not here to rescue people. Blue dragonic sorcerers… black dragonic ninjas… add in some desperate mercenaries and a marauding dragon and you are good to go! See page 192 for adventurer-tier *Agents of the Three*, or page 196 for champion-tier versions of these adversaries.

Druids & Beasts?

If the High Druid was responsible for Vantage's fall, it is reasonable to assume you'll find her minions in the area immediately afterward. Even if the Druid's followers had nothing to do with the fall itself, it's possible they are drawn to the surges of wild magic released by vanquished wards.

We confess that we've weighed the amount of new material we created to support the High Druid's forces in this book and decided we don't have enough to justify the many pages of reprints required to flesh this out as an adversary group. You'll find one druidic menace in the *Wizards & Spellcasters* adversary group on page 218; otherwise, if this is the path you're set on, you can recruit from the many beasts in our bestiaries, the *13th Age Monthly* article called *High Druid's World*, and the upcoming *Icon Followers* book.

Orcs of the Orc Lord

Aren't most orcs working for the Orc Lord? Typically, yes, but one of the major plotlines you may choose to exploit in your campaign involves a powerful spawning pit called the Orcwell. If the Orc Lord was involved in the fall of Vantage, the Orcwell may be his target.

You'll find a new adventurer-tier orc that's right for the *glitterfall* on page 214. If you eventually plan to deal with the Orcwell, you'll find notes on its creatures on page 215.

Undead

The Lich King has his agents in place. Maybe they attacked Vantage, maybe he resurrected the dead as his servants, or maybe the undead were *always* here in Redfield Valley, just waiting…. Notes on an undead adversary group appear on page 217.

Wizards & Spellcasters

Survivors from Vantage, assassins sent to cover up the fall, corrupt servants of the Archmage who turned traitor, or magical backup for another adversary group—wizards and their servants make excellent antagonists. Who knows? Several rival groups could be in the *glitterfall* at once. We include enough diverse spellcasters in the *Wizards & Spellcasters* adversary group on page 218 that they need not have much connection to the Archmage, if that's your preference.

Random Glitterfall Wanderers

Other antagonists the party must face during their pass through the *glitterfall* could be deserters from Vakefort, opportunistic mercenary bands who just happened to be passing by, soldiers of the Crusader, creatures of the Prince of Shadows, or even villagers out to scavenge whatever they can.

If this is the case, the PCs have it easy: use the stats for the Villagers and Tough Villagers/Vakefort Soldiers from page 9 for these adversaries.

Adventuring in the Glitterfall

The *glitterfall* is a dungeon that comes to the adventurers. Simply moving from one end of a village to the other becomes its own quest, with adventure locations literally drifting or falling from the sky. With that in mind, we created a wandering dungeon table you can use whenever the PCs move through the valley on the way to their next adventure.

Roll once or twice on the tables below as the adventurers stir from the ashes to begin the next phase of their adventure. Treat a total of five rolls on the *Glitterfall Wandering Dungeon* table as the equivalent to a single battle for the purposes of tracking when the PCs should get a full heal-up.

There are over a million possible "dungeons" you can create with just five random *glitterfall* incidents, so feel free to use the *Glitterfall Wandering Dungeon* table a few times as the adventurers move about Redfield Valley. The *glitterfall* could drag on for weeks.

GAMEMASTER

Eventually, adventurers are going to reach a high enough level that the *glitterfall* is no longer an active threat. That's fine—it's perfectly acceptable to use the *glitterfall* as an adversary at lower levels and as a narrative device or background color at higher levels, as the PCs' focus naturally shifts from survival to longer-term goals.

RANDOM GLITTERFALL EVENTS

When adventuring in the *glitterfall*, roll a d20 on the *Glitterfall Wandering Dungeon* table up to five times to discover what the party faces this time. A result of 20 indicates you should introduce a plot element you invent, choose from the *Glitterfall Plot Point* table (starting on page 50), or roll to select from the table randomly.

As you can see, there's a great deal of variation within single results, though there are certain events you won't want to use twice. If you're inspired to create your own *glitterfall* events, may the PCs survive. . . . Barely.

1. Treasure: The party stumbles upon some form of treasure. We recommend using the fading items that appear in the *Magical Treasures* appendix on page 189. Fading items were either a part of Vantage, or powered by Vantage, and are usually glowing twists of sharp, unidentified metal or hunks of broken, rune-carved stone. They are initially extremely powerful, but their power fades over time. Thus, the PCs get a taste of power, but not the full meal!

2. Red Glowball: A glowing, red sphere of light drifts down from the sky. When it touches a solid object, it makes a tiny popping sound and leaves a mote of red light. The mote slowly expands, and starts to pull mud, rubble, sharp twists of metal, and adventurers toward it. PCs must make a DC 15 check to hang on to something solid; failure means they suffer 2d6 points of damage from internal organ collapse and being pelted with detritus. Anybody foolish enough to grab on to somebody or something stuck to the mote gets stuck themselves and also takes the 2d6 damage.

After a minute or so, the mote begins to drift upward, shedding its gathered load as it does so (anybody attached to the mote suffers 3d6 falling damage). The mote expands back into a fuzzily-glowing sphere of light and drifts away.

3. Falling Masonry: Avoiding chunks of falling masonry requires a DC 15 skill check for each character, whether that means avoiding the area or seeking cover once the masonry tumbles from the sky; failure means the falling masonry attacks the

GLITTERFALL WANDERING DUNGEON TABLE

1. Treasure
2. Red Glowball
3. Falling Masonry
4. A Wall
5. The Tunnel
6. Magical Defenses
7. Bridge Over Danger
8. Golden Glowball
9. Radiant Spire
10. Blue Glowball
11. The Mirage
12. Hidden Danger
13. The Archway
14. A Sudden Drop
15. The Waterfall
16. The Crystal Door
17. The Lodestone Spinner
18. Green Glowball
19. Golden Storm
20. Plot Point

adventurer. **Vantage masonry chunk +5 vs. AC—2d6 damage;** *miss:* 1d6 fire damage.

4. A Wall: A huge remaining section of Vantage crashes down directly in front of the adventurers, blocking their way (roll a d6):

1. It's a section of floor with a mosaic pattern that landed on its side, creating a wall.
2. It's a piece of one of the sky roads that led to Vantage.
3. It's a wall with a door in it, but the impact jammed the door shut (DC 20 check OR 20 points of damage dealt in a single attack to open the door; failure causes **Falling Masonry**—see above).
4. It's a huge metal cylinder, glowing with runes. Anybody who approaches takes 2d4 cold damage.
5. It's a congeries of parts—cogs, cracked and smoking crystals, dead lifeless runes, metal tubes, melted stone, etc.
6. The same as 5, but also re-roll a d20 twice on the *Glitterfall Wandering Dungeon* table to see which effects accompany it.

5. The Tunnel: The way ahead is blocked by a wall of rubble and twisted metal. A pipe sticks out of the wall, large enough to crouch-walk through. It looks like there is light at the end of the pipe—a possible way through (roll a d6):

1. It's a pipe; it's a bit slippery with rain water, but it provides passage to the other side.
2. It's a part of Vantage's former sewers. It stinks, and there is a metal grate at the far end preventing further passage. Adventurers must make a DC 15 check to kick out the metal grate; failure causes the kicker to skid and fall over in filth.
3. The pipe is a dead-end, but there is a monster with glowing eyes at the far end (it's your call whether this is a serious battle or an unusual interlude).
4. The pipe is a dead end, but there is a glowing crystal mounted at the far end. Mud and other similar muck that touches the crystal disappears, though dropping the crystal into mud causes it to overload and explode; everybody nearby takes 1d10 force damage. If the adventurers also remove the portion of pipe on which the crystal is mounted along with the crystal, it won't explode when dropped in mud (though the metal pipe section does get hot).
5. The pipe leads to a chamber that has other pipes leading out of it; roll a d3 + 1 to determine the number of other pipes; then, re-roll a d6 on this table to describe each pipe.
6. The pipe leads to a mirror covered in runes (roll another d6):
    1. When touched, the mirror produces a duplicate of the adventurer who touched. The duplicate then attacks the party (use the adventurer's current stats). If the living reflection escapes or is subdued there is a 50% chance it just fades away; otherwise, it becomes a real being and later attempts to either kill or befriend its creator.
    2. The mirror is a portal that allows passage to a mirror in another pipe elsewhere in the *glitterfall*.
    3. Anybody who touches the mirror with a bare hand takes 1d8 cold damage.
    4. The mirror shows an image that is somehow flipped or reversed from the truth—maybe each character appears as a close member of their own family, or the party's reflections show what the PCs would look like if they served different icons.
    5. The mirror is just a mirror, nothing special or magical about it.
    6. Roll a d4 on this table twice. The adventurers encounter both results.

6. Magical Defenses: A piece of wreckage drifts slowly down to one side; as it does so, its magical defenses activate (roll a d6):

1. Everybody is confused and rolls initiative (easy save ends). Hilarity ensues, for bragging rights, if nothing else.
2. Everybody is stuck (save ends) and takes 5 fire damage at the end of their turn until they can free themselves and move away from the wreckage, as their kinetic energy is transmuted to heat.

3. The wreckage unfolds to reveal a golem (or golems). Set up a fight from the *Golems* adversary group (page 207).
4. The party teleports 10 feet into the air; everybody takes 1d6 falling damage from the resulting fall. After the PCs hit the ground, the defenses activate again on the next round, and the next, and the next. Roll initiative to see if the PCs can wreck the wreckage before it wrecks them. The wreckage has Initiative 22, AC 16, PD 16, is immune to attacks that target MD, and has 20 hp. Until they destroy the piece of wreckage, the party continues to take damage on the wreckage's initiative count. From a distance, it probably looks funny. Up close—not so much.
5. Glowing defenders appear from the wreckage. Set up a fight using the *Golems* (page 207) or *Wizards & Spellcasters* (page 218) adversary groups. (They are magical projections and cannot move away from the wreckage). The defenders' creature type changes to "spirit".
6. The chunk of wreckage doesn't touch down; rather, it hovers in front of the party, slowly rotating in place. As it turns, it reveals a hidden pit trap that attempts to suck in the adventurers, who must make a DC 20 check to resist. Those sucked into the pit trap find their gravity re-aligned so they are subjectively at the bottom of the pit, no matter the hovering chunk's relation to the ground. To get out of the wreckage, the PCs must make a DC 15 check to jump "up" toward the ground; failure means they take 1d6 + 2 falling damage as they fall back into the floating wreckage, success means they take only 3 falling damage from launching headfirst into the ground. (The PCs must make a DC 25 check to jump to the ground without taking the 3 falling damage).

7. Bridge Over Danger: Jagged metal spires heat up the ground, boiling mud and melting rock. The only way across is to walk on a long piece of fallen wreckage. As each adventurer crosses, (roll a d6):

1. They slip. They must make a DC 15 check to avoid the jagged metal on the wreckage; failure means they take 1d6 damage from a strange metal spike.
2. A burst of gas from below sends scalding fumes upward. Scalding fumes +5 vs. PD—2d6 poison and fire damage.
3. A red-hot mud bubble bursts; the PC either takes 1d6 fire damage OR is targeted by the following attack. Burning mud +5 vs. PD—2d6 fire damage.
4. Nothing happens; the adventurer gets across without incident.
5. The wreckage shifts. All further rolls on this table use a d4 instead of a d6.
6. The adventurer spots treasure dangling from a nearby jagged spire and must make a DC 20 check to "rescue" the treasure instead of dropping it in the lava—a DC 25 check to do so without taking 1d12 + 8 points of fire damage while reaching for the treasure. It's your call whether the treasure is a true magic item, a fading item, or something weirder.

8. Golden Glowball: A glowing, gold sphere drifts down from the sky, illuminating everything around it. As it moves toward the ground, it expands. The PCs must make a DC 20 check to get out of the sphere's area of influence, otherwise (roll a d6):

1. Everything within the sphere's area of influence changes to shades of a single color, including the adventurer's equipment, their hair and eye color, and even the mud on their cloaks (roll a d12). 1-Red, 2-Orange, 3-Yellow, 4-Green, 5-Cyan, 6-Blue, 7-Purple, 8-Magenta, 9-Black, 10-White, 11-Grey, 12-re-roll with a d8, but the color is now metallic. The effect is harmless and will *probably* wear off, eventually.

2. Everybody becomes weightless for the next few minutes. Though they drift over the next obstacle, they must make a DC 15 skill check to land safely; failure indicates they drifted into danger (re-roll a d20 on the *Glitterfall Wandering Dungeon* table to find out what they drifted into).

3. The adventurers' senses are switched about. Adventurer A visually perceives what adventurer B smells, and hears what adventurer C touches, etc. The DC for all skill checks is raised by 10 until this effect wears off (after the next obstacle or the next rest).

4. Everybody rolls a d6 and receives a +5 boost to the indicated attribute for their skill checks; however, using said attributes inflicts 1d10 damage each time a roll is made. (1-Str, 2-Con, 3-Dex, 4-Int, 5-Wis, 6-Cha). The effect ends after the party's next rest.

5-6. Everybody gets ill and takes 3d6 negative energy damage.

9. Radiant Spire: A twisted spike of stone and metal juts up above the landscape, a new landmark in the transformed geography. Glowing runes flicker at the base of the spike, but there is no immediate danger. There are several voids or "rooms" in the spike for the PCs to explore (roll a d6 twice):

1. A hollow crystal hemisphere offers shelter and a good view.

2. A space within the spire is much larger on the inside than the outside. Chains are strewn about the room; it would seem they fell from one of several holes in what is now the ceiling. The PCs can hear muffled voices through one of the holes, their words indistinct and their tone ominous. For a fun twist—the holes lead to the future; if the characters shout through the holes, they pass by some holes later in the adventure and hear their past selves shouting at them.

3. An interior space reveals what was once a garden, though the soil now slopes toward one end of the askew floor and all the plants are uprooted. Glowing crystals hang in nets from the ceiling. Anybody who holds one of these crystals gains +1 to attack and +1 damage when using any magic that involves plants (the bonus doesn't stack with bonuses from magical implements).

4. A room that looks like a storeroom contains a jumble of smashed wooden crates full of broken glassware. Some of the jars' contents (mostly pickles) might be salvageable. A door in the opposite wall leads to a twisted metal plank that was once a walkway.

5. A room that contains a hovering, polished wooden board. The board can carry the same amount as a fully-laden mule, hovers about 3 feet above any solid surface, and—if pulled or pushed—moves as though it carries no extra weight at all. It might only work in Redfield Valley, but perhaps it can roam.

6. A door is set into the spire at an angle. Behind the door, you find (roll a d4):
    1. Wreckage blocking an internal corridor.
    2. An internal corridor leading to 2 more rooms (re-roll a d6 on the table above for each room).
    3. Fire! The room is on fire! The PC who opened the door takes 2d6 fire damage, and the fire continues to belch forth for the next week.
    4. A storeroom containing salted meat, dark rye bread, and large, live snails in jars. There is a door on the far side of the room (re-roll a d6 on the table above to see what's in the next room).

10. Blue Glowball: A glowing sphere of blue light descends gently toward the ground (roll a d6):

1. All adventurers heal up to maximum hit points; however, if they linger near the glowing sphere, their orifices begin to seal shut: eyelids fuse to eyeballs, nostrils pinch shut, lips won't open, ear holes close, etc.! Those who don't run away suffocate and die before becoming blobby corpses of undifferentiated, smooth flesh. It takes a steady hand and 1d6 points of damage, or a hurried blade and 1d10 points of damage, to reopen sealed orifices. The cosmetic damage fades, if the victim seeks magical healing and a decent surgeon. The blue sphere floats away after the adventurers encounter it.

2. The sphere explodes, blinding anybody who doesn't make a DC 20 skill check to shield their eyes. The blindness is magical in nature—those blinded see only sky wherever they look. The blindness fades, but those blinded face the next obstacle with a –5 penalty.

3. The adventurers find themselves suddenly attracting every piece of metal in their vicinity. **Metal storm +5 vs. AC (four attacks, each against a different adventurer)**—4 damage.

    Hereafter, the adventurers can stick coins to their faces as a party trick.

4. The ground beneath the adventurers liquefies, and the blue sphere fades away as the ground solidifies once more. The adventurers must make a DC 15 check to avoid being trapped; failure means they take 10 damage as they pull free from the solidifying ground.

5. The sphere just hovers there, humming softly. It does nothing unless the adventurers poke it or otherwise interfere with it; then, re-roll on this table using a d4.

6. The sphere follows the adventurers around for five minutes, providing illumination so they can see. After five minutes, or the first time an adventurer pokes it, re-roll on this table using a d4.

11. The Mirage: A group of wizards stands around a plinth, discussing weighty matters. Behind them, the adventurers can see Vantage. This is a magical illusion that masks some other

feature (re-roll a d20 on the *Glitterfall Wandering Dungeon* table—all DCs and attack bonuses for the new event are 3 higher than usual).

12. Hidden Danger: It looks like a normal patch of ground, slightly scorched, between two heaps of debris and rubble (roll a d6):

1. It *is* a normal patch of ground.
2. Whenever anybody tries to pass through (or throws something metal through) lightning arcs between the debris. **Lightning arc +10 vs. AC**—8 lightning damage.
3. The piles of debris are unstable, and pieces fall on unwary adventurers. **Rubble avalanche +10 vs. AC**—2d6 damage.
4-6. A piece of debris lies on the patch of ground. The PCs need a DC 25 check to spot it, as it is out of phase with reality. Adventurers walking through must dodge the debris as it phases in and out of existence. **Phasing debris +15 vs. PD**—14 damage.

13. The Archway: An archway sits askew in the mud, surrounded by hot spikes of metal that are moving and fusing together. The archway is the only way through (roll a d6):

1. The archway teleports anybody who walks through it to an identical archway, high in the sky on a mote of rock. The adventurers can see the devastated Redfield Valley far below. There isn't much space to stand up here, and the floating rock wobbles in the wind. The only ways down are to go back through the archway. . . or jump!
2. The archway has a force-field in it, which repels anybody who tries to walk through it. It does allow non-living items through, but not back. Any weapon an adventurer sticks through it is either lost or trapped half-in-half-out. Anybody who walks unknowingly into the field takes only minor damage (maybe 1-2 points), but finds that the front of their clothes, parts of their armor, and possibly parts of some of their weapons passed through the field. They can only retrieve these items if they find a way to the far side of the archway.
3. Anybody walking through the archway emerges thoroughly clean, though this is a painful process and feels like being attacked by scrub-brushes.

4. The archway causes anybody who tries to pass through it to move ahead one minute in time. As far as anybody watching is concerned, the person disintegrates (*GMs, have fun with this, but don't over-exasperate your players*).
5. The archway is just an archway—the adventurers pass through without issue.
6. The archway has crackling runes on it that cause 1d6 damage of a random type to anyone who touches them. It is otherwise just a normal archway.

14. A Sudden Drop: A piece of debris carved a huge ravine in the earth, coming to rest some distance away. The ravine's sides are baked clay—Redfield Valley's rich mud solidified by the intense heat. Coals still burn at the bottom of the trench. Getting across it takes time, during which two new obstacles fall from the sky (roll a d20 on the *Glitterfall Wandering Dungeon* table twice more).

15. The Waterfall: A torrent of water gushes out from beneath a piece of wreckage, spraying the adventurers as they pass (roll a d6):

1-4. The water is cold—it seems a portal deep within the wreckage is still linked to a mountain stream somewhere. The water is drinkable—a vital resource in the post-fall valley.
5. The water is boiling—it sends up a cloud of steam and scalds anybody who gets too close to the wreckage. Once cooled, it is drinkable, though it has a slightly metallic taste.
6. The water stops gushing as soon as the adventurers approach, reducing its flow to a trickle. As soon as they pass, it begins to spray out of the wreckage again.

16. The Crystal Door: A large, crystal door survived the fall, still in its frame. The door presents a possible way past a wall of rubble (roll a d6):

1. A magical eye appears above the door and shoots a ray at the party: **Eye of judgement +15 vs. PD (1d3 targets)**—10 force damage.
2. The door vanishes when the adventurers get within six feet of it and reappears when they retreat. Other than that, it is a normal door in all respects.
3. A stuttering illusion appears and either loudly declares that this is a restricted area or greets the adventurers and welcomes them to Vantage (50% chance either way). Moments later, the door shatters harmlessly.
4. A magical eye appears above the door and a wide beam shines from it, examining the party. Then, the eye shuts, and the door magically opens for all party members except one, who must find another way around. If the lone PC chooses to climb the rubble, they must make a DC 15 skill check; failure sends rubble down on other party members.
5. It leans at an angle, providing shelter from the *glitterfall* long enough for the party to rest.
6. Roll a d4 on this table twice. The adventurers encounter both results.

17. The Lodestone Spinner: A piece of rubble spins on its tip in the dirt, spraying mud and sending up a cloud of dust. Rubble obstructs most other routes (roll a d6):

1. The rubble just spins there, a harmless oddity.

2-3. As the party attempts to pass, the rubble spins faster and faster until it finally spins apart: **Exploding rubble chunk +10 vs. PD (2d3 targets)**—5 damage.

4-5. The spinning rubble repels metal items the party carries, even non-ferrous items. Adventurers who attempt to move around the object as far away as possible must make a DC 5 – DC 15 skill check (depending on how much metal they are carrying); failure means they are flung backward and take 2d6 + 3 force damage.

6. Combine the results from 4-5 and 2-3; after the rubble explodes, it reforms and continues to spin.

18. Green Glowball: A glowing energy field descends from the sky, verdant light seeping from it in tendrils (roll a d6):

1. The field hovers in place. Plants begin to grow nearby. Lichen covers the rubble, grass grows up from the dirt, and flowers bloom. Finally, saplings begin to sprout. After about an hour, the former rubble is a lush forest clearing, with only a few moss-covered stones sticking up here and there.

    Adventurers who stick around can shape the growing saplings, weaving huts from the living wood if they so choose.

2. Events happen as above, but much more rapidly. Anything wooden the adventurers carry (such as a bow, wand, or staff) begins to bud tiny flowers and leaves. Then, golems made of moss, stone, and living wood burst from the ground and attack the adventurers (use the *Primal Golem* on page 59).

3. Any cuts or wounds the adventurers had re-open and anything leather they carry begins to bleed and flop about. All adventurers lose a recovery, but regain their recovery value in hp, plus an additional 2d6 temporary hp. Their reanimated leather goods "die" if they leave the area. If the party has a recently deceased character with them, that character can make a death save; on a success, they return to life with 1 hp.

4. Everybody nearby suffers from a terrible headache. **Cognizance barb +10 vs. MD (2d3 targets)**—5 psychic damage and the next obstacle they face requires an additional +5 DC to their skill check. The orb drifts away after it attacks.

5. The rubble begins to move in a futile attempt to repair itself. Any broken items the party carries mend themselves, and dents "ping" out of armor. If the party remains here for too long, their equipment starts to fuse together—swords "mend" with scabbards, clothing stitches to clothing, chainmail links unite, etc.

6. The glowing sphere splits into three: one red, one gold, and one blue (see results 2, 8, and 10 on the *Glitterfall Wandering Dungeon* table for what each glowing sphere does).

19. Golden Storm: The *glitterfall* intensifies—instead of stinging glitter drifting down from the sky, sharp grit and gravel starts to fall. The *glitterfall* also glows, making it harder to see. As the rain of debris becomes harder and larger, the adventurers must make a DC 15 check to seek immediate cover; failure means they take 5 damage. They continue to take this damage each round until they succeed at finding adequate cover.

20. Plot Point: Something interesting is about to happen.... The plots described in the following *Glitterfall Plot Point* table can continue as narrative threads throughout the adventure. We expect you'll want to look through them and choose one that fits your campaign or use this moment to introduce something new you've got cooking. But, if you prefer to leave it to fate, grab a d12!

GLITTERFALL PLOT POINT TABLE

1. Prism Break
2. A Traitorous Archmage
3. Detective Stories
4. The Control Stone
5. For Gold and Glory!
6. For Honor!
7. The Rivals
8. The Race
9. Survival
10. Noble Hearts
11. Glitter-War
12. Shattered Wards

FRONT-LOAD, BUT DON'T OVERLOAD

If you like one of these plots and you want to make it a central plot in your campaign, use foreshadowing to front-load it pre-fall. Don't overload the party with plots, though—pick two or three and make them recurring themes.

1. Prism Break: Vantage held demonic prisoners onboard as harmless refracted light within crystalline prisms. The prisoners (or *"prismers"*) are now loose—they landed safely on the ground while imprismed but were freed when some of the prisms broke. This could be an ongoing plot as different flavors of demons with escalating agendas get free. (See page 116 for more on the *Great Prism*, and page 200 for the *Demons of the Prism* adversary group.)

2. A Traitorous Archmage: Vantage was a huge power-sink for the Archmage's fading magic. The adventurers find something in the ruins showing that the traitorous Archmage allowed Vantage to fall. Maybe Vantage was attacked, and he made the decision to withdraw his power; or maybe this is just the latest of his wards from which he has had to withdraw his arcane might. This is a serious scandal—the Archmage apparently let hundreds of his wizards die to preserve his own life.

Perhaps the adventurers find a letter that contains a warning about the Archmage's intentions, addressed to his favorite wizard; or maybe they find a dying familiar who relays the tale. Or, perhaps magical assassins attack the adventurers, determined to silence any survivors of the "unforeseen" disaster. Sounds like a job for the Wizards & Spellcasters adversary group on page 218, perhaps in company with an agent of the icons such as Rezlorkis (page 13), Lients (page 10), or Irkma (page 11).

3. Detective Stories: The adventurers uncover a clue that shows *someone* bought down Vantage. The clue is inconclusive, but it's highly likely that if they keep searching the *glitterfall,* they'll uncover enough evidence to prove what they are starting to suspect. Clues could include:

- A dead attacker, whose body is mangled beyond recognition but provides some small yet vital clue (a scrap of cloth, a tooth, a feather, a skeletal hand, etc.).
- A weapon used by an attacker, twisted by magic but revealing its likely point of manufacture (a grave-goods sword, a wooden club studded with obsidian flakes, a dagger forged in hellfire, etc.).
- A dying attacker, injured and delirious, but able to answer a few questions—albeit cryptically.
- Distinctive damage to some part of Vantage—something that could only be done by a specific icon's forces.

If you decide to go with this plot and your players engage with it, scatter the clues throughout the adventure—provide enough clues to keep them engaged, so they don't lose the thread, but not so many that they are tripping over clues and no mystery remains. The "why" of how Vantage fell won't undo the damage, but it could lead to an icon being brought to justice (at epic-level) and might allow the adventurers to find out where that icon will strike next and prevent another disaster.

Non-Detectives

Not every adventuring group is interested in playing *CSI: 13th Age.* If your players shrug at the clues they uncover and go looking for "the action," this is definitely not the plot for them.

When Rob's early playtest group encountered this as a plot hook, they entirely failed to engage with it, because with the sky falling and the world burning there were too many other interesting things to do.

If, however, your players love solving puzzles and riddles, this plot might be ideal—it has them running through the rubble with shields above their heads, trying to gather evidence before the rain of debris obliterates it, and piecing together what happened and why Vantage fell.

4. The Control Stone: Vantage used to move about through the sky; however, it ossified above Redfield Valley long ago. Whatever control widget it used (a magical ship's wheel, a giant crystal throne, a crown, etc.), somebody somewhere wants it. Here are some ideas:

- The adventurers must race to prevent unfriendly forces (from an adversary group of your choice, starting on page 191) from finding and capturing the control stone. If they fail, the villains could build a new flying battle-fortress.
- An icon sends the adventurers to fetch the control wheel; they must risk life and limb to secure the magical wheel before the enemy does.

If you introduce this plot, there are a lot of frantic chases through the *glitterfall,* as the adventurers search for signs of Vantage's lost control mechanism. Finding it involves some detective work, but also high-speed archeology, vaulting over and through obstacles, and fighting battles.

As the GM, you must decide who the opposing party is, and then sprinkle signs of their passage throughout the *glitterfall* for the adventurers to find (ropes attached to large detritus for scaling walls of rubble, chalk arrows they left so they wouldn't get lost, etc.).

5. For Gold and Glory!: There is bound to plenty of treasure in the *glitterfall.* Corpses have pockets, and pockets contain loose change. There could even be chests of treasure or magical items.

Of course, it all depends on whether the adventurers can get there before other looters. Villagers, soldiers from Vakefort, even survivors from the fall (or attackers) all have the same idea.

This plot works well for groups with ties to the Dwarf King—he might even send a message asking them to retrieve specific items.

6. For Honor!: The inverse of *For Gold and Glory!*, this plotline involves the adventurers' attempts to prevent others from looting the dead. Groups allied with the Lich King or Priestess might want to stop others from desecrating the dead (or have orders from their icon patron to protect the dead).

7. The Rivals: A rival group loots whatever they can in the *glitterfall* and endangers people or places the PCs care about; the adventurers must hunt them down either as revenge for bringing down Vantage, or to safeguard the remaining wards. This plotline can easily flip into *The Race*, or invert into *Glitter-War*.

8. The Race: A rival group spots a juicy treasure and is determined to get to it first. The adventurers must race against their rivals to get to the treasure, choosing the quickest route through the *glitterfall* and weighing risk against reward. This plot can flip into *The Rivals*.

9. Survival: The adventurers don't care about helping other survivors, looting, or exploring. . . they just want to get where they're going with minimal pain and anguish. Unfortunately; this means they must avoid powerful enemies, probably from an adversary group of your choice starting on page 191.

10. Noble Hearts: The adventurers are heroes, damn it! They aren't going to let civilians die on their watch!

This plotline involves herding survivors through the wreckage to places the adventurers vet as safe; finding them food, water, and medicine; and attempting to care for those who are injured.

The fact that new pieces of debris constantly rain from the sky complicates matters—what was once a "safe path" may no longer be safe the next time they try it.

11. Glitter-War: Somebody is out to get the adventurers; and they're not interested in loot or personal safety. Every turn the adventurers make leads to a potential ambush; every pile of detritus is a potential booby-trap. The adventurers don't even know how many enemies are out there—they might not even know *who* the enemy is.

When darkness falls, the hunt begins in earnest—unless the adventurers find a safe place to hide.

12. Shattered Wards: The adventurers receive advance warning that a ward is about to fail. Maybe they find a slab of crystal that displays certain images, meet a dying wizard who warns them of the danger with his last breath, or receive a warning directly from an icon (see *Icon Messengers* in the *Iconic Angles* section on page 40). Or, perhaps they uncover evidence of the failing ward while they explore Vantage's ruins. Don't overload players with the threat of potential doom, rather allow them to discover and deal with the failing wards one or two at a time.

Major Warded Areas

Here, we provide a list of the major warded areas, along with what information a failing-ward warning might convey. The area notes include level ranges. If you choose to provide champion-tier warnings to an adventurer-tier group, you may also want to warn them the problem is way above their heads!

Redfield Rising

(3rd and 4th level) The valley is the site of an ancient battle that was frozen in time and shifted out of phase with reality. The magic is not perfect; the battle has raged on for untold centuries in slow motion, drops of blood providing the soil its fertility and rich red color.

Once the ward fails, the whole valley becomes an active battlefield again.

Old Tusk

(5th and 6th level) A mountain visible in the distance is in fact a volcano, held dormant by the wards Vantage maintained. Now that Vantage fell, the volcano is reawakening. It was sealed to begin with because it has the potential to collapse into a full-blown hellhole, a portal to a demonic netherworld filled with monsters and demons.

Stampede

(3rd and 4th level) Long ago, someone discovered a land that time forgot—it was one of the first things sealed away in Redfield Valley. Once the ward fails, all the monsters who were frozen in time awaken and spill out into the valley.

The Orcwell

(3rd to 5th level) The battle in Redfield was over control of something known as the *Orcwell*, a spawning pit for orcs of all types. The Orcwell's influence is what leads to the birth of so many half-orcs near Redfield Valley. If the ward on the Orcwell slips, hundreds of orcs pour forth and rampage across the land.

The Great Prism

(any level) Vantage trapped thousands of demons as refracted light in a giant crystal. When Vantage fell, the crystal shattered. Now, demons are escaping from the shards.

The Forest of the Dream Princess

(adventurer-tier, best at 3rd and 4th level) Evidence proving a lost icon from a previous age's existence lies north of Redfield Valley in the Vakevale. Once the wards slip, anybody could find the evidence, which might upset the Elf Queen. So, maybe this failing ward isn't really all that terrible... it could be semi-comic relief: *"Wait, that's all? The Elf Queen gets a bit embarrassed?"*

The Repository

(adventurer-tier—best at 2nd and 3rd level, and champion-tier) Part magically-radioactive dump and part warehouse, the Repository hidden in the Vakevale stores magical items too intriguing to destroy, but too dangerous to let out into the world. Once the wards on the Repository fail, the unstable magics it contains spill into the world, warping reality and birthing monsters.

The Corpse of Kroon

(6th and 7th level, or a bit above) Kroon was a giant that implanted magical items into its body and declared itself a living god. The giant was frozen in time moments after somebody dealt it a mortal blow. The giant itself is dead (or will be soon after the stasis wards on it fail), but the magical items inside it could unleash their energy all at once in a chaotic and destructive wave. Who knows what monsters might spring forth from Kroon's corpse?

CHAPTER 5:

SHATTERED SECRETS

ADVENTURES FOR 1ST AND 2ND LEVEL CHARACTERS

This chapter contains two low-level adventures suitable for 1st and 2nd level PCs and introduces *tension table* rules. If the PCs decide to move around outside between these adventures, they must pass through the *glitterfall* (see page 45 in Chapter 4).

THE SHATTERED SPINE

The Shattered Spine was once a tower on Vantage. It fell on its side in the valley and is partially broken, making it ripe for exploration. Altruistic heroes may want to search for survivors in the ruins, whereas less heroic adventurers may loot the bodies.

Certain parts of the Shattered Spine also make a suitable place for the adventurers to keep refugees safe while they wait out the *glitterfall*, if the adventurers can get them there in one piece.

THE LOST TOMB

The Lost Tomb is the resting place for one of the Archmage's first apprentices. While we present it as a 1st and 2nd level adventure, the tomb does become more dangerous beyond the fake throne. The *Inner Tomb* portion of this dungeon is aimed at 3rd and 4th level characters. Treat 1st and 2nd level PCs who manage to infiltrate this area as though they were at least 3rd level characters.

Plotlines for entering the tomb may be slightly more complicated than usual. The current Archmage might send the adventurers into the tomb to move the body to a safer place or obtain magical items to help them with other quests.

Alternatively, if the adventurers do not care about the Archmage (or oppose him), looting a tomb is always good, dungeoneering fun.

TENSION TABLE RULES

Several dungeon locations in this book use a mechanic called *tension tables*. Most tension tables function as combined random event/wandering monster generators, requiring a roll each time the adventures enter a new area. The source of the building tension varies from dungeon to dungeon.

In some dungeons, the tension roll becomes more dangerous depending on how high the escalation die rose in the previous battle. In other dungeons, the tension roll becomes more dangerous for each battle you fight toward a full heal-up.

It's worth mentioning that we assume GMs will use the standard *13th Age* rule that the adventurers gain a full heal-up and regain their daily powers after four significant battles, even if they're still in the middle of the dungeon.

Earlier playtest versions of the tension tables used more punishing rules that pushed groups toward fleeing. That's not the intent of the final tension tables; so, if you played with earlier versions, follow the new rules for each dungeon precisely and don't add the half-remembered problems from earlier drafts!

Complications in areas that already have complications: If you're satisfied with the narrative impact of an area's already detailed encounters, denizens, or traps—or the complications you've come up with for the PCs thanks to ongoing events in the dungeon crawl—it may be unnecessary to roll on the tension table. However, if you feel like doubling up on potential problems or running three-way battles, go for it.

Turning back: It's your call as a GM whether to keep rolling on the tension table when PCs are on their way out of the dungeon. Sometimes it's fun to turn retreats into fighting retreats. Other times, you may just want to move on to a different section of the adventure.

Bored now: Some of the results on the tension tables are purely atmospheric, a slightly more interesting way to say, "nothing else unusual adds to the strange things you already find in this new area." If you keep rolling the same atmospheric result, skip it or come up with new riffs on the theme.

If you or the players get tired of using the tension table in a dungeon, you should go back to GM-loaded complications or your wandering monster system of choice.

THE SHATTERED SPINE

Level range: Aimed at 1st and 2nd level; but also works for 3rd and 4th level, due to the design of adversary groups and building battles tables.

The Shattered Spine is a tower that fell from the sky and landed on its side—a broken column that now sits at the bottom of a river valley. When the PCs get close enough, it's obvious many sections of the tower landed right-side up, so the whole thing looks like a huge, multi-tiered wedding cake that slid to one side. The tower partially blocks the Red River, which finds new routes around and through the tower.

DUNGEON GOAL

The theme of the Shattered Spine is exploration: wandering about, seeing what there is to see, and looting the place. If your PCs are 3rd or 4th level, you may want to slightly bump up the DCs for skill checks.

ENTRANCES TO THE SHATTERED SPINE

The Shattered Spine maps refer to the area under the tower—a mixture of rubble and river water—as Area Z.

The map has a cheat-code: if an area's name rhymes with "Zee" it leads to Area Z—in other words, areas B, C, D, E, G, V, and T lead to the river. Likewise, all areas with vowel names contain an entrance/exit (Y has an entrance/exit if you force your way in/out).

The Shattered Spine has 6 possible entrances to the fallen tower's interior.

- At its southern end, a circular doorway leads inside [to Area A].
- A large crack in an exterior wall leads to a partially flooded library [Area E].
- A small crack in the wall leads downward into the ruins and descends into a darkened room [leads to Area I].
- An entire section of the tower is open to the air—it looks like there might be a way to go deeper inside from there [leads to Area O].
- There's a shattered crystal dome at the North end of the tower; the crystal shards move around, making the area rather dangerous [leads to Area U].
- Ravens fly in and out through a stone wall with holes carved in it; if the PCs can make a DC 20 skill check to bash in the wall, they gain entrance via a rookery [Area Y].

ADVENTURING IN THE SHATTERED SPINE

Each area in the Shattered Spine is potentially dangerous. Each time the adventurers enter a new area, they should roll a d12 on the tension table. As a bonus to the d12 roll, add twice the number of battles the adventurers have fought toward their next full heal-up. For example, if the adventurers have fought two significant battles since their last full heal-up, the tension table roll is 1d12 + 4.

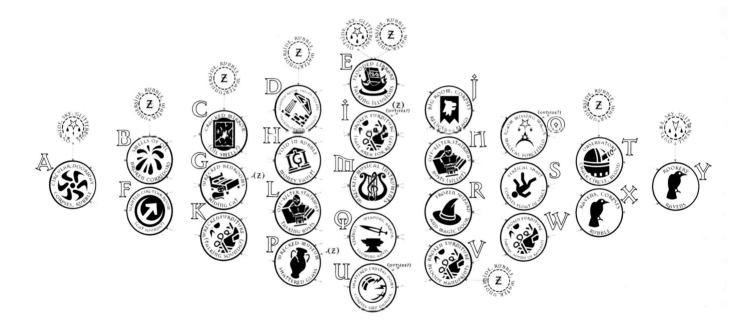

SHATTERED SPINE TENSION TABLE (D12)

1-4. Nothing of note happens. Add +2 to the group's next tension table roll in the Shattered Spine.

5. The PCs hear a grinding noise. It's the tower, settling into the clay of the river bed.

6. The PCs hear sounds of ravens coming from a couple of rooms away.

7. Dust falls from the ceiling as the tower's integrity weakens

8. The PCs hear a faint groaning sound coming from underneath the nearest pile of rubble—it may be a dying survivor or just the rubble settling (GM's call).

9. The PCs find a group of survivors who are not looking for a fight and are in no shape to do so.

10. The room shifts as the tower settles.

11+ *odd.* A magical defense activates. Roll on the *Shattered Spine Magical Defense* table, but don't count this encounter as a fraction of a battle for purposes of tracking heal-ups; the Shattered Spine's magical defenses are more of a nuisance than a threat.

12+ *even.* The PCs encounter a wandering monster. Roll on the *Shattered Spine Wandering Monster* table, choose a result, or make up your own monster. The battle should count as a standard fight.

SHATTERED SPINE MAGICAL DEFENSE TABLE (D6)

1-2. A forcefield seals off one of the exits to this area. It takes a DC 15 check to destroy the barrier by force or circumvent it by making a hole in a wall; failure means the adventurer takes 2d6 force damage.

3. A shimmering field suddenly appears in one of the exits to this area. Any character who passes through the lightning barrier takes 1d10 lightning damage. Eventually, the barrier burns itself out; but that takes about half an hour and just as the lightning ceases, it's time to make another roll on the tension table.

4. An orb appears in the room and attacks the adventurers before flying away. It takes a DC 15 skill check to hide as the orb enters the area. **C: Thunder orb +10 vs. PD (1d3 enemies)**—1d10 thunder damage

5. A magical eye appears and attempts to hypnotize an adventurer (**+15 vs. MD**). If successful, the adventurer immediately makes their best basic or at-will attack against a random ally within range.

6. A vortex teleports the adventurers to a new area they have not yet visited.

SHATTERED SPINE WANDERING MONSTER TABLE (D10)

1-4. Magical defenders of the Shattered Spine. Use the specific monsters and battles in the next section.

5-8. Shattered Spine constructs. Use the specific monsters and battles on page 58.

9. Defenders of Vantage. Use a battle from the *Wizards & Spellcasters* adversary group on page 218. They assume the adventurers are attackers and adopt a shoot-first, ask-questions-later policy. If you prefer, and if the adventurers can somehow make a DC 25 check to prove they are friends or allies, there's a slight possibility they can talk the defenders around to their side.

10. An adversary group. Perhaps whoever brought down Vantage is here, poking about in the ruins looking for something, or perhaps this is an opportunistic enemy. Choose an adversary group from the *Appendix* starting on page 191 that seems interesting or fits with the party's icon relationship rolls.

55

MAGICAL DEFENDERS OF THE SHATTERED SPINE

Use a battle from this section when you roll a result of 1-4 on the *Shattered Spine Wandering Monster* table or whenever you feel like engineering a fight with leftover defenders of the towers' magical system. The battles are a bit tougher than usual, but nowhere near double-strength. Levels 2-4 have multiple battle options to keep things fresh during extended adventuring.

#/Level of PCs	Lesser Homunculus	Greater Homunculus	Minor Living Spell	Spell-Warrior	Living Spell
3 x 1st level	2	1	1	0	0
4 x 1st level	8	1	1	0	0
5 x 1st level	5	1	1	1	0
6 x 1st level	8	0	1	2	0
7 x 1st level	8	1	1	2	0
3 x 2nd level	0	1	1	1	0
3 x 2nd level	2	0	0	0	1
4 x 2nd level	0	2	1	1	0
4 x 2nd level	2	0	0	1	1
5 x 2nd level	3	3	1	1	0
5 x 2nd level	2	0	0	2	1
6 x 2nd level	5	3	2	1	0
6 x 2nd level	2	0	0	1	2
7 x 2nd level	8	4	2	1	0
7 x 2nd level	2	0	0	2	2
3 x 3rd level	0	2	0	2	0
3 x 3rd level	0	2	0	0	1
4 x 3rd level	0	4	0	2	0
4 x 3rd level	0	3	1	0	1
5 x 3rd level	0	4	0	3	0
5 x 3rd level	0	3	1	0	2
6 x 3rd level	0	5	0	4	0
6 x 3rd level	0	3	3	0	2
7 x 3rd level	0	6	0	5	0
7 x 3rd level	0	3	1	0	3
3 x 4th level	0	3	0	3	0
3 x 4th level	0	2	0	0	2
4 x 4th level	0	4	0	4	0
4 x 4th level	0	4	0	0	2
5 x 4th level	0	5	0	5	0
5 x 4th level	0	3	0	0	3
6 x 4th level	0	6	1	6	0
6 x 4th level	0	3	0	0	4
7 x 4th level	0	6	1	8	0
7 x 4th level	0	4	2	0	4

LESSER HOMUNCULUS

This was one of the near-mindless servitors on Vantage. It may have more of a mind of its own now, but it's not a sane mind.

0 level mook [CONSTRUCT]
Initiative: +3

Tiny sharp claws +5 vs. AC—3 damage

R: Alchemical blurp +4 vs. PD (1d3 nearby or far away enemies in a group)—2 acid damage
  First natural 16+: The next ally to attack the target gains +2 to hit.

AC 16
PD 14   HP 5 (mook)
MD 10

Mook: Kill one homunculus mook for every 5 damage you deal to the mob.

GREATER HOMUNCULUS

"Go away. Farther! Farther!"

2nd level troop [CONSTRUCT]
Initiative: +5

Sharp claws +5 vs. AC—7 damage

R: Alchemical blurp +7 vs. PD (1d3 nearby or far away enemies in a group)—6 acid damage
  First natural 16+: The next ally to attack the target gains +2 to hit.

AC 18
PD 16   HP 36
MD 12

MINOR LIVING SPELL

This roiling ball of energy is intelligent and eager to defend Vantage, quite unaware that it fell.

2nd level archer [SPIRIT]
Initiative: +7

Magefire +10 vs. PD (1d3 attacks)— 3 fire damage
  Natural odd miss: The target pops free.

C: Spell burn +10 vs. PD (2 nearby or far away enemies in a group)—5 force damage
  Natural even hit: The target becomes vulnerable to fire and force damage until the end of the battle.

Mana burn: When a magical attack or a weapon attack with a magic weapon targets the minor living spell, the attacker takes force damage equal to their level.

Flight: The minor living spell floats about, paying no mind to minor things like gravity.

Immaterial: The minor living spell has *resist damage 16+* to attacks against AC and PD, except those that do force damage. It can also drift through walls, phase through floors, and otherwise defy solidity, though it can't end its turn in solid objects.

AC 16
PD 16   HP 24
MD 18

SPELL-WARRIOR

Is it a spell that became a warrior? Or a warrior who became a spell?

3rd level archer [SPIRIT]
Initiative: +6

Lightning staff +8 vs. AC—10 lightning damage
  Natural roll equal to or less than the escalation die: The spell-warrior pops free and makes a *mana blast* attack as a free action

R: Mana blast +8 vs. PD (one nearby or far away enemy)—6 force damage
  Natural even hit: The spell-warrior may make another *mana blast* attack as a free action. The attack must be against an enemy who was not attacked with a *mana blast* this turn. The spell-warrior may keep making *mana blast* attacks in this way until it fails to roll a natural even hit or there are no more valid targets.

Air-walking: The spell-warrior can't fly, but it can ignore pits and sudden drops by gliding right over them.

AC 19
PD 17   HP 44
MD 13

LIVING SPELL

It blasts intruders for the glory of the Archmage. That is all.

5th level archer [SPIRIT]
Initiative: +10

Magefire +10 vs. AC (1d3 attacks)—8 force and fire damage
Natural odd miss: The target pops free.

R: Spell burn +10 vs. AC (2 nearby or far away enemies in a group)—14 force damage
Natural odd hit: The target becomes vulnerable to force damage

Mana burn: When a magical attack or a weapon attack with a magic weapon targets the living spell, the attacker takes force damage equal to their level.

Flight: The living spell floats about, paying no mind to minor things like gravity.

Immaterial: The living spell can drift through walls, phase through floors, and otherwise defy solidity, though it can't end its turn in solid objects.

AC	18	
PD	21	**HP 72**
MD	21	

SHATTERED SPINE CONSTRUCTS

Heroes who notice that the golems they're fighting in the Shattered Spine seem less puissant than the iron and stone golems they've heard of might deduce that these wicker and primal golems were designed to perform magical maintenance functions in the tower.

Several rooms contain magically illuminated wall recesses that are just the right size to hold these golems. After the players fight some golems, let them find others that are still snug within their alcoves, interfaced with the tower's magical system.

If the fights against these specific constructs become repetitive, mix in creatures from the *Golems* adversary group (page 207).

#/Level of PCs	Wicker Golem	Clockwork Automaton	Primal Golem	Larger Primal Golem
3 x 1st level	0	0	1	0
4 x 1st level	2	0	0	0
5 x 1st level	1	0	1	0
6 x 1st level	3	0	0	0
7 x 1st level	0	0	2	0
3 x 2nd level	2	0	0	0
4 x 2nd level	0	0	2	0
5 x 2nd level	2	0	1	0
6 x 2nd level	4	0	0	0
6 x 2nd level	0	0	3	0
7 x 2nd level	2	0	2	0
3 x 3rd level	0	0	2	0
4 x 3rd level	1	0	0	1
5 x 3rd level	2	0	2	0
6 x 3rd level	1	3	0	1
7 x 3rd level	2	3	2	0
3 x 4th level	0	2	0	1
4 x 4th level	0	2	1	1
5 x 4th level	0	2	2	1
6 x 4th level	0	0	2	2
7 x 4th level	0	2	2	2

WICKER GOLEM

It burns well, you'd just better hope you are not inside it at the time. Some use wicker golems as a means of capturing rather than killing, others to sacrifice their enemies mid-battle.

Huge 0 level wrecker [CONSTRUCT]
Initiative: +4
Vulnerability: fire

Wicker hands +5 vs. AC (two attacks)—5 damage. If at least one attack hits a target, the target is grabbed.

> *Entrap:* If a grabbed target does not escape the grab by the end of its next turn, the golem stuffs the target into its body cavity. Once a target is in the golem's body cavity, it moves with the golem until it escapes and is stuck, dazed, and unable to affect anything except the wicker golem. The target also takes any fire damage the wicker golem takes. If the target deals 5 or more damage with an attack, the golem's body cavity briefly pops open and the target can make a disengage check to try to escape.

Golem immunity: Wicker golems are immune to effects. They can't be dazed, weakened, confused, made vulnerable, or touched by ongoing damage (except fire damage).

Burning man: Whenever the wicker golem takes fire damage, it also takes 5 ongoing fire damage. While the wicker golem takes ongoing fire damage, a natural even hit with *wicker hands* does the same amount of ongoing fire damage to its target.

Deliberate conflagration: If the golem has an enemy trapped inside, it may set itself on fire (5 ongoing fire damage) at any time.

Blood sacrifice: If a non-mook creature is reduced to 0 hp while within the golem's body cavity, the golem immediately heals to 55 hp.

AC 14
PD 14   **HP 55**
MD 10

CLOCKWORK AUTOMATON

Gears grind and the thing moves forward on a pair of spoked, iron wheels. Each of its metal arms ends in a sharp point.

2nd level troop [CONSTRUCT]
Initiative: +4

Spear-hands +6 vs. AC—6 damage
> *Natural even hit:* The automaton can make a second *spear-hands* attack as a free action (but not a third).

Made of gears and cables: When an attack crits against it or when it's staggered, the automaton must roll an easy save (6+). On a failure, the construct's internal workings fail, and it breaks apart in a small explosion of metal and gears. Drop the automaton to 0 hp and make an *exploding gears* attack.

> **C: Exploding gears +6 vs. PD (each creature engaged with or next to the automaton)**—2d12 damage

AC 17
PD 14   **HP 40**
MD 12

PRIMAL GOLEM

This stone golem is carved with spirals and covered in moss. It resembles a toppled pile of standing stones in its inactive state; but, when it's active, the spirals glow. The Archmage occasionally uses primal golems to guard against magic users. Some have destructive magical stomp attacks, but generally not those working in towers!

Large 2nd level wrecker [CONSTRUCT]
Initiative: +5

Stony fists +8 vs. AC (two attacks)—8 damage
> *Miss:* 4 damage.

Golem immunity: Non-organic golems are immune to effects. They can't be dazed, weakened, confused, made vulnerable, or touched by ongoing damage. You can damage a golem, but that's about it.

Resist spells 16+: When a spell targets this creature, the attacker must roll a natural 16+ on the attack roll or it only deals half damage.

Empowered by magic: Each time you roll a *natural odd hit* on a magical attack (a spell or magic weapon) against the primal golem, it gains a cumulative +1 attack bonus until the end of the battle.

AC 19
PD 17   **HP 52**
MD 12

LARGER PRIMAL GOLEM

This massive stone golem is carved with spirals and covered in moss. It resembles a toppled pile of standing stones in its inactive state; but, when it's active, the spirals glow.

Large 4th level wrecker [CONSTRUCT]
Initiative: +7

Stony fists +10 vs. AC (two attacks)—12 damage
> *Miss:* 6 damage.

Golem immunity: Non-organic golems are immune to effects. They can't be dazed, weakened, confused, made vulnerable, or touched by ongoing damage. You can damage a golem, but that's about it.

Resist spells 16+: When a spell targets this creature, the attacker must roll a natural 16+ on the attack roll or it only deals half damage.

Empowered by magic: Each time you roll a natural odd hit on a magical attack (a spell or magic weapon) against the primal golem, it gains a cumulative +1 bonus to attack until the end of the battle.

AC 21
PD 19   **HP 90**
MD 14

SHATTERED SPINE AREAS

Now that you have a basic description of the *Shattered Spine* and an understanding of how to use the tension table and wandering monster table for this location, we'll dig into the dungeon layout. Don't forget—areas whose letter names rhyme with "Zee" connect to Area Z, and those with vowel names have entrances/exits!

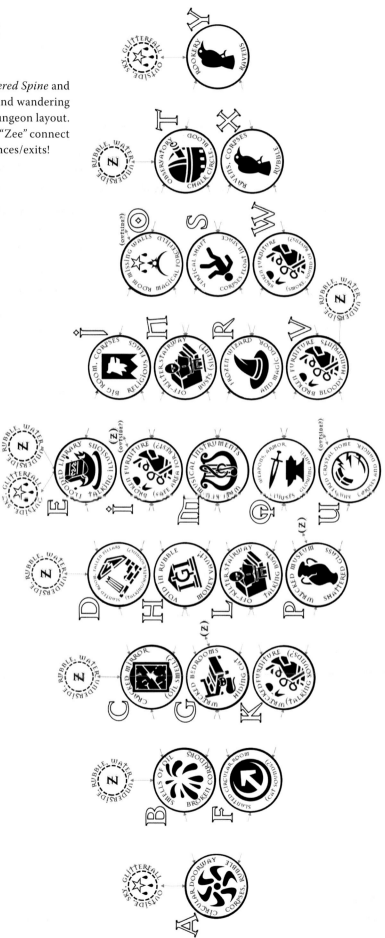

A: THE CIRCULAR DOORWAY

First impressions: Large, round room on its side with a spiral staircase.
Second glance: Corpses under rubble.
Joins to areas: B, F, and outside

This is an entrance to the *Shattered Spine*. The circular doorway has no door, but a slight blurring effect covers the entrance and a powerful magical fan, whirring away at high speed blows outward from the interior, which keeps it free of *glitterfall*. Spotting the fan when investigating the doorway requires a DC 25 skill check; otherwise the fan inflicts 3d6 damage to the oblivious adventurers as they step through. The adventurers can jam something big and solid into the fan's metal blades to stop it long enough for the party to get through; however, any mundane item placed in the fan either shoots free or is chopped up by the blades soon after, and the fan restarts.

Beyond the doorway is a cylindrical chamber (the room is on its side, so is about 10 feet wide but 60 feet tall) with doorways all around its curved perimeter—most of which are completely blocked by rubble. The doorway near the floor is accessible, though [*adventurers must drop through or lower themselves on a rope. The doorway leads to a corridor that leads to* B].

Halfway up the "wall" is a spiral staircase, which exits the room through the center of the opposite "wall" (previously the ceiling when the tower was upright) [*leads through various shattered rooms choked with rubble to* F; *the adventurers need a rope to climb up to the now horizontal staircase*].

The room itself is full of rubble piles, with the occasional corpse poking out from underneath. Looting the bodies yields 5d20 gp-worth of random stuff (a gold monocle, a shattered hourglass filled with silver powder, etc.).

B: THE SEED OF FIRE

First impressions: Long, dark room—mostly upright.
Second sniff: Smell of lamp oil, crack in the floor.
Joins to areas: A, C, G, and Z

This 20-foot by 6-foot room landed mostly upright, though the corridors that lead to it are shattered. You can glimpse the Red River through a wide crack in the floor [*leads to* Z], and three shattered corridors lead from the room [*lead to* A (*upward climb involved, DC 15 check*), C, *and* G].

The room itself contains the shattered remains of barrels that stored lamp oil. The oil is everywhere—anybody carrying a lit torch or casting a fire spell risks starting a conflagration that the flow of air will draw back through to Area A. Adventurers likely smell the oil and know what it is (DC 15); the question is, do they notice in time? The conflagration from any misadventure deals 1d10 fire damage to each party member, unless there is some good reason why the fire wouldn't blast somebody.

Fighting here: If the PCs fight wandering monsters here, all it takes is one attack dealing fire damage or a loose point of lightning to blow things up good! If the PCs won't get it done, surely a monster will oblige. In the unlikely case in which the PCs are getting wrecked in their first fight in the dungeon, you could even make the conflagration deal a bit more damage to the monsters.

C: THE LENS OF THE AVATAR

First impressions: Square room, with doors and a heavy curtain—something might be moving inside.
Second sniff: Mirror on the wall, faint smell of lamp oil.
Joins to areas: B, D, H, and Z

This 10-foot by 10-foot chamber is resting upright. Two doorways lead away from it [*to* D *and* H], and a corridor with no door but a heavy curtain also provides an entrance to another room [*leads to* B]. A crack in the floor shows the dry riverbed of the Red River [*leads to* Z].

An upright mirror in this room shows each adventurer in an idealized form: taller, braver, more confident, better dressed, etc. However, a crack in the mirror causes a distortion in the reflection: the adventurer is a different race, a different class, or has an obviously opposed alignment. The mirror is part of a magical "cosmetic" device that temporarily transforms a person into their idealized self (the shattered floor tiles still show the magic circle), but it is either broken—each glass shard reflecting an increasingly wrong image—or no longer works and is merely an oddity. The mirror is heavy and ungainly, but it could fetch a good price in a city (3d4 x 100 gp) if the adventurers can rescue it and bring it to market. Even if the mirror is broken, the gold on the frame is worth 5d20 gp.

Behind the mirror is a safe, hidden in the wall by illusion magic. The safe contains a large bag of silver coins (3d20 gp-worth) and a true magic item. Spotting the safe takes a DC 20 skill check, opening it requires a DC 25 skill check.

Fighting here: Wandering monsters, especially adversary group creatures, might show up in strange reversals. Perhaps the mirror's images of the PCs' enemies hold clues to hidden alliances?

D: THE PILLARED HALL

First impressions: Semi-circular hall at a 45-degree slant, plenty of fallen stone pillars.
Second glance: There are corpses under the rubble, and the faint sounds of talking and water from somewhere nearby.
Joins to areas: C, I, E, and Z

Many of the pillars in this slanted, semi-circular hall came loose, shattered, and rolled downhill to block the exits there. At the "top" end of the hall are two doors *[lead to C and I]*—a slight breeze comes from under one of them *[leads to I]*. The adventurers hear sounds of splashing water and voices from a side corridor *[leads to E]*.

Exploring the hall requires a DC 15 check if the adventurer lassos a rope to an intact pillar, or a DC 25 check if they try to just grip the smooth tile floor; failure means they take 2d8 falling damage.

Several wizards' bodies lay crushed at the "bottom" of the hall—the pillars crumbled and killed them. Looting the bodies yields a magic item, and possible information about Vantage's last minutes before the fall. The adventurers can hear a trickle of water beneath the pillars—rolling a few aside reveals a doorway that faces the Red River's mostly-dry riverbed *[leads to Z]*.

E: THE FLOODED LIBRARY

First impressions: A wrecked library, the sound of voices, hip-deep flowing water, crack in the wall that leads outside.
Second glance: Illusionary docents flicker in and out, high in the air.
Joins to areas: D, J, Z, and outside

The library provides an entrance to the Shattered Spine, through a large crack in a wall that has a minimal amount of rubble on it. The Shattered Spine's interior is full of water here, and the room itself has irregular dimensions (several rooms collapsed into one another). Further inside, a side-room has a window *[leads to Z]* that now faces downward and shows the Red River's dry riverbed, while gaps in the rubble lead further into the structure *[to D and J]*.

Library docent illusions illuminate the whole area; the docents were magical constructs that answered questions. Now, the illusionary docents are as broken as the tower, flickering in and out of existence and spouting nonsense phrases. Interrogating a docent requires a DC 25 skill check (they interact with anybody; but trying to squeeze sense out of their fading-construct minds is difficult)—a successful roll could reveal facts about the fall of Vantage.

The library's books and scrolls float around the room in the hip-deep water. Some might be salvageable—the adventurers could rescue one or more. Here's a quick list of the most likely survivors:

- *On Foolish Messes* (a book on scrying and divination)
- *Cooking with Fireballs* (a book about using battle magic for peaceful purposes)
- *What is not Forbidden* (a lengthy work regarding necromancy).

The rescued books are worth 3d20 gp in a city, and twice that in Horizon.

Fighting here: Maybe the PCs' enemies have a much better idea which books they want to salvage from the wreckage?

If you love to use Latin words as mystic-sounding titles, ASH's original book titles are Sincere de pulmentum, Caedes sine otium, *and* Sedentem ad pedes umbrae.

F: THE POTTER'S WHEEL

First impressions: Circular room at a 30-degree slant, with a spiral staircase that goes from floor to ceiling.
Second glance: Lots of windows barely holding back rubble—this area is dangerous. The sound of a cat mewing.
Joins to areas: A, G, K, and kitchen

This 60-foot wide, circular room slants at a 30-degree angle, resting as it does against Area A. A twisted spiral staircase comes from the center of the floor *[eventually leads to A]* and exits through the ceiling *[leads to K]*. A door in the curved wall halfway around the sloped room is jammed partially open by its twisted frame *[leads to G]*. At the bottom of the slanted floor at other end of the room is another door *[leads to small dead-end kitchen we're not bothering to map]*.

Much of the curved wall is lined with windows, through which the adventurers can see mud and rubble. Occasionally, a window shatters under the weight, sending a shower of rubble and glass into the room. **Rubble and glass +5 vs. AC (1d3 attacks against random targets)**—5 damage.

The floor itself is a huge, circular mosaic that used to rotate under its own power, but now that the room is tilted, the floor shifts and spins unpredictably when adventurers try to cross it to get to or from the doors or spiral staircase. It takes a DC 25 check to cross the floor; failure sends the adventurer tumbling toward the door at the other end of the room.

The door can support two adventurers' weight—a third adventurer causes it to come away from its frame, and each adventurer nearby must make a DC 15 check or take 2d6 falling damage as they tumble into the ruins of a kitchen. There is no other way out of the kitchen—it takes a DC 15 check to climb back out, followed by a DC 25 check to navigate the shifting, mosaic-disk floor.

G: THE UNMADE BED

First impressions: Suite of rooms, wrecked. Silk sheets, expensive carpets. Magical doors.
Second glance: There is a cat here, and a corpse.
Joins to areas: B, F, H, L, and Z

These rooms were an important wizard's private chambers. The area consists of an antechamber, a meeting room, a bedroom, a bathroom, and a dressing room. Each room has a pillar at the center with nine magic doors set into it—which lead to one of the other rooms in the suite, another area *[F, B, H, or L]*, or to an outside balcony. The adventurers can hear what sounds like a conversation from behind one of the doors *[leads to L]*. The outside balcony became detached and was crushed under the collapsed tower *[leads to Z]*.

The adventurers hear meowing coming from the bedroom. The wizard lies crushed beneath his four-poster bed, his cat familiar pawing at his body. Wrapped around the cat is a faintly glowing belt (anybody wearing it takes no damage the next time they fall, after that, the magic fades—there is no need to attune to the consumable item to use it). The wizard obviously used the magic item to save his familiar's life instead of his own. The cat is injured (but not badly so) and is understandably freaked out. If a player character befriends the creature, it could become a party member's familiar. The tag on the cat's collar reads *"Kippers"*.

A magic staff (your choice, or a player's!) lies next to the wizard and the adventurers can find 1d3 + 1 consumable magic items by searching the room. There's a notebook with many scribbled notes in the corpse's back pocket; the notes are mostly astronomical observations, recipes for fish, and random lists of words (all of which are crossed out, except the word *"Kippers"*).

This section of the adventure has the potential to include a lot of loot. Don't feel constrained by that—if everybody has at least one item by the end of 2nd level, then you are kind of on track and don't need to include more treasure.

I'm a generous GM, which comes through in the early parts of Shards of the Broken Sky. If you are a bit less generous, or if your campaign is less magic-item heavy, go with what feels best to you. Maybe the treasure was already looted, maybe it was destroyed, or maybe it was lost during the fall of Vantage and some farmer might find it half-buried in a field years from now.

H: THE VAULT

First impressions: Huge void in the rubble, it seems several rooms collapsed into this single space.
Second glance: The area is unstable. A metal treasure vault is lodged half-way up/down the void—it came crashing through here during the fall.
Joins to areas: C, G, I, and M

This area is a void in the rubble, where several rooms collapsed. There's a large metal cylinder jammed halfway down the void—a treasure vault. The vault door is open, and the adventurers can see the glow of treasure inside. Getting down or up to the vault requires a DC 20 check; failure indicates the adventurer takes 3d6 falling damage when they fall onto rubble OR everybody takes 1d6 damage from dislodged rubble—player's call. Gaps in the shattered walls lead to other areas *[C, G, I, and M]*.

The vault itself is still magically guarded—a carving on the vault door is, in fact, a guardian statue that attacks anybody who tries to open the door and enter the vault without giving the password (**+15 vs. AC**—8 damage). It takes a DC 25 check for a character to disable the statue or deduce the password (*"kippers"*) if the players can't do so.

As adventurers climb into the vault, they feel it shift slightly; there is another void beneath the vault into which it could tip.

The vault is full of silver and gold bars—far more than the party can feasibly remove in one trip (especially considering the vault is in the middle of a void). These bars are easily worth a couple hundred thousand gp. Each character can easily carry a number of bars equal to their strength modifier—each additional bar after that gives a cumulative -1 penalty to all physical skill checks, AC, PD, attack rolls, and initiative.

Once the adventurers remove any amount of gold and start to leave Area H, the vault shifts and spills its remaining gold bars down into the muddy-bottomed void below, where they sink out of sight forever. Clever adventurers can empty the vault as a team, stacking the gold in a more secure location (in which case, when they return to retrieve it, d4 x 10 bars are still accessible). Each gold bar is worth 500 gp; we might assume the PCs choose gold over silver, but if not, silver bars are worth about 50 gp each.

Groups that obsess over the treasure and come up with an astoundingly clever way to loot it all and carry it out of the dungeon should be allowed to do so, *at a cost*: lugging around wheelbarrows full of gold attracts every scavenger out in the *glitterfall* and severely slows down the adventurers.

Fighting here: This could be your chance to confront the adventurers with a hugely superior enemy force . . . that has crippled itself by trying to carry too much treasure out of the vault! As the enemy realizes its mistake and uses actions to reduce its load, the escalation die rises, and the PCs seize the momentum.

The adventurers in one campaign I played in took all the gold and ended up crashing several villages' economies! This is a lot of gold.

If the adventurers try to spend it all in one place, the local prices shoot sky-high: a tankard of ale suddenly costs several hundred gold pieces, as the locals become flush with the cash the adventurers pump into their economy.

Other potential problems include thieves, tax assessors, and the like. If the adventurers are not wary, millions of gold pieces can vanish more quickly than hundreds ever would.

The adventurers' best bet is to purchase something big—perhaps a castle or fort—or invest in several businesses (trade caravans are good, high-value investments).

Of course, all the gold in the empire won't stop the icons from wanting the adventurers to lead their own treasure hunters back into Redfield Valley, especially once word of the treasures there gets out. Mid-way through their spending spree, you can rely on a messenger to draw them back to Redfield Valley's ruinscape.

The other option for controlling out-of-control spending is to curse the gold in some interesting way—a curse the adventurers can only lift by going on another adventure in Redfield Valley.

I: THE INKWELL

First impressions: A collection of partially collapsed rooms.
Second glance: One of the rooms is intact, its ceiling held up by a bunk bed.
Joins to areas: D, H, J, N, and outside

This short, 10-foot x 20-foot room landed more-or-less upright. It contains a triple bunk-bed, three desks, and some shattered furniture that might have been wardrobes. The room is full of scrolls, books, and papers, all of which were ruined by a carboy (10-gallon container) of ink that shattered and spilled on them during the wreck.

The room was part of a larger network of rooms, all of which partially collapsed. The adventurers must crawl through on their bellies to investigate the other rooms, which all contain corpses of those killed in the fall. One of the rooms has a crack in the floor *[leads to Z]*, and the collapsed rooms eventually lead to other areas *[D, H, J and N]*. A crevice in the still-standing room's ceiling lets in fresh air and draws out any smoke. The crevice is a possible entrance/exit.

This area could be a good place for adventurers to rest and roleplay a moment, but that won't help them gain their next full heal-up!

J: THE CHAPEL

First impressions: 80 foot wide, circular room, lots of dead bodies.
Second glance: Religious iconography, a place of worship.
Joins to areas: E, I, and O

The 80-foot wide room collapsed on one side, making it a semi-circle. The magic-blasted corpses of ten wizards face the shattered and rubble-choked windows. Looting their bodies allows the adventurers to recover 100 gp-worth of low-denomination coins, and 1 or 2 magic items. Many of the corpses clutch burnt wand stumps—they died trying to stop Vantage from falling.

Three doorways lead from the room. The first is choked with rubble and requires crawling on hands and knees to get through *[leads to I]*; the sound of water comes from the second *[leads to E]*; and the third is locked, though the adventurers can see sunlight through the keyhole *[leads to O]*. It takes a DC 20 check to pick the lock or break down the door.

The chapel is dedicated to the Gods of Light, and embroidered flags around the room depict the major Gods.

GODS OF THE CHAPEL

We've not really said much about religion in the Dragon Empire. The Priestess serves the Gods of Light, the Crusader worships dark gods, the Diabolist consorts with demons, and there are devils and other terrible things. We leave the details to you as the

GM, and to those players whose characters are clerics or paladins or who otherwise care about the gods.

If your campaign features a monotheistic "light" god or goddess, the banners in the chapel are of that deity (and perhaps their saints); if your "light" gods are modeled after the Norse pantheon, then these banners have the symbols of Odin, Thor, Freya, etc. If your game has many pantheons, these banners probably depict the most notable "light" members of each pantheon (Odin, Perun, Zeus, Helios, Athena, Epona, Sulis, Raven, Anansi, Bran, Herne, Nyame, Asase Ya, Ra, Ma'at, Isis, etc.).

ASH's home campaign contains a mish-mash of conflicting religions: cat-worshiping gnomes, apotheosis-seeking princesses, tree-worshiping pantheist druids, and actual-factual-one-unique-thing children of gods—this chapel would have banners depicting all of them. It's not that the banners magically shift based on the beliefs of those who enter the room (or perhaps they do!), but rather that those gods and their symbols are what is true and appropriate for your campaign.

In an early draft of this book, the banners were magic items useable by clerics and paladins—you could reintroduce this in your game by making them into magic holy symbols PCs can wear as cloaks.

Fighting here: Some enemies may be too busy trying to desecrate the chapel to pay attention, allowing the heroes to slip into the room and take them by surprise . . . .

K: The Star Chamber

> **First impressions:** 60-foot circular room, with holes in the center of the ceiling and floor.
> **Second glance:** Stars on the ceiling, lots of broken chairs, light and sounds of talking through some double doors.
> **Joins to areas:** F, L, and P

This circular room is 60 feet wide, with holes through the center of the ceiling and floor where a spiral staircase once ran. The ceiling is painted blue with gold stars. Heading down through the hole in the floor leads to a twisted section of the spiral staircase *[leads to F]*.

Pieces of broken furniture—mostly former large chairs—are scattered around the room, which was obviously a grand meeting chamber of some sort. At first, the ceiling exit *[leads to P]* looks like the only way out; to use the exit, the adventurers must find a way to fly, use rope tricks, or stack the broken chairs high enough to reach it. However, moving some of the chair pieces reveals another, hidden exit—a large set of double doors—through which the adventurers can see light *[leads to L]*. It is difficult to stack the chairs in a stable configuration to reach the ceiling exit (DC 15 check; failure causes 1d10 falling damage). Once they notice them, the double-doors provide an easier exit.

Fighting here: If the game needs some comic relief, the PCs could catch their enemies in the middle of stacking chairs toward the ceiling. Or maybe the PCs are balancing on chairs when their enemies burst into the room; that's funny for you!

L: The Lower Stair

> **First impressions:** Off-kilter stairs, sounds of talking, daylight shining through unbreakable crystal enclosure.
> **Second glance:** Lots of rubble on the outside, talking marble busts at the bottom of the stairs.
> **Joins to areas:** G, K, M, and Q

This long staircase is slightly off-kilter. It originally wound around the tower outside, a magically reinforced glass enclosure holding the elements at bay. The enclosure held together in the fall, allowing daylight to shine through and giving those inside a view from the tower, but no exit to the outside.

The stairway has regular alcoves, which once held talking marble busts that are now piled at the bottom of the stairs. They seem to be engaged in conversation with each other. The busts are piled by a door *[leads to G]*. Anyone who listens to them for long realizes they're not really talking, they're reciting famous sayings of long-dead wizards.

A set of double-doors further up leads to a meeting chamber *[leads to K]*, as evidenced by the brass plaque on the door, and two more doors on the stairs lead to other areas *[M and Q]*. One of the doors *[leads to Q]* is thick and locked; requiring a DC 30 check to get through from this side.

Flickering force fields—part of Vantage's emergency magical defenses—prevent further progress down or up the stairs.

M: The Music Room

> **First impressions:** Lots of instruments, most of them broken. Large gap in one wall.
> **Second glance:** Faint sounds of music.
> **Joins to areas:** H, L, N, and R

This room has a huge hole in one wall—peering through it reveals a rubble-filled void with a cylinder at the bottom *[leads to H]*. Otherwise, there are three doors in the room, two of which have daylight showing through them *[lead to L and N]*. The third door is stuck tight *[leads to R]* and requires a DC 15 check to open by force.

The room itself is a jumble of broken instruments and sheet music. Faint sounds of music with no discernable source echo throughout the room.

N: THE HIGHER STAIR

First impressions: Stairs, rubble covering the crystal enclosure.
Second glance: Animated marble busts are mute, very faint sound of music.
Joins to areas: I, M, O, and S

A twin to the lower stair, this staircase has many doors leading from it, most of which open into collapsed rooms; however, three of the doors allow adventurers to proceed *[to M, O, and S]*. A fourth door leads to a partially collapsed room that they can crawl through to reach another area *[leads to I]*.

The busts in this area are silent, though their mouths move constantly.

O: THE OPEN ROOM

First impressions: Area open to the outside.
Second glance: Despite being open, glitterfall flakes bounce off the area.
Joins to areas: J, N, and T

This tower room was ripped open—one of the walls is entirely missing. This is a potential entrance to the tower. The *glitterfall* bounces off an invisible field that surrounds the area.

Magical defenses still work in this area—a force field flickers across the missing wall. Getting through the flickering force field takes a DC 25 skill check; failure means the person attempting to pass through takes 5 force damage, plus 5 ongoing force damage until they pass the roll (an ally can try to push or pull them through, which lowers the difficulty by 10; however, if the roll is still a failure, both characters are stuck in the field and take the damage until freed).

Doors lead further into the tower *[to J, N, and T]*.

The contents of this room were lost in the fall, scattered to the winds.

P: THE MUSEUM

First impressions: Long gallery, a former museum. Exhibits scattered everywhere.
Second glance: Some of the museum exhibits might be magic items.
Joins to areas: K, Q, U, and Z

This long gallery is full of shattered glass cases. Treasures from past ages lie scattered across the room—here a shattered vase, there a carved wooden figurine collection, over there a woven cedar hat. To the right collector, they would be priceless; to an adventurer, they are worthless. Still, there are one or more actual treasures hidden among the culturally significant *objets d'art*.

The remains of a spiral staircase in one corner end just as they pass through the floor *[leads to K, though it is quite a drop without stairs]* and lead upward through the ceiling to a room bathed in daylight *[leads to U]*. A door in the corner nearest the staircase flickers in and out of reality—one moment, there is a blank wall, the next, a door appears *[leads to Q]*. If an adventurer grabs hold of the doorknob on the flickering door (DC 15 check; failure indicates 5 force damage), it stabilizes long enough to open it and jump through. The windows at the far end of the room—across from the staircase and door—are shattered and choked with rubble, but adventurers can still climb through them to get under the tower *[leads to Z]*.

Fighting here: Maybe it doesn't have to be a fight. There's enough interesting treasure here that a temporary truce and the desire to proceed in opposite directions might circumvent hostilities. . . .

Q: THE ARMORY

First impressions: Dead soldiers everywhere, lots of weapons and armor in disarray.
Second glance: An anvil, faintly glowing.
Joins to areas: L, P, R, and V

This thick-walled room contains the corpses of a dozen dead soldiers who were killed in the fall. There's also a jumble of swords, spears, and armor.

A glowing anvil is bolted to the floor. If the adventurers manage to pry it free, it requires an ox and cart (or equivalent) to transport over long distances; though a single character with 20 strength, two with 18 strength, three with 16 strength, etc., can lift and slowly move it. (The anvil isn't something you can take adventuring with you, but you could haul it away and install it elsewhere.)

WONDROUS ITEM

You can attune multiple wondrous items. They don't fill up a chakra.

Enchanted anvil: This glowing anvil is powerfully magnetic. 1d3 times each day, when you strike a weapon or piece of armor against the anvil, the struck item gains a random, tier-appropriate rune that you can later activate for one battle. Quirk: Sing while you work.

There is also a heavy door in the armory, which is locked from this side *[leads to L]*. Next to it, another door flickers in and out of reality *[leads to P]*. If an adventurer grabs hold of the doorknob on the flickering door (DC 15 check; failure indicates 5 force damage), it stabilizes long enough to open it and jump through. Another door—this one open—leads into a short corridor, in which the adventurers can hear water trickling *[leads to V]*; a stairway in the corridor leads up to a door *[leads to R]*.

R: THE MASTER'S CHAMBER

> **First impressions:** Wizard's sanctum (complete with wizard), frozen in time.
> **Second glance:** The door is magic and opens to different locations.
> **Joins to areas:** M, Q, S, and W

This room is frozen in time, stuck mid-fall. A powerful female wizard stands in the middle of the room, frozen off-balance at the moment she cast her final spell.

This is obviously a wizard's sanctum. Several objects are frozen mid-air; navigating around the shattered glassware and flying books proves difficult. Because the objects are immovable, paper edges cut like steel and dust itself becomes an obstacle (DC 25 check; failure indicates 1d6+5 damage from walking eye-first into an immoveable drop of the wizard's sweat or an errant dust-mote).

Magic weapons aplenty line the walls; sadly, they are as stuck as the rest of the items in the room. Players accustomed to the game's *anything is possible* trope may be certain there is some way to get around the wizard's *time-stop* spell; but, if there is, it's way beyond the capabilities of the player characters and their icon connections. As a story option, it's likely there are ways to discover the wizard's name, and there are certainly people in Horizon who would want to know about her "survival." Still, a spell this powerful isn't likely to be solved without high-powered assistance from the Archmage's top individuals.

The room has a single door that leads to one of four locations, depending on how you turn the handle *[leads to Q, M, S, or W]* The door sticks for one of the options *[M]*; it requires a DC 25 check to pop it open.

Fighting here: Characters who roll a 1 or a 2 on an attack probably need to make a save against running into an immoveable part of the room as detailed above. Play up these failed interactions with the time-stuck environment.

S: THE SHAFT

> **First impressions:** Empty vertical shaft with dead bodies floating in it.
> **Second glance:** A magical elevator.
> **Joins to areas:** N, R, T, and X

When the adventurers open a door to this area, it reveals a shaft that flickers with light. Corpses float in the shaft, their limbs broken as though they suffered a great impact.

Anybody who steps into the shaft can will themselves up or down it—it's a magical elevator.

Many doors lead into the shaft, most of them sealed shut with rubble from the other side. Only five doors open—one leads to a corridor where doors shrink and disappear as the adventurers approach, only to grow back as they move away (a magical defense against intruders); the other four lead onward *[to R, N, T, and X]*.

Every time an adventurer enters the shaft, there's a 25% chance the magic in the shaft goes crazy and slams them (and the corpses) about. **Gravity slam +10 vs. PD (each adventurer who enters the shaft)**—1d10 damage.

Fighting here: Enemies make the same rolls as the PCs for triggering crazy gravity magic. A fight in the shaft should come across as a crazy, zero-g experiment with people slamming into walls, flyers having trouble with conditions that aren't actually flight, and new corpses colliding with the original supply.

The area also feels a lot different if the enemies are hungry undead. . . .

T: THE OBSERVATORY

> **First impressions:** A room with a dome, a bewildering array of astronomical instruments and telescopes.
> **Second glance:** Trail of blood that leads to a chalk circle.
> **Joins to areas:** O, S, Y, and Z

This domed room contains astronomical charts, lots of telescopes (a few are even intact) and several bent brass instruments (an astrolabe, a sextant, a device like a series of dials set into a table, some complex orreries, and a mechanical calendar that calculates moon phases and tides).

Somebody survived the fall here—a trail of fresh blood leads to one corner and pools near a chalk circle, where it appears a wizard teleported out of the room.

A hatch in the domed roof—through which you can see daylight and hear birds—is open; there's a ladder nearby.

There are two doors in the room *[lead to O and S]*, and a smashed window that leads to a drop down beneath the tower *[to Z]*.

Fighting here: Smash complex astronomical equipment with every miss (and half the hits)! If the PCs try to keep the equipment intact, they'll deal slightly less damage with each attack, and then you'll have to figure out whether you want to reward them for their care.

U: THE HIGH DOME

First impressions: Shattered crystal dome, an entrance to the tower, there are corpses here.
Second glance: The crystal in the dome whirls about every so often, this area is dangerous.
Joins to areas: P, V, and outside

This was previously the tower's highest point: a glittering, glass dome 100 feet in diameter. Most of the dome's panes are shattered, and the whole thing tilts at a slight angle. Dozens of corpses—soldiers, wizards, and a few guests—lie here in the dome.

The glass from the broken panes keeps trying to mend itself—every few minutes, it spins itself into a frenzy and futilely attempts to fit into one of the empty panes. It's difficult to time attempts to move through or near the dome to coincide with periods when the glass is not moving (DC 20 check; failure indicates 5 damage, and 5 ongoing damage—you didn't get through yet).

A spiral staircase leads down from the dome *[leads to P]*, and a concealed hatch in the floor that requires a DC 20 check to spot from this side leads to a lower room *[leads to V]*.

V: THE BARRACKS

First impressions: Lots of long rooms, bunks everywhere.
Second glance: Bloody handprints
Joins to areas: Q, U, W, and Z

These long rooms are full of broken wooden bunks.

It's obvious somebody survived here and pushed a bunk over to a hatch in the ceiling *[leads to U]*; there are bloody handprints in the vicinity.

Two doors lead to and from the room *[lead to Q and W]*; it looks like someone pushed the bunks up against the doors post-crash and then pulled them back. A third door hangs off its hinges; the room beyond the door (a communal wardrobe) is mostly collapsed *[leads to Z]*.

W: THE MESS HALL

First impressions: Scattered tables and chairs.
Second sniff: Smell of fire, sounds of ravens nearby.
Joins to areas: R, V, and X

There are plenty of overturned tables and chairs in this semi-circular chamber, and its many windows are choked with rubble.

An open door leads to a small kitchen, in which an uncontrolled fire recently raged. Another door leads to the stables *[leads to X]*, and a third only partially opens—there are bunks stacked behind it *[leads to V]*. A fourth door floats eerily in mid-air *[leads to R]*.

X: THE STABLES

First impressions: A stable for something that could fly, exit to outside blocked by rubble.
Second sniff: Smell of blood and fire, animal corpses, ravens eating.
Joins to areas: S, W, and Y

Soldiers who were stationed here used these stables high in the tower for their flying mounts. Most of the mounts are missing, though more than a couple died in the fall and are still in the stables.

All the straw and blood strewn about this room make it hard to tell at first that the mounts were griffons; ravens now peck at their bodies.

A doorway (the door is off its hinges) leads into a burned-out kitchen *[leads to W]*, another door is closed *[leads to S]* and a third open door leads to a rookery *[leads to Y]*. Though the stables originally led to the outside, a wall of rubble blocks that exit.

Y: THE ROOKERY

First impressions: Ravens, darkness.
Second glance: Bird droppings, daylight.
Joins to areas: X, T, and possibly outside with some effort

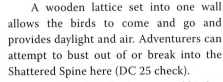

This dark chamber is full of ravens that are cawing and flapping about. The rookery's interior is a confusion of shelves, perches, and ladders.

A wooden lattice set into one wall allows the birds to come and go and provides daylight and air. Adventurers can attempt to bust out of or break into the Shattered Spine here (DC 25 check).

An open door leads to a stable that smells of blood *[leads to X]*; and a ladder lies next to a hatch in the floor, which leads downward *[leads to T]*.

Z: THE UNDERSIDE

First impressions: Rubble, riverbed, darkness.
Second glance: Danger, a quick way to bypass certain areas by crawling under the tower.
Joins to areas: B, C, D, E, G, P, T, and V

The tower fell directly into the Red River, and the water diverted around and partially over the rubble. An area of riverbed under the tower provides a crawl-space, though moving under the tower involves crawling on hands and knees through the freezing water in a confusing maze of rubble and darkness.

Crawling around under the tower requires a normal save (11+) for each character who attempts it. Failure deals 1d8 damage somehow, perhaps as rubble shifts and falls, or perhaps as the character cuts themselves on something hidden in the darkness.

Several voids large enough to let an adventurer stand exist, and there are a couple of tower rooms open to the underside *[leads to areas B, C, D, E, G, P, T, and V]*.

THE LOST TOMB

Level range: Adventurer tier, ideally 1st and 2nd level; but, a hidden portion of the tomb is aimed at 3rd and 4th level. If lower level characters get in there, too bad for them!

The Lost Tomb is the final resting place for one of the Archmage's first apprentices. The tomb is rigged with tricks and traps designed to dissuade intruders.

No tension tables: Unlike some of the exploration-oriented dungeons in this book, this dungeon has enough going on with traps and monsters that tension table additions aren't required.

THE OUTER TOMB

The tomb entrance—a stone slab with turf over top that leads down into a rough, rock tunnel—is hidden in the side of a hill. All other entrances were long ago filled in with rock and earth or erased using magic—this is the only remaining way inside.

The hill itself is the mound that the village of Crownhill crowns! If it wasn't for Vantage wrecking the place, the tomb would have remained hidden forever—the town's inhabitants above completely unaware that the big lump of earth on which their town sat was the hollow resting place for an icon's favorite apprentice.

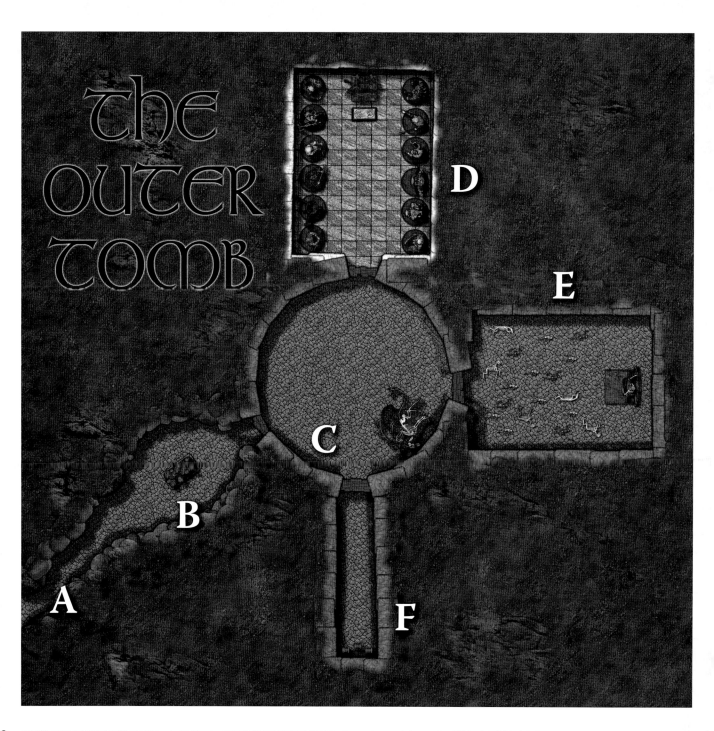

The back of the now cracked stone slab that covers the entrance holds a powerful warding spell, designed to turn away the minds of any who consider the hill. The mind-turning magic is so strong that it's still hard to think about the hole leading into the hill that the slab concealed—villagers (and other no-level NPC types) avert their gazes and have trouble holding coherent conversations while standing in its presence. The stone slab is too massive to easily carry away as loot; but, if the adventurers can round up a team of carthorses, they could haul it away and use it to conceal another entrance somewhere.

Behind the stone slab lies a sloping, earthen tunnel, lined with other stone slabs. . . .

A: THE NARROW PASSAGE

The walls of the stone-lined sloping tunnel down into the hill are uneven and form a narrow passage through which adventurers must walk single-file.

The stones were carefully rigged to collapse as people walked past—the stone slabs underfoot rock the wall supports causing ceiling rocks (and a ton of earth) to drop on intruders' heads. Each adventurer must roll a DC 15 skill check to notice the danger in time and dodge the falling rocks. **Falling rocks +5 vs. AC**—1d10 damage.

Simple designs, intended to give the impression that this is the tomb of some tribal chieftain, are carved in the walls. There are clues that all is not as it seems; it requires a DC 20 check to spot the deception.

B: THE CHIEFTAIN'S TOMB

The narrow passage ends in a slightly taller chamber with the same rough stonework as before. A doorway in the stone was bricked up with red clay bricks, preventing further passage forward.

A cairn stands in the center of the area; beneath it lies a corpse wearing the burial gear of a tribal chieftain (worth 4d20 gp). The door is not only the way forward, it is also a trap that requires a DC 20 check from the group's trap expert to discern and disarm. The bricks are part of the room's structural integrity and removing them brings the ceiling down! If the group's trap specialist doesn't take care of the trap, everyone in the area is attacked. **Falling ceiling +10 vs. AC**—1d8+5 damage.

If the adventurers do not brace the doorway before they start to remove the bricks, they'll have several hours of digging ahead of them before they can go deeper into the tunnel. The "chieftain" is, in fact, a magical construct (though, not an undead creature). Its job is to wait until there are no living creatures present, then reset any traps that need to be reset (this includes digging out the tunnel if it has collapsed). The "chieftain" is a mindless drone—if any characters attempt to interact with the bone construct, it plays dead. Destroying the "chieftain" is trivial; the magic repairs it within 1d3 days.

C: THE PIT

This is a circular chamber with four doorways: the one the adventurers just came through *[leads back to B]*, and three others that are also bricked up *[lead to D, E, and F]*. Removing the bricks

from the doorways is not difficult, as the mortar is basically mud.

The stonework here is close-fitting dressed stone—much different than the crude stone in the areas that led here *[A and B]*.

The center of the room's ceiling is marked with a star chart. The chart has no meaning or purpose beyond luring explorers into the center of the room, which is a pit trap that goes down about 60 feet. It takes a DC 15 skill check from the first character near the trap to discern and disarm it, otherwise the floor might collapse on anybody who walks across the center of the room. **Pit trap +5 vs. AC**—2d6 damage.

The desiccated bones of a long-dead dragon rest at the far side of the circular room. A chain runs from an iron collar on its neck to a ring in the wall. The chain is long enough to lower into the pit; this, too, is a trap. When somebody pulls on the chain (such as while using it to climb out of the pit), the chain pulls on the ring. The ring is connected to a mechanism in the wall that releases concealed ceiling hatches and drops quicklime—a white acidic powder that burns flesh and blinds anybody who gets it in their eyes. Fortunately, most of the quicklime decomposed over the centuries, otherwise this trap would strip the adventurers' flesh right off their bones. It requires a DC 20 check (a DC 25 check if the PCs are in the pit) to discern and disarm the quicklime trap. **Quicklime +10 vs. PD (all adventurers in the area)**—1d12 acid damage. *Natural 20*: The target is dazed until their next full heal-up, or until they receive magical healing (any healing from a spell or magic item, or healing that doesn't involve using a recovery—though free recoveries are fine).

D: THE HALL OF STATUES

This long hallway is constructed from white stone and carved with battle scenes that show the fall of a great king. Thirteen statues line the hall: six on each side and one at the far end of the hallway. The statue at the far end is the largest—it is the mighty king. The other statues are imposing-looking humanoid figures—they are either gods or icons of a previous age, as the symbols on the statues are not those of the current icons.

A shiny stone box resembling a sarcophagus or altar rests at the foot of the largest statue. Carved lines run across the box in geometric patterns.

The square floor tiles in this room are spring-loaded, and between each tile is a razor-sharp blade. Those who step into the room need a DC 15 check to react quickly to the trap, otherwise they are thrown off-balance and fall on the blades in the cracks between tiles! **Blades +10 vs. AC**—2d6 damage.

Two possible ways the adventurers can avoid being sliced into cubes are to jump from statue to statue (DC 15 check) or make a carpet of chainmail and shields to walk across.

The stone "box" is actually one or more golems, which unfold from their compressed form and attack once the characters are close enough that the golems can easily knock them off statues or their impromptu pathway back into the trap. The golems prefer to stay in the hall of statues; but, if they can, they try to kick adventurers near the doorway into the pit *[center of C]*.

GM: This fight becomes tougher for big adventuring parties, but that's good, for a change.

#/Level of PCs	Box Golem	Tougher Box Golem
3 x 1st level	1	0
4 x 1st level	1	0
5 x 1st level	2	0
6 x 1st level	0	1
7 x 1st level	1	1
3 x 2nd level	2	0
4 x 2nd level	0	1
5 x 2nd level	3	0
6 x 2nd level	1	1
7 x 2nd level	2	1
3 x 3rd level	2	0
4 x 3rd level	1	1
5 x 3rd level	2	1
6 x 3rd level	0	2
7 x 3rd level	1	2
3 x 4th level	2	2
4 x 4th level	0	3
5 x 4th level	2	3
6 x 4th level	2	4
7 x 4th level	4	4

BOX GOLEM

It seems that whoever this dead apprentice was, they were the type of person to appreciate the time spent on magical research & development to construct a golem that can fold into a box.

Triple-strength 1st level wrecker [CONSTRUCT]
Initiative: +4

Fists of Steel +8 vs. AC (2 attacks)—6 damage
  Miss: 3 damage.

Golem immunity: Non-organic golems are immune to effects. They can't be dazed, weakened, confused, made vulnerable, or touched by ongoing damage. You can damage a golem, but that's about it.

Back in the box: As a move action, the box golem can assume a sturdy cube shape, gaining *resist damage 16+*. While in box form, the box golem can't make any attacks. The box golem can assume its normal shape as another move action.

AC	19	
PD	15	**HP 60**
MD	11	

TOUGHER BOX GOLEM

Same box, more golem.

Triple-strength 3rd level wrecker [CONSTRUCT]
Initiative: +6

Fists of Steel +10 vs. AC (2 attacks)—12 damage
  Miss: 6 damage.

Golem immunity: Non-organic golems are immune to effects. They can't be dazed, weakened, confused, made vulnerable, or touched by ongoing damage. You can damage a golem, but that's about it.

Back in the box: As a move action, the box golem can assume a sturdy cube shape, gaining *resist damage 16+*. While in box form, the box golem can't make any attacks. The box golem can assume its normal shape as another move action.

AC	21	
PD	17	**HP 104**
MD	13	

E: THE THRONE ROOM

This room is a long chamber. Many long-dead knights and horses are arranged here as though they are paying homage to the throne at the far end of the room. The king's corpse sits upon the throne, with a sword in one hand and a crown on his head. It is obvious from their broken bones and smashed skulls that these long-dead warriors and their king died in battle.

There are a couple of true magic items on the king's body, and his crown is worth 300 gp. If the adventurers already went through the Shattered Spine and have a load of loot, skip the magical treasure.

The area around the throne is strangely clear of the dust that coats the rest of the room. There is a hatch underneath the throne that leads to the Inner Tomb. Adventurers examining the throne area can easily spot the hatch.

F: THE TREASURE ROOM

This room is long, plain, and empty except for a series of chests at the far end. There is one chest per adventurer (this is not magic, just a handy meta-gamey coincidence to make sure everybody gets their share of loot).

The chests are made of thick oak, with sturdy iron and gold bands; they lack any sort of locking mechanism and are worth about 25 gp each.

Each treasure chest is full of silver and copper coins (over 600 silver and 6000 copper coins per chest: about 125 gp-worth), as well as a smattering of jeweled golden brooches and torcs.

The room itself is a trap—the whole hall pivots at its center point. When the adventurers move a chest toward the exit (or when most of the party stands at the exit) there is enough weight to tip the room's balance and flip it from a hallway into a vertical shaft. It takes a DC 20 check to discern the trap before it triggers and a subsequent DC 15 skill check to disarm the trap. Otherwise, moving the chests triggers the pivot.

Sudden drop +10 vs. PD—2d6 damage, mostly from heavy treasure chests falling on the characters.

It is possible to get the treasure out of the chamber without setting off the trap by moving heavy objects into the far end of the corridor as counterweights. However, once the room flips vertically, there is no way in or out. The adventurers must make a DC 25 skill check to climb to the top of the shaft (hauling treasure chests there) and rock the room back into a horizontal position; failure results in 2d6 damage from falling and dropping heavy chests on themselves.

Adventurers who were outside the trap when it activated can try to maneuver the trap back into place (DC 20 check; alternatively, lower the DC for those inside the trap by 5). Icon relationship rolls can also help here.

STUCK?

The old-school way to deal with adventurers getting stuck at the bottom of a vertical shaft was for the adventurers to starve to death while bemoaning their poor life choices. If that is your group's preferred playstyle, then this may be a potentially deadly trap.

However, we're not permanently enrolled in the old-school, we just take a couple of classes there. After a day of trial and error, most competent adventurers should be able to get out of the trap—though they may develop an aversion to treasure chests and coins in the process.

Another option is to allow the dungeon's age to work in the party's favor—perhaps the trapped unfortunates feel a breeze coming from a crack in the wall of the shaft (previously the corridor's ceiling). A couple of well-placed kicks at the stonework in the bottom of the shaft lets the adventurers into Area G of the Inner Tomb.

THE INNER TOMB

The adventurers can access this area of the dungeon through a hatch under the throne in the Outer Tomb. You should warn 1st and 2nd level parties that the tenor of the area beneath the hatch is a step up from that of the tomb they just plundered.

In other words, we don't present 1st and 2nd level stats for the battles that follow. Low-level characters who push on are about to start their legends.

FOOL'S GOLD

The first thing the adventurers see in the Inner Tomb are piles of gleaming gold coins, and this is something the adventurers keep coming across—lots of lovely gold, just sitting there.

The Archmage who built this tomb long ago figured that anybody persistent enough to get this far in the tomb won't give up without finding treasure, and lots of it. There are no treasure chests here, just coins scattered about that require tomb robbers to bend over and pick them up off the floor. Most of the "gold" coins in the Inner Tomb are actually lead coins enchanted to seem like gold—once they leave the tomb, they lose their golden luster.

However, there are just enough gold pieces down here to ensure greedy adventurers keep wandering into traps, and to convince them to take what they've gathered and leave. There are over a million lead "gold" pieces in the Inner Tomb, but only 1000 gp in *actual* coins. Unfortunately; adventurers need to haul out all the coins to sort out the worthwhile from the dross.

G: THE TREASURE POOL

This square room contains a pool of coins. A ladder leads down into the pool, and there's even a diving board. The pool is not trapped, but those diving into it take 3d6 falling damage from smacking face-first into a pile of metal objects.

The Archmage, or some joker who worked for him, rigged up a magical mouth that appears whenever anybody dives into the pit. The mouth laughs and mocks those who choose to dive into the pit:

"Ha, ha, ha! Stupid tomb robber. What did you think would happen?"

"You are as stupid as you are ugly. Ha, ha!"

"Hey you. Hey. Yeah. You. You're the dumbest adventurer I've ever seen."

The wall behind the mouth contains a section of glass, painted to look like stone. Adventurers must make a DC 20 check to discern that the wall is glass, otherwise, those who attack the mouth risk breaking the glass and releasing thousands of hornets from magical stasis within the glass tank. **Hornets +10 vs. PD—3d6 poison damage.**

There are two exits from the room. The first is a portcullis that leads into a dark corridor that looks like a dead end *[leads to H]*. Lifting the portcullis takes a DC 20 skill check and activates a pair of ankle-height scythe blades. It's a DC 25 check for each PC to dodge the blades, and a DC 25 check for a trap expert to disarm it and prevent it from firing again whenever the portcullis is lifted. **Foot removal +10 vs. AC—3d4 damage.** *Miss:* Half damage.

The other exit from this area is a ladder that leads back up to the fake throne in the Outer Tomb *[leads to E]*.

H: THE DARK CORRIDOR

At first, this corridor appears to be a dead end—the end of the dungeon. There are a few coins on the floor, but not much else of interest.

However, as the adventurers approach the corridor's far wall, it flickers slightly—just long enough to let the canny adventurers know there is magic here. A wall of force and an illusion block further passage; only two DC 20 skill checks (one to overcome the wall of force and one to penetrate the illusion) can lower the barrier.

As soon as the barrier is down, the stasis field behind it reveals the monsters the Archmage placed here and they attack. Note that this counts as a double-strength fight for 1st and 2nd level characters, who must take their chances at being treated as though they were at least 3rd level.

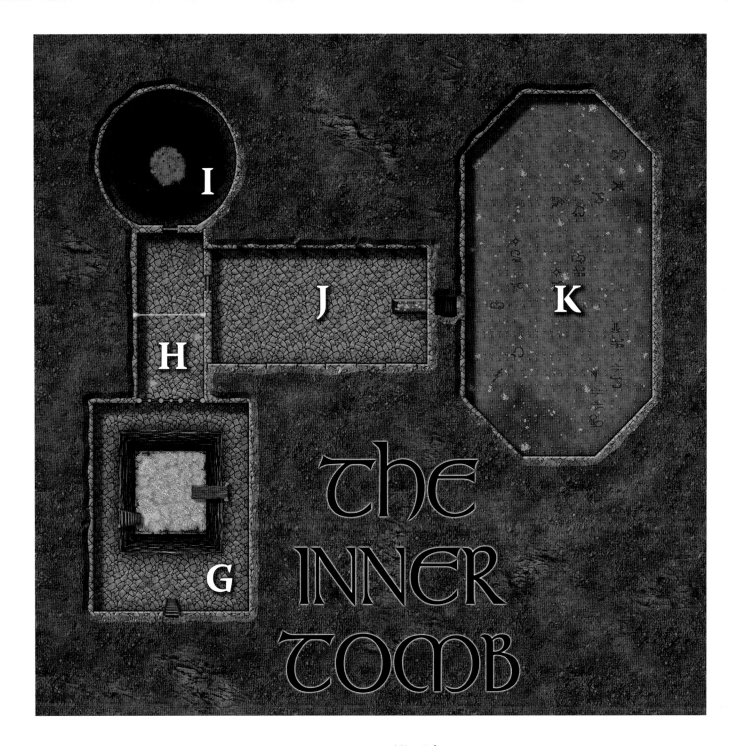

THE INNER TOMB

LESSER GRAY OOZE

These oozes look like slick flowing stones. They can be found in volcanic dungeons, wizard's towers on mountain peaks, quiet swamps, and sadistic death traps.

3ʳᵈ level troop [OOZE]
Initiative: +2

Hungry mass +8 vs. AC—10 damage
 Natural even hit: The target is grabbed.

**Acidic constriction (one creature the ooze has grabbed) + 9
 vs. PD**—6 acid damage

Miss: 3 damage.
Quick use: 1/round, as a quick action.

Resist cold and fire 16+: When a cold or fire attack targets this
 creature, the attacker must roll a natural 16+ on the attack roll
 or it only deals half damage.

AC	18	
PD	16	**HP 40**
MD	12	

Behind the monsters is a pair of doors. Both are locked and trapped. Their surfaces are coated with contact poison (preserved by the same stasis field that kept the monsters in place). Anybody

#/Level of PCs	Lesser Gray Ooze
3 x 3rd level	3
4 x 3rd level	4
5 x 3rd level	5
6 x 3rd level	6
7 x 3rd level	7
3 x 4th level	4
4 x 4th level	6
5 x 4th level	7
6 x 4th level	8
7 x 4th level	10

who inhales too near the doors (for example, a thief trying to pick the locks or a character trying to kick down the doors) risks being poisoned. The adventurers can throw water on the doors and wait for a bit to get rid of the poison, though they must still make a DC 20 check to open them. **Poisonous fumes +10 vs. PD**—2d10 poison damage.

The door to the left opens to a pit with a 60-foot drop *[leads to I]*, where gold and gems gleam at the bottom. The door to the right leads into what looks like a tomb, complete with sarcophagus *[leads to J]*.

I: THE MONEY PIT

This 60-foot deep pit is filled with coins and what look to be gems. It takes a DC 25 skill check by the most observant adventurer to discern that each "gem" is hollow glass and contains a spell—disturbing a gem causes it to explode. **Exploding gem +15 vs. PD**—2d12 force damage.

It also takes a DC 25 skill check to discern and disarm the doubly-trapped pit—a counterweight mechanism causes the ceiling to slam down if the pit becomes too light (for example, if the adventurers remove a lot of the coins). **Ceiling slam +15 vs. AC**—1d12 damage.

Once the ceiling slams down, the mechanism resets—it then takes a DC 20 skill check by each adventurer, one at a time, to get out of the pit without setting it off again, although throwing enough coins or other heavy objects in to balance the counterweight allows adventurers to climb out without making a roll.

J: THE CRUSHING TOMB

This room is a tomb; a sarcophagus is clearly visible at the far end. There are coins on the sarcophagus, but not on the floor leading to it.

The central part of the room is a trap: if the adventurers put any weight on the walls, floor, or even ceiling, the stonework shifts slightly.

For every adventurer who steps on the floor, there is a 1 in 4 chance the trap activates. When the trap activates, the floor and walls rotate—dropping anybody in that section of the room into a pit before slamming a stone slab down on them from the ceiling. Fortunately, the trap has not aged well; its creaking motion allows adventurers a chance to dodge out of the way. Unfortunately, the trap resets itself and has four separate slabs it can drop into the pit. It requires a DC 20 check by the most perceptive adventurer to discern and outsmart the trap. **Spin and slam pit +15 vs. AC (each adventurer stepping when the trap activates)**—4d6 damage, again each time a new slab drops into the pit.

The sarcophagus lies beyond the trap. Mechanical "hounds" and clockwork automatons spring out and attack as soon as the adventurers open the sarcophagus lid. This is another 3rd or 4th level fight. Under the place where the constructs hid in the sarcophagus, there's a heavy stone door that leads to steps headed downward *[leads to K]*.

#/Level of PCs	Clockwork Automaton	Diamond Pup
3 x 3rd level	2	2
4 x 3rd level	3	3
5 x 3rd level	4	3
6 x 3rd level	4	4
7 x 3rd level	5	5
3 x 4th level	3	2
4 x 4th level	4	3
5 x 4th level	5	5
6 x 4th level	6	6
7 x 4th level	8	7

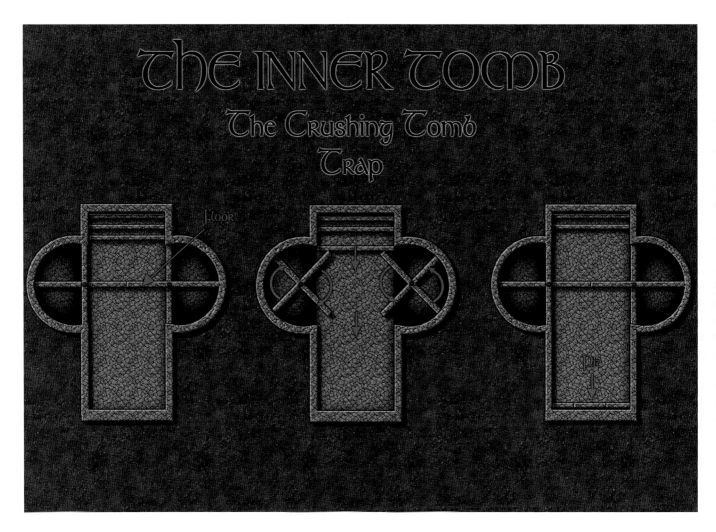

THE INNER TOMB
The Crushing Tomb
Trap

CLOCKWORK AUTOMATON

Gears grind and the thing moves forward on a pair of spoked, iron wheels. Each of its metal arms ends in a sharp point.

2nd level troop [CONSTRUCT]
Initiative: +4

Spear-hands +6 vs. AC—6 damage

Natural even hit: The automaton can make a second *spear-hands* attack as a free action (but not a third).

Made of gears and cables: When an attack crits against it or when it's staggered, the automaton must roll an easy save (6+). On a failure, the construct's internal workings fail, and it breaks apart in a small explosion of metal and gears. Drop the automaton to 0 hp and make an *exploding gears* attack.

C: Exploding gears +6 vs. PD (each creature engaged with or next to the automaton)—2d12 damage.

AC	17	
PD	14	**HP 40**
MD	12	

DIAMOND PUP

These small quartz quadrupeds aren't all that hound-like, but "crystalline lion-lizard thing" is a mouthful.

3rd level blocker [CONSTRUCT]
Initiative: +9

Bite +8 vs. AC—7 damage

C: Crystal-forming breath +8 vs. PD (one nearby enemy)—5 damage

Natural even hit: The target is stuck (save ends).
1st failed save: Target is stuck, dazed, and vulnerable (save ends all).
2nd failed save: Target is stuck, dazed, vulnerable, and must begin making last gasp saves (hard save ends all).

Climber: The diamond pup can run on any surface that can support it; it can even use its claws and crystal-forming powers to run upside-down along ceilings.

Burst of speed: Twice per fight, the diamond pup can pop free and immediately move to intercept any moving character, even if it would not normally be able to intercept that character.

AC	21	
PD	17	**HP 45**
MD	13	

K: The Hall of Flame

This elongated octagonal room is lined with metal spikes on all surfaces (about one every foot); among the spikes are scattered coins, golden torcs, and jeweled golden brooches.

There are a couple of true magic items and 1d4 x 100 gp in this area. Some of the gold items are attached to hidden chains that activate the room's trap: when pulled, the chains cause a hidden mechanism to heat up the spikes and shoot jets of flame from between the floor's flagstones. The trapped gold attacks everybody in the room when it is disturbed. It takes a DC 25 skill check by the most perceptive adventurer to discern and work around the trap. **Sudden oven +15 vs. PD (each adventurer in the room)**—2d12 fire damage.

A series of runes is hidden among the coins and iron spikes and requires a DC 20 check to translate. Once the runes are read aloud, the flames and spikes vanish, revealing the final resting place of the Archmage's apprentice.

Final Rest?

I leave the appearance of the first apprentice's tomb up to you. In one early playtest, it was a richly appointed burial chamber with a glass coffin and many musty books of magic; in another, it was an orichalcum-lined chamber where the apprentice's deeds were inscribed on the walls, but there was no body. Your final resting place—and exactly how you reveal it—might be completely different.

Whatever your story needs, this is a good place to fulfill it. If the Elf Queen is important to your group, then maybe the first apprentice was an elf and the final resting place is a glass coffin in the branches of a tree that rises from the floor. If the Lich King is important, then maybe the walls slide back to reveal trophies of the conflict that destroyed the Wizard King. If the Dwarf King is important, then perhaps the first apprentice was a dwarf and the final resting place is a carved, stone hall the adventurers can only access through a secret door, which is revealed when the runes are read aloud. It's up to you and what you believe can help the campaign sing.

CHAPTER 6:

THUNDER & LIGHTNING

ADVENTURES FOR 3RD AND 4TH LEVEL CHARACTERS

As the wards come down one by one, they reveal various dungeons and adventure environments. *The Lightning Spires* are an accidental consequence of Vantage's fall. The other three adventure locations in this chapter—*Great Beasts*, *Redfield Rising*, and *The Orcwell*—are now accessible because of broken wards.

Broken wards: Opening *all* the wards at once can overwhelm players with options and make the problems their adventurers face seem unmanageable. Present a couple of failing or failed wards at a time and let the players choose which one to chase after. Once they are done dealing with a ward, reveal two more to give them more options. Try to keep the players' options to a few possible adventures at a time; but, be open to them coming up with alternate ideas about where to go and what to do beyond the options you present. Make their choices meaningful, but not so dire that they despair.

You also shouldn't feel constrained by our material. You don't have to use all our locations and even if you do, mixing your own cool ideas in keeps things fresh for players who can't help peeking at source books.

THE LIGHTNING SPIRES

The Lightning Spires are a set of towers that fell from Vantage. They crackle with energy and threaten everything nearby.

An attempt to shut down the Lightning Spires is a good reason to go exploring there, as the lightning is endangering parts of the valley.

Then again, looting the ruins before enemies can do so is a good reason to be there, too.

THE GREAT BEASTS

The Great Beasts takes place in a newly revealed land-before-time, with dinosaurs galore. Preventing enemies from obtaining dinosaur mounts could be a worthy goal.

REDFIELD RISING

Redfield Rising is a time-locked battlefield—exploring the area reveals clues about the past, but some groups of adventurers might blunder into a frozen battle by accident.

THE ORCWELL

A potential threat to the Dragon Empire, the Orcwell must be dealt with; unless the adventurers work *for* the Orc Lord, in which case they must capture and control it.

By this point in the adventure, the adventurers may have accumulated quite a bit of gold. The lost city of Magaheim shows up in the valley when the adventurers reach 5th level; but some groups might have an issue with waiting until they are at champion-tier to spend their loot.

If adventurers want to leave the valley for a respite, let them. The worst of the glitterfall is over, and the brave adventurers deserve a rest from constant danger. Leaving is fine, provided they have a reason to return.

Give the adventurers time and space to fence their loot in Glitterhaegen, sell their treasures to the monsters of Drakkenhall, report to their secret masters in Axis, or whatever it is they wish to do.

Leaving the valley needn't be the end of their time in Redfield—any icon might conceivably send the adventurers back to recover an artifact, guard something, solve a problem in the valley, or figure out what went wrong with Vantage. The adventurers might even end up being hired as guides and guards to bring NPCs into the valley.

Gareth Ryder-Hanrahan's Eyes of the Stone Thief adventure offers a few other possibilities. An adventure for 4th to 7th level characters, it focuses on a living dungeon that surfaces to consume other cities or dungeons. You can easily adapt that adventure's modular design to have the monstrous living dungeon swallow the adventurers (and whatever dungeon or ruin they are currently investigating). Perhaps the fall of Vantage revealed secrets the Stone Thief wants for itself, possibly even leads on how to recover its eyes. The Shards of the Broken Sky sandbox could be a great zone for the Stone Thief's rampages.

The Lightning Spires

Level range: 3rd to 4th

Five great spires fell upright and intact into Redfield Valley's deep mud. The spires are between twenty and 200 yards of each other. Rainbow-hued lightning arcs between the orichalcum-filigreed walls of the five towers. Unless they manage to pull surprising information out of an icon relationship advantage with the Archmage, the PCs won't know anything about the towers' names or configuration, but no one can miss that each tower has its own distinctive appearance.

The Red Hand Tower: The tower's exterior is covered with tiles in many different shades of red. From a distance, the lightning flares make discerning the shape of the tiles difficult; but, as you get closer, it becomes clear that the apparently stable configuration of tiles is made up of all different sizes, positions, and shapes of hands, merged together.

The Tower of the Elements: The PCs may be able to figure out this tower's name, given that it's painted with extremely vivid representations of the elements. Four elements? Five? Six? That's up to you.

The Tower of the Mind: The tower's white paint is now scorched and splattered with mud; however, the filigree appears to be intact. It's still spraying lightning.

The Golden Tower: Apparently, the people of Vantage referred to this as the Golden Tower; but the well-worked vines twisting below the filigree look more like brass—because they are.

The Tower of Power: You can't really tell what this tower is made of—or if it's painted—because the exterior is crawling with balls of lightning.

As the PCs might guess from the fearsome lightning bolts dancing around the fallen towers, they were originally part of Vantage's defense system. Occasionally, the lightning storm builds up and devastates part of the surrounding valley. It's an awesome display, but it's generally not fatal if you take cover. What adventurers likely care more about is that the windows on the lower floors are shattered, allowing easy entrance.

Presentation and reality: Our diagrams are laid out as though the towers were side-by-side, when they're actually scattered across almost a mile of the valley floor. We've detailed the towers, left to right, starting with the Red Hand Tower; but the PCs can enter the towers in any order and access the other towers through magical portals in many of the rooms.

Dungeon Goal

The theme of this dungeon is exploration—the adventurers should wander about and see what there is to see (and loot the place). If you want to make this dungeon into something a bit more than that, drop the lightning spires somewhere where their random storms endanger something the characters want to protect.

Interior Overview

Each spire contains a series of rooms, and each room in the spires is identical in shape—a 40-foot wide circular room with curved stairways leading down on one side of the room and up on the other. Each room also has high, narrow windows around the exterior.

There is one exception: the missing tower that's buried deep in the mud, not visible from the surface, and all but destroyed. This missing tower has only one room left, and the only way in is through a magic portal.

Entrances to the Lightning Spires

Where each spire sank into the deep, red mud its windows are shattered (*Areas A, F, K, P, and U*). Wading from tower to tower—heck, getting close to the towers in the first place—is slow going, and the characters must make a DC 25 check to find cover or dodge when lightning discharges to avoid it blasting them. **Rainbow lightning +10 vs. PD (each adventurer who fails the skill check)**—2d6 + 4 lightning damage.

ADVENTURING IN THE LIGHTNING SPIRES

Each time the adventurers enter a new, potentially dangerous area in the Lightning Spires, they should roll a d12 on the tension table. As a bonus to the d12 roll, add twice the number of battles the adventurers have fought toward their next full heal-up. See page 53 for detailed instructions on using (and when not to use) tension tables.

LIGHTNING SPIRES TENSION TABLE (D12)

1-4. Nothing of note happens. Add +2 to the adventurers' next roll on this table.

5. The hum of lightning oscillates into a zap. Outside, luckily.

6. Rolling thunder!

7. One or two random PCs take 1d4 lightning damage from static . . . lightning.

8. A random magic item the party carries grows temporarily more conscious and demanding about its quirk.

9. Flickering spirits shift through the room. Ghosts? Memories?

10. The nearest magical portal cycles through the colors of the rainbow. And then, through colors that aren't in the rainbow.

11+ *odd*. A magical defense activates. Roll on the *Lightning Spires Magical Defense* table..

12+ *even*. Wandering monster encounter. Choose from or roll on the *Lightning Spires Wandering Monster* table.

Vantage's ruins still have a few active magical defenses, though they "go offline" often. Still, they may activate in any area at any time, attacking the adventurers while they explore the ruins. When they do, roll on the *Lightning Spires Magical Defense* table. The defenses with delayed effects can "stack," accumulating to make the problem worse when they fully trigger.

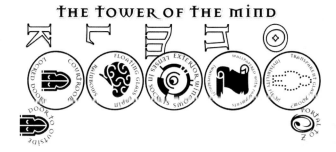

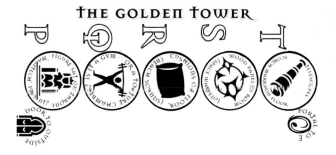

LIGHTNING SPIRES MAGICAL DEFENSE TABLE (D4)

1. *Suppression field:* Randomly choose a PC and ask to see their character sheet. Look it over and more or less randomly choose a power. Invent a lightning-oriented trap or zap that triggers against the PC. The next time the PC is in combat in the Lightning Spires, they are unable to use the power you chose until the escalation die reaches 2+.

2. *Lightning "batteries":* Strange lightning magic hisses around the adventurers. Each PC rolls a normal save. Those who fail are surrounded by subtle lightning fields that trigger the next time the PC rolls initiative for combat. **Lightning "batteries"**—5 ongoing lightning damage (save ends).

3. *Thunder orb:* An orb appears in the room and attacks the adventurers before flying away. It takes a DC 20 skill check to hide as the orb enters the area.
C: Thunder orb +15 vs. PD (1d3 enemies)
—1d12 thunder damage

4. *Hidden alarms:* Magical glyphs flash and lightning sparks *just* outside the adventurers' visual range. Most characters feels like a light flashed briefly in the corner-of-the-back-of-their-eyes, but a forgeborn or other construct PC sees the alarms clearly and probably recognizes them for what they are. The alarms have no immediate effect, but the next wandering monster battle the PCs fight in the Lightning Spires (unless it's against an adversary group) is harder than it would have been: add monsters worth at least 1 or 1.5 additional PCs and don't give the PCs increased credit for a tougher battle.

LIGHTNING SPIRES WANDERING MONSTER TABLE (D10)

1-3. Magical defenders of the Lightning Spires. Use the specific monsters and battles in the next section.

4-6. Lightning Spires constructs. Use the specific monsters and battles on page 86.

5-7. Defenders of Vantage. Use a battle from the *Wizards & Spellcasters* adversary group on page 218. They assume the adventurers are attackers and adopt a shoot-first, ask-questions-later policy.
If you prefer, and if the adventurers can somehow make a DC 25 check to prove they are friends or allies, there's a slight possibility they can talk the defenders around to their side.

8-10. An adversary group. Perhaps whoever brought down Vantage is here, poking about in the ruins looking for something, or perhaps this is an opportunistic enemy. Choose an adversary group from the Appendix starting on page 191 that seems interesting or fits with the party's icon relationship rolls.

MAGICAL DEFENDERS OF THE LIGHTNING SPIRES

The arcanites in this section are from Gareth Ryder-Hanrahan's *Book of Ages* (page 28). Previously, the arcanites served the Wizard King as magical custodians, so it doesn't feel like much of a reach to bring them here to the Lightning Spires. The Archmage had a lot of things hidden—turns out some of them were people!

#/ Level of PCs	Tiny Lightning Elemental	Spell-Warrior	Arcanite Custodian	Arcanite Guard
3 x 3rd level	0	0	1	1
3 x 3rd level	2	2	0	0
4 x 3rd level	0	1	1	1
4 x 3rd level	3	2	0	0
5 x 3rd level	0	0	1	2
5 x 3rd level	2	2	1	0
6 x 3rd level	2	0	1	2
6 x 3rd level	2	3	1	0
7 x 3rd level	0	0	2	2
7 x 3rd level	2	3	2	
3 x 4th level	1	0	1	1
3 x 4th level	4	2	0	0
4 x 4th level	0	2	1	1
4 x 4th level	3	2	0	1
5 x 4th level	0	2	1	2
5 x 4th level	2	2	1	1
6 x 4th level	0	2	2	2
6 x 4th level	3	2	2	1
7 x 4th level	2	2	2	2
7 x 4th level	4	0	2	2

TINY LIGHTNING ELEMENTAL

Webs of lightning repeatedly streak in all directions, outlining the form of the creature and then dissipating. Each flash happens so fast, it leaves the thing's image burned into your eyes.

2nd level spoiler [ELEMENTAL]
Initiative: +9

Lightning zap +7 vs. AC—7 lightning damage
Natural odd hit: The target is dazed until the end of its next turn.
Metal affinity: The attack gains a +1 bonus against enemies wearing metal armor or wielding metal weapons.

R: Lightning strike +7 vs. PD (one nearby enemy or a far away enemy at −2 attack)—8 lightning damage
Metal affinity: The attack gains a +1 bonus against enemies wearing metal armor or wielding metal weapons.

Flight: Lightning elementals zip from place to place as quick as lightning, hovering above the ground to avoid being grounded.

Resist lightning and thunder 16+: When a lightning or thunder attack targets this creature, the attacker must roll a natural 16+ on the attack roll or it only deals half damage.

AC	17	
PD	17	**HP 34**
MD	11	

SPELL-WARRIOR

Is it a spell that became a warrior? Or a warrior who became a spell?

3rd level archer [SPIRIT]
Initiative: +6

Lightning staff +8 vs. AC—10 lightning damage
Natural roll equal to or less than the escalation die: The spell-warrior pops free and makes a *mana blast* attack as a free action

R: Mana blast +8 vs. PD (one nearby or far away enemy)—6 force damage
Natural even hit: The spell-warrior may make another *mana blast* attack as a free action. The attack must be against an enemy who was not attacked with a *mana blast* this turn. The spell-warrior may keep making *mana blast* attacks until it fails to roll a natural even hit or there are no more valid targets.

Air-walking: The spell-warrior can't fly, but it can ignore pits and sudden drops by gliding over them.

AC	19	
PD	17	**HP 44**
MD	13	

ARCANITE CUSTODIAN

Age-old keepers of the Wizard King's wonders, patiently waiting for a master who must never return.

4th level caster [HUMANOID]
Initiative: +7

Spell-charged staff +9 vs. AC—7 damage
  Spell-charged: The custodian may choose to expend a spell-charge to deal an extra 2d6 damage.

[interrupt action] C: Spell-snatch +9 vs. MD (one nearby or far away enemy who just cast an arcane spell)—On a hit, the spell is countered, and both the enemy and the custodian take 3d6 psychic damage. The custodian gains one spell-charge.

R: Rain of magic +9 vs. PD (1d4 + 1 nearby enemies or allies)—This ability may target both enemies or allies of the custodian. When targeting allies, the custodian does not need to make attack rolls for those targets—the chosen ally automatically gains a spell-charge. When targeting enemies, the attack deals 3d6 damage.
  Limited use: The custodian must expend one spell-charge to use *rain of magic.*

Spell-charge: An arcanite custodian starts with 1d4 spell-charges, and it can hold up to four.

Gather power: As a standard action, the arcanite custodian may gain 2 spell-charges.

Fragile form: The custodian loses one spell-charge when it suffers a critical hit or when it is staggered.

Nastier Specials
Spell-charged death: If an arcanite custodian is killed while holding a spell-charge, it automatically deals 2d6 damage to a number of nearby enemies equal to the number of spell-charges held.

AC	19	
PD	14	HP 50
MD	19	

ARCANITE GUARD

Sentries and guardians of the Wizard King's lost sanctums and laboratories.

4th level blocker [HUMANOID]
Initiative: +8

Spell-Charged Sword +9 vs. AC—12 damage
  Spell-Charged: The guard may choose to expend a spell-charge to deal another 2d6 damage.

Spell-Charged Intercept: Once per round, an arcanite guard may expend a spell-charge to intercept an enemy who is moving to attack one of his nearby allies. He can pop free from up to two enemies to move and intercept the attack.

Spell-Charge: An arcanite guard starts with one spell-charge, and it can hold only one charge at a time.

Nastier Specials
Spell-Charged Death: If an arcanite guard is killed while holding a spell-charge, it automatically deals 2d6 damage to one nearby enemy.

AC	20	
PD	18	HP 58
MD	14	

Lightning Spires Constructs

Appropriately, the sword juggler is from the Age of Towers in *Book of Ages* (page 55)! You'll find its full writeup and illustration there.

The zorigami first appeared in the *13th Age Bestiary* (page 224). It's up to you whether these are real zorigami or facsimiles the Archmage managed to cobble together on Vantage. Either way, we're sure the zorigami were especially interested in goings-on within the Golden Tower.

#/Level of PCs	Clockwork Automaton	Dawn Zorigami	Sword Juggler	Apex Zorigami
3 x 3rd level	3	1	0	0
3 x 3rd level	2	0	1	0
4 x 3rd level	3	2	0	0
4 x 3rd level	2	1	1	0
5 x 3rd level	3	3	0	0
5 x 3rd level	2	0	2	0
6 x 3rd level	3	1	0	1
6 x 3rd level	2	1	2	0
7 x 3rd level	3	2	0	1
7 x 3rd level	2	0	3	0
3 x 4th level	3	2	0	0
3 x 4th level	2	0	0	1
4 x 4th level	4	3	0	0
4 x 4th level	1	0	1	1
5 x 4th level	4	2	1	0
5 x 4th level	2	1	1	1
6 x 4th level	4	2	2	0
6 x 4th level	2	0	2	1
7 x 4th level	5	2	2	0
7 x 4th level	0	0	2	2

Clockwork Automaton

Gears grind and the thing moves forward on a pair of spoked, iron wheels. Each of its metal arms ends in a sharp point.

2nd level troop [CONSTRUCT]
Initiative: +4

Spear-hands +6 vs. AC—6 damage
  Natural even hit: The automaton can make a second *spear-hands* attack as a free action (but not a third).

Made of gears and cables: When an attack crits against it or when it's staggered, the automaton must roll an easy save (6+). On a failure, the construct's internal workings fail, and it breaks apart in a small explosion of metal and gears. Drop the automaton to 0 hp and make an *exploding gears* attack.
  C: Exploding gears +6 vs. PD (each creature engaged with or next to the automaton)—2d12 damage.

AC	17	
PD	14	**HP 40**
MD	12	

Dawn Zorigami

This egg-shaped thing sticks close to the other creatures. As you approach it, a strange numbness comes over you, like time itself is fighting on the little guy's side.

3rd level spoiler [CONSTRUCT]
Initiative: +6

Headbutt +8 vs. AC—10 damage, and the target moves down 1d6 points in initiative order.

R: Ray of wasted time +8 vs. MD (1d3 nearby enemies or one far away enemy)—5 psychic damage, and 5 ongoing psychic damage.
  Natural 16+: The target also moves down 1d6 points in initiative order.

A moment of silence: The escalation die does not increase the round after a dawn zorigami drops to 0 hp.

On pause: A creature reduced to a negative initiative count in a battle involving one or more dawn zorigami moves forward in time, disappearing and then reappearing somewhere nearby in a number of minutes equal to their negative initiative count—presumably long after the current battle is over. The target may be confused by this effect, since the ways of zorigami are mysterious.

AC	22	
PD	13	**HP 30**
MD	17	

SWORD JUGGLER

The wizards of Highrock pulled down archons and sylphs from the overworld, girded them in steel and runes of binding, and fitted them with whirling blades.

5th level wrecker [CONSTRUCT]
Initiative: +10

Spinning sword +10 vs. AC—15 damage
  Natural 16+: The sword juggler may make a *spinning sword* attack on a different target that it's engaged with as a free action. If there aren't any valid targets, the sword juggler regains 1d10 hit points.

R: Thrown sword +12 vs. AC (one nearby target, or one far-away target at a −2 penalty)—25 damage. The sword juggler permanently loses one *spinning sword* attack, to a minimum of one.

Spin faster! When the sword juggler is staggered, it gains another *spinning sword* attack.

Spin even faster! When the escalation die becomes even, the sword juggler gains another *spinning sword* attack.

Nastier Specials
Rolling charge: Once per battle, the sword juggler may make a double move action and add the escalation die to all its attacks made that round.

Death blossom: When the sword juggler is killed, it immediately makes one *thrown sword* attack for every *spinning sword* attack available to it.

AC	22	
PD	18	**HP 64**
MD	14	

APEX ZORIGAMI

The clockwork man moves with a fluidity you've never seen. Every blocked attack offers a perfect chance to react. Every cut is precise and deadly. You would weep at its beauty if it weren't trying to kill you.

6th level spoiler [CONSTRUCT]
Initiative: +11

Multi-geared mace +11 vs. AC—20 damage
  Natural even hit or miss: Randomly select one of the target's true magic items. The target can't use the item's bonuses and powers until the end of the battle.

R: Spray of sharpened gears +11 vs. AC (1d3 nearby enemies or one far away enemy)—15 damage
  Miss: 8 damage.

Lethal parries: When an enemy engaged with the apex zorigami misses it with an attack, the apex zorigami may roll a normal save; on a success, it can make a *multi-geared mace* attack as a free action.

Take five: The escalation die does not increase the round after an apex zorigami is staggered or drops to 0 hp.

AC	24	
PD	17	**HP 75**
MD	19	

THE RED HAND TOWER

This tower contains Areas A-E. Its exterior is covered in red tiles, most of which are shaped like hands. What sort of hands? That's your call.

A: THE CRYSTAL SHARDS

> **First impressions:** Red, crystalline growths slowly form out of the walls.
> **Second glance:** Rhythmic sounds of a hammer on an anvil coming from upstairs.
> **Joins to areas:** B, and outside

This room's original purpose is obscured by the crystalline growths that sprouted all over it since the fall. The crystals are fragile, you can easily break them off by hand, and they are growing over obscured lumps. Yes, the lumps under the crystals are a mixture of furniture and corpses.

The crystals themselves are not gems, they are huge salt crystals. They draw their color from the red mud that flowed into this room after the crash. It takes a DC 15 check to realize you can sell the salt at market for half its weight in silver, a DC 20 check to avoid saying it out loud and marking yourself as an adventurer who is a little too desperate for treasure.

Exits: A stairway leads upward *[to B]* and shattered windows allow outside access.

B: The Hammer

First impressions: A large, solid metal cylinder repeatedly levitates up and down, smashing against metal disks mounted in the ceiling and floor. The noise is deafening. A swirling magical portal hovers off to one side of the room.
Second glance: The metal cylinder has writing on it; it moves too fast to read the writing.
Joins to areas: A, C, G, and V

The clanging hammer in this room makes conversation all but impossible. It's a good place for a fight, though!

Any creature caught between the hammer and the floor plate when it falls takes 4d8 damage per round until someone pulls them out or they roll out. Items (other than true magic items) placed under the hammer are usually destroyed in a single blow; adventurer-tier magic items are eventually destroyed (2d4 rounds or at the GM's discretion).

There was a field here to contain discharged magic from destroyed magic items, but it was deactivated during the fall to divert power elsewhere. One possible effect: make a **+10 vs. MD** attack against each nearby creature; the target hit by the greatest margin becomes confused, possessed by the destroyed item's bonuses and powers, and acts out the item's quirk (save ends all). Other possible weird effects that destroying a true magic item might have on bystanders are up to the GM.

A crate in the corner of the room contains 1 to 3 cursed items that were due for destruction.

Exits: One stairway leads downward *[to A]*, another leads upward *[to C]*. A swirling magical portal leads to other towers *[G and V]*.

C: The Hall of Elegance

First impressions: Swirls of light are embedded into the stone walls, lots of shelves full of fabric. A swirling magical portal hovers off to one side of the room.
Second glance: Rhythmic sounds of a hammer on an anvil coming from downstairs.
Joins to areas: B, D, and Z

The hall is lined with shelves that hold bolt after bolt of fabric. Below the shelves are drawers full of needles, thread, ribbons, measuring tape, and paper patterns. Six or seven dressmaker's dummies lie toppled over in one corner. A stone dais rotates slowly under its own power in the center of the room, and full-length mirrors (most shattered, but not all) and dressing screens surround the dais.

This was the tailor of Vantage's workroom. The room retains its magic—anybody who stands on the dais is "attacked" by a swarm of cloth bolts, ribbon, needles, scissors, etc. Roll a d6 to determine the outcome:

1. The character gains a fancy wizard's robe. Roll a d6 for details about what makes it so fancy:
   1. High collar
   2. Wide-brimmed hat
   3. Hidden pockets
   4. Conical, brimless hat
   5. Huge wizard's sleeves
   6. Velvet skull cap
2. The character gains a dress or gown. Roll a d6 for details:
   1. Silk
   2. Satin
   3. Velvet
   4. Ribbon and lace
   5. Matching hat and shoes
   6. Embroidered traveling dress
3. The character gains a richly embroidered doublet and cape. Roll a d6 for details:
   1. Hunting scenes
   2. Character's personal heraldry
   3. Trees
   4. Geometric patterns
   5. Slashed doublet
   6. Velvet
4. The character gains a new cloak. Roll a d6 for details:
   1. Fur-lined
   2. Woolen and heavy
   3. Leather and rain-proof
   4. A long-coat
   5. Hidden pockets
   6. Displays character's personal heraldry
5. The character gains a soldier's uniform and boots, like those worn in Vantage. Roll a d6 for details:
   1. Simple guard's uniform
   2. Sergeant's uniform
   3. Captain's uniform
   4. Captain's uniform with medals and ribbons
   5. No-rank uniform
   6. Griffon-rider's uniform
6. The character receives several cuts and scrapes from the scissors and needles—2d6 damage

Any existing non-magical clothing worn or carried by the character is torn to shreds in the process, though the room ignores magical items and the invisible tailors attempt to match the fabrics, patterns, or colors of their new creation to the magical items. Stepping off and then back on the dais reactivates it.

Fun with rituals: Any adventurer capable of using ritual magic or with a background related to tailoring can direct the room and choose what it creates—on their own behalf or that of others. They must roll a skill check to direct with finesse; their results depend on their final check result:

1-4. Misshapen clothes that quickly fall apart

5-9. Roll a d6 on the above table, then roll a second d6 on the details for another clothing type *[cloak made of ribbons and lace, leather dress with many hidden pockets, doublet with wizard's sleeves, wizard's robe trimmed with military medals, etc.]*

10-14. Clothing that doesn't look ridiculous

15-19. Elegant or well-made clothing

20-24. (Once per character) perfectly tailored and extremely well-made clothing that matches the wearer's desires exactly *[player chooses results instead of rolling]*, and is also very valuable (worth d100 + 100 gp)

25+. (Once per "tailor") a true magic item, a *raiment of iconic splendor* (see below).

Raiment of Iconic Splendor (light or no armor): When you first attune this item, randomly select one of your icon relationships. When interacting with creatures strongly associated with that icon, you gain a +2 bonus to social skill checks, to your defenses against their attacks, and to your attacks against their MD. This bonus stacks with other magic items.

Other goodies: It takes a DC 15 check to spot that one to three bolts of cloth here are enchanted. If used to make clothing, each bolt can create up to two sets of magical clothing (light/no armor or cloaks).

Exits: One stairway leads downward *[to B]*, another leads upward *[to D]*. A swirling magical portal crackles with lightning *[leads to Z]*.

During early playtesting, my players had great fun with the Hall of Elegance! They spent an hour jumping on and off the podium trying to get it to make them guard uniforms and laughing whenever a character ended up in an outfit in which they wouldn't be caught dead.

D: THE HALL OF THE ORB

First impressions: A dozen life-sized statues collectively hold an orb on their backs. A swirling magical portal hovers off to one side of the room.
Second glance: The orb cracked, recently.
Joins to areas: C, E, and Z

The statues turn their heads to watch the adventurers as they enter, but they are otherwise inanimate.

This orb was used to scry on far-off locations, revealing living dungeons rising to the surface and the movement of magic items. Now, it is cracked and simply reflects the adventurers, though magic items they carry glow brightly in the orb's reflection. Cursed items glow a sickly green or purple color. Touching the orb triggers an attack: **+10 vs. MD**—2d6 psychic damage. Otherwise, the orb does not react if the adventurers hit, poke, or prod it. The orb is either too large—or magically woven into this room—to loot.

Exits: One stairway leads downward *[to C]*, another leads upward *[to E]*. A swirling magical portal crackles with lightning *[leads to Z]*.

E: THE ROOM OF MIRRORS

First impressions: Mirrors line the walls, and the floor is a kaleidoscope of shifting colors. A swirling magical portal hovers off to one side of the room.
Second glance: The mirrors show alternate versions of this room.
Joins to areas: D, and T

The characters' alternate-reality reflections have only small differences (a cut in a different location, a cloak tied slightly differently, etc.).

The wizards originally used this room to advise themselves, by looking into the enchanted mirrors and talking to slightly different reflections of themselves.

The mirror versions of the characters can advise them, too: if the characters offer information about where they have explored so far, their alternate selves can give them information about 1d3 other rooms in another tower. If the characters react with suspicion toward their alternate selves, then their alternate selves do likewise. If a character has an unused icon relationship result with the Archmage or one of the suspects in the fall of Vantage, they can use it to gain a clear (a result of 6 on an icon relationship die) or possibly misleading (a result of 5) message from their future self. A clear message might accurately detail an upcoming enemy's capabilities, while an unclear message might be vague about said capabilities or to which enemy they refer. Smashing the mirrors has no effect beyond breaking them.

Exits: One stairway leads downward *[to D]*. A swirling magical portal leads to other towers *[leads to T]*.

Fighting here: A battle in which both sides have alternate selves offering advice and critiques offers roleplaying opportunities seldom encountered outside Vantage.

The Tower of the Elements

This tower consists of Areas F-J. The tower's exterior is painted with representations of the elements. If you're using the *Lightning Spires* tension table (page 82), keep on rolling.

F: The Burning Room

First impressions: This room is on fire!
Second glance: The fire gives off only a little heat. There is a clear path from the shattered windows to the stairs.
Joins to areas: G, and outside

The flames don't burn as hot as they should in this room. Closer inspection reveals the flames come from burning human, elven, dragonic, and gnome corpses partially buried in the mud. There's no explanation as to why these slow fires haven't fully consumed the bodies yet.

Characters who choose to stick around in this area (either to examine the corpses or to fight a wandering monster group) are subject to an attack: +15 vs. PD—4d6 fire damage. If your plot focus is figuring out who attacked Vantage, these corpses might provide a clue as to the attackers' identity.

Exits: A stairway leads upward *[to B]* and shattered windows allow outside access.

G: The Sphere of Water

First impressions: A sphere of water hovers in the middle of the room, and a swirling magical vortex floats off to one side.
Second glance: The sphere appears to be bigger on the inside, something is moving inside it.
Joins to areas: B, F, H, and V

The sphere is a gateway to an elemental water world. Buckets and barrels surround the edge of the room—it seems the wizards drew water directly from the sphere for use in magical rituals (or perhaps just to run their baths).

The creature the adventurers can see in the sphere is merely a large fish that is curious about the light the sphere emanates on the other side. Living creatures cannot pass through the sphere, but anything they drop into the sphere falls into the depths of a lightless ocean on a far-off alien world and is (probably) lost forever.

The water from the strange ocean is fresh, not salty, but it has a strange metallic aftertaste.

Exits: One stairway leads downward *[to F]*, another leads upward *[to H]*. A swirling magical portal leads to other towers *[leads to B and V]*.

H: The Map Room

First impressions: A circular table in the center of the room contains a relief map.
Second glance: The map is a life-like, to-scale model of Redfield Valley, complete with fallen portions of Vantage.
Joins to areas: G, and I

The map is life-like, down to miniscule figures that move across the landscape and flames that burn here and there. Whenever a new piece of Vantage falls from the sky, the adventurers can probably see it, but there also holes and messy areas where the map, or perhaps the world, appears damaged. If the adventurers pick up or poke at a piece of the map, they can see it is made from magical clay and reforms itself afterward. Things that happen to the map have no effect on Redfield Valley: for example, punching it doesn't cause a huge fist to descend from the sky.

There's no way to remove the table from the room, and if there were, the map wouldn't work any longer. Still, there are other things to loot! There are drawers under the map table that contain scroll maps of various parts of the empire—taking these maps gives the adventurers +5 to one skill check during their adventures in *Shards of the Broken Sky* when having an accurate map would be of help. (Of course, even if the map was truly accurate, it won't be all that accurate now that Vantage is wrecked. It's as accurate as *you* want it to be, GM, not as accurate as the PCs hope!)

Exits: One stairway leads downward *[to G]*, another leads upward *[to I]*.

Fighting here: If you need a good place for an encounter with a wandering monster group, this could work—the PCs are not the only ones who find the great map worth studying.

I: THE ROOM OF RAVENS

> **First impressions:** A large orb in the center of the room shows the sky. There are ravens perched about the room.
> **Second glance:** *Glitterfall* is coming through the orb—it's a portal to the sky.
> **Joins to areas:** H, and J

The orb in this room is indeed a portal to the sky. Characters who linger here must make a DC 25 check to avoid getting hit by chunks of the *glitterfall*: **+15 vs. PD**—4d6 damage.

It is possible to pass through the portal, though doing so dumps the adventurers out mid-air over Crownhill; they suffer 4d8 falling damage and must make their way back to the rest of the party (if they end up taking only a little damage, they were lucky enough to fall on a haystack that is only partially on fire or land in a pool of water feet-first!).

Characters who choose to go through the portal (it is almost impossible to go through accidentally, as there is a slightly yielding magical barrier they must "push" through) can make a DC 25 skill check to perform mid-air acrobatics or a feat of strength to grab hold of the magical field and get back to the room of ravens before they fall.

Exits: One stairway leads downward *[to H]*, another leads upward *[to J]*.

J: THE ROOM OF STARRY DOORS

> **First impressions:** A central column in the room has a dozen doors in it.
> **Second glance:** Each door displays a constellation symbol and is cold to the touch.
> **Joins to area:** I

The room's exterior is lined with locked cabinets (DC 15 check to open) full of star charts and books about astrology and astromancy. Each door in the central column is also locked (DC 25 check to open) and they are cold to the touch.

If the characters open a door, the air rushes out of the room, through the door, and into the inky blackness of the astral void. Each character next to the door is attacked: **+15 vs. PD**; on a hit, they are sucked through the doorway and must begin making last gasp saves (they have hold of the doorframe but are being sucked through). Pulling a character back through the door requires a DC 25 skill check, lowered by 5 for each additional ally trying to rescue them.

If a character fails their last gasp save, they lose their grip and are sucked into the void; then, the door slams shut and locks. What exactly happens in the void is up to the GM, but the character is almost certainly dead, or at least missing for the rest of the campaign.

If exploring this room results in more than one last gasp save being rolled, it should probably count as a battle.

Exits: A stairway leads downward *[to I]*.

THE TOWER OF THE MIND

This tower consists of Areas K-O. The tower's exterior is painted white, though it has recent scorch marks and mud splatters from its crash-landing.

K: THE ROOM OF SECRETS

> **First impressions:** Locked doors built into a central column, thousands of keys mounted on the chamber walls.
> **Second glance:** The furniture indicates this was a courtroom.
> **Joins to areas:** L, and outside

Red mud and shattered glass cover the floor of what was once a testing chamber for apprentice wizards. If a character chooses a key from the wall and opens one of the doors, several cloaked figures enter the room through the door. The figures throw back their hoods to reveal that they are people from the character's past (possibly even the character themselves). The figures put on a little one-scene play about an important part of the character's life; then they bow and exit back through the door. The other side of the door is complete darkness, and only the cloaked figures can pass through the doors.

If characters question the cloaked figures about the scene they act out, they elaborate and explain anything their audience does not understand; they can also repeat lines or actions from their little play. The figures know nothing beyond their scene— they have no memories, opinions, or desires—they only wish to act out their scene and leave.

If the characters interfere with the figures in a way that prevents them from acting out their scene or leaving afterwards (which includes attacking them) they collapse in a heap on the floor. The figures have no blood or internal organs, they are solid flesh-toned "stuff" the whole way through.

Exits: A stairway leads upward *[to L]* and shattered windows allow outside access.

L: THE PRISMATIC BRAIN

First impressions: A glass brain floats in the middle of the room.
Second glance: Light that passes through the brain splits into colored rays, and the brain's main color changes every few seconds.
Joins to areas: K, and M

This was another testing chamber for apprentices, designed to teach them combat skills. Each fight with a prismatic brain is different than the last. Unfortunately for the adventurers, the brains are still active.

When the party enters the room, additional brains appear to match the number of party members. They assume different colors (by rolling their *prismatic foe* ability—see the stats below), then attack.

Testing combat observation skills: When a character attacks using a spell or an attack that deals the wrong type of energy damage to the brain, have them roll a DC 15 skill check to determine the energy type to which the brain is presently vulnerable. Obviously, they don't need to roll this skill check if they attacked with the correct energy type.

If the PCs are nearly all spellcasters who find this battle *intriguing*, feel free to make it a little tougher. As written, it's an easier-than-usual battle, partly because characters who don't cast an assortment of spells may not get to tap into what makes the fight interesting, and partly because the battle doesn't have lasting consequences. See *this is only a test* below!

#/Level of PCs	Prismatic Brain, Third Rank
3 x 3rd level	2
4 x 3rd level	3
5 x 3rd level	4
6 x 3rd level	5
7 x 3rd level	6
3 x 4th level	3
4 x 4th level	4
5 x 4th level	5
6 x 4th level	6
7 x 4th level	7

PRISMATIC BRAIN, THIRD RANK

This creature appears to be an oversized red (or orange, yellow, green, blue, or purple) crystalline brain, but its brain power seems entirely devoted to zapping you with magic rays.

3rd level troop [CONSTRUCT]
Initiative: +8
Vulnerability: random (see *prismatic foe*)

R: Prismatic Ray +7 vs. PD or MD (one nearby enemy)—10 damage of a random type (see *prismatic foe*).

Prismatic resistance: The brain has *resist damage 16+* of a random energy type (see *prismatic foe*).

Flight: The prismatic brain can levitate and hover about. It's your call whether the chamber is tall enough to let one or more prismatic brains escape melee attacks from the floor.

Lost opportunity: This creature can't make opportunity attacks.

Prismatic foe: A prismatic brain changes each time it enters battle. For each brain, roll a d6; or, choose a result from the table below:
1. *Red*—Vulnerability: cold; attack vs. PD; damage type/resistance: fire; PD/MD are 15/15.
2. *Orange*—Vulnerability: force; attack vs. MD; damage type/resistance: psychic; PD/MD are 11/19.
3. *Yellow*—Vulnerability: thunder; attack vs. PD; damage type/resistance: lightning; PD/MD are 15/15.
4. *Green*—Vulnerability: psychic; attack vs. PD; damage type/resistance: force; PD/MD are 11/19.
5. *Blue*—Vulnerability: fire; attack vs. PD; damage type/resistance: cold; PD/MD are 15/15.
6. *Purple*—Vulnerability: holy; attack vs. MD; damage/resistance: negative energy; PD/MD are 11/19.

Super-vulnerable: All the prismatic brain's defenses have a -3 penalty against attacks that deal damage of the type to which it is presently vulnerable.

Nastier Special

When the prismatic brain is first staggered by an attack, it changes its *prismatic foe* result (if possible) to one that makes it resistant to the damage type of the attack that staggered it, which grants a higher defense (PD or MD) against the triggering attack.

AC	19	
PD	15 or 11	HP 45
MD	15 or 19	

This is only a test: This battle isn't entirely real. It's some sort of arcane projection of magic that's far beyond the PCs' capabilities to even recognize. Creatures that "die" in this room "revert" to a previous version of themselves just before they entered this room. This means characters revive and regain any recoveries, powers, or spells they expended during the fight (consumable items and expended magic item powers are still gone). If any party members die, characters that *don't* die get an incremental advance for their trouble. Defeated brains vanish after the battle, but one reappears in the center of the room once the party leaves.

If the adventurers beat the brains, a voice announces that they passed the test and are worthy of the third rank of wizarding in the Order of the Pure Mind; if they fail the test, the voice announces they are not yet worthy of the third rank of wizarding in the Order of the Pure Mind (if you're feeling charitable toward the PCs, you could treat this "rank" as an icon relationship advantage with the Archmage, hovering as a resource in some future necessity.)

If the party decides to re-enter the room at any point, the brains have tailor-made *prismatic foe* results to give them an advantage against the party members. If party members die in subsequent fights, they are still revived, but the battle does not count toward reaching a full heal-up and they don't receive incremental advances.

It's true that experiencing an actual battle in this room, with true enemies, could turn out very differently than anyone expects. Perhaps the enemies are the ones being tested.

Exits: One stairway leads downward *[to K]*, another leads upward *[to M]*.

M: THE ROOM OF LENSES

First impressions: The room's exterior windows all have built-in lenses.
Second glance: The lenses can be repositioned, they are mounted in brass sockets.
Joins to areas: L, and N

The lenses in the windows view the present and the past. Skillful manipulation allows characters to view exterior scenes up to a mile away and up to one day in the past.

If the adventurers care about the mystery of who caused Vantage to fall, this room could provide a vital clue; otherwise, the adventurers view only peaceful fields and skies (which throws the devastation they see through the windows into sharp relief).

One stairway leads downward *[to L]*, another leads upward *[to N]*.

N: THE ROOM OF WRITING

First impressions: The walls are papered with parchment and the whole room is covered in writing.
Second glance: A faint whispering sound.
Joins to areas: M, and O

Adventurers who read the parchments on the walls gain knowledge about the history of Vantage. Most of it is fairly dry stuff—records of long dead wizards carrying out important, but highly arcane, tasks.

Still, taking the time to read the walls grants the party one +5 bonus to a single skill check sometime during this adventure due to the knowledge they gained here.

Exits: One stairway leads downward *[to M]*, another leads upward *[to O]*.

O: THE PANOPTICON

First impressions: It looks like the room is empty, and it's made wholly of glass. A swirling magical portal hovers off to one side of the room.
Second glance: Anybody who steps into the room becomes transparent, and the ruins of Vantage likewise look transparent to them. There's a strong smell of blood.
Joins to areas: N, and Z

The room is indeed invisible, as is everything in it. The ruins of Vantage (including the tower beneath the adventurer's feet) are see-through, though seeing into individual rooms is impossible.

The corpses of four wizards who died in the fighting are in the room. Their heads are missing, though the adventurers would need to make a DC 15 check to locate the bodies and a DC 20 check to discover they're headless. Looting the bodies yields at least one true magic item, possibly more.

One or more glassteel golems also lurk in this room. They're invisible until they attack, though an icon relationship advantage might somehow clue in a PC that there's more going on here than headless invisible corpses. The golems attack once a party member notices them, fails a skill check to search the room, or starts to leave the room.

Tough fight: Technically, the golems don't have the invisible ability; however, the fact that the characters have difficulty seeing them is factored into their stats and the *glassteel advantage* ability, which also gives creatures who can see invisible things a big attack bonus against the golems. If none of the PCs can see invisible things and none of them have worthwhile attacks against PD or MD, these golems may be too tough for them. It's your call as the GM whether you'd prefer to use the suggested nicer special *flawed mirror*, skip the fight altogether, or encourage the PCs to flee.

#/Level of PCs	Glassteel Golems
3 x 3rd level	1
4 x 3rd level	1
5 x 3rd level	2
6 x 3rd level	2
7 x 3rd level	2
3 x 4th level	1
4 x 4th level	2
5 x 4th level	2
6 x 4th level	2
7 x 4th level	3

GLASSTEEL GOLEM

You won't see many glassteel golems outside what's left of Vantage. For that matter, you won't see many glassteel golems anywhere.

6th level troop [CONSTRUCT]
Initiative: +9

Glassteel fists +11 vs. AC (2 attacks)—9 damage

Golem immunity: Non-organic golems are immune to effects. They can't be dazed, weakened, confused, made vulnerable, or touched by ongoing damage. You can damage a golem, but that's about it.

Glassteel advantage: Glassteel golems are unaffected by invisibility, which means they can attack invisible creatures normally (as well as characters under effects like those from the *blur* spell) and being invisible does not grant the golem any additional defensive bonuses. Creatures that can see invisible enemies gain a +4 bonus to attack the glassteel golem.

Glassteel disadvantage: Critical hits against the glassteel golem do triple damage instead of double.

Nicer Special

Flawed mirror: The glassteel golem's surface has cracks from previous damage. The cracks become increasingly apparent, so the PCs can double the escalation die this fight.

AC 28	
PD 24	HP 50
MD 20	

Exits: A stairway leads downward *[to N]*. A swirling magical portal crackles with lightning *[leads to Z]*.

THE GOLDEN TOWER

This tower consists of Areas P-T. The tower's exterior is covered in brass vines beneath the orichalcum filigree.

P: THE ROOM OF WISDOM

> **First impressions:** A humanoid figure draped in a green robe sits on a throne, her hair long and white.
> **Second glance:** The woman is an automaton.
> **Joins to areas:** Q, and outside

When adventurers enter the wrecked room, the automaton whirs to life. She is a self-aware and life-like golem, with moving joints made of magically strengthened porcelain. Once she awakens, she wants to know what happened.

The automaton's name is **Muse**, and her task was to further the personal development of the wizards who ran Vantage. She wandered Vantage's halls giving encouragement to wizards in many endeavors, frequently directing them to the golden tower to train their bodies and minds. Many of her memories are missing.

Muse's throne has driveshafts that interface with cogs in the back of her neck, which is how she stored her memories and gained knowledge about happenings elsewhere on Vantage. During the fall, the system went haywire; now, her memories are scrambled. She knows the golden tower is for training, but believes the higher levels were off-limits to apprentices. She knows Vantage was attacked, but her memories of that are hazy, at best (if your players are trying to solve the mystery of who attacked Vantage, Muse can give them clues; otherwise, she either doesn't know at all or she knows and can tell the adventurers). If the PCs invite Muse to join the party, she refuses; she prefers to wait here until her throne is repaired.

If the PCs attack Muse, it's won't be much of a fight. She's not a warrior, so it's probably not even worth rolling for the battle. But, feel free to have Muse broadcast descriptions of her attackers to all functioning Vantage systems and poison the party's supposedly positive icon relationships with the Archmage!

Exits: A stairway leads upward *[to Q]* and shattered windows allow outside access.

I wrote that Muse definitely would not join the party; but, when I ran this adventure as the GM, I ignored what I'd written and went a different way.

During playtesting, the players in my group convinced Muse to join the party. I had Muse malfunction at critical points (fights, puzzles, etc.) so her being with the party would not be a huge advantage, but she did still give the PCs minor help here and there (usually a couple of +1s each session).

When one of the PCs died, the player took over playing Muse. Muse-as-PC was a Forgeborn Cleric-of-Vantage, and we re-flavored her "divine" powers as tools and weapons concealed in sliding hatches in her body (she shot her javelin of faith *from her hand like a sci-fi beam weapon), or as her calling upon the mystic powers of the still-functioning sections of Vantage.*

So, as a designer, I don't think you should let Muse tag along—but as a GM, I think Muse joining the party is a great idea.

Q: THE ROOM OF EXCELLENCE

First impressions: Strange apparatuses are bolted to the floor around the room, possibly torture devices?
Second glance: This is a gymnasium.
Joins to areas: P, and R

This is a magical gymnasium filled with treadmills that create moving terrain for people to run on, golem arms for arm-wrestling, weights that change mass depending on the strength of the person using them . . . that sort of thing.

Most of the equipment is still functional, though it is bolted in place. A pair of padded suits of armor used for sparing rest in one corner. At least one of the suits is light magical armor; the PCs can discover this with a DC 15 check and loot it.

Exits: One stairway leads downward *[to P]*, another leads upward *[to R]*.

R: THE ROOM OF HIGHER THOUGHT

First impressions: The room is empty, except for some cushions scattered here and there.
Second glance: There is a faint sound, like waves on a beach.
Joins to areas: Q, and S

This is a meditation chamber. Any arcane spellcaster who meditates here for five minutes regains the use of an expended daily or recharge spell, but they may only use the chamber once per day. Other characters may also, once per day, use the chamber to recover an expended magic item power.

Exits: One stairway leads downward *[to Q]*, another leads upward *[to S]*.

S: THE ROOM OF TRANSFORMATIONS

First impressions: The light warps and shifts in this room, as though viewed through rippling water. The walls are wood-paneled.
Second glance: Reality in this room is unstable. There are patterns on the wall panels.
Joins to areas: R, and T

Passing into this room causes the characters' bodies to warp and shift like the reflections in a funhouse mirror. Bright lights and loud sounds emanate from the characters' equipment.

Wizards used this room to practice casting spells while under duress. Any changes to the characters are reversed when they leave the room. Skill checks and attack rolls they make in this room are at a -4 penalty, and any magic they cast in this room fizzles when it hits a wall panel.

The PCs could conceivably use the wall panels as magic shields (see below), if they can make a DC 15 check to carefully pry a single panel loose without breaking it (the DC increases by +5 for each attempt; after the first failure, the party can no longer harvest more panels).

Funhouse shield (1/day): When hit by a ranged attack against your PD or MD, the attacker must reroll the attack with a −4 penalty. If the result is an *odd miss*, the attack has no effect on you and instead hits the attacker. After use, the *funhouse shield* attempts a normal save; if the save fails, the shield breaks and there is no longer a reason to carry around this awkward wood panel.

A false wood panel is hidden in one corner of the room (DC 15 check to spot the false panel), behind which is a safe (DC 20 check to open the safe). Inside the safe is a magic item.

Exits: One stairway leads downward *[to R]*, another leads upward *[to T]*.

T: THE ROOM OF REVELATIONS

First impressions: Telescopes on swivel mounts bolted to the window frames. A swirling magical portal hovers off to one side of the room.
Second glance: The telescopes are hot to the touch. There are human-shaped scorch marks on the floor.
Joins to areas: E, and S

This room was an observatory and lookout post. The acolytes in this room were some of the first killed in the attack—vaporized as soon as they spotted the enemy.

The last scene viewed through each telescope (the attack) is burnt into the now-opaque lenses, though the captured scenes are indistinct behind blurs of light.

Exits: A stairway leads downward *[to S]*, and a swirling magic portal leads to another tower *[leads to E]*.

THE TOWER OF POWER

This tower consists of Areas U-Y. Balls of lightning bob and crawl over the tower's surface.

U: THE HALL OF CONTRADICTIONS

First impressions: The elemental balance is off in here, things freeze and heat up simultaneously.
Second glance: This room is actively dangerous, but there is a clear way across it.
Joins to areas: V, and outside

Anybody who ventures into the room begins to simultaneously smolder and freeze; further, there is light where there should be shadows. The room is a magical generator with silver inlaid walls. With the tower now wrecked, the energy has nowhere to go—except through wandering player characters.

Arrays of crystal and silver wire now lie ruined in the foot-deep mud that coats the floor. The silver wires are worth 50 gp, and a couple of the crystals still hold magical energy. Characters who explore the room take 2d10 cold or fire damage (*even* damage total is cold; *odd* damage total is fire) for every skill check they make in the room, or if they search long enough to find the *power-stones*.

Magus' power-stones: These semi-precious gemstones hold reserves of magical energy. When mounted to a weapon or implement, the power-stone grants +1 to attack and damage rolls (champion: +2; epic: +3).

When mounted to armor, the power-stone grants +1 AC (champion: +2 AC; epic: +3 AC). When you roll a critical hit with a stone-mounted weapon, or when a critical hit is rolled against you while you wear stone-mounted armor, the stone cracks and is destroyed—it deals 5 force damage to you as it breaks (champion: 15 force damage; epic: 35 force damage).

Exits: A stairway leads upward *[to V]* and shattered windows allow outside access.

V: THE ROOM OF THE SILVER CIRCLE

First impressions: A silver circle inlaid on the floor. Benches arranged in tiers around the room's exterior. A swirling magical portal hovers off to one side of the room.
Second glance: The silver circle is of intricate design.
Joins to areas: B, G, U, and W

This room is a certamen chamber—an area set aside for wizards to engage in magical duels. Magic cast within the circle does not reach outside the circle, and vice-versa. The circle simply absorbs any magic cast *at* the circle itself. An actual fight with spellcasters in this room could prove interesting . . . .

The silver circle is magically charged; attempting to loot it causes a magical energy discharge—2d6 force damage to whomever is attempting to loot it. If the adventurers continue to attempt to remove the circle, they take 2d8 force damage, then 2d10, then 2d12, then 2d20, then 3d20, then 4d20, etc.

Exits: One stairway leads downward *[to U]*, another leads upward *[to W]*. A swirling magical portal leads to other towers *[leads to B and G]*.

W: THE ROOM OF COGS AND CRYSTALS

First impressions: The ceiling is made of cogs, they seem to be jammed and move back and forth with a shudder.
Second glance: Many cogs have tiny crystals mounted in them.
Joins to areas: V, and X

This area used to take the magical energy from the generator chamber (and any absorbed in the certamen chamber) and process it for safe use.

The mechanism jammed when the tower hit the ground; it now whines and clunks. The cause of the jam is not discernable from within this room.

Exits: One stairway leads downward *[to V]*, another leads upward *[to X]*.

X: THE PUZZLE ROOM

First impressions: The floor is made of blocks that can be repositioned.
Second glance: The blocks have tiny lines that join up and form pathways. Copper wires run upward from the edges of the puzzle-floor to the ceiling.
Joins to areas: W, and Y

The puzzle blocks connect to the cogs and crystals in the chamber below. It takes a DC 25 skill check to make repairs.

If the adventurers manage to make repairs, they may ignore any natural roll of 11 or 12 when rolling on the tension table for the rest of the time they explore the Lightning Spires. Touching the copper wiring on the walls deals 3d6 lightning damage.

Exits: One stairway leads downward *[to W]*, another leads upward *[to Y]*.

Y: THE ROOM OF LIGHTNING FISTS

First impressions: There's a large floating model of a pre-fall, intact Vantage in the middle of the room.
Second glance: Metal gauntlets on the floor near the model join to the model with copper wire.
Joins to area: X

This was the control room for the lightning weapon. Unless the PCs fixed the blocks in the puzzle room, touching the model or the gauntlets inflicts 3d6 lightning damage.

Donning the pair of gauntlets (once the room below is repaired) allows an adventurer to mystically view the ruins' exterior and direct the lightning that crackles around the spires to hit anything in the immediate vicinity of the spires' exterior: **Dex + level vs. PD**—4d8 lightning damage.

There isn't really anything important the PCs need to hit near the towers, but if there is an NPC antagonist group wandering around outside, they are in for a nasty surprise. Operating the broken weapon is draining—every attack the character makes using the gauntlets deals 2d6 psychic damage to them.

It is possible to shut down the lightning that arcs from the towers and threatens Redfield Valley in this room.

Exits: A stairway leads downward *[to X]*.

THE MISSING TOWER

This tower consists of Area Z. The tower is missing—it sank deep into the mud in another part of Redfield Valley.

Z: THE ROOM OF LIGHTNING

First impressions: A circular room wracked with rainbow lightning, doors that appear and disappear around the exterior. A swirling magical portal hovers off to one side of the room.
Second glance: A voice speaks through the lightning.
Joins to areas: C, D, and O

The room is partially collapsed, and the dark red Redfield Valley clay is visible through the windows.

The voice in the lightning seems to speak gibberish; it takes a DC 15 check to understand that it is an evacuation warning. Lightning crackles everywhere (treat as a result of 2 on the *Lightning Spires Magical Defenses* table on page 83).

Exits: There are three glowing portals that lead to other towers *[leads to C, D, and O]*. There are no mundane exits here—the stairs that lead from this room are choked with mud and impassable.

THE GREAT BEASTS

Level range: 3rd and above

It's not entirely clear how these scaled behemoths became hidden under the wards. One possibility is that a few were still around when the first wards went up in Redfield, and they were frozen in a land that time forgot—a lost world. However it happened, the magical barriers that once trapped them in their time-slowed kingdom, cut off from the world, are now gone.

As you'll see, the combat stats for these great beasts are quite fearsome, but they have an Achilles heel that explains why they didn't flourish to rival the dragons and serpent archons as the dominant reptilians of primordial aeons: the great beasts are vulnerable to magic. This *vulnerability: magic* flaw includes spells, magical abilities such as dragons' and dragonics' breath weapon attacks, and even attacks by magical weapons.

Other dinos: In the time *Shards of the Broken Sky* spent gestating, other *13th Age* supplements introduced ancient thunder beasts! For several detailed options on how to handle dinosaur-like creatures in your campaign, see **13B2: 268**. The creatures in that book don't share the same problems with magic as these great beasts. . . .

GREAT BEASTS PLOTS

The great beasts could launch several events in Redfield Valley. Instead of providing detailed plotlines and building battles tables, we suggest a few options, provide the monster stats, and let you stampede the great beasts through your campaign as you like.

SOUND OF THUNDER

The adventurers are minding their own business when suddenly hundreds of monsters stampede toward them, trampling everything in their path.

JURASSIC RESCUE

The great beasts surround somebody or something important that needs rescuing. The adventurers are the only ones on the scene who can mount said rescue.

THE CAVE-IN

The beasts fell through a hole into an area under Redfield Valley. Maybe it's a lost tomb, maybe it's a dwarven tunnel, or maybe it's an opening to another part of this adventure. Dinosaurs in the dungeon!

DINO ATTACK

You smell like food, or you're wearing red, or you've somehow annoyed the great beasts. They attack!

THE HERALDS

The great beasts presage the coming of the serpent archons (see *Tomb of the Serpent Archons* on page 162). Some of the beasts carry brands that give clues to the serpent archons' eventual return.

ORC CAVALRY

Orcs who work for the Orc Lord get distracted from their investigation in the Orcwell; they decide the great beasts would make fantastic steeds and are attempting to tame them. Lots of orcs die during this process, but the orcs don't care. If they can gain the great beasts as (semi-) tame mounts, the orc hordes could do a great deal more damage on future rampages.

You'll find stats for a rhinosaur howdah in the *Orcs of the Orc Lord* adversary group on page 215.

THE GREAT BEASTS

The great beasts themselves could be dinosaurs or other strange beings. You can flavor them as old-school reptilian dinosaurs, feathered dinosaurs, furry Neolithic giant beasts, or proto-dragons.

FEATHERBACK

These bipedal reptiles hunt in packs, though one on its own is enough to put a clubtail to flight.

Double-strength 4th level troop [BEAST]
Initiative: +9
Vulnerability: magic

Bite +9 vs. AC—28 damage
 Miss: Other featherbacks gain +1 to hit this target until the end of their next turn.

Pack tactics: Featherbacks gain a cumulative +1 to hit for every featherback engaged with the target (to a maximum of +4).

Clever girl: Featherbacks are smart. They can lay ambushes, create distractions, and even open doors.

Leaps: Featherbacks can't fly, but they can perform surprisingly agile jumps for something so large.

AC 21	
PD 19	**HP 110**
MD 14	

CLUBTAIL

This well-armored herbivore likes to meet threats tail-first.

Huge 5th level troop [BEAST]
Initiative: +7
Vulnerability: magic

Headbutt +8 vs. AC—44 damage
  Miss: 22 damage.

C: Swinging tail +8 vs. AC (1 nearby enemy)—36 damage
  Natural even hit or miss: Repeat the attack against a different target.

Nastier Special
Plateback: The clubtail takes no miss damage from attacks against AC or PD.

AC 21	
PD 20	**HP 264**
MD 13	

FANGMAW TYRANT

If this creature could cope with magic it would have rivaled the dragons.

Huge 7th level wrecker [BEAST]
Initiative: +12
Vulnerability: magic

Huge bite +12 vs. AC—80 damage
  Natural odd hit or miss: 20 ongoing damage
  Natural even hit against a smaller-than-large creature when the fangmaw tyrant does not have a creature swallowed: The target is swallowed whole and cannot move, use move actions, or interact with anything except the fangmaw tyrant. While swallowed, the target is dazed and hampered, and takes 8d10 damage at the start of its turn. While the fangmaw tyrant lives, the target can only escape by inflicting at least 35 damage in a single attack—this forces the fangmaw tyrant to free the target by disgorging it.

AC 22	
PD 21	**HP 360**
MD 16	

THUNDER STOMPER

This long-necked beast is nearly unstoppable.

Huge 10th level spoiler [BEAST]
Initiative: +13
Vulnerability: magic

Squish +15 vs. AC (1d3 attacks)—40 damage

C: Whipcrack tail +15 vs. PD (2d3 nearby enemies)—40 thunder damage, and a target with less than 80 hp is stunned until the end of its next turn.

Nearly unstoppable: The thunder stomper ignores opportunity attacks and interception attempts from normal-sized or smaller creatures, and such creatures can disengage from the thunder stomper with an easy save (6+).

AC 25	
PD 26	**HP 700**
MD 18	

REDFIELD RISING

Level range: 3rd and 4th

THE SECRET OF REDFIELD VALLEY

Everyone knows Redfield Valley got its name from its rich red clay. Crops grow much faster here than elsewhere, some shoot up overnight as healthy stands of abundant food.

What almost everyone forgets is that long ago there was a mighty battle in the valley. The then-emperor died in that battle, and the Archmage sealed the area in time behind a ward that lasted for untold centuries.

The ward around the battlefield is starting to fail, creating curtains of shimmering air between the farmers' fields, splicing strange new terrain in the middle of what was calm farmland, and cutting off travel routes for adventurers trying to get from one part of the valley to another. Strange smells and noises come from behind the translucent curtains. Birds fly into the shimmering air and don't fly back out for several minutes, and the *glitterfall* vanishes unexpectedly only to blow out from behind the curtains at an odd angle.

The barriers do yield—it is possible to push through them to the other side. Even a glance through the barriers makes it possible to see the "real world" that was carefully hidden for so long—the area known as Redfield Valley is part of a careful illusion.

Time moves differently on the other side of the failing wards—all around, a battle is frozen in mid-carnage. Behind the curtains, war machines stand in the muddy trenches of a different age. Corpses, frozen in time, have bled into the mud for centuries—enriching the soil with blood and power that would otherwise be used for destruction.

When adventurers push through the barrier, the scene in front of them twists and distorts: the reality the ward hid for so long is overlaid with what the world was fooled into seeing. The vast *red fields* are a battlefield that stretches as far as they can see. The farmers' fields were but patchwork-green oases, separated by ruins and trenches. The soil is sodden, red with the blood of the fallen, and sucks at the boots of those who step through. The wards kept the battlefield bottled up in time and space, so the stench of fresh death is still evident. Arrows and spells hang suspended in the air, the ward still holding back the flow of time in some places. There are corpses everywhere; everything smells of blood.

Forgeborn and humans were (or rather still are—things get confusing with time-frozen battlefields) on one side of the battle. They're all wearing archaic armor with early Dragon Empire colors and sigils, and they're armed with weapons the characters don't recognize—relics from a lost time (the weapons are beam-wands, and as the crystals needed to power them were drained long ago, any surviving examples are now museum pieces). Looting the combatants' weapons is not possible; the figures are frozen in time, and their weapons are as immobile as they are.

Players who notice that it's weird for entirely immobile battlefields to smell of blood should be commended for their analytical skills, but this isn't a logical form of time-stop magic. It breaks all its own rules all the time. We're playing for dramatic effect, after all, not *Timewatch*-worthy effects!

Creatures the adventurers do not recognize fight on the other side of the battle. These huge creatures have stone-like skin, a hunched posture, and spiral carvings all over their bodies. Most have horns, tusks, or armored plates. Some look like humanoid rhinos or elephants, others resemble living rock complete with moss, and still others have cracks in their grey flesh where fire shows through. These enemies wield crude weapons—massive stone-headed axes and gargantuan bone clubs—and have wooden armor lashed to their bodies with makeshift rope.

Whatever or whomever these ancient enemies were, someone drove them from the empire long ago.

ADVENTURING IN REDFIELD

As the heroes push through the barriers and slog across the blood-wet mud, they encounter the detritus of a titanic, final battle—they may even find themselves face-to-face with a dying war-machine that's stumbling into a deep trench or being attacked by undead. Some war-machines may even come back to life!

The adventurers have encounters in Redfield equal to twice their level (so a 3rd level party faces six events). Roll a d20 on the *Redfield Random Events* table for each encounter on their journey (reroll any repeat results); and choose something interesting from one or two "twists" for the journey, as well.

REDFIELD RANDOM EVENTS TABLE

1. The Behemoths

2. A Patch of Green and Gold

3. The Trench

4. Death Gas

5. Falling Arrows

6. War-Spells

7. Blood Mire

8. The Fourfold Dragon Banner

9. The Bombardier Banner

10. War Spell

11. The Time Warp

12. The Wreckage

13. The Leaping Giant

14. The Spell-Knights

15. The Trench-Knights

16. The Beasts

17. Imperial Steed

18. The Canopic Golem

19. The Thresher

20. The Verdant Wave

1. The Behemoths: A monstrous combatant is frozen, its club hovering in mid-swing toward an equally large forgeborn. Motionless human soldiers cower in a nearby trench, dwarfed by the lumbering fighters.

As the adventurers get closer, they notice time is beginning to leak back into this area. One of the human soldiers blinks ever so slowly as a stray wave of time passes over him. A glittering ball of energy hangs nearby, a spell cast eons ago that is only just now reaching its target. Lingering in this area is probably a bad idea—if time unfreezes, the spell will hit and turn everything into a smoking crater.

Twist...

One of the soldiers unfreezes and joins the timestream once more. How does the soldier react to seeing the frozen battle around them? How do they react to the adventurers? How do they react to passing through one of the failing wards into the outer Redfield Valley? The world the soldier knew is gone, the emperor they fought for is dead, and the war is long over—how do they cope with that knowledge? This could be an interesting encounter with an NPC, or a prime opportunity to introduce a new player character.

2. A Patch of Green and Gold: With a "pop," the adventurers pass through a ward back to the mundane world of farmers and peace. A rectangular field sits among the desolation, the *glitterfall* still raining down overhead. All around, the falling wards that contain the battle shimmer.

Twist...

This would be a good point to introduce a stranded farm family, lost and scared. Or not. Your call.

3. The Trench: Frozen spell effects crisscross this area—deadly beams and shimmering fields battle against conjured spirits and living shadows. Fortunately, there are trenches dug into the mud, which allow the adventurers to duck out of the way of the motionless destruction.

Inside a small hut built into the side of the trench there is a kettle on an iron stove; a frozen fire burning below it. Paralyzed smoke comes from the stove's chimney, and the water in the kettle is still warm. A lone soldier sits in a chair next to the fire, clutching at a mortal wound. The wards kept this scene of carnage preserved.

Twist...

What happens when you burn something in a frozen fire? If the adventurers could lift the frozen fire and take it to a forge, could they make it into a sword forged of frozen fire?

4. Death Gas: The only sounds the adventurers hear in this area are those of crows feasting on some freshly revealed well-preserved dead that recently became unfrozen in time. Close by, a storm of crows rises from a trench full of bodies, then falls out of the sky as it flies into a strange, oil-slick-colored smoke cloud.

Twist...

The cloud of smoke unfreezes, as well; the birds' death broke the spell holding it in time.

The cloud begins to drift toward the party as though it is following them. The adventurers cannot outrun it, but a DC 25 skill check allows a character to hold their breath as it passes. Failing the check means the character takes 1 poison damage for each point by which they failed.

5. Falling Arrows: A cloud of spears and arrows hangs in mid-air, drifting slightly with the breeze as time begins to unfreeze.

Twist...

When passing by the arrows, there is a cumulative 2-in-20 chance for each adventurer present that their passage unravels the failing ward (a seven-member party triggers the effect on a 1-14). If an adventurer does unravel the ward, the arrows make an attack. **Falling Arrows +8 vs. AC (2 attacks against each party member)**—4 damage.

6. War-Spells: Spells are frozen here and there in mid-air, while the ward still stops time. Portals are half-open, fireballs shed yellow light across the red mud, and spirits are frozen mid-combat. The light near some of these frozen magical effects is bright enough you could read by it. The wizards who cast these spells long ago stand at the edge of a trench, their gestures half-completed.

Twist...

When passing by the spells, there is a cumulative 1-in-20 chance for each adventurer present that their passage unravels the failing ward (a seven-member party triggers the effect on a 1-7). If an adventurer does unravel the ward, the explosion of stale magic makes an attack. **Force-wrack +5 vs. PD (each party member)**—8 force damage. *Miss:* Half damage.

7. Blood Mire: Deep trenches cut across the landscape, and craters full of blood pock-mark the soil. Walking is a slow slog; running is almost impossible. Blood and soil cake the party as they stumble and crawl across the ruined battlefield. Corpses lie about everywhere.

Twist...

Each PC must make a normal save or lose at least one boot or other piece of equipment to the mire.

8. The Fourfold Dragon Banner: A great banner displaying four golden dragons intertwined on a field of blue, their tails encircling a burning eye at the center, is thrust into an outcrop of rocks. As the wind stirs the banner, golden lightning arcs forth from the tattered fabric. The balls of lightning roll over the ground, and grass grows wildly and flowers bloom wherever they touch the ground. The only sound is a faint sizzle-and-pop as the flowers burst to life.

Twist...

If you have an idea which icon the empire was fighting, the adventurers can gain a clue from this banner with a DC 30 skill check (though getting to a library lowers it to a DC 20 check). The ancient enemy's identity is up to you as the GM.

 Personally, I feel that the enemy and banner in this part of the adventure fit a previous incarnation of the High Druid, but you may prefer to use a (past or present) icon here instead—maybe the Orc Lord in his first life, or perhaps the fallen Wizard King?

Twist...

The ball lightning suddenly flares wildly and strikes one or more adventurers near the banner. Getting hit by the golden lightning *hurts* and deals 1d12 damage each round they remain near the banner.

The golden lightning's effects seem life-giving, at first; but the powered-up version that hits the adventurers "gives life" indiscriminately (non-magical wooden equipment splits, and sprouts leaves and roots; non-magical leather armor begins to bleed and tries to reknit itself around a hypothetical animal; maps lose their markings as cells attempt to regrow as plants, characters spout new, useless body parts, etc.).

Staying near the banner for too long is deadly—soon, new organs and body parts grow wildly out of control. Getting hit once causes nothing more than an odd skin condition where the lightning struck; successive hits cause increasingly severe mutations. Remaining near the banner eventually causes a person fall over dead—as a fleshy lump covered in eyes and lungs and filigrees of veins. Yuck!

9. The Bombardier Giant: A vast, grey-skinned bipedal creature, covered in carved spirals, looms over the landscape—frozen mid-lumber. The giant's wooden armor is held on by leather straps, and smaller figures stand on platforms attached to the armor by ropes. These small figures are mid-throw—their lit, clay-ball bombs motionless in the air. Wherever the bombs hit—the ground explodes!

As the adventurers approach the area, some of the bombs hanging in mid-air begin to move. Suddenly, the great beast unfreezes and continues its forward motion in battle. It roars, and spirits fly out of its mouth. The unleashed spirits use their teeth and claws to tear apart rocks and shatter wood. The spirits last only seconds before they fade; but, in those brief moments, they created much devastation.

The great giant slows, as though wading through treacle, then freezes once more mid-step.

Twist...

Adventurers who approach the Bombardier Giant are hit by the falling crude bombs (little more than clay jars filled with burning pitch). **Falling bombs +10 vs. PD (three nearby adventurers)**—5 ongoing fire damage.

Adventurers must endure three rounds of falling bombs as they pass the giant.

Twist...

The giant momentarily continues to move and spit out destructive spirits. The adventurers must find cover (DC 15 check) or take damage equal to twice the amount by which they fail the roll.

10. War Spell: The adventurers hear a high-pitched, whistling sound. A deadly spell cast eons ago just unfroze.

Twist...

The spell misses the adventurers completely, blasting a crater in the nearby ground and harmlessly showering dirt into the air.

Twist...

The spell gets stuck mid-air in an area of frozen time and burns away its fury like a second sun.

Twist...

The spell hits very close to the adventurers. They all lose their hearing for d8 rounds and are struck by flying rocks and waves of elemental magic. **Elemental magic +7 vs. AC (each adventurer)**—5 damage. *Natural 16+*: 5 ongoing fire damage.

11. The Time-Warp: The failing wards release time and space back onto the battlefield. Roll 1d8 twice:

1. Sudden nightfall—the sun slips rapidly down in the sky.
2. Double sunrise, two days happen at once. If that's too crazy for you, make this doubled-up-day a very temporary situation.
3. Localized winter—the adventurers must try to find shelter (DC 20 check) or take 1d12 damage for every 1d6 hours of exposure.
4. "Youthening"—the oldest party member suddenly becomes the youngest. This is painful, but not otherwise harmful.
5. The sky flickers and strobes as days pass by too quickly.
6. The adventurers see their past selves up ahead for an instant. Eerie.
7. The adventurers have the sense they are being watched, but when they turn around nobody is there.
8. The adventurers stumble upon a mirage that shows their possible future selves dying. This might give them a clue about another danger here that they have not yet faced.

Twist...

This event could presage further sections of the battlefield unfreezing or the monstrous enemy moving another couple of stumbling steps forward. Roll a d20 again and apply the danger from that result.

12. The Wreckage: A pair of brightly painted steel-and-wood vehicles form a makeshift, crumpled bridge over a trench—one of a series of trenches that run across the battlefield. The vehicles look as though they were pulled by beasts, which are now missing—caught in a different timestream.

Not far from the wreckage lies a skeleton, wrapped in cords and attached by a harness to a great quantity of silk. The corpse seems to move, but that may just be the wind blowing the silk and tugging on the cords that wrap around the dead warrior's limbs. The silk might have been a giant pair of wings, but it's too ripped and torn to make any clear identification.

A large egg blocks most of the entrance to a small hut built into the side of the trench.

Twist...

The large egg contains a spell effect it was meant to be catapulted over the enemy's front line, guided by a brave fool with a silk wing strapped to their back.

Moving the egg likely unleashes the spell effect within, though its potency decreased with the passing of the ages. It takes a DC 25 skill check to avoid activating it when interfering with it. Failure means it activates, producing a mist that causes everybody in the area to become confused, initiate combat, gain +4 to attacks, and take a -4 penalty to defenses (save ends). Those who save may attempt to defend themselves without attacking their confused friends (+4 to defenses).

13. The Leaping Giant: A spiral-carved giant silently hovers over the battlefield, frozen mid-leap. It hangs in the air, eerily motionless. Forgeborn cling to it, mid-struggle, heroically trying to wrestle the giant.

Twist...

The leaper's spirals begin to glow with green bale-fire. The adventurers must make a DC 15 skill check to run for safety or find cover. If they fail, the bale-fire attacks. **Bale-fire +7 vs. PD (each adventurer not at a safe distance or behind cover)**—5 ongoing fire and lightning damage.

14. The Spell-Knights: The red soil is full of soldiers in blue coats, armed with archaic swords. Rank insignia is visible on their uniforms, which have faded to grey on the exposed sides and become a blackish-purple where the blood-rich mud encases their bodies.

Each soldier wears a leather mask with glass lenses. Some of them died clutching their throats; others have huge wounds, as evidenced by the gashes in their uniforms.

Crows peck at the corpses, most of which look like they were trampled. Large footprints nearby are full of rain that leaked into the time-stuck battlefield over the centuries.

Twist...

The adventurers notice some of the bodies are no longer frozen in time and have started to decay rapidly, the centuries finally catching up with them. Provided they don't mind robbing corpses, there is treasure of a kind to be had here: the non-magical swords are so well-made, they grant +2 to damage. The swords do start to decay once the adventurers remove them from the battlefield, and they become useless within 1d3 days.

15. The Trench-Knights: Knights in leather coats slump in a deep trench that runs across the battleground, their bodies caked with the red mud. The metal plates sewn onto their coats are either battered or missing completely.

A grey behemoth stands blocking the trench, frozen mid-battle with the last of the knights. A strange, oil-slick-colored mist clings to the bottoms of the deeper trenches—an unwholesome miasma that doesn't stir with the wind.

Twist...

The adventurers notice that some of the corpses are almost fully decayed; their remaining bits of hair flap in the wind. It seems these few corpses are unfrozen from time. A bit of corpse-robbing might provide useful treasure.

16. The Beasts: Vaguely humanoid orc-like figures are hip-deep in mud. They are surrounded by hundreds of dead soldiers wearing blue uniforms.

Twist...

These are horrific proto-orcs that fought against the empire. They might all be dead and frozen in time, or they might unfreeze and attack the adventurers! Use the *Orcwell* adversary group on page 215.

17. Imperial Steed: A beast unfamiliar to the adventurers is stuck deep in the mud. It's larger than a human, wears bone-white armored plates, has a gold and velvet saddle on its back, and is covered in gem-like protrusions that flicker with a strange glow. The beast shudders when the heroes get close, as waves of time melt off it. Its hindquarters are soaked in blood, and a fallen battle-standard lies nearby in the mud.

Twist...

The beast is indeed becoming slowly unfrozen in time—and as it does, the battle-standard and saddle become retrievable loot.

The standard is that of the long-dead emperor; this may be the very place where he died! Exactly what the saddle and standard are worth is up to you—they might be worthless (simply gold paint on a wooden saddle), or priceless.

Exactly how much trouble the saddle and standard cause for the party with those who recognize them is also up to you.

There are 1d3 magic items scattered around the area.

18. The Canopic Golem: This creature is a lumbering, armored construct with a living brain—which is partly visible through its heavy, armored plates. A legendary canopic golem, this creature is part mobile tomb, part life-support system, and all weapon of war. While the golem is physically frozen, its undying mind inside is fully aware of the long centuries it has been trapped—and it's totally insane.

Twist...

The golem's undying mind cries out to the party; the adventurers hear its insane thoughts as they pass by it.

Twist...

The golem's undying mind is angry and insane. Though it cannot move, it can attack the adventurers psychically as the party gets close.

Likewise, the party can't really harm the time-frozen engine of destruction unless they make attacks that target its MD.

Time-Frozen, Insane Canopic Golem

Eternal pain compressed into a tight window of opportunity.

Huge 4th level wrecker [CONSTRUCT]
Initiative: +8 (it likely ambushes the party)

C: Ego disintegrating idea +9 vs. MD (one nearby or far away enemy)—30 ongoing psychic damage, and the target feels crushing despair.

Shame field: Anybody who misses with an attack that targets MD feels shame and takes 12 psychic damage, or 24 psychic damage if their attack roll was a 1. Yes, it is possible to literally die of shame trying to fight this thing.

Temporary problem: Assuming the party attempts to move away from the time-frozen golem, roll 1d6 at the start of every round. If the result is equal to or less than the escalation die, the party escapes the golem's attack window. Feel free to use an icon relationship or a skill check to advise groups intent on slugging it out that there is a better way.

AC: N/A*
PD: N/A   HP: 140
MD: 20

* The golem is frozen in time and is, therefore, immune to physical attacks.

19. The Thresher: A hundred human and forgeborn soldiers are frozen mid-rush in their charge toward grey-skinned brutes. Spells from a cadre of wizards sizzle mid-air. The monstrous enemies of the Dragon Empire are hauling a time-frozen monolith, from which verdant energies crackle.

Adventurers who move across the battlefield must duck beneath motionless sword-blows, move carefully around mid-flight arrows, and maneuver beneath spells.

Twist...

The adventurers carry their own little pocket of "real" time with them. It may not affect everything on the battlefield, but all it takes is one temporarily unfrozen spell or no-longer motionless sword at the wrong moment, and things end up going very poorly for the party.

Three adventurers, chosen at random, are unlucky:

Unfrozen weapon +9 vs. AC—14 damage.

Magical meteor strike +10 vs. PD (two adventurers)—9 thunder damage.

Mental blast +9 vs. MD—7 ongoing psychic damage.

20. The Verdant Wave: Grey brutes that seem smaller and more humanoid than the others surround a stone monolith covered in moss and carved spirals; they are frozen in the act of worshiping it.

It's fairly obvious from the marks on the ground and the huge brutes with ropes nearby that the monolith was dragged onto the battlefield and erected as part of the enemies' battle plan against the Dragon Empire. A green light emanates from the top of the monolith, rolling sluggishly outward through the air.

Twist...

The adventurers' presence may be just enough to partially restore time, or at least kick the monolith into high gear. Trees and other plants sprout all around the adventurers, literally exploding out of the ground in showers of soil. Those standing above a plant as it grows get impaled. Each adventurer in the area is attacked.

Wild growth +9 vs. AC—7 damage, and the target is stuck (save ends). Each round an adventurer remains stuck, the area makes a *growing trees* attack. **Growing trees +9 vs. PD**—7 damage, and the target must save or lose a recovery

THE ORCWELL

Level range: Mostly 3rd and 4th, with occasional bursts of higher-level problems

It may well be that the Archmage originally moved Vantage to Redfield Valley to defend against the Orcwell, back when Vantage was merely a flying fortress freshly captured from the defeated Wizard King. The Orcwell is really nothing more than a huge pit in the ground, from which climb orcs. There's nothing fancy about it—deep hole, dark magic, orcs come out.

What exists at the bottom of the hole is up to your imagination as the GM. *A meteor with strange magical energies? A dark god's severed head? Tunnels that lead to the orc dimension? The Orc god's temple? Pulsating orc eggs? Cocoons where the orcs drag unfortunate victims for transformation? Maybe there's nothing at all—just a lot of mud with orcs crawling out of it. . . Really, it's your call.*

Five great obelisks, the focus of the ward that kept the Orcwell shut down and hidden from view, stand several hundred yards from the pit's edge. The adventurers must repair the obelisks to shut down the pit again, and quickly, before the area is overrun with orcs.

Orcs of all shapes and sizes have overrun the area around the Orcwell. We include an *Orcwell* adversary group in the *Adversary Groups* section starting on page XX, and we suggest you apply it here. There are lots of orcs! These orcs are (probably) wild and (probably) not under the Orc Lord's control, but they know enough to attack the adventurers on sight.

THE ORCWELL AND THE ICONS

Which icons might have a special interest in the Orcwell?

THE ORCWELL AND THE ORC LORD

Of course, the Orc Lord is interested in the Orcwell—if he can control it and fully remove the wards surrounding it, he could raise entire armies with amazing speed by simply calling them forth from the Orcwell. The Orc Lord may even manage to create-to-order new orc variants if he controls the Orcwell. Is the world ready for an orc centaur cavalry, flying orcs, or giant orcs? The Orc Lord might even be able to direct the Orcwell's energies to transform certain human populations into something orc-like.

If the Orc Lord gains possession of the Orcwell, the age could end—badly.

THE ORCWELL AND THE ELF QUEEN

The elves created the Orc Lord; and it's possible the Orcwell is his birthplace (or place of transformation). The Orc Lord defeated the Wizard King, at the cost of the world being burdened by the orc race.

The Elf Queen almost definitely knows the Orcwell is here and wants to control it—if for no other reason than to prevent the Orc Lord doing the same. If she is responsible for bringing Vantage down, it may be because she has a plan to destroy the Orcwell forever—and she needs the wards down so her agents can enact it.

THE ORCWELL AND THE DWARF KING

Suppose the Dwarf King discovered a lost dwarven treasure was corrupted to create the Orcwell—not only does this mean someone stole a priceless artifact from the proud warriors of the under-mountains; they used it to create the dwarves' most persistent enemies! The Dwarf King's boundless rage might have led him to destroy Vantage as the first step toward enacting vengeance against his ancient enemies.

THE ORCWELL AND THE THREE

The obelisks are the same colors as the five great dragons (now reduced in power and known as The Three). Why is this? Did The Five (as they might have been known then) create the ward around the Orcwell? If they did, do The Three wish to mend the ward, or did they crash Vantage to recover something from the Orcwell once the ward was down? Did they willingly raise the wards on the obelisks, or were they coerced into doing so?

THE OBELISKS

The five obelisks kept the ward around the Orcwell intact. If the adventurers want to keep the Orcwell hidden, the wards must be repaired; however, if the adventurers want to free the Orcwell so an icon can take possession of it, they need to crash the wards. We list the required DC for skill checks to mend each ward under *Obelisk Rituals*. If your group is the oddball group that wants to permanently destroy the wards that suppress the Orcwell, assume that destroying the wards takes an identical amount of effort. Whether they're working to mend or destroy the wards, a successful ritual at one obelisk provides a cumulative +2 bonus to ritual skill checks at other obelisks.

Denizens and rivals: The creatures associated with each of the obelisks are not wandering monsters—they're locals who benefit from the obelisk's magic spillover, though they may not be entirely aware of the obelisk's role in their ecosystem. Some of the locals are absolutely monsters, and they're likely to respond to adventurers exactly as they should. But, depending on your player characters' composition and icon relationships, one or two of the interactions at the obelisks could be non-violent encounters instead of battles. Given that rituals to mend the obelisks look a lot like rituals that could break the obelisks, this isn't certain!

If you decide the locals are not all hostile, you could replace a battle against the obelisk's defenders with a battle against an adversary group intent on destroying (or saving) the obelisk. Obviously, this could involve followers of the *Orc Lord* (page 214) and creatures from the *Orcwell* (page 215) itself, but you might have even more devious plans.

Orcwell antagonists: The areas around the obelisks may be somewhat less troubled by orcs from the Orcwell, but getting from one obelisk to the next probably takes the adventurers through areas where any wandering monsters are Orcwell creatures. . . who didn't have to wander far.

The White Obelisk

The area around the white obelisk is frozen, and the snow forms deep drifts that prevent fast movement. A frozen lake surrounds the obelisk, beneath which slumbers a huge white dragon. The ice is thick and magical; it's so tough that even the druidic white dragon that lives in the area can't get the huge elder dragon out—if, in fact, it wanted to.

The white dragon and some pet wolves hunt in this area, picking off orcs that come out of the Orcwell. Welcome to the ecosystem.

#/Level of PCs	White wolf	Dire wolf	Druidic White Dragon
3 x 3rd level	0	0	1
4 x 3rd level	1	0	1
5 x 3rd level	2	0	1
6 x 3rd level	2	1	1
7 x 3rd level	2	2	1
3 x 4th level	1	0	1
4 x 4th level	1	1	1
5 x 4th level	0	2	1
6 x 4th level	3	2	1
7 x 4th level	2	3	1

White Wolf

2nd level troop [BEAST]
Initiative: +6

Bite +6 vs. AC—6 damage

Pack attack: This creature gains a +2 bonus to attack and damage for each other ally engaged with the target (max +4 bonus).

AC 18
PD 16   HP 34
MD 12

Dire Wolf

Large 3rd level troop [BEAST]
Initiative: +6

Vicious bite +8 vs. AC—18 damage
Miss: 3 damage.
Miss while staggered: 6 damage.

Pack attack: This creature gains a +2 bonus to attack and damage for each other ally engaged with the target (max +4 bonus).

Chilling howl: Whenever a dire wolf's attack drops an enemy to 0 hp or below, all dire wolves in the battle can *howl* as a free action. When the wolves howl, each enemy in the battle takes a penalty equal to the number of living dire wolves in the battle (max −5) to all attacks and defenses until the end of the attacking wolf's next turn. New howls extend the duration of the current howl rather than downgrading the howl's effect if dire wolves are slain in the meantime.

AC 18
PD 17   HP 80
MD 13

DRUIDIC WHITE DRAGON

Maybe this started out as a path to power, but what was once opportunistic is now life.

Large 5th level troop [DRAGON]
Initiative: +11

Claws and bite +9 vs. AC (2 attacks)—16 damage
First natural 16+ each turn: The white dragon can make an *ice breath* attack as a free action.
First natural 1–5 each turn: The white dragon can cast an additional spell this battle, provided it has not already cast all its spells.

[Special trigger] **C: Ice breath +9 vs. PD (1d3 nearby enemies in a group)**—12 cold damage
Natural 18+: The target is stuck (easy save ends, 6+). If the target is already stuck, it is instead hampered (easy save ends, 6+).

Dragon magic: The druidic white dragon can cast one 5th level spell, chosen from the list below, during each battle. As a special trigger of the dragon's *claws and bite* attack, it can cast additional 5th level spells during a battle. Specific spells can't be cast more than once per battle.

Resist cold 16+: When a cold attack targets this creature, the attacker must roll a natural 16+ on the attack roll or it only deals half damage.

AC	20	
PD	18	**HP 160**
MD	17	

DRUIDIC WHITE DRAGON SPELLS

DRAGON'S ICE SHIELD (5TH LEVEL)

Close-quarters spell
Daily
Quick action to cast
Target: You
Effect: Until the end of the battle, when an enemy engaged with you attacks you and rolls a natural 1–10, it takes 4d6 cold damage after the attack.
7th level spell (huge) 6d10 damage.

ICE SHARD (5TH LEVEL)

Ranged spell
Daily
Target: One nearby or far away creature
Attack: +9 vs. PD
Natural Even Hit: 40 cold damage, and the target is hampered (easy save ends, 6+).
Natural Odd Hit: 40 cold damage, and the target is stuck (easy save ends, 6+).
Miss: Half damage, and the target is stuck until the end of its next turn.
7th level spell (huge) +12 vs. PD, 80 damage.

WHITE FOG (5TH AND 7TH LEVEL)

Ranged spell
Daily
Targets: Each creature in the battle, including you
Effect: Until the start of your next turn, when the target attempts to attack, ready an action, or delay, it must roll a hard save (16+). If the save fails, the target expends that action to no effect.

Obelisk rituals: A magical ritual and a DC 15 skill check from the ritualist are required to mend the obelisk. A mirror shard from Area C in the *Shattered Spine* (page 61) lowers the difficulty by 5, which is obvious to the ritualist if they previously visited that area.

THE GREEN OBELISK

The green obelisk is in the middle of a deep and tangled forest, and it's covered in vines. The forest is full of animals and the plants bloom and die unnaturally fast here—a side-effect of the obelisk's magic. Lizardmen live in the forest. Their village is a fair distance from the obelisk, but they most certainly have patrols around the holy stone.

#/Level of PCs	Lizardman Savage	Lizardman Hunter	Lizardman Champion
3 x 3rd level	2	0	1
4 x 3rd level	2	1	1
5 x 3rd level	1	2	1
6 x 3rd level	3	2	2
7 x 3rd level	3	3	2
3 x 4th level	2	1	1
4 x 4th level	2	2	1
5 x 4th level	2	2	2
6 x 4th level	2	3	2
7 x 4th level	3	4	2

LIZARDMAN SAVAGE

Stone through bone.

2nd *level wrecker* [HUMANOID]
Initiative: +6

Stone-tip spear +7 vs. AC—7 damage
  Natural 16+: The lizardman can make a *bite* attack against the target or another creature engaged with it as a free action.

[*Special trigger*] **Bite +7 vs. AC**—5 damage, and the lizardman savage can make a *ripping frenzy* attack against the target as a standard action if it's engaged with that target.

[*Special trigger*] **Ripping frenzy +9 vs. AC (3 attacks)**—5 damage.

R: Thrown spear +6 vs. AC—5 damage.

AC 17
PD 16   **HP 32**
MD 12

LIZARDMAN HUNTER

In her ecosystem, you're prey until proven otherwise.

4th *level spoiler* [HUMANOID]
Initiative: +9

Javelin +10 vs. AC—10 damage, or 16 damage against a stuck or hampered enemy.

R: Barbed net +10 vs. PD (one nearby enemy)—Target is stuck (save ends), or hampered (save ends) if already stuck. Each failed save deals 5 damage to the target.
  Limited use: 2/battle.

R: Thrown javelin +10 vs. AC—8 damage.

AC 19
PD 18   **HP 56**
MD 14

LIZARDMAN CHAMPION

These lizard people couldn't possibly remember the serpent archons, but they know that great scales are shifting beneath the earth.

5th *level wrecker* [HUMANOID]
Initiative: +10

Barbed spear +10 vs. AC—14 damage
  Natural 16+: The lizardman can make a *bite* attack against the target or another creature engaged with it as a free action.

[*Special trigger*] **Bite +10 vs. AC**—10 damage, and the lizardman savage can make a *ripping frenzy* attack against the target as a standard action if it's engaged with that target.

[*Special trigger*] **Ripping frenzy +12 vs. AC (3 attacks)**—10 damage.

R: Thrown spear +9 vs. AC—10 damage.

AC 20
PD 19   **HP 70**
MD 16

Obelisk rituals: A magical ritual and a DC 20 skill check are required from the ritualist to mend the obelisk. A shard of green glass from Area V in the *Winding Gyre* (page 136) lowers the difficulty by 5, which is obvious to the ritualist if they previously visited that area. Given the level guidelines it's not likely to play out this way, but we mention it in case you upgun the obelisks for use later in your campaign.

THE BLUE OBELISK

The blue obelisk stands on a rock outcropping in the center of a still lake. Ogres live on the island with their goblin slaves.

#/Level of PCs	Goblin Grunt	Goblin Shaman	Ogre	Ogre Berserker
3 x 3rd level	5	1	0	0
4 x 3rd level	3	1	1	0
5 x 3rd level	4	1	1	1
6 x 3rd level	4	1	2	1
7 x 3rd level	4	2	2	1
3 x 4th level	0	1	1	1
4 x 4th level	0	1	2	1
5 x 4th level	0	2	2	1
6 x 4th level	0	2	2	2
7 x 4th level	0	2	3	2

GOBLIN GRUNT

1st level troop [HUMANOID]
Initiative: +3

Club +6 vs. AC—6 damage, if the goblins and their allies outnumber their enemies; 4 damage if they don't.

R: Shortbow +6 vs. AC—4 damage.

Shifty bugger: Goblins gain a +5 bonus to disengage checks.

```
AC 16
PD 13        HP 22
MD 12
```

GOBLIN SHAMAN

2nd level caster [HUMANOID]
Initiative: +6

Pointy spear +6 vs. AC—5 damage.

R: Shaking curse, +6 vs. PD—8 damage, and until the end of the shaman's next turn, the target takes 2 damage whenever an enemy engages it or disengages from it.
Natural even roll: Choose another nearby enemy; it also takes the *shaking curse* engage/disengage damage until the end of the shaman's next turn.

Shifty bugger: Goblins gain a +5 bonus to disengage checks.

```
AC 17
PD 12        HP 34
MD 16
```

OGRE

Large 3rd level troop [HUMANOID]
Initiative: +5

Big honkin' club +7 vs. AC—18 damage
Miss: Half damage.

Big shove +7 vs. PD (each enemy engaged with the ogre)—1d6 damage and the target pops free
Quick use: 1/round when the escalation die is even.

Nastier Specials
Tough skin: Whenever the ogre takes weapon damage, reduce the damage by 1d8 points.

```
AC 19
PD 17        HP 55
MD 12
```

OGRE BERSERKER

This is not a fight you can escape without blood on your hands. And your face. And your knees, backside, and elbows.

Large 4th level wrecker [GIANT]
Initiative: +9

Giant axe or sword +8 vs. AC—28 damage
Natural 5, 10, 15, or 20: The ogre berserker gains the *escalator* ability (it adds the escalation die to its attack total) until the end of the battle.
Miss: Half damage, and the ogre berserker takes 1d6 damage.

You shouldn't have done that: When an enemy engaged with the berserker scores a critical hit against it, that enemy takes 7d6 damage.

Incidental damage: When an enemy makes an opportunity attack against the berserker, hit or miss, that enemy takes 2d6 damage.

Rauguguggh: Once per battle as a free action, when the ogre berserker fails a save, it can take 3d6 damage to succeed at the save, instead.

```
AC  18
PD  18       HP 120
MD  15
```

Obelisk rituals: A magical ritual and a DC 25 skill check from the ritualist are required to mend the obelisk. Water from Area E in the *Winding Gyre* (page 132) lowers the difficulty by 5, which is obvious to the ritualist if they previously visited that area.

THE BLACK OBELISK

The black obelisk is deep within a swampy area; the black mud and fog makes it hard to see the mist dragons that lurk there. A female gnoll's head is in this area, near the body of a slain basilisk.

Depending on how the battle plays out, you may want lizard folk that worship (or at least highly respect) the mist dragons to accompany them.

If you use our Building Battles table below, this is a double-strength fight.

#/Level of PCs	Mist Dragon	Lizardfolk Teethripper
3 x 3rd level	1	2
4 x 3rd level	1	5
5 x 3rd level	2	3
6 x 3rd level	3	1
7 x 3rd level	3	4
3 x 4th level	2	0
4 x 4th level	2	4
5 x 4th level	3	2
6 x 4th level	3	0
7 x 4th level	4	4

MIST DRAGON

Is this a unique dragon, mutated by its prolonged exposure to the obelisks? It's unclear. Can you reason with it? No, clearly not.

Large 5th level spoiler [DRAGON]
Initiative: +12

Sharp vicious teeth +10 vs. AC— 30 damage
  Miss: 15 damage.

Mist breath: As a move action, the dragon can breathe out a heavy mist. All attacks against creatures with which the attacker is not already engaged take a −5 penalty.

Flight: Mist dragons can fly. They are not agile, but they hunt by performing high-speed dives toward aerial prey. Occasionally, they hunt travelers on high mountain roads.

Sticky pads: Mist dragons have gecko-like sticky pads on their feet, which allow them to cling to vertical surfaces like sky road pylons or cliff faces.

Evasive: +5 bonus to disengage checks.

AC 21	
PD 17	**HP 150**
MD 19	

LIZARDFOLK TEETHRIPPER

This lizardfolk has a mouthful of oversized teeth that look almost too big for its jaws.

7th level mook [HUMANOID]
Initiative: +9

Ripping teeth +12 vs. AC—15 damage
  Natural 16+: The teethripper can make another *ripping teeth* attack this turn as a free action (no limit).

R: Poisoned javelin +12 vs. AC—6 damage, and 8 poison damage
  Natural odd hit: The target is dazed, and takes 5 ongoing poison damage (save ends both).

AC	23	
PD	21	**HP 28 (mook)**
MD	15	

Mook: Kill one lizardfolk teethripper mook for every 28 damage you deal to the mob.

Obelisk rituals: A magical ritual and a DC 30 skill check from the ritualist are required to mend the obelisk. A bottle full of *mordent miasma* from Area M in the *Winding Gyre* (page 134) lowers the difficulty by 5, which is obvious to the ritualist if they previously visited that area.

THE RED OBELISK

The red obelisk stands in the middle of a lava field; its reddish-black stone is warm from the magma that flows beneath it.

Guarded by demons: Strangely, the red obelisk is the power source for a deviant little lava demon pod. Use a battle from the *Lava Demon* adversary group on page 211.

Obelisk rituals: A magical ritual and a DC 25 skill check from the ritualist are required to mend the obelisk. A piece of frozen fire from an area in the *Redfield Rising* battle zone (page 102) lowers the difficulty by 5, which is obvious to the ritualist if they previously visited that area.

INTERLUDE: THE SKY ROADS

There were *sky roads* that led from the ground up to Vantage; during the fall, at least one of them became visible, and others may begin to show up later. Some become visible as they collapse, others remain in the air. Some appear to be supported by hitherto invisible pylons, like great bridges. Others just float freely.

Here are some "big picture" questions the GM should answer:

- Did Vantage truly fly, or was it held up by these invisible roads?
- Where do the roads lead? Do they touch down somewhere? If so, where?
- Is there a whole network of roads in the sky? If so, are they only visible here or are they becoming visible all over the Dragon Empire?
- Are Vantage's attackers still on one or more of the roads? If so, who comes to aid them or attack them?
- Who built the sky roads, and why?

THE PYLONS

Climbing up one of the roads' support pylons requires at least a DC 15 check *[if the adventurers are still at adventurer-tier and if they can find ladders]*, but possibly up to a DC 30 check *[if the adventurers are champion-tier, there are no ladders, and high winds and glitterfall are issues]*.

Climbers might face attacks from aerial foes, such as Vantage's attackers, the defenders of Vantage, or aerial predators. Falling from a pylon is a last gasp roll—the adventurer tries to grab hold of something as they fall—but a check from an ally with the same DC requirements as the climbing roll (unless they are roped together, in which case it is 5 lower) allows them to rescue a falling ally. Of course, an ally who rolls a 1 on an attempted rescue also falls! Falling from such great heights is deadly.

THE PLATFORMS

There are rest areas on the way up the pylons; some are nothing more than ledges, while others are wide platforms with built-in huts that provide shelter from the freezing sky.

Unless you have more combative plans for the pylon platforms, this is a good place to introduce one of the Archmage's odd creations. Technically, they're called *volansims*, but most people call them flying monkeys. They're smart, understand language, perform mimes, and often enjoy serving powerful magic users. Unfortunately, they have a habit of abandoning tasks mid-way through, which could explain why the Archmage kept a few around near Vantage while preventing them from spreading across the Empire.

We include the stats here, but this doesn't have to be a battle—it could be a social interaction with flying monkeys who communicate with gestures and growls, requesting food and shiny things. If the PCs treat the flying monkeys badly, we recommend bringing them back as ongoing nuisances that turn up whenever the PCs *really* don't want to have a lever pulled or an item scooped up before they can reach it.

FLYING MONKEY

It's a cold, hard world that has a niche for owlbears and barely recognizes flying monkeys.

6th level mook [BEAST]
Initiative: +13

Scratch or bite +11 vs. AC—8 damage

Natural even hit or miss: The target or one of the target's allies suffers from some surprising or embarrassing minor problem, starting with monkey poo and moving up to awkward stumbles or hampering. It's comedy time.

R: Surprising dropped object +13 vs. AC (one nearby enemy)—15 damage

Limited use (group—see below): Only when flying above the target.

Group ability: For every four flying monkeys in the battle (round down), one can use *surprising dropped object* once during the battle.

Flight: Flying monkeys fly well, but they can't hover.

Scatter!: When one or more flying monkey mooks are dropped to 0 hp, each surviving flying monkey can attempt to disengage as a free action, adding a bonus equal to the number of flying monkey mooks that were just slain. Does it surprise you to know that they fly away as quickly as possible instead of staying to fight?

AC	21	
PD	20	**HP 25 (mook)**
MD	19	

Mook: Kill one flying monkey mook for every 25 damage you deal to the mob.

SURPRISING THINGS?

Here's a partial list of somewhat heavy things flying monkeys might drop on you:

- Corpse of an NPC who died when Vantage fell.
- A living NPC.
- The severed head of a marble golem.
- An item the PCs lost a while ago.
- An Archmage symbol pried from a fallen tower.
- A crystalline magic item (see page 189; and bump up the attack bonus and damage of the *surprising dropped object* attack!).

THE PERIPHERY

Adventurers who climb the pylons must face the sky roads' defenses as they attempt to get to the road itself. These defenses are designed to knock anybody who is not supposed to be on the roads off them.

SPINNING BLADES

The adventurers must climb through a series of blades; the wind turns the blades, which cut anybody passing through them to ribbons.

Each adventurer must make a DC 15 skill check to dodge the blades. **Slice 'n dice +5 vs. AC—1d10 damage.**

EVER-SLICK PAINT

The pylon's surface was prepared with a substance designed to make adventurers lose their grip. They must make a skill check with a DC 5 higher than a normal climb skill check (adventurer: 20; champion: 25; epic: 30) to compensate for the slick surface. Failure means the adventurer falls (see *The Pylons*).

BLAST WARDS

Champion-tier adventurers could unknowingly climb into an area with runes designed to kill climbers by blasting them clear of the pylons.

Each adventurer needs to make a DC 20 check dodge the blast. **Blast off +10 vs. AC—2d12 thunder damage,** and if any one die result is a 12, the adventurer falls (see *The Pylons*).

FORCE SPHERES

Higher-level champion-tier climbers might meet force spheres—bubbles of energy that scoop up climbers and crush them as the bubble descends toward the ground. Each adventurer must make a DC 30 check to dodge the spheres. **Bubble trouble +5 vs. AC—3d10 force damage,** and if any one die result is a 10, the bubble plucks the adventurer from the pylon and carries them swiftly back to the ground.

What's On The Road?

Exactly what the adventurers find on the road is up to you, the GM. The only certainty is that they don't find Vantage, because Vantage is on the ground below. . . and falling past you, still.

Up here, adventurers are at least out of the *glitterfall*, and they can see the whole of Redfield Valley laid out below them.

The adventurers could meet evacuees from Vantage, Vantage's enemies, or those who regularly use the hidden network of sky roads.

The nature of roads is that they are used for travel; this means any section of sky road the adventurers explore may contain different NPCs (and monsters) the next time they visit.

The sky roads might be empty stretches of glass-smooth road or green fields, or they could be lined with houses and little shops that cater to travelers. There might be military checkpoints, toll booths, and inns with "stables" for the Empire's dragon riders to use during long patrols.

If the adventurers (and players) are done with Redfield Valley for now, I recommend the sky roads as a great avenue to lead them toward adventure elsewhere (or flee the mess they've made).

If the players are not ready to move on yet, then the section of road they are on spirals back down to Redfield Valley in one direction, and it is broken in the other.

If the players are fed up with constantly worrying about the glitterfall, *but you still want to use the* glitterfall *and aren't ready for it to stop just yet, then both sides of the road are broken; this now-isolated section of road is a safe-haven for adventurers, high above (most) danger. If this is the case, allow the adventurers to come and go as they please once they have made their first ascent. If you use the safe-haven option but come to regret it (because the adventurers constantly retreat to the sky roads rather than adventuring in the valley below), just have the "safe" road section collapse while they are away.*

CHAPTER 7:

LOST & FOUND

ADVENTURES FOR 5ᵀᴴ AND 6ᵀᴴ LEVEL CHARACTERS

The Great Prism is an adventure that involves demons escaping from a crystal prism. Those who align themselves with good icons want to stop the demons, but there are also options for ambivalent heroes.

Old Tusk & Magaheim is more of an adventure setting than a dungeon. It is a volcano (Old Tusk) that houses a lost dwarven city (Magaheim), where dwarves and demons have long interbred. If the Diabolist or Dwarf King are important icons in your game, then this is a good area to explore.

The Winding Gyre is a huge spiral of floating wreckage—a flying-tumbling-falling dungeon. No matter which icons are front and center, this is a great area to explore and loot.

Rynth is a true dungeon; an Archmage captured it long ago and put it to use to provide a self-replenishing force of sentient oozes that were willing to die to protect the First Emperor's tomb. Those who oppose the Archmage may wish to kill the living dungeon; but perhaps the Archmage sent the adventurers to help his oozefolk fanatics against common enemies, or to help him finally bring the oozefolk into the wider world.

THE GREAT PRISM

Demons and other captured enemies of the Empire were imprisoned in a great crystal as refracted light. Vantage harbored that crystal.

When Vantage fell, the prism cracked; and chunks of it exploded outward and fell across the valley. The demons are now escaping from the crystal pieces, finding angles through which they can refract and escape. Rainbows shoot out of the crystals—but demons appear at the end of them, not gold.

We present several plot elements that play off the Great Prism. The first, *Over the Rainbow*, is a roleplaying-centered character study that doesn't have much to do with the imprisoned demons. The remaining three plot elements focus on the demons and the problems a broken prism might present.

OVER THE RAINBOW

During a somewhat restful moment, a chunk of crystal accompanies the *glitterfall* to complicate the adventurers' lives. A beam of light shoots out from the crystal and separates one or more of the adventurers into several different people, each embodying part of that adventurer's personality. The "reflections" remain together (none of them wander off), but they might begin to argue. Only one of the reflections is physically present at a time—the others circle like spirits or shift in and out of the body while they argue. In other words, the player still has only one character, but with very different split personalities!

This is a good opportunity to explore the characters' personalities: have the player write down the three most important or prominent personality aspects for their character on index cards. Then, everybody else (players and GM) writes down an aspect that is minor or entirely suppressed (spread these out between the cards). Until the issue is resolved, the affected player shuffles the index cards after each rest and plays whichever "reflection" they draw, while the other reflections hang in the background. The GM might play them, the other players probably kibitz with them, and the "active" personality should spar with them.

It's up to the GM and the player to decide what happens if a personality aspect "reflection" dies. Exactly how a character can re-integrate their reflections we leave to you, the GM. Below are some ideas:

- It wears off with time or requires some sort of reconciliation between personality aspects.
- The adventurers must find an intact crystal, so the character can recombine their various aspects.

- Once the personality aspects get recombined, the adventurer is profoundly changed somehow (emotionally, and perhaps physically) by the experience.
  - The personality aspects never get recombined; eventually the rest leave, creating a very focused personality. We think this would require player buy-in.

GETTING INDIE IN THE DUNGEON

This type of thing is too "artsy" for some groups, so keep in mind your group's sensibilities. Then again, if everybody is agreeable, you could run a session where everybody gets to play a reflection of the character as a separate adventurer.

This plot places a lot of focus on one player and their character—some players might not be comfortable with that. Further, if the character's reflected personalities become the focus of the game, it can present problems for the other players whose characters are sidelined. If spotlighting or sidelining become a problem, then just have the magic wear off and the split character merge back together.

Treasure: The crystal itself could be considered treasure of a sort, though it is treasure with a story value rather than a traditional value. When it is time to level up, characters could use the crystal to train with themselves (imagine sparring with somebody who knows all your moves), discover hidden talents, or otherwise gain insight and wisdom. It might even be possible to split and recombine characters: *"Remember my dying, elderly wizard friend? We had a chat—I now know some new spells and his knowledge need never die."*

RAINBOW DELIVERY: DEMONS

A rainbow touches down near the adventurers, depositing a bunch of confused and angry demons. The demons have a lot of pent up energy from spending centuries as beams of light and are keen to work some of it off on the adventurers. Unfortunately for the escapees, they are still suffering from the effects of their "Imprisment" and start the fight dazed (save ends).

Use a level-appropriate battle from the *Demons of the Prism* adversary group on page 200.

CRYSTAL-SMASHERS

A bunch of demons and other escapees have decided to hunt down and break any crystal shards that they can find, to prevent being recaptured. The characters first find out about them through the many problems they cause (NPCs slain, areas attacked prior to the adventurers' arrival, vital items and resources destroyed, etc.). The demons cross paths with the adventurers several times—in multiple dungeons and *glitterfall* refuges—until one side or the other decides to force a climactic battle.

Use a level-appropriate battle from the *Demons of the Prism* adversary group on page 200.

RECAPTURE

If the adventurers stand against the Diabolist they want to recapture the demons. Doing so involves finding portable crystal shards, pushing demons into the shards, and then fitting the shards back into the Great Prism. This involves a lot of fighting demons, hunting down shards (and demons), and solving a giant, crystalline puzzle. The demons themselves eventually get wind of what is happening and set traps and ambushes for the adventurers. As an ongoing plot, it becomes even more complicated when you splice it with adventures in Magaheim.

If this sounds perfect for your campaign, we recommend picking up *Book of Demons*. It's got demon stats to flavor all tiers and the demonologist class comes in handy on this hunt.

DOUBLE-CROSS

If the adventurers are in league with the Diabolist, they meet a group of demons that claim she is their queen. These demons direct the adventurers to attack a group of "disloyal" demons. Of course, if they do, the "disloyal" demons claim it is *they* who really serve the Diabolist, and the other group are "renegades." The two (or more) demon groups keep encouraging the adventurers to attack the other groups, which inevitably turn out to be ambushes, double-crosses, or mistaken identity.

Who really works for the Diabolist? Maybe none of them, or maybe all of them.

OLD TUSK & MAGAHEIM

Level range: 5th and 6th and beyond

There is more to the mountain known as Old Tusk than it seems. Old Tusk is a volcano, held dormant by the Archmage's power.

Now that the wards are tumbling down, Old Tusk erupts with sudden fury—darkening the sky with a plume of smoke and sending fireballs high into the air.

You decide what sort of threat you want the volcano to pose.

Trouble with lava demons: One of the simplest roles the reawakened volcano could play is that of an erupting volcano that's threatening to be a hellhole! There's nothing subtle about this approach: simply follow the lava with lava demons that threaten a new hellhole.

We don't do much to support this simple approach other than nod to it a couple times; but, as mentioned in the *Great Prism* adventure on page 116, books like *13 True Ways*, *Book of Demons*, and *The Crown Commands* are brimful of demons—and devils you could reskin as demons. You probably don't need much coaching to set up a hellhole that operates out of a volcano. Recruit the *Lava Demon* adversary group on page 211 as your main adversaries and give most of your attention to the sections below that are flagged with the words "lava demons."

If you opt for the lava demon approach, you may be happy with a simpler story that pivots around the Diabolist, Crusader, and perhaps the Great Gold Wyrm. You won't need the city of Magaheim for this campaign, save it for when you want something more involved.

Magaheim: Our more developed approach makes Old Tusk home to a dwarven city that was lost to demons; worse still, they negotiated their own peace.

The Old Tusk and Magaheim material that follows presumes you're interested in introducing a strange city of demonic dwarves and dwarven demons to your campaign. If neither the Diabolist nor the Dwarf King are central to your campaign, you may have more fun skipping this section to focus on other parts of this campaign.

OLD TUSK AND THE ICONS

Which icons might have a special interest in the volcano? The Dwarf King, the Diabolist, and the Crusader, of course. Of the three, the interests of the Dwarf King and the Diabolist fit well with our presentation of Magaheim as a detailed urban-roleplaying setting.

McHUGH

OLD TUSK AND THE DWARF KING

Old Tusk is a forgotten colony of dwarves, cut off from the outside world by the Archmage's wards. While the Dwarf King might be keen to re-establish contact (did he crash Vantage to lift the wards and free his subjects?) the dwarves from Old Tusk are. . . different. Volcanic. Demonic. The centuries they spent trapped beneath a volcano that hosts a portal to hell warped their bodies and minds.

OLD TUSK AND THE DIABOLIST

We mention elsewhere how the Diabolist may well have brought down Vantage to uncork chaos on the Dragon Empire.

But... suppose she didn't? While she has pacts with demons and devils of all sorts (it is unclear who serves whom, as with all really twisted dark pacts), she may not have pacts with *this* particular faction of demons. Even now, she might be rushing to *seal* the hellhole so a faction of demons that are not in league with her won't compete with "her" demons. Or maybe she's busy desperately negotiating pacts to bring Magaheim under her control and would be grateful to the adventurers if they could help her keep everything under control until she can do so.

How the Diabolist relates to the dwarves of Magaheim is up to you: are they potential recruits, fodder for her torture chambers, or both?

OLD TUSK AND THE CRUSADER

The Crusader wants to know how the Archmage kept Old Tusk sealed, and he's more than willing to launch a crusade to stop the flow of demons from the nascent hellhole.

. . . or maybe he's not. What if the Crusader bought Vantage down to unseal Old Tusk? What if the Crusader believes he already knows how the Archmage kept it sealed and unsealed the volcano/hellhole to test his theory?

. . . or what if opening a hellhole on his own schedule, conquering it at his leisure, and building a fortress out of Vantage's ruins is just a way for the Crusader to expand his army? A victory is a victory, after all, and conquests are easier when *everything* goes according to your plan.

OLD TUSK: GEOGRAPHY

THE APPROACH

The way to get to the volcano is over a landscape that was blackened in the recent eruption. Though the initial eruption has stopped, there are constant rumbles from Old Tusk. The lava flows have mostly cooled, but still pose a danger to unwary adventurers here and there. Lava continues to flow under the solidified crust, just waiting for an unwary foot belonging to an inattentive adventurer to break through.

Use the *Impromptu Damage by Environment* chart in the 13th *Age* core book (page 319) to determine the difficulties and damage of the hazards unwary travelers might face. Unless you want to make things more difficult for the PCs, the approach could lead straight to the caldera.

If you're using the lava demon hellhole storyline, this is a good place to introduce the *Lava Demon* adversary group (page 211), since higher up the mountain, there are just demons and more demons. If you're intent on introducing Magaheim, though, maybe don't bother.

THE LAVA TUBES

The warm lava tubes are an alternate entrance to the volcano. Here and there, lava flows behind the glass-thin rock walls and provides a bit of light.

The main problem with the tubes is that minor lava-based monsters have begun to leave the newly de-warded Old Tusk hoping to expand their territory. If the adventurers enter the volcano through the lava tubes, they avoid the caldera entirely. If you're using Magaheim in your campaign, the PCs introduction to Magaheim's residents comes from the encounter in the Mines (below), instead of from the city itself.

Whether you're using the lava demon hellhole plotline or not, feel free to dial up a battle from the *Lava Demon* adversary group (page 211).

THE MINES

If you're using the Magaheim plotlines and the PCs sneak through the lava tubes, they might encounter Magaheim's unfortunate miners deep within the volcano. Old Tusk is honeycombed with mine-shafts where slaves extract minerals from the rock that are vital to the dwarves of Magaheim.

The merest infringement of the law in Magaheim can land offenders in the mines. Most inhabitants can expect to find themselves in the mines at one point or another—for an unpaid debt, for not filling out paperwork correctly, or for tardiness in their daily tasks. Prison terms are not overly long; most offenders spend a few weeks at most in the mines (although attempting to escape results in far harsher punishments). Most Magaheimers simply accept being sent to the mines as part of life in their city.

For truly heinous crimes (such as murder, theft, insurrection, etc.) prisoners are tortured daily in addition to their mining duties.

It's not entirely certain this must be a battle: after all, the Magaheim dwarves and demons have been isolated for a long time, so they *might* not greet newcomers as enemies immediately.

Use Magaheim dwarf warriors (page 124) as the main enemy if there is a battle, which is probably more likely if one of the more demonic-looking creatures on that page accompanies these dwarves! It's your call.

THE CALDERA

The volcano's caldera is a huge crater with almost unnaturally steep sides. At its center is a city, suspended above the lava.

Because of the recent volcanic explosion, the city's rulers sent out scouts to assess the damage (they do not yet realize that the ward that keeps them trapped in/on Old Tusk was broken).

If you want to use a battle with the scouting party to introduce the PCs to Magaheim's creatures, a battle follows. If you'd rather find a less straightforward way to make introductions, consider a mostly peaceful encounter, or allow the PCs to get much closer to Magaheim before the fighting starts.

Use Magaheim dwarf warriors and a Magaheim tiefling (page 125) or two for the scouting party.

OLD TUSK: PLOT POINTS

You can use any of the following plot points that work in your campaign.

THE NIGHT HAS A SINGLE EYE

The demons of Old Tusk want to reopen the gateway to the hells. Unfortunately, an ancient prophecy depicts outsiders being the key to opening the gateway; they intend to kidnap and sacrifice the adventurers to fulfil the prophecy. A rival group of cultists believe that whoever opens the eye will be rewarded, so they rush to "save" the adventurers (so *they* can sacrifice the adventurers, instead).

Meanwhile, the Crusader sent agents to Old Tusk to kill the adventurers before anybody can sacrifice them.

THE DAMNED DON'T CRY

An escapee from the Diabolist's infamous *maze of seven dooms* fled to Old Tusk, somehow finding her way past the ward. The Diabolist's chief hunter approaches the adventurers—help find the escapee, and the Diabolist promises not to interfere with Old Tusk. The escapee is an elf named Eleanor Rose; she is currently masquerading as a tiefling with the help of her illusion magic (if you need stats for her, use the stats for Lients Recharche on page 10.)

VOLCANIC LEGION

The demons, lava dwarves, and elemental monsters of Old Tusk are on the march. They pour through the lava tunnels in a glowing wave, searching for new territory to conquer.

With the might of the rulers of Magaheim behind them, it looks like Redfield Valley may only be the first stop for this conquering army.

Someone saw figures who wore the Crusader's mark in the lava tunnels. Are these the Crusader's stalwart warriors trying to stop a demonic incursion? Are they deserters who joined up with a new side? Or are they agent provocateurs?

THE SIEGE

The Crusader used secret paths to march his army into Redfield Valley. They lay siege to Old Tusk, but an army in the tunnels prepares to break the siege.

The adventurers know the layout of the valley, so the Crusader asks them to lead a covert strike force on Old Tusk and Magaheim.

MAGAHEIM: CITY OF GOLD AND FIRE

The details about Magaheim that follow presume one of two things: either you're going to find ways to make this information relevant to the PCs, or you just like reading stuff about weird demon cities in volcanoes. We can hope for the second possibility, but to ensure the first, you might want to introduce the PCs as the first emissaries of the outside world to make it to the city.

Geography: The city of Magaheim is suspended above a roiling lake of lava with great chains. From a distance, the city looks like it is made of gold; however, that is just the lava reflecting off the many polished steel plates that deflect heat away from the city. Though it is in name and function a city, Magaheim is far smaller than Horizon or Axis. It's probably about the size of Shadow Port or Old Town.

You can gain entrance to the city via one of the many chains—beneath each mighty link is a wide, chain bridge with metal slats. A cart and horse can easily pass over one of the chain bridges without causing it to sway (the passage of mere mortals is not enough to offset the weight of a city).

THE UPPER CITY

The upper part of Magaheim is the furthest from the lava, making it the most exclusive place to reside. High towers quite unlike normal dwarven architecture stretch toward the circle of blue sky far above. The upper castes of Magaheim society inhabit this area; they believe they are normal, high-class dwarves with no demonic aspects. They're wrong, of course.

THE BURROWS

The bustling center of Magaheim is the Burrows—the district where the chains meet the ancient plug of volcanic pumice that forms the bulk of the city. Tunnels run through the porous rock and widen into streets and thoroughfares, where shops and houses are built into the rock itself. Tieflings and dwarves—and the occasional hybrid—inhabit this area.

You can catch glimpses of the sky from a few open places in the Burrows, but the towers in the Upper City crowd most areas.

UNDERTOWN

The volcanic gasses from the lava below sear the city's underside, and the lowest of the low inhabit the hanging buildings here.

Part lava demon dwarves and dwarf-tiefling hybrids are common in Undertown, because they can withstand the heat. Undertown is considered the worst district to live in out of the three main districts.

THE IRON WATCHERS

A gateway to hell—currently sealed—lies at the center of the city. This gateway is the reason demonic forces originally constructed Magaheim: so that they could reach the mid-air rift between worlds. A great, red swirling vortex hovers between nine, pitted iron obelisks; the locals call it "The Eye."

For the moment, the gateway is closed; but with the wards down, it may soon open and allow passage to the deep under-realms once more.

LIFE IN MAGAHEIM

BRIEF HISTORY

Magaheim was a dwarven mining outpost—until the volcano erupted, and demons started to appear in mid-air above the magma pool. The demons and dwarves fought over possession of the area. The demons constructed a huge rock platform under the portal ("The Eye"); then, the dwarves recaptured the area and built a fortress on the platform, calling it "Magma Home". The demons and dwarves continued to retake and recapture the area for about a century.

Eventually, a past Archmage sealed the whole thing under a ward and magically transported the volcano to Redfield Valley. Dwarves and demons alike were trapped in the ward; and, after a brief period of adjustment (i.e. generations of warfare), they learned to coexist. The city that sprang up in Old Tusk became known to its inhabitants as *Magaheim*.

THE FIVE KINDEN

The dwarves, half-demons, and other races of Magaheim call themselves *kinden*. Each kinden has a different lineage. The important thing to remember is that no lineage is pure-blooded anymore, no matter how insistently they may claim so; they're all a unique mixture found only in Magaheim.

The kinden conduct themselves much like crime families—with the kinden being the *most* important thing—and it's crucial to know who is allied with whom.

- The *demons* are descendants of the demonic soldiers who came through The Eye just before the Archmage sealed it and set up the ward. Though they claim to be full demons, they are now just "mostly demonic," due to a century of inbreeding.
- The *tieflings* are the descendants of the demonic soldiers, human cultists, and a bit of dwarf here and there.
- The *dwarves* believe they are still as dwarven as the day they were trapped in Magaheim. And maybe they are. But they've also intermarried with demons, a fact that won't be lost on anyone else in the Dragon Empire.
- *Hybrids* are a mix of different races, usually short demons or taller-than-usual dwarves with demonic features.
- *Lava dwarves* are dwarves who developed an elemental affinity for volcanism, to the point that they are partially composed of glowing rock. If someone in your group wants to play a lava dwarf, you can find a PC lava dwarf writeup on page 185.

GOVERNANCE & THE SEVEN GUILDS

An elected mayor and a city council rule the city. The council is—in theory—freely elected; however, thanks to voter intimidation, the Five Kinden control each district. The mayor is usually the biggest criminal in town, but the Five Kinden leave the mayor alone—mayors make great fall-guys when things go wrong, and all mayors inevitably go down in flames (sometimes, literally).

Seven guilds manage the economic life in Magaheim:

- The Guild of Pride *(accounting, metalworking, playwrights, magic)*
- The Guild of Liars *(mining, herbalism, criminal law, and the fire brigade)*
- The Guild of Traitors *(quarrying, civil law, surgery, and banking)*
- The Guild of the Wicked *(singers, food production, roads, and archives)*
- The Guild of Mischief-Makers *(roofing, brewing, messengers, and musicians)*
- The Guild of Deceit *(actors, private entertainment, education, and housing)*
- The Guild of Discord *(architecture, sewage, religious persecution, and medicine)*

The guilds' overlapping portfolios mean you must pay bribes to several of them to accomplish anything.

FOOD AND DRINK

The city's wizards perfected the art of making stones and metals edible. They are able to grow a few plants with the little rainwater that comes in through the ward and the little sunlight from above, but these are expensive. Plant growth is a regulated activity, and guards regularly raid illegal farms that sell mushrooms to brewers. Meat exists, is illegal to sell, and is most often former citizenry.

ECONOMY

The *scrip*—a seashell sometimes found in the mining tunnels—is the city's trade coin. Metals are plentiful in a volcano, but seashells are rare. The city does not trade with the outside world (obviously), so all economic activity focuses around entertainment and what we would call "consumer goods."

MAGAHEIM NOIR

Magaheim is perfect for *noir* adventures. The city is corrupt and evil, though lawful on the surface. Bureaucracy is important, as is the practice of offering bribes to get things done. Almost everybody is corrupt; but you only get punished if you *get caught*. The guards are incompetent bullies who are likely to arrest the first bystander or witness they find.

You must hire a *private inquisitor* (or "private eye") to accomplish pretty much anything. Demonic evil tinges everything and volcanic fumes and smoke often obscure the streets. Everybody is cynical, and more than a little fatalistic. The city even sits above a volcano, so it's literally hard-boiled.

ADVENTURES IN MAGAHEIM
THE OUTSIDERS

The adventurers' arrival sparks a full-scale revolt by Magaheim's downtrodden masses. The heads of the Five Kinden want to retain power, but a former mayor, Grayson Burr, seeks a comeback and wants to lead the citizens out of Magaheim. If the Five Kinden get their way, they'll re-establish the ward from the inside, trapping the citizens once more. If Grayson's followers flood into Redfield Valley, they'll endanger themselves and those already in the valley. Both sides alternately threaten the adventurers and make overtures of peace.

THE THIN DWARF

Dashiel Brinson, a clan-head of the lava dwarves in Undertown, has a problem: he wants to know who killed his predecessor and father, Brin Hammett, but cannot risk investigating the issue himself lest he tip off the murderer. Officially, everyone blames Dashiel for the murder—he spent years in the mines and on torture racks before he took up his current position.

Powell Redbeard, now head of the lava dwarves' kinden, oversaw the original investigation back when he was captain of the guard. The adventurers are outsiders who can risk upsetting the status quo without making it look like an investigation, so Dashiel promises them aid if they solve the murder for which he was blamed (without *looking* like they are investigating, of course).

DEMONS WITH DIRTY FACES

The demon Boss Madvig, crooked chief guard of the mines, has known about a way in and out of Old Tusk for some time—an underground river through a lava tube that exits into the Vakevale. He smuggles prisoners out in exchange for a hefty bribe (blindfolded, of course, so they cannot return without bribing him again).

Beaumont, a tiefling, was his latest "fare" out of Old Tusk; but now, Boss Madvig needs Beaumont back. Beaumont took out huge loans before his exit, loans secured on many of Madvig's friends' interests and in Madvig's name. Madvig must bring Beaumont back to Old Tusk before the loans come due and Madvig's friends and allies turn on him.

Remember that the dwarves of Magaheim use scrip (seashells) rather than metal coins or gold—adventurers who spend outsider cash in Magaheim get only 3d10% (3–30%) of what their gold would purchase elsewhere.

Cunning players who want to find an alternative to world-saving might decide to set up a get-rich-quick seashell trade—bringing in shells from the outside world to trade for cheap gold. Such endeavors could entangle the PCs in multiple plots from this section.

KING OF THE UNDERWORLD

Baelthazar Shim, owner of the Plucky Duckling Alehouse, has been creating a web of informants and agents throughout the city for some time. He intends to create a scandal surrounding the current mayor, Malthaza Trasa, to bring her down so he may run for the position.

The adventurers present the perfect opportunity to enact his plan—if Baelthazar can maneuver the adventurers into attacking Mayor Trasa, she must fight back; and if the mayor fights the first outside contact in generations, her support could shrivel. Baelthazar sends word to the adventurers that he is glad to provide food and lodging, in the hopes he overhears something he can use to his advantage to put his plan in motion.

THE GREAT ESCAPE

The Dwarf King has a plan to save his lost subjects: the adventurers must find the crystal that held Vantage aloft and use it to break Magaheim's chains and fly it to the fort of Anvil. Dwarven rangers will "attack" Magaheim as a distraction, while the adventurers carry out their plan.

THE DWARVEN FALCHION

The Dwarf King knew Old Tusk would become accessible, so he sent a diplomat (Sturm Finebeard) with a bejeweled weapon (the falchion) as a gift to Magaheim's rulers.

When the adventurers arrive, the diplomat has just turned up dead and the falchion is missing. All signs point to Dusque Shale, a dwarven femme fatale. Dusque says she didn't kill Sturm, but the diplomat had secretly come to Magaheim for years, *long before the ward came down.* Dusque suggests that the adventurers speak to her husband—Rift Darkbringer, a tiefling wizard—as he was meeting with Sturm.

Unfortunately, Rift is missing, his laboratory was wrecked, and all signs point to a kidnapping. When the party begins to investigate, various kinden heads' agents either lean on them to solve the case, threaten them to try to get them to leave town, or provide half-true clues to try to confuse them. Where is Rift? Who killed Sturm? Why (and how) did Sturm secretly visit the city for years? And who has the falchion now?

KISS, KISS; CHOP, CHOP

The Diabolist sent a favored "pet" to sign a treaty with the dwarves of Old Tusk. The demon signs the treaty and leaves, but then the only copy is stolen. The Diabolist lets it be known she will not sign another, but she will hold the dwarves to the minutiae and fine print of a treaty they can no longer double-check.

The Dwarf King hires the adventurers, through an imperial diplomat called Elmore Chandler, to find the treaty. Unfortunately, Elmore is killed, and the adventurers are blamed for her death. The Dwarf King claims no knowledge of Elmore.

OF ALL THE GIN JOINTS IN ALL THE WORLDS. . .

The adventurers arrive in the city just as demons start to come through The Eye, the gateway to hell. The infernal forces quickly gain control of the city and install a puppet government.

They immediately put Old Tusk's common folk to use as slave labor to create weapons and armor for the rest of their demonic army coming through The Eye. The new arrivals do not deem the demons in the city "pure-blooded" enough and imprison the "impure" demons in the mines.

The adventurers end up at a tavern called the House of White Bones, where the occupiers treat them well. Eblis Soulflayer of the "demon resistance" secretly contacts the adventurers and asks them to pass through The Eye and shut it from the other side. Do the adventurers have what it takes to sacrifice all for others' freedom, or do they side with the invading forces of hell?

If ASH's noir in-jokes trip you up, change the names of the characters in Magaheim. If you didn't notice them, well, forget I said anything!

Magaheim Monsters

Below, we list some of the lost dwarven city of Magaheim's inhabitants. Of course, lower-level people also live in Magaheim, but these creatures are the ones you'll probably find most useful for the 5th and 6th level adventures in this *Old Tusk & Magaheim* section.

We don't present specific battles here, since urban adventures in Magaheim are far more open than the rest of our dungeons.

Magaheim Dwarf Warrior

There is more than a little demon in this dwarf's bloodline, not that she would admit it.

5th level troop [HUMANOID]
Initiative: +8

Twin axes +10 vs. AC—18 damage.
  Miss with natural 2–4: Reroll the attack; if it hits, deal half damage.

R: Throwing axe +9 vs. AC (one nearby enemy)—18 damage.

Nastier Specials
Demonic heritage: When in an area containing fire, or when the dwarf spends a standard action to pour flaming oil on her axes; gain +2 to attacks.

AC 22
PD 20
MD 14
HP 68

Magaheim "Demonic" Citizen

It claims to be pure demon; but, it is more mortal than it lets on.

5th level spoiler [DEMON]
Initiative: +10

Hellblade +10 vs. AC—10 damage, and 8 ongoing fire damage
  Natural 16+: Target is vulnerable to hexes until the end of the fight.

C: Hex of mind-bending +10 vs. MD (2 nearby or far away enemies in a group)—9 psychic damage, and each target must include the other target in its next attack or take 20 psychic damage.

R: Hex of soul-melding +10 vs. MD (one nearby or far away enemy)—9 psychic damage, and the target makes a basic melee or ranged attack against a target of the demonic citizen's choice as an immediate free action.
  Natural 18+: Target is confused (easy save ends).

Unusual locomotion: As a move action, this demon can teleport to any point it can see, nearby or far away. Perhaps it isn't teleportation—maybe it steps through shadows, or turns into smoke, or walks through mirrors, or becomes a swirling pillar of fire. . . but, functionally, it is the same as teleportation.

Flight: The demon can fly, though not with any great agility. It usually lands to attack.

AC 21
PD 19
MD 15
HP 72

Magaheim Street-Mage

Part demon, part dwarf, part everything else.

5th level caster [HUMANOID]
Initiative: +9

Rusty pick +10 vs. AC—10 damage, and 5 ongoing damage.

C: Hex of fire +10 vs. MD (1d3 nearby enemies in a group)—13 psychic and fire damage
  Miss: Gain +2 attack bonus with the next use of *hex of pain*.

R: Hex of pain +10 vs. MD (one nearby or far away enemy)—18 negative energy damage.

Demonic specials (choose one or two)
Tail: The street-mage has a prehensile tail that grabs at enemies' weapons; +1 to defenses against enemies with whom the street-mage is engaged.
Hooves: 6 miss damage with *rusty pick* attacks due to kicking.
Horns: These are larger than normal. +2 to damage when attacking an enemy that was intercepted.
Wings: The street-mage can fly (or at least jump really well), glide, and maybe ride thermals.
Hellfire: Add +1d8 fire damage on a natural 16+ hit.

AC 19
PD 21
MD 16
HP 40

MAGAHEIM TIEFLING

Dwarf, human, demon. Yep.

6th level spoiler [HUMANOID]
Initiative: +9

Trident and net +11 vs. AC (2 attacks)—10 damage
If both attacks hit the same target: The target is stuck OR hampered (save ends, GM chooses which effect to use).

R: Creaking crossbow +11 vs. AC (one nearby or far away enemy)—16 damage
[Special] It takes a move action to reload the crossbow.

Demonic specials (choose one)

Tail: The tiefling has a prehensile tail that grabs at enemies' weapons; +1 to defenses against enemies with whom the tiefling is engaged.

Hooves: 4 miss damage with trident and net attacks due to kicking.

Horns: These are larger than normal. +2 to damage when attacking an enemy that was intercepted.

Wings: The tiefling can fly (or at least jump really well), glide, and maybe ride thermals.

Hellfire: Add +1d8 fire damage on a natural 16+ hit.

AC 22	
PD 20	**HP 96**
MD 18	

OCTAVE OF TERROR

From one perspective, this is the longest-running experiment in which mortals and demons have cohabited. That explains this demon's pitch-perfect understanding of mortal frailty.

7th level wrecker [DEMON]
Initiative: +10

Touch of sin +12 vs. MD (2 attacks)—14 psychic and negative energy damage.

Crescendo of pain: Whenever the demon misses with an attack, it gains a cumulative +1 attack bonus and deals +1d6 damage until the end of the battle (maximum bonuses: +4, +4d6).

Demonic specials (choose one)

Envy: When the demon rolls a 16+ on an attack, it pulls a nearby enemy into engagement, popping that enemy free.

Gluttony: The demon may choose to deal 4 less damage on an attack to heal 10 hp.

Greed: The demon knows which enemy has the lowest hp, and which has the lowest PD. Unlike most of the GM's creatures, this demon always acts ruthlessly on the information.

Lust: Disengaging from this demon is a hard save (16+).

Pride: If the demon misses with an attack, it gains +1 to hit that target with its next attack but −2 to disengage from that target until the end of the fight.

Sloth: If the demon did not move on its last turn it gains +1 to hit this turn.

Wrath: When the demon crits, it deals double damage AND, as a free action, makes a second attack against the same target.

AC 23	
PD 17	**HP 108**
MD 21	

MAGAHEIM HORDE DEMON

It wears a uniform of hot iron and flayed skin.

9th level mook [DEMON]
Initiative: +12

Chains and spikes +14 vs. AC—32 damage
Natural 16+: As a free action, the demon can make up to two *whipping chains* attacks as quick actions on its next turn.

C: Whipping chains +14 vs. AC (1 nearby enemy)—15 damage.

R: Barbed iron javelin +14 vs. AC—20 damage, and 7 ongoing damage.

AC 23	
PD 21	**HP 45**
MD 17	

THE WINDING GYRE

Level range: 5th and 6th level

This floating maze is a spiral of wreckage that stretches up to the sky. Some portions of the wreckage are large enough to contain intact rooms or areas worth exploring, others are merely fist-sized chunks of rubble. Getting from one part of the maze to another involves using the floating rubble as stepping stones. Some larger parts of the aerial ruin have their own gravity—they tumble dizzily while those inside or standing on them experience no motion and feel as though their feet are planted on solid ground.

The residual magic that holds the shattered stonework aloft catches any character who falls for any reason while exploring the skyward spiral. They take 4d8 damage as they tumble up into the sky and loop back to slam down near their previous position in the maze.

Flying: We suspect the magic that holds the Gyre together might make flying outside or above the Gyre difficult, in which case flying characters must progress along the dungeon's natural course.

If only one or two characters can fly, you could let them move ahead and meet enemies meant to challenge the entire party. If you somehow have an entire party of flying characters, you must choose whether to reward them for their talents, let them move around as they like throughout this dungeon, or come up with interesting problems they must solve. The simplest solution might be to dial up some nasty encounters from the *Raptors* adversary group (page 216).

DUNGEON GOAL

The theme of this dungeon is exploration: wandering about and seeing what there is to see (and looting the place). However, you could change things up—if the characters are looking for a specific treasure, they find out it is at the highest point of the Winding Gyre. If the adventurers are looking for a location in Redfield Valley, then the top of the gyre is the perfect place to spy on the whole valley: they can spot wards as they start to fail, see troop movements, and watch for emerging living dungeons.

ADVENTURING IN THE WINDING GYRE

See page 53 for our advice on how and when to use tension tables.

Every time the adventurers enter a new area, they should roll 1d12 on the tension table. As a bonus to the tension table roll, add twice the number of battles the adventurers have fought since their last full heal-up.

WINDING GYRE TENSION TABLE (D12)

1-6. Nothing of note happens; add a +2 bonus to the next roll on this table.

7. Gravity suddenly gets stronger; raise the DC of all physically-oriented skill checks by 5 in this area.

8. Gravity is slightly off-kilter; floors and walls do not feel level. Emphasize movement problems if the PCs fight in this area.

9. At some point while in this room, a random character must make a DC 30 skill check to avoid "falling" and taking 4d8 damage as gravity flickers and shifts around them.

10+ *even*. The PCs encounter a wandering monster. Roll on the *Winding Gyre Wandering Monster* table, choose a result, or make up your own monster.

11+ *odd*. Encounter defenses. Roll on the *Winding Gyre Magical Defenses* table.

WINDING GYRE WANDERING MONSTER TABLE (D12)

1. An adversary group that is probably associated with an enemy icon. By this time, the PCs should have plenty of enemies to choose from; if not, start a new hostile relationship to freshen the plot.

2. Survivors/Defenders of Vantage. Use a battle from the *Wizards & Spellcasters* adversary group (page 218). Given the Winding Gyre's strange physics, they may be having problems of their own. Also, given that the PCs may have done good things in the *glitterfall*, it's possible this won't be a fight, but play it as you like.

3. An enemy adversary group (or the Gyre's magical defenders), already badly injured by their experiences in the Winding Gyre or elsewhere (they have −1 to hit and only 70% of their normal hp).

4. A group of survivors. They surrender without a fight. Introduce an interesting NPC or someone who knows something about pieces of this "dungeon."

5-7. A group of constructs. They either assume the adventurers are enemies or they no longer care. That is, assuming they ever cared. Choose a battle from the Golems adversary group (page 207).

8. Roll on this table again with a d4; the creatures the adventurers encounter are dead (they have 1 magic item with them, and 2d20 gp).

9-12. Magical defenders of the Winding Gyre. Use the specific monsters and battles in the next section.

Vantage's ruins still have a few active magical defenses, though they "go offline" often. Still, they may activate in any area at any time attacking the adventurers while they explore the ruins. When they do, roll on the *Winding Gyre Magical Defense* table:

WINDING GYRE MAGICAL DEFENSE TABLE (D6)

1-2. Improvise a magical trap or accidental side-effect of this area's unique characteristics and randomly select one PC to attempt a DC 20 skill check. Failure deals 4d6 damage of a type whatever you concoct suggests.

3-4. Sputtering magical defenses zap one random PC with a ray that should paralyze or kill them, but instead applies a −2 penalty to their skill checks and attack rolls until the next time the escalation die reaches 2+.

5. Long-distance force cannons stutter into operation from somewhere in the floating wreckage. Each PC can attempt a DC 30 skill check to hide or magically shield themselves; failure means they take 2d8 force damage. Further, the cannons hit each PC who rolls a 1 on the skill check twice, for 4d8 force damage instead.

6. A dampening field or metaphysical siphon turns off 1d3 of the party's true magical items, while failing to turn off whatever communication abilities they possess. Choose items randomly among the PCs, and roleplay item-distress if your group finds that amusing. A separate easy save for each item (6+) after each battle restores the item to its true nature.

MAGICAL DEFENDERS OF THE WINDING GYRE

The rest of the wandering monsters here are taken care of by the adversary groups. As an extremely diverse swirl of wreckage, the gyre has an equally diverse group of magical defenders. You don't have to stick with the flavor the original names of these creatures provide—reflavor them in ways that will amuse your players.

For the record, we're already amusing ourselves by counting a creature like the *couatl* as a possible magical defender (see **13B**: 52 for more on this bright option).

If you know the first *Bestiary* book, you already know the wibble, a nasty little byproduct of bungled magic. The fall of Vantage counts as a catastrophic case of bungled magic, so we've added catastrophic wibble mooks to the roster of possible defenders in the Winding Gyre.

#/Level of PCs	Living Spell	Catastrophic Wibble	Lightning Elemental	Couatl
3 x 5th level	2	6	1	0
3 x 5th level	1	6	0	1
4 x 5th level	1	5	2	0
4 x 5th level	1	5	1	1
5 x 5th level	2	8	2	0
5 x 5th level	1	0	1	2
6 x 5th level	3	7	1	1
6 x 5th level	2	0	1	2
7 x 5th level	1	10	2	1
7 x 5th level	2	5	1	2
3 x 6th level	2	7	2	0
3 x 6th level	3	0	1	1
4 x 6th level	3	10	2	0
4 x 6th level	3	0	2	1
5 x 6th level	3	10	3	0
5 x 6th level	2	0	2	2
6 x 6th level	2	10	3	1
6 x 6th level	2	0	3	2
7 x 6th level	4	10	3	1
7 x 6th level	3	0	2	3

LIVING SPELL

It blasts intruders for the glory of the Archmage. That is all.

5th level archer [SPIRIT]
Initiative: +10

Magefire +10 vs. AC (1d3 attacks)— 8 force and fire damage
Natural odd miss: The target pops free.

R: Spell burn +10 vs. AC (2 nearby or far away enemies in a group)—14 force damage
Natural odd hit: The target becomes vulnerable to force damage.

Mana burn: When a magical attack or a weapon attack with a magic weapon targets the living spell, the attacker takes their level in force damage.

Flight: The living spell floats about, quite unheeding of minor things like gravity.

Immaterial: The living spell can drift through walls, phase through floors, and otherwise defy solidity, though it can't end its turn in solid objects.

AC	18	
PD	21	HP 72
MD	21	

CATASTROPHIC WIBBLE

The 4th, 13th, and 237th laws of magic prove that it is impossible to create a wibble larger than the tiny glitches so often created by apprentices and hedge wizards. The 27th and 587th laws similarly proved that Vantage would never fall.

6th level mook [CONSTRUCT]
Initiative: +6

R: Force burp spell +11 vs. PD—12 force damage.

Disengaged: Wibbles gain a +5 bonus to disengage checks. They also don't remain engaged with their foes and move every turn in battle. When they fail a disengage check, a wibble moves away anyway.

Eruptive blorp: When an enemy hits a wibble with a melee attack, it takes force damage equal to double its level.

Flight: Wibbles waft about. They can fly well enough to ignore most wind, but not strong gale winds.

Whiff and wibble: When a creature makes a non-spell attack against a catastrophic wibble and rolls a natural 1–2, 1d3 new catastrophic wibbles are created in the same area. These new wibbles typically melt back into their "parent" at the end of a battle if not destroyed, but sometimes they remain separate and drift off on their own.

AC	18	
PD	18	HP 20 (mook)
MD	18	

Mook: Kill one catastrophic wibble mook for every 20 damage you deal to the mob.

LIGHTNING ELEMENTAL

Webs of lightning repeatedly streak in all directions, outlining the form of the creature and then dissipating. Each flash happens so fast, it leaves the thing's image burned into your eyes.

7th level spoiler [ELEMENTAL]
Initiative: +14

Lightning zap +12 vs. AC—20 lightning damage
Natural odd hit: The target is dazed until the end of its next turn.
Metal affinity: The attack gains a +1 bonus against an enemy wearing metal armor or wielding a metal weapon.

R: Lightning strike +12 vs. PD (one nearby enemy or a far away enemy at −2 attack)—24 lightning damage
Metal affinity: The attack gains a +1 bonus against an enemy wearing metal armor or wielding a metal weapon.

Flight: Lightning elementals zip from place to place about half-as-quick as lightning, hovering above the ground to avoid being grounded.

Lightning storm transformation: Roll 1d8 at the start of each of the lightning elemental's turns. If you roll less than or equal to the escalation die, it shifts into lightning storm form until the end of the battle. While in this form, it gains the following improved attack (and you stop rolling *lightning storm transformation* checks):

C: Storm strike +12 vs. PD (up to 2 nearby enemies)—20 lightning damage
Natural even roll: The elemental can include an additional target in the attack (requires attack roll) that hasn't been hit by storm strike this turn, but the attack only deals half damage.
Metal affinity: The attack gains a +1 bonus against an enemy wearing metal armor or wielding a metal weapon.

Resist lightning and thunder 16+: When a lightning or thunder attack targets this creature, the attacker must roll a natural 16+ on the attack roll or it only deals half damage.

AC	22	
PD	22	HP 100
MD	15	

COUATL

The couatl doesn't want your soul. It wants you to use your soul in interesting ways that would not have occurred to you. Or anyone else.

Large 8th level spoiler [BEAST]
Initiative: +14

Rippling scales +13 vs. PD (each enemy engaged with it)—10 damage, and the couatl must pop free from the target
Quick use: 1/round as a quick action.

Serpent strike +13 vs. AC (one dazed, confused, staggered, or stunned enemy)—60 damage, and 20 ongoing poison damage.

R: Forked devastation +13 vs. PD (one nearby or far away enemy)—50 fire, holy, or lightning damage (couatl's choice)
Natural even hit or miss: The couatl can make a *forked devastation* attack against a different enemy as a free action.

C: Striking comets +13 vs. PD (each nearby creature)—40 damage
Natural even miss: The target is dazed (save ends).
Natural odd miss: 20 damage.
Limited use: 1/battle, when the escalation die is 2+.

Resist holy and poison 16+: When a holy or poison attack targets this creature, the attacker must roll a natural 16+ on the attack roll or it only deals half damage.

Flight: Couatls fly and hover so smoothly on their multi-colored wings that other flyers get jealous.

Cyclic escalator: When the escalation die is even, the couatl adds the escalation die to its attack rolls

Flee: Once per campaign, the couatl can take a "campaign loss"—similar to the PC-oriented flee special action (*13th Age* core rules, page 166)—to escape from certain death, along with its allies.

AC	24	
PD	21	**HP 300**
MD	21	

WINDING GYRE AREAS

The only two areas accessible from the ground are Area A and Area N.

A: THE SPINNING CUBE

> **First impressions:** A huge chunk of rubble, obviously a deep interior piece of Vantage. It hovers above the ground, rotating slowly.
> **Second sniff:** There is blood somewhere nearby.
> **Joins to areas:** B, N, and the ground

The exterior of this floating ruin has its own gravity, which means the characters can partially walk around it. Walking on the surface of this rubble means the character is upside-down—though, from their perspective, the ground is "above" them. The characters cannot navigate the whole cube, rubble and the artificial gravity prevent access to its far side, so passing through the cube is the only way to progress from this area.

Two doorways in the masonry lead inward *[to B and N]* and a good jump takes the characters back to the ground.

B: THE CORPSE ROOM

> **First impressions:** Lots of dead bodies on the ceiling here.
> **Second glance:** Some of the bodies bump around a bit.
> **Joins to areas:** A, C, and O

This room is perfectly normal except for the fact that the ceiling is covered in easily a hundred corpses. These are some of Vantage's defenders (and maybe attackers). Pools of blood on the floor drip upward, toward the ceiling. The characters' possessions are attracted upward, while the adventurers themselves remain on what is to them the "floor." Anything the adventurers drop in this room falls upward toward the ceiling. Characters who carry a lot of weight (tons of looted gold, wearing full plate armor, etc.) must make a DC 25 skill check or become weightless and float slowly toward the ceiling, where they must crawl over the corpses to reach the edge of the room.

The corpses are moving due to tiny eddies in gravity (unless there is a wandering monster in the room, in which case it might be under the bodies feasting or waiting to ambush the characters). Attacking the bodies sprays gore everywhere (it drips upward, so be careful not to get any under your nostrils)!

If the characters insist on carefully searching all the bodies, they might find something worthwhile; still, feel free to make their next battle harder than it should be without giving them credit, since they dawdled.

One doorway leads outside *[to A and C]*, another leads further into the floating ruins *[to O]*.

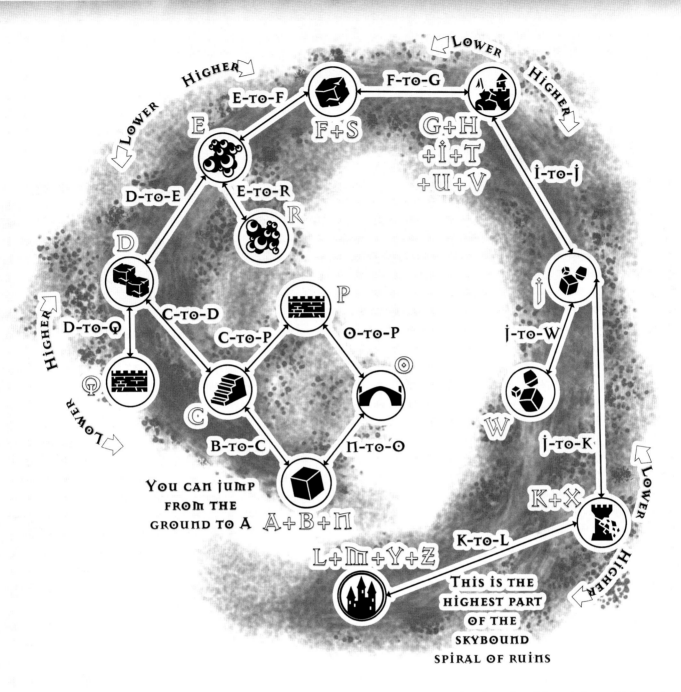

LOWER HIGHER

E-TO-F

F-TO-G

LOWER HIGHER

E

D-TO-E

E-TO-R

F+S

G+H
+I+T
+U+V

R

I-TO-J

D

HIGHER

C-TO-D

P

J

D-TO-Q

C-TO-P

O-TO-P

J-TO-W

LOWER

C

W

B-TO-C

N-TO-O

J-TO-K

You can jump
FROM THE
GROUND TO A

A+B+N

K+X

L+M+Y+Z

K-TO-L

This is the
HIGHEST PART
OF THE
SKYBOUND
SPIRAL OF RUINS

LOWER HIGHER

C: Stairway to Heaven

First impressions: The exterior of the floating ruin, a grand staircase that leads into thin air.

Second glance: The stairs have pressure plates under them, though the mechanism looks damaged.

Joins to areas: B, D, and P

These stairs stretch upward; the topmost of them are completely broken away from the rest of the staircase—just floating planks of wood in mid-air. There's a field of floating rubble on the far side of the stairs *[D]*. The damage to the stairs shows hidden mechanisms underneath—pressure plates and bladders filled with some sort of liquid. This is a trap that someone activated too late to effectively defend Vantage. Anybody who walks on

the stairs gets sprayed with sticky oil from below, which sparks and then ignites. Despite their damage, the stairs still have three attacks remaining; characters who walk up the stairs are subject to an attack. **Fantasy napalm +15 vs. PD (each adventurer in area C)**—3d10 fire damage.

Disarming the traps requires three successful DC 30 skill checks (each success disarms one set of pressure plates and oil bladders, removing one potential attack). Those who choose to run up the stairs trigger the attacks against everybody in the area, but avoid being a target themselves; however, it takes a DC 25 skill check to avoid falling off the floating stairs into the sky and crashing back down into them (4d8 damage).

The stairs rest between two areas *[lead to B and D]*, and characters can leap from them to an open doorway *[leads to P]*.

Funny story. . . during playtests, one of the party rogues—played by my friend Wes—rolled well enough to disarm all three traps in the stairway to heaven area. However, he wanted to loot the traps instead of simply disarming them, so I offered him the choice to loot two but be unable to find the third, instead of disarming all three.

He agreed and as he carried the oil-filled bladders up the stairs at the head of the party, he triggered the third trap (which rolled a natural 20 on its attack), and the two bladders he was carrying exploded at point-blank range for maximum damage. Then, while half the party was on fire, the monsters attacked.

Ahh . . . good times.

D: THE RUBBLE FIELD

First impressions: A swarm of floating masonry; most pieces are large enough to stand on.
Second glance: When somebody steps on the rubble, it turns.
Joins to areas: C, E, and Q

The spinning rubble motes are difficult to traverse (DC 20 check; failure causes 3d6 damage) because they spin every which way in the wind. None of the rubble motes are much larger than a dinner plate. At the lower end of the rubble is a floating staircase *[C]*, at the higher end is a wobbling sphere of water as large as a house *[E]*. An opening to the interior of a long chunk of ruin is also reachable by walking across the rubble field *[leads to Q]*.

E: THE FLOATING POOL

First impressions: A floating pool of water, with a floating piece of ruin in the center.
Second glance: The piece of ruin has chains that lead to other areas, if one can get to it.
Joins to areas: D, F, and S

This pool of water surrounds a large chunk of rubble wrapped in chains. Two of the chains stretch away from the rubble: one upward to a field of broken statues floating above *[F]*, and one downward to a part of the ruin that looks like it contains doors *[leads to S]*. The pool trails rubble *[D]* as it orbits in the spiral. To pass through this area, the characters must swim through the blob of water.

Due to the strange gravity that holds the blob in place, the water tries to flow over anything with which it comes in contact. It takes a DC 25 skill check to avoid drowning; for every point by which the roll fails, the character takes 1 damage due to water inhalation). If the GM agrees, certain creatures that may not need to breathe (probably forgeborn, maybe twygzog, some characters with *uniques* such as being one of the living dead) can maneuver through the water without risk of drowning.

F: THE BROKEN STATUES

First impressions: A field of broken statues, tumbling around in the air.
Second glance: Magic sparks from some of these statues.
Joins to areas: E, G, and S

These statues were part of Vantage's defenses; they stood in alcoves along an outer wall and fired beams of lightning from their eyes at intruders who passed before their gaze. They are broken now, but the severed marble heads still hold their magic. If the PCs decide to go through the field of statues, they attack the lead character without warning. **Lightning eye beams +20 vs. PD**—2d20 lightning damage.

Additional characters who pass through the field of statues can make a DC 30 skill check to avoid the statues' gaze, once they are aware of the danger.

One of the larger statues has a chain wrapped around it *[leads to E]*, which spirals upward in the sky toward a semi-intact piece of Vantage *[leads to G]*. A long piece of Vantage tumbles in the sky in the middle of the statue field *[leads to S]*.

G: THE GRAND HALL

First impressions: A huge chunk of Vantage, a grand hall with a missing roof.
Second glance: This area is level with the lower clouds; the stonework is wet here.
Joins to areas: F, H, and T

This was once a grand ballroom, with mirrors lining the walls and windows providing a view of the sky. The piece of Vantage that the ballroom occupies is upside-down and the roof is missing, which means those exploring this area have a vertiginous view if they glance upward: the ground looms far "above" them.

This area is relatively free of oddities (beyond the view) and would be a good place to rest were it not for the clouds depositing water onto the stonework.

A doorway leads deeper into the floating ruin, to a corridor missing its floor *[to H]*. A mirrored side-door leads in the opposite direction *[to T]*. Climbing out of the ballroom leads to a field of shattered statues *[leads to F]*.

H: THE GREAT CORRIDOR

First impressions: A huge chunk of Vantage—a long corridor with pillars—with most of the floor missing.
Second glance: It looks like the floor was a mosaic.
Joins to areas: G, I, and U

A throne room is on the far side of the corridor [*leads to I*] and a ballroom is on the other. During the fall of Vantage, most of the floor in this area fell away. It takes a DC 25 skill check to move through this corridor without falling "down" (up into the sky), and then being flung by the strange gravity back into the ruin (4d8 damage).

Most of the doors in the corridor were magically sealed shut during the attack, but one handle still turns [*leads to U*].

I: THE THRONE ROOM

First impressions: A huge chunk of Vantage—a throne room with a missing wall.
Second glance: This area is full of Dragon Empire symbols.
Joins to areas: H, J, and V

This was where the Emperor and his predecessors held court in Vantage. The room is lavishly decorated, with velvet wallpaper (ruined by dampness from the clouds), exquisite floor tiles, and a throne gilt in gold and studded with rubies.

The throne is magically anchored to this spot, but if the PCs pry the rubies free, they are worth 300 x 1d10 gp. One of the rubies has a protective spell cast into it (DC 20 check to notice the slight glow) and is hard to pry loose—but, once loose, is almost indestructible (we're sure adventurers can think of a couple of uses for a stone that can't be easily destroyed).

A gap in the wall leads into the sky, where a shattered mosaic floats in mid-air [*leads to J*], which in turn leads to a section of outer wall. A corridor leads deeper into the floating ruin [*leads to H*]. A concealed door (DC 25 check to spot it) leads to a side-room [*V*].

J: The Colored Tiles

> **First impressions:** A shattered mosaic, floating in the sky.
> **Second glance:** The tiles form a pattern, but it is hard to see from below.
> **Joins to areas:** I, K, and W

These tiles were once part of a corridor *[in H]* but broke free during the fall of Vantage. They are part of Vantage's enchanted defenses: roll on the *Winding Gyre Magical Defenses* table (page 128). The tiles stretch between three large floating pieces of Vantage *[lead to I, W, and K]*.

K: The Battlements

> **First impressions:** A section of Vantage, floating in mid-air.
> **Second glance:** There is blood here; it looks like defenders died in this area.
> **Joins to areas:** J, L, and X

This is one of Vantage's more conventional defenses: a section of wall with an intact round tower and castle battlements. Atop the round tower stands a working trebuchet (a counterweighted catapult).

A very large area of Vantage floats overhead *[leads to L]*, and it is possible to reach the area if adventurers are willing to fling themselves from the battlements toward the overhead ruins. It requires a DC25 skill check to correctly aim the trebuchet; failure causes the hapless adventurer to launch into a high-speed orbit around the battlements until they finally crash through the window of the tower *[leads to X]*. The PCs can also access the tower by climbing down a ladder bolted into its side.

A field of tiles trails in a widening spiral beneath the battlements *[leads to J]*.

L: The Lectory

> **First impressions:** A dark chamber with figures at desks inside, a large hole in the wall.
> **Second glance:** The figures are automatons, and they are speaking.
> **Joins to areas:** K, M, Y, and Z

Automatons recited charms over and over in this room to keep various wards intact. Some are still at their task, mindlessly reciting the words on the parchments in front of them. At some point in the recent past, however, someone or something hurled a large round stone through the wall of this room and set fire to many of the automatons who were not crushed.

The automatons look like porcelain humans, but they don't have the ability to move beyond scanning their glass eyes over a space in front of them and working their artificial lips, tongues, and billows-lungs (they don't even have legs under their robes, and their arms only move to turn pages). They are truly mindless and do not react to anything beyond reading aloud whatever is put before them. This wasn't the central method of maintaining the wards, but it was certainly one of the ways in which the wards were supported.

This is a good location for GMs to reveal some upcoming problems, such as the collapsing wards across Redfield Valley. Players can read some of the charms or listen to them being spoken and get clues about upcoming events regarding the fall of various wards. For a more dramatic show-and-tell, perhaps the adventurers can now see the shimmering and collapsing magical barriers in the valley below.

Stairs lead upward from this room *[to Y and Z]*, and a short corridor leads to a door *[leads to M]*. A good running jump out of the hole in the wall takes characters back to the battlements *[leads to K]* but it takes a DC 20 check, otherwise the odd gravity flings them back through the hole (3d6 damage).

M: The Mordant Miasma

> **First impressions:** The area is full of green smoke. It has a flagstone floor.
> **Second sniff:** The miasma is acidic. The room looks empty.
> **Joins to areas:** L, Y, and Z

This room is full of green smoke. **Acid cloud +12 vs. PD**—15 acid damage. The room seems empty except for the smoke; however, exploring reveals a loose flagstone that covers a trapdoor in the floor. Beyond the trapdoor is a treasure vault (DC 20 skill check to open the vault), in which there are several magical tomes.

Stairs lead upward toward the sounds of birdsong *[leads to Y and Z]* and a door leads deeper into the ruin *[to L]*.

N: The Narthex of Dirges

> **First impressions:** A lobby area with many pillars and marble floors, open on one side and accessible by leaping from the ground.
> **Second glance:** The sounds of mournful singing echo through the chamber.
> **Joins to areas:** A, O, and the ground

This area was once the entrance to a chapel on Vantage. Most of the chapel is now rubble, but the narthex remains. A sad song resounds in the chamber; it mourns the fall of Vantage and the deaths of those who defended it. If you are running a mystery plot revolving around who attacked Vantage, this could be the final clue that reveals everything—otherwise, it is just a spooky song that seems to come from everywhere at once.

A doorway leads deeper into the ruin *[to area O]*, and a gap leads into the open air *[to A or the ground, depending on whether the PCs climb out or leap]*.

O: THE BRIDGE OF OMENS

First impressions: A bridge over a floorless chamber.
Second glance: The bridge is unmoored, it is floating in the air.
Joins to areas: B, N, and P

The bridge floats in mid-air, unattached to anything else. Characters who cross it must make a DC 30 skill check; failure means the bridge tips and they fall *[to P]*. The bridge leads to the remains of a chapel *[to N]* and a room deeper in the ruins *[leads to B]*.

P: THE PONTIFF'S SCALES

First impressions: A room with a floor of brass tiles.
Second glance: The tiles shift and move in the wind, they are part of a magical mechanism.
Joins to areas: C, and O

This area was part of Vantage's magical defenses. Those crossing it must step on the tiles in a specific pattern (DC 20 skill check), or the tiles open and dump the character into the sky. Fortunately, this trap is now very close to the ground and inflicts only 3d8 falling damage on those who fail to step on the tiles correctly. Characters who jump can reach a bridge above the tiles *[leads to O]*; the only other exit or entrance in this area is an open doorway above a set of stairs. Moving to or from the stairs involves jumping; but, thankfully, the strange gravity in the area aids jumpers (no roll required).

Q: THE ALCHEMICAL QUARREL

First impressions: A long hallway with a series of holes in the wall.
Second glance: Cracks in the plasterwork show a mechanism hidden in the walls.
Joins to area: D

This long corridor is inside a rapidly rotating piece of Vantage that speeds up when the characters land on it. Walking over the ruin is not possible (it is surrounded by a cloud of rubble that would surely dash in the skulls of anybody who attempted it).

Despite the ruin's rapid rotation in the sky, adventurers in the corridor feel no motion (though, looking out at the spinning sky might make some queasy).

The corridor has many rooms along it, most of them resembling monastic cells. At the far end is a stairway that leads downward and ends in the open air, leading to nowhere. Under the stairs is a heavy door—it's open, though it has many locks on it. Inside is a potion store-room—somebody was obviously here recently, as there is evidence they scooped armloads of potions off the shelves. 1d6 + 4 champion-tier healing potions and 1d3 of each other type remain in the room.

The corridor has a mechanism hidden in the walls; a quick examination shows that this area is trapped with pressure plates and crossbows. *It is also obvious the mechanism is jammed.* Characters who fiddle with the mechanisms risk reactivating the trap (DC 20 check to render it permanently broken); otherwise there is a 50% chance that the trap spontaneously unjams when they return to the rubble field from which they entered the corridor *[D]*. If/when the trap activates, it attacks. **Crossbows trap +10 vs. AC** (each creature in Area Q)—2d12 damage.

R: THE RIPARIAN CHAMBER

First impressions: A stream of water flows through this chamber, out through a crack in the wall, around the ruin, and then waterfalls back in through another crack.
Second glance: Something golden glistens in the stream of water.
Joins to area: E

Water circles this chunk of Vantage rubble, which floats below and is connected by a chain to the main globe of water *[E]*. Within the water swim golden-scaled koi fish. The fish are not made of gold, they are merely golden in color; the characters can easily catch and cook the koi. The chamber is probably a safe place to rest.

S: THE SKEWBALD CIRCLE

First impressions: A collection of rooms with broken windows that open to the sky.
Second glance: The shadows in here move in unnatural ways.
Joins to area: F

This part of Vantage tumbles end-over-end amidst a field of broken statues *[F]*. The external surface of the ruin constantly bashes against statues and other sky-bound rubble, but the rooms inside are accessible through empty doorways and shattered windows.

Anybody inside the tumbling ruin does not feel motion, though looking out the window might give them motion-sickness.

The internal area is a collection of a dozen rooms that were once offices; they were completely wrecked during the battle that brought Vantage tumbling down. The shadows in this area move rather oddly; it takes a DC 25 check to notice the odd movement is not just because the ruin is tumbling. If your campaign features any recurring shadowy antagonists, bring them in here. Otherwise, if the adventurers haven't had many battles in the Winding Gyre, this is a good place for a battle with flying creatures from the *Raptors* adversary group (page 216).

T: THE TRIGON VOID

First impressions: A circular area lined with triangular tiles on the floor.
Second glance: There is not much beneath the tiles—the wind whistles through gaps between them. There is faint music.
Joins to areas: G, and U

The floor in this curved hallway has triangular marble slabs lining it; stepping on them produces musical notes. As adventurers put their weight on the tiles, they notice there is nothing below the tiles, just sky.

This area is part of Vantage's magical defenses. Anybody who moves across the corridor must step on the tiles in such a way that they produce the imperial anthem; failure to do so sets off a magical trap. It requires a DC 30 skill check to work out how to walk down the corridor and avoid setting off the trap (jamming it takes a DC 20 check, if the character attempting to do so can cast ritual magic); failure to play the correct tune teleports everybody in the area outside Vantage. Fortunately, the trap teleports characters into the sky and they end up falling back into the ruins *[at I]* and taking 3d8 falling damage.

The curved hallway stretches between a grand ballroom *[leads to G]* and a series of doors *[one leads to U; the others open into the sky]*.

U: THE UNHALLOWED SANCTUM

First impressions: A wizard's sanctum; the floor mostly fell away, leaving just the edges of the room navigable.
Second sniff: The hair on the back of the adventurers' necks stands up as they enter this area.
Joins to areas: H, T, and V

This was obviously a wizard's inner sanctum (based on the wall decorations); and its floor is missing. Only a narrow lip around the edge of the room remains, which requires a DC 25 skill check to walk along without falling into the sky.

All adventurers who enter this area get an uncanny feeling. As soon as more than two adventurers are in the room, a cloud of roiling darkness appears in mid-air at the center of the room.

If you have the *13th Age Bestiary*, run a battle using the entire "family" of chaos beasts that appear on page 38. If you don't have access to that book, use the 4th level version of the fight against spell-warriors and living spells that occurs in the Nightmare Prince's realm (page 23), but add one of the villainous NPC agents of the icon who appeared in the first chapter (page 10) to make the battle more challenging.

This circular room has four doors *[lead to H, T, V, and the sky]*.

V: THE VIRIDESCENT GLASS

First impressions: A room made partially of green glass bricks.
Second glance: The green is spreading, more of the area is becoming green glass.
Joins to areas: I, and U

This room is little more than a closet. It has one regular door *[leads to U]* and a door with eyeholes in it *[looks into I]*. The door with eyeholes is hidden from the other side, this chamber was used to spy on diplomats who met in the adjoining throne room *[I]*.

This whole room is slowly transmuting into green glass, though the cause is not apparent.

W: THE CHUUL'S REMEMBRANCE

First impressions: This room contains the corpse of a monstrous creature.
Second glance: The creature is stuffed and mounted. Words are scratched all over its carapace.
Joins to area: J

This ruin of Vantage floats beneath a field of mosaic tiles *[J]*. It has a series of rooms, which are mostly uninteresting until the inner room, where there is a stuffed and mounted monstrous chuul corpse.

This was a chuul-worshiping cult's inner sanctum, hidden on Vantage. Words of praise and veneration are scratched into the chuul's carapace. If you own the *13th Age Bestiary*, feel free to stock this sanctum with some chuul symbiote magic items (**13B:** 49).

X: The Xylographic Secret

> **First impressions:** A wood-paneled room.
> **Second sniff:** The area reeks of magic, even to untrained senses.
> **Joins to areas:** K

This room is in a tower that's attached to a section of floating battlements *[K]*. The characters can access it by climbing out the window and up a ladder that's bolted to the side of the tower. The tower's interior is a series of rooms that contain books, presses, paper, inks, and tools for carving woodblocks—this area was used to create woodblock-stamped books. None of the completed books or raw manuscripts are magical in nature, but some of them might fetch a good price in Santa Cora, Concord, or Horizon (about 1d20 x 1d100 x 10 gp) if a character empties out their pack to fill it with books. They won't know how much they'll get for the books until they get to a city—it could be anywhere from 10 gp to 20,000 gp. . . a bit of a gamble).

It takes a DC 20 skill check to spot the false wall in the tower behind which there's a hidden room. The room contains a golden tome (worth 1000 gp if sold for gold, worth 1d20 times that in Horizon). This book is the forbidden *Libro Flavo*. If forces loyal to the Emperor or Archmage catch anybody carrying it, they'll confiscate it and possibly punish the individual. It's said that encoded within the book are illustrated instructions for creating a hellhole.

Y: The Yearn

> **First impressions:** An empty plaza, with a still-functioning fountain. There are fruit trees around the edges of the plaza.
> **Second glance:** Birdsong fills the area; the birds are nesting in the fruit trees.
> **Joins to areas:** L, M, and Z

One of Vantage's subtler defenses attacks adventurers who explore this plaza: an enchantment that relaxes intruders. In fact, they become so relaxed that they forget all their worries and eventually forget everything. Then, the plaza attacks. **The yearning +20 vs. MD (against each adventurer)**—Each target starts to roll last gasp saves. Failure means the target wanders around the plaza aimlessly, eating fruit from the trees and drinking from the fountain. After each day (or each full heal up) spent in the plaza, the target may roll a normal save (11+) to break free from the spell.

When Vantage was intact, guards checked the plaza for bamboozled intruders daily; but now, no guards come. For each day the adventurers spend in the plaza, introduce an additional campaign loss (another ward breaks, a new set of enemies shows up, etc.). It takes a DC 30 skill check to break another character free of the spell; one attempt per entrapped adventurer, per day.

Pacing: If your campaign doesn't have the patience for this long a delay, shorten the period for saving on your own or getting slapped out of it to an amount of time that makes sense for your story.

Stairs lead upward from the plaza to a tower *[leads to Z]* and downward into the floating ruin *[leads to L and M]*.

Z: The Zenith

> **First impressions:** The highest portion of the rubble; the room is locked.
> **Second glance:** A glimmer of gold through the keyhole. Far above, glimpses of the Overworld, just out of reach.
> **Joins to areas:** L, M, and Y

The door to this room is obviously locked and trapped (any rogue or magic user in the party instantly notices this). It takes a DC 30 skill check to pick the lock; failure sets off a trap. **Mind-taker +20 vs. MD**—target becomes confused and initiates combat, or flees if there is nobody to fight (hard save ends).

If the characters use magic to unlock the door, they always succeed; but, they trigger a magical dart trap. It requires a DC 25 skill check to notice and disarm or otherwise negate the dart trap. **Acid dart +20 vs. PD (person who set off the trap)**—16 ongoing acid damage.

Bashing down the door takes a DC 20 skill check but does not trigger either trap; those who once protected this room had guards to hear any attempts to break down the door, but the guards either died or fled.

A huge golden throne, inset with gems of every color, is inside the room. Anybody who sat on the throne was filled with magical energy; alas, the throne no longer works properly due to the fall. Roll a d6 three times (re-roll any duplicate results) to discover what abilities the throne gives the one who sits on it:

1. May enchant any one object to become a champion-tier magic item from the *13th Age* core rulebook, the *Book of Loot*, or *Loot Harder*.
2. May teleport everybody present (including themselves) to any open-air area in Redfield Valley.
3. May create mundane items out of thin air (not treasure or magical items though), OR heal all the party's wounds (restore full hp), OR turn lead into gold.
4. Instantly gains the benefits of a full rest.
5. Infinite cosmic knowledge. Sadly, being one with the universe induces complete paralysis and it is almost impossible to remember what infinite cosmic knowledge is like once one has lost it.
6. Random, uncontrollable minor magical effects (roll a d6):
   1. Doves and rabbits appear out of clothing.
   2. Vomits 3d100-worth of gems.
   3. Emits puffs of colored smoke.
   4. Causes flashes of light, apparitions, and levitation.
   5. Eyes shoot light beams and voice becomes resonant and impressive.
   6. Reality seems to peel away for a moment, revealing an infinite star field.
   7+. The chair explodes, causing 3d20 damage to everybody in the area.

Every person after the first who sits in the chair adds a cumulative +1 to their rolls.

There are also 2d4 true magic items in this room.

Two sets of stairs connect the tower to the plaza below *[lead to area Y]*.

For what it's worth, you can *see* the overworld through the windows in the throne room. It's out of reach, but it probably wasn't when Vantage was intact.

RYПTH

Level range: 5th and 6th

Long ago, an Archmage shackled a living dungeon to his will and bought it to Redfield Valley to serve as a source of guardians for the Imperial Tomb.

Depending on how you want to present Rynth, it is either a random dungeon that an Archmage captured, a captured living dungeon, or the end-result of experimentation with oozes and slimes. All the creatures in the dungeon are oozes or oozefolk.

We provide details for the highest and lowest regions of this location, and a handy generator for any rooms you'd like the PCs to explore in-between.

Upper Level: Entrances to Rynth get you into the Upper Level, composed of three different areas: the shattered zone, the ooze pools, and the upper shrine. There are no maps for these areas, but we describe them below.

The Labyrinth: Beneath the Upper Level is the labyrinth, a mazy sequence of rooms that you can generate anew for each campaign (or session!) by rolling dice on our labyrinth generator.

Temple of the Archmage: The lowest level contains three carefully mapped, detailed rooms that compose the living dungeon of Rynth's tri-part heart: the Arena, the Hall of Prophecy, and the Sacred Temple. Each is centered around a pillar of magical energy. Adventurers intent on slaying the living dungeon must snuff out all three magic pillars.

THE CULT OF THE ARCHMAGE

The oozefolk have a distant memory of when the dungeon was shackled by the Archmage and have formed a religion around the event. They venerate the Archmage as their god and believe that those who are worthy will be taken to fight in the heavens on his behalf.

Their faith is a time-distorted remembrance of a pact made between them and the Archmage—that he would leave them in peace in exchange for several of them being teleported away when there was need to serve him as guardians for the Imperial Tomb.

The name of the dungeon, "Rynth" is a corruption of "Labyrinth". The oozefolk have never seen sky, know nothing of trees, in fact the world beyond their sprawling dungeon is unknown to them—though over the long centuries some have escaped their dungeon and found their way into the wider world, or at least up to Vantage.

For more on oozefolk and using oozefolk as player characters, see page 186.

ADVENTURING IN RYПTH

Rynth's Tension/Wandering Monster table uses a d20, instead of a d12, as it combines the tension and wandering monster tables for the random, oozing fun of it. As with earlier dungeons, add a bonus to the tension/wandering monster table roll equal to twice the number of battles the adventurers have fought since their last full heal-up.

RYПTH TEПSIOП/WAПDERIПG MOПSTER TABLE (D20)

1-10. Nothing of note. A few glowing oozes slime their way across the ceiling and walls, providing illumination. Add +2 to the next roll on this table.

11-13. Many glowing oozes slime their way across the ceiling and there is an abundance of plants and bugs—a tiny eco-system. Nothing in this area is harmful if the characters leave it alone. Some of the larger beetles might attempt to bite if somebody picks them up and handles them. The area looks cultivated, it might be an oozefolk farm.

14-15. Curious oozefolk. They've never seen another race, so adventurers appear as figures from their legends. Depending on how the adventurers behave, they might be met with cowering fear, religious adulation, or cautious curiosity.

16-19. Oozefolk warrior-priests, almost certainly eager to kill on behalf of their god, or because they are having a bad day. See the section about Oozefolk Warrior Battles on page 145. Alternatively, if you are saving the oozefolk from your worst adversaries, this is a battle with those adversaries, instead.

20+. A monstrous ooze or many monstrous oozes. They're against you no matter what your purpose in the dungeon. Use grey ooze (page 30), lesser black puddings (page 30), and perhaps a rainbow pudding (page 178).

DUNGEON GOAL

You have a choice on how you approach Rynth. Most groups, even if they are aligned with the Archmage, probably don't have any trouble breaking into it like a normal dungeon and causing havoc. This is especially true for a group that is not really on the Archmage's side.

Still, we present the oozefolk as somewhat sympathetic creatures. So, maybe this isn't a living dungeon the PCs must slay. Maybe their enemies are trying to slay the dungeon to eliminate the Archmage's oozefolk allies?

No one is entirely certain why the Archmage went to such lengths to set up the oozefolk's living dungeon. Maybe he felt guilty about something, or maybe he has seen a future when a great oozefolk hero sets the world right. (That's your cue, player character oozefolk!)

If your adventurers are on the oozefolk's side or decide to be on their side midway through the dungeon, use attacking adversary group antagonists instead of oozefolk defenders as the main enemies.

ENTRANCES TO RYNTH

It is up to you how the adventurers gain access to Rynth. The entrance may be in a tomb or through a magic portal, or maybe it's just a simple crack in the ground. Because Rynth is below Redfield Valley, the crash of Vantage might open several pathways to Rynth.

As this is a living dungeon, albeit one that is "tamed," it could be that wards breaking caused it to start awakening and climbing upward to the surface. The intelligent dungeon inhabitants know something is happening, but they're not sure what, exactly. Some believe it is their prophesied end-of-days, so they look for their god's return (the Archmage) and prepare to fight his enemies. A clever wizard might be able to convince the oozefolk that she (or he) is their god, though it would require at least several DC 30 skill checks and a few good icon relationship results to do so.

THE UPPER LEVELS

The upper levels of Rynth are fairly mundane, mostly empty, and interlinked.

THE SHATTERED ZONE

This could be the entrance to the dungeon. Rynth collided with something—perhaps another dungeon, a natural cavern, or a piece of Vantage's wreckage that impacted deep in the valley. The ceiling is collapsed in this area, the walls have holes in them, and dust pours down from above. There are no injured oozefolk here, they just "oozed out" from under the rubble.

If you end up running a battle here because of wandering monsters or the tension tables, fill the area with rubble, rockslides, and odd holes that end up as dead ends for anyone with a corporeal form.

THE SLIME POOLS

This area is full of deep pools of differently colored slime. Occasionally, the slime shifts, ripples, burps, or bubbles; but for the most part, the slime is quiescent. These are the birthing chambers for the non-sentient slimes in the dungeon. Adventurers who venture into the pools (for whatever foolish reason) take 3d6 damage of a random type (roll a d12):

    1-6. Acid
    7-8. Lightning
      9. Fire
     10. Force
    11-12. Roll twice more using a d10 and add 1d6 to the damage

If you end up running a full battle here, have fun with slime pools in a palette of wild colors seldom seen in dungeons.

THE UPPER SHRINE

This is a huge room, dedicated to worship of the Archmage. Acid-etched pictures cover the walls and pillars; they tell the story of their god and how he created them, and how at the end of days he will bring his chosen people to heaven to fight armies of monsters who try to invade heaven. There's a map of "heaven" on the ceiling—which is actually a partial map of the Imperial Tomb).

OOZEFOLK NAMES

In ASH's game, the standard naming pattern for individual oozefolk of Rynth is based on their color and their parentage. The oozefolk appreciate very fine gradations of color!

Amber Out-of-Jade, Auburn From-Clementine, Azure From-Celadon, Blue From-Indigo, Cherry Out-of-Bianca, Cyan From-Cherry, Cyan From-Marigold, Green Out-of-Hyacinth, Hazel Out-of-Magenta, Ice Out-of-Magenta, Ivory From-Lavender, Jet Out-of-Jet, Lilac From-Coral, Mauve Out-of-Moss, Olive From-Olive, Pearl Out-of-Pink, Raven Out-of-Rose, Red From-Pink, Rust From-Saffron, Sage From-Scarlett, Sienna From-Ruby, Slate From-Goldie, Violet Out-of-Ebony

THE LABYRINTH OF RYNTH

For the labyrinth itself, we include a random generator. First, roll a d12 to establish the *Dungeon Level Shape*; then, roll a d6 to determine the *Exit to the Temple of the Archmage*; then, roll a d10 five times on the *Rynth Dungeon Generator* to stock the dungeon levels.

The dungeon has as many levels as you need, all stocked with oozes or enemies according to the *Wandering Monster* table. When you decide the party has delved deep enough, they finally reach the lowest level—the Temple of the Archmage.

The first nine labyrinth layouts owe their names and categorization to Matthew J. Neagley of *Gnome Stew* fame, from his essay "*The Nine Forms of the Five Room Dungeon.*" The final three are loops that I named myself. In this table, Area A is always the entrance to the level. The exact locations, layouts, and shapes of the areas are unimportant—what is important is how they connect to each other.

DUNGEON LEVEL SHAPE (D12)

1. The Railroad

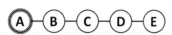

2. Foglio's Snail

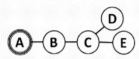

3. The Fauchard Fork

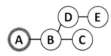

4. The Moose

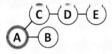

5. The Evil Mule

6. The Paw

7. The Vendetta

8. The Arrow

9 The Cross

10. Law's Box

11. Ash's Hourglass

12. The Everything's Connected Star

Exit to the Temple of the Archmage (d6)

1. Area A
2. Area B
3. Area C
4. Area D
5. Area E
6. More than one area has a link to other parts of the dungeon: roll twice more. Multiple results for the same area indicate there are multiple exits to new dungeon areas from the same area. For each 6 you roll after the first, add another room to this level that's connected to Area A.

Rynth Dungeon Generator (d10 x 5)

1. A corridor area. There is a 50% chance it leads to 1d6 + 1 rooms (roll a d6):
    1. Store rooms
    2. Empty rooms
    3. Slime-pool/breeding chambers
    4. Cells (possibly a jail?)
    5. Barracks
    6. "Farm" rooms
2. A guard area (roll a d6 twice):
    1. Guard room
    2. Checkpoint with heavy door
    3. Armory
    4. Monster pen
    5. Training area
    6. Barracks
3. A living area (roll a d4 twice):
    1. Homes (2d6 doors; each leads to an area that contains a kitchen, bedroom, living area, etc.)
    2. Workshop
    3. Communal area
    4. Civic area (roll a d4):
        1. Gymnasium
        2. Courtroom
        3. Sports arena
        4. School
4. A small, natural cavern
5. A maze of empty corridors with no discernable purpose
6. A mine (with domesticated oozes dissolving the metals out of the mine walls)
7. A former mine now used as a rubbish dump for anything that the oozes can't dissolve
8. A shrine to the Archmage
9. A foundry (roll a d3):
    1. Metal
    2. Glass
    3. A substance produced from acid-dissolved stone called "Rynth Metal"
10. A large, natural cavern (roll a d20 twice):
    1. An entrance to the underdark, which the oozefolk priests sealed and kept secret
    2-10. A deep underground lake
    11-15. Fantastic crystalline formations
    16-19. A shallow underground lake and wide shale beach
    20. Walls painted and acid-etched by the oozefolk

THE TEMPLE OF THE ARCHMAGE

This is the living heart of the dungeon. All three areas—the arena, the hall, and the sacred temple—are connected to each other as integral elements of the great temple. Each area/room centers on a magical pillar. To "kill" this living dungeon, the PCs must do 100 points of damage to each of the three pillars. The pillars regenerate at a rate of 10 hp per round in which they don't take damage; however, if the adventurers manage to drop a pillar to 0 hp, it "stays dead" for a couple hours, then dies forever if all three pillars are extinguished.

THE ARENA

This looks startlingly like the gladiatorial arenas in Axis. Around the periphery are many glass-topped pits that contain ooze monsters. The creatures are slumbering, awaiting the next match. The oozefolk priests practice here for their end-times battle on behalf of the divine Archmage. Battles are not normally fatal, but they can make an exception for the adventurers.

The Pillar: A twisting shaft of water and fire is in the center of the arena (touching it does 4d6 fire and cold damage).

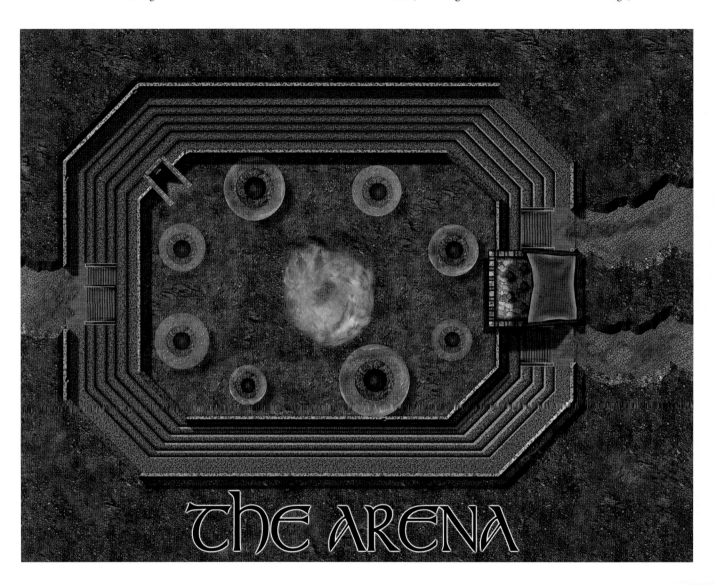

THE ARENA

THE HALL OF PROPHECY

Oozefolk priests come here to meditate and receive visions from their god. The hall is guarded (the priests are aware by now that the adventurers or their other enemies are on their way). Use an *Oozefolk Warrior Battle*. . . unless you're staging an adversary group invasion instead.

    The Pillar: A vertical shaft of light and air is in this hall (touching it does 4d6 force and lightning damage).

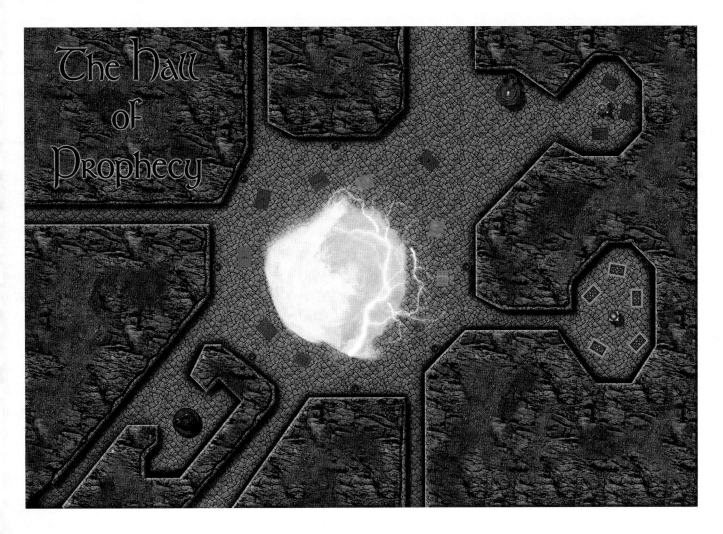

THE SACRED TEMPLE

The oozefolk consider this area the holy of holies. All around the temple are acid-etched depictions of the Archmage, and the prophecies and laws given to them by their priesthood are written in the archaic script of the oozefolk.

   The Pillar: A pillar of roiling clouds and darkness is at the center of the temple (touching it deals 4d6 thunder and negative energy damage, which applies to melee attacks against the pillar as well—it's better to send a spellcaster to destroy this pillar than a sword-swinger).

The Sacred Temple

FOLK YES, OOZES NO

Oozefolk are not technically oozes because we got all logical for a moment and gave specific abilities to all oozes on page 241 of the *13th Age* core rulebook. Oozefolk shouldn't have those abilities. Well, there's also the fact that they're humanoid.

CITIZEN OF RYNTH

Just your everyday ooze person.

5th level archer [HUMANOID]
Initiative: +9

Rubbery fist +9 vs. AC—8 damage, and the target takes 5 ongoing acid damage that ends when the target is no longer engaged with any oozefolk.

R: Thrown rock or spear +11 vs. AC (1 nearby or faraway enemy)—14 damage.

AC	19	
PD	17	**HP 45**
MD	13	

OOZEFOLK WARRIOR

This tough customer has trained its whole life to fight the "evil solids."

Double-strength 5th level troop [HUMANOID]
Initiative: +10

War-spade +10 vs. AC—30 damage
  Natural even hit: +12 damage
  Natural odd hit: Target pops free.

R: Throwing club +10 vs. AC (one nearby enemy)—20 damage
  Natural even hit: +10 damage.

Oozefolk form-shifting tricks: Once per round when intercepted or about to suffer an opportunity attack, the warrior can ignore the interception or attack, but then receives a −2 attack penalty until the end of its next turn.

Nastier Specials
Armor: Armor plates stuck to its body provide +3 AC.

AC	21	
PD	19	**HP 144**
MD	15	

OOZEFOLK WARRIOR BATTLES

#/Level of PCs	Citizen of Rynth	Oozefolk Warrior	Oozefolk Templar	Oozefolk Priest
3 x 5th level	2	2	0	0
3 x 5th level	1	0	2	1
4 x 5th level	3	1	0	1
4 x 5th level	0	1	2	1
5 x 5th level	3	2	0	1
5 x 5th level	0	1	2	2
6 x 5th level	4	2	0	1
6 x 5th level	0	1	3	2
7 x 5th level	3	2	0	2
7 x 5th level	0	2	2	2
3 x 6th level	4	2	0	0
3 x 6th level	2	0	3	1
4 x 6th level	4	2	0	1
4 x 6th level	0	2	3	1
5 x 6th level	4	3	0	1
5 x 6th level	0	2	3	2
6 x 6th level	4	3	0	2
6 x 6th level	0	3	3	2
7 x 6th level	5	3	1	2
7 x 6th level	0	3	3	3

OOZEFOLK TEMPLAR

This warrior oozes conviction.

6th level wrecker [OOZE]
Initiative: +12

Flaming spear +11 vs. AC—16 damage
Natural even hit: +10 fire damage.

Surprising reach +9 vs. AC (1 nearby enemy)—10 damage
Natural even hit: +10 fire damage.

Close is too close: Deal 2d6 acid damage to any enemy engaged with the oozefolk templar that rolls a natural odd melee attack roll against it.

AC	21	
PD	20	**HP 94**
MD	18	

OOZEFOLK PRIEST

Its religion says you need to die. It is nice to see faith in action.

7th level leader [OOZE]
Initiative: +13

Sacrificial spiked hammer +12 vs. AC—20 damage
Natural even miss: 10 holy damage.

C: Bolstering word +12 vs. MD (1d3 nearby or far away enemies in a group)—20 holy and acid damage
Natural even hit: One oozefolk heals 10 hit points, or once per bolstering word attack, one random "dead" non-mook oozefolk "schlops" back together with 15 hit points
Limited use: Only when the escalation die is odd

R: Word of rebuke +12 vs. MD (one nearby or far away enemy)—Target pops free, target must immediately move far away from the priest as a free action and is then stunned (easy save ends)
First failed save: Target becomes vulnerable to acid (hard save ends) and the save against stunned becomes a normal save
Aftereffect (immediately after the target saves against the stunned condition): Target takes 20 psychic damage
Miss: 20 psychic damage
Limited use: Enemies can only be hit by *word of rebuke* once per battle; after that, each attack counts as a miss and no attack roll is made.

Oozefolk form-shifting tricks: Once per round, when intercepted or about to suffer an opportunity attack, the priest can ignore the interception or attack, but receives a −2 attack penalty until the end of its next turn.

AC	23	
PD	21	**HP 108**
MD	17	

OOZEFOLK NPCs

If your campaign begins treating the oozefolk of Rynth as NPCs to interact with instead of villains to slay, here are some characters to get you started.

Amber Out-of-Slate-From-Goldie—Amber is an oozefolk leader from a long line of such leaders and oversees several levels of Rynth.

Azure From-Azure—Azure is a teacher, helping educate young minds about the wonders of the Archmage and the triumphs of oozefolk history. Amber is shocked to meet non-oozefolk and learn that there is a world beyond Rynth.

Celadon From-Cherry—Celadon is a young oozefolk who works as a miner but dreams of exploring newly discovered caverns.

Coral From-Mauve—Coral is a warrior-priest, trained by birth to serve the Archmage should the oozefolk ever be called into service. Coral secretly does not believe that the Archmage is real.

Cyan Out-of-Indigo—Cyan is a wizard-priest of the Archmage who prays daily that the Archmage will return and show the oozefolk the wonders of magic.

Indigo Out-of-Pearl—Indigo is an architect, working with miners and oozeherds to expand the dungeon of Rynth.

Jade Out-of-Rust—Jade makes a living as a dancer and entertainer and is often called upon to perform religious plays featuring the Archmage.

Magenta From-Red—Magenta is an oozeherd, training and caring for the many domesticated lesser oozes that live in Rynth.

Rose From-Red—Rose is an oozefolk farmer who tends the many underground gardens of the levels surrounding its own.

CHAPTER 8:

PAST AND FUTURE

ADVENTURES FOR 6TH AND 7TH LEVEL CHARACTERS

THE GRAND SPIKE

The Grand Spike is a huge, semi-intact piece of wreckage from Vantage. It's not just any piece of wreckage: it contains the control crystal that directed the energy that kept Vantage aloft! No matter who the adventurers are working for or against, everybody is after the crystal (so the adventurers had better get there first)!

THE TOMB OF THE SERPENT ARCHONS

The Tomb of the Serpent Archons is the last refuge of an evil that predates even the Dragon Empire. Almost every icon wants to prevent the emergence of the serpent archons . . . though they may have worshipped The Three or perhaps even the Great Gold Wyrm in a past age.

THE GRAND SPIKE

Level range: 6th and 7th

A huge, oil-sheen metal pyramid looms over the smashed and rubble-filled landscape. There are rents and tears in the metal, which allow access to the interior. Waves of colored energy splash over and out of the pyramid, mostly from its apex.

The Grand Spike was part of the underside of Vantage that fell from the sky and landed upside-down; most of it is completely wrecked and buried deep in mud, but the uppermost part of the ruin is intact. On Vantage, it resembled an elongated, downward-pointing four-sided pyramid; now, it is a mass of twisted metal and broken mechanisms that rises from a sea of mud.

MAGICAL MARVEL OR MECHANICAL WONDER?

The Grand Spike is obviously a machine, but is it *magical* or *technological*? Well, it's as much of one or the other as you like.

Fantasy is full of lost civilizations with superior technology than those that came after (such as Atlantis, Mu, Jack Vance's Dying Earth); this may be one of the few surviving pieces of high technology from a lost age that predates the Dragon Empire's counting system.

Then again, all those turning cogs could be lining up glyphs in just the right order, mixing the right potions at the correct time, or staying in tune with the cosmos itself; in other words, it might be a giant, magical engine that automagically casts thousands of spells every second.

Maybe it's both—a giant-scale "arcanotech" engine that combined ancient lost science and cutting-edge magic to both hide Vantage and keep it afloat.

Two things are certain: the great machine's inner workings are most likely far beyond the adventurers' understanding, and it is thoroughly and completely broken.

ADVENTURING IN THE GRAND SPIKE

The Grand Spike's interior is a confusing mass of brass pipes, cogs, glowing crystals, and chains. There are no internal doors, just huge interconnected chambers with catwalks magically suspended in the air.

It is important to note that because the Grand Spike is upside-down, the catwalks are upside-down, too; thus, there are no hand-rails when the characters walk on them. Thankfully, they can still traverse the underside of the stairs.

Falling and walking outside catwalks: Walking around in places other than on the catwalks is dangerous: the cogs are sharp, mechanisms can move unexpectedly, and the glowing crystals randomly discharge magic. If the PCs still want to chance it, it takes a DC 30 skill check to move through a non-catwalk area without taking damage; failure means they take an amount of damage equal to the amount by which they failed the roll, and this applies each round they remain in a non-catwalk area. The same applies when a character falls off the catwalks into the mechanisms; although, in this case, the first skill check

is a DC 40 check! It's not hard to get back on the catwalk, the PCs automatically do so with a single check no matter how low their result, but if they fail they'll get hurt in the process.

Several traps and magical defenses in the Grand Spike can knock adventurers into the cogs, so you'll want to keep track of these skill checks. Not surprisingly, the Grand Spike's servitor creatures have no problem moving safely through the cogs, but in a fight against adversaries, enemies forced into the cogs should probably take 2d10 damage to get back onto the catwalk.

Tension in the Grand Spike: The tension table rules inside the Grand Spike are slightly different than the other dungeons. Every time the adventurers enter a new area, they should roll a d12 on the tension table. Add the higher of two possible bonuses to the roll: either twice the number of battles the PCs have fought in the Grand Spike since their last full heal-up, or the value of the escalation die when their most recent battle in the Grand Spike ended.

See page 53 for our general advice on how and when to use tension tables. Here in the Grand Spike, we advise against rolling on the tension table for *every* new area you enter. The Grand Spike's strange rooms have many odd things going on already, so it's a good idea to assess your group's progress and experience before adding more. If you've got a sneaky group that manages to avoid most fights, and it seems like they're getting off easy, keep rolling on the tension table until they're not. If it's already a tension-filled bloodbath, rolling on the table for every other area may be enough.

Starting higher up: On the other hand, don't go easy with the tension table if the PCs somehow manage to enter higher up in the pyramid. If, for instance, the adventurers enter the pyramid by climbing up to Area U, you may want to roll 2d12 for each tension table roll and use the higher roll.

GRAND SPIKE TENSION TABLE (D12)

1-8. Nothing of note happens; add +2 to the next roll on this table.

9. A "safe" area, devoid of dangers beyond the immediately obvious problems listed in the area writeup.

10. The crystals in this area pulse with light—they're dark one moment and blindingly bright the next.

11. The mechanisms shift, rearranging themselves into a new configuration. Anybody who tarries here is in danger. If the PCs end up fighting a battle here, apply result 12 below when the escalation die reaches 2+.

12. The mechanisms briefly whirl into action, though exactly why is hard to discern. The catwalk begins to shake; choose two or three affected PCs who need to make a DC 30 skill check to avoid falling off into the mechanisms.

13+ *odd*. Encounter defenses. Roll on the *Grand Spike Magical Defenses* table.

14+ *even*. Encounter a wandering monster. Choose or roll a monster from the *Grand Spike Wandering Monster* table.

Vantage's ruins still have a few active magical defenses, though they "go offline" often. Still, they may activate in any area at any time attacking the adventurers while they explore the Grand Spike. When they do, roll on the *Grand Spike Magical Defenses* table.

GRAND SPIKE MAGICAL DEFENSE TABLE (D6)

1. A forcefield seals off one of the exits to this area. It takes a DC 30 skill check to destroy the barrier by force or circumvent it by making a hole in a wall; failure means the adventurer takes 3d8 force damage. A ritual caster who spends half an hour unpicking the magic of the forcefield automatically succeeds, but at the end of that half hour just as the barrier comes down, it's time to make another roll on the tension table.

2. A shimmering field suddenly appears in one of the exits to this area. Any character who passes through the lightning barrier takes 4d8 lightning damage. Eventually, the barrier burns itself out; but that takes about 5 minutes to half an hour and just as the lightning ceases, it's time to make another roll on the tension table.

3. An orb appears in the room and attacks the adventurers before flying away. It takes a DC 30 skill check to hide as the orb enters the area. **C: Thunder orb +20 vs. PD (1d3 enemies)—2d20 thunder damage.** Adventurers who successfully hide are not among the targets.

4. The pyramid's "machinery" interacts badly with the adventurers' magic items, causing crystal feedback. Choose 1d3 random PCs and deal 1d4 lightning damage to each chosen PC per true magic item that PC has attuned.

5. Each adventurer feels a strange wave of arcane energy, but it's unclear what happened, at first. **Strange wave +12 vs. PD (each PC who lacks a positive or conflicted icon relationship with the Archmage)**—inflicts a −2 penalty to all skill checks, until the target rolls a natural 1 or 20 on a skill check or attack.

6. Each adventurer feels a draining wave of arcane energy, but it's unclear what happened, at first (tell affected PCs they feel "drained"; they'll find out what it means soon enough). **Draining wave +12 vs. MD (each PC who lacks a positive or conflicted icon relationship with the Archmage)**—the target is hampered (normal save ends, 16+), but the effect does not kick in until the next time the target rolls initiative.

GRAND SPIKE WANDERING MONSTER TABLE (D12)

1-3. An adversary group that is probably associated with an enemy icon that hopes to get to the crystal first. There'll be another adversary group battle at the top of the pyramid, so decide which you want to pit against the PCs here (use the *Adversary Groups* appendix that starts on page 191).

4-5. Golems that served on Vantage; they now perceive the PCs as intruders, no matter how well-intentioned they try to appear. Use the Golems adversary group on page 207.

6-9. A mixed group of Grand Spike constructs on roving clean-up duty. Use one of the battles from the next section.

10-11. Elemental defenders of the Grand Spike (see page 153).

12. Lucky adventurers: no battle for you! Instead, you find 1d3 champion-tier magic item(s) of a highly random nature scattered in the cogs (consider using crystal items from page 189).

GRAND SPIKE CONSTRUCTS

These creatures served inside Vantage's underbelly, servicing the arcane mechanisms and fulfilling the rituals that kept Vantage hovering in place.

Several of the encounters here specify which creatures you should use; in cases where you're fighting several of one construct type, we leave the math to you. The battles we list below are for instances in which you mix all the constructs together.

#/ Level of PCs	Drill-bird	Quartz Quadruped	Glass Spider	Crystal Crab	Machine Acolyte
3 x 6th level	1	1	0	1	0
3 x 6th level	2	0	3	0	1
4 x 6th level	1	1	0	2	0
4 x 6th level	2	0	8	0	1
5 x 6th level	1	2	0	2	0
5 x 6th level	2	0	8	0	2
6 x 6th level	3	2	0	2	0
6 x 6th level	4	0	8	0	2
7 x 6th level	4	2	0	3	0
7 x 6th level	4	0	8	0	3
3 x 7th level	1	1	0	2	0
3 x 7th level	3	0	3	0	1
4 x 7th level	2	2	0	2	0
4 x 7th level	3	0	8	0	1
5 x7th level	2	3	0	2	0
5 x7th level	5	0	8	0	1
6 x 7th level	3	3	0	3	0
6 x 7th level	6	0	8	0	2
7 x 7th level	4	4	0	4	0
7 x 7th level	6	0	10	0	3

DRILL-BIRD

It looks like a giant hummingbird with a drill for a head. Or a saw. Or a hammer.

6th level spoiler [CONSTRUCT]
Initiative: +11

Tool attack +12 vs. AC—18 damage
  Natural even hit: Choose one tool effect (below).

Flight: The bird can dart swiftly in and out of tight spaces or hover in place.

Tool Effects
Hammer head: Target must save (11+) or be weakened until the end of its next turn.
Drill beak: Target must save (11+) or take 10 ongoing damage.
Saw beak: Target must save (11+) or take a cumulative −2 to AC until the end of the fight.
Welding torch: Target must save (11+) or take 10 fire damage.

AC 22
PD 20   HP 84
MD 16

QUARTZ QUADRUPED

Call them diamond dogs if you must, but they're still more like crystalline leonine lizard-things.

Large 6th level blocker [CONSTRUCT]
Initiative: +12

Claw and bite +11 vs. AC—42 damage.

C: Crystal-forming breath +11 vs. AC (1d3 nearby enemies in a group)—34 damage, and the target is stuck (save ends)
  1st failed save: Target is hampered (save ends stuck and hampered)
  2nd failed save: Target is helpless (save ends stuck, hampered, and helpless)
  Limited use: Only when the escalation die is odd.

Climber: The quartz quadruped can run along any surface that can support it; it can even use its claws and crystal-forming powers to run upside-down along ceilings.

Burst of speed: Twice per fight, the quartz quadruped can pop free and immediately move to intercept any moving character, even if it would not normally be able to intercept that character.

AC 22
PD 20   HP 180
MD 16

GLASS SPIDER

This tiny menace can chew metal, stone, and glass, and spin strands of the same stuff from its body. Given enough time, it can create cogs, complex machines, traps, walls. . . anything, really.

7th level mook [CONSTRUCT]
Initiative: +14

Chew, chew, chew +13 vs. AC—10 damage, and the target takes a cumulative –1 to their attacks for the rest of the battle (up to a maximum of –4). Characters can normally repair chewed weapons and implements during a short rest.

C: Weaver +12 vs. PD (1d3 nearby or far away enemies in a group)—Target is stuck (hard save ends, 16+). Each failed save deals 6 damage to the struggling character.

AC 23	
PD 19	**HP 27 (mook)**
MD 19	

Mook: Kill one glass spider mook for every 27 damage you deal to the mob.

CRYSTAL CRAB

It's a squat and highly functional energy engineer, adept at removing inferior components. That's you, *in case you're wondering.*

7th level wrecker [CONSTRUCT]
Initiative: +9

Sophisticated claws +12 vs. AC (3 attacks)—8 damage
Natural even hit: 10 ongoing lightning damage.

R: Energy field +12 vs. PD (1d3 random nearby enemies)—20 energy damage, of a type that was last used in an attack this battle (or lightning, if none).
Limited use: Only when the escalation die is odd.

Reactive programming: The crystal crab gains a cumulative +2 bonus to its AC and PD each time it is hit by an attack. When the bonus reaches +4, the crab gains a +4 bonus to attacks on its next turn, but its defensive bonus resets to 0 at the end of that turn.

Climber: The crystal crab can scuttle along any surface that can support it; it can even use its claws and engineering skills to run upside-down along ceilings.

AC	21	
PD	19	**HP 100**
MD	17	

MACHINE ACOLYTE

An acolyte of metal, lightning, and recycled fleshy bits from willing wizardly donors.

8th level spoiler [CONSTRUCT]
Initiative: +13

Telekinetic grasp +15 vs. AC—28 force damage, and the target pops free and is slammed about
Natural 18+: The target is moved to an unfortunate position (target must roll twice for its next attack and use the worst roll).

R: Reorganize matter +15 vs. PD (one nearby or far away enemy)—22 damage, and the target is dazed (save ends).

Wall of metal and crystal: Once per round, as an interrupt action, the machine acolyte can make a gesture to create a small wall in front of a moving character, ending movement for all but insubstantial creatures. The wall dissipates at the start of the next round.

Reshape environment: The machine acolyte can walk anywhere in the Grand Spike it pleases, creating temporary stairs and bridges as it moves. This is probably not as useful outside the Spike.

AC 23	
PD 21	**HP 118**
MD 17	

ELEMENTAL DEFENDERS OF THE GRAND SPIKE

The Grand Spike was never a hospitable environment for squishy organic servitors. Carefully bound elementals handled most of the communication and security tasks that wizards ordinarily would have. An added bonus were the elemental power boosts whenever the Grand Spike required them.

For more on flux elementals, see *Bestiary 2*, page 76.

#/Level of PCs	Big Air Elemental	Big Flux Elemental	Lightning Elemental	Epic Air Elemental	Greater Flux Elemental
3 x 6th level	1	1	1	0	0
3 x 6th level	0	0	1	0	1
4 x 6th level	0	2	0	1	0
4 x 6th level	1	0	1	0	1
5 x 6th level	0	0	2	1	1
5 x 6th level	2	2	2	0	0
6 x 6th level	2	3	0	1	0
6 x 6th level	1	0	2	0	2
7 x 6th level	0	2	3	2	0
7 x 6th level	3	1	1	1	1
3 x 7th level	0	0	0	1	1
3 x 7th level	0	2	3	0	0
4 x 7th level	0	0	2	1	1
4 x 7th level	2	2	2	0	0
5 x7th level	0	0	2	1	2
5 x7th level	3	0	3	0	1
6 x 7th level	0	0	2	2	2
6 x 7th level	4	0	4	0	1
7 x 7th level	0	1	3	2	2

BIG AIR ELEMENTAL

7th level wrecker [ELEMENTAL]
Initiative: +14

Slam +13 vs. AC—20 damage

C: Swirling winds +13 vs. PD (1d3 random conscious nearby enemies)—18 damage
Natural even hit: The target pops free from the elemental.

Flight: It's quick and direct.

Resist non-spell damage 16+: When a non-spell attack targets this creature, the attacker must roll a natural 16+ on the attack roll or it only deals half damage.

Whirlwind transformation: Roll a d8 at the start of each of the air elemental's turns. If you roll less than or equal to the escalation die, it shifts into whirlwind form until the end of the battle. While in this form, it gains the following improved attack (and you stop rolling *whirlwind transformation* checks):
Elemental whirlwind +15 vs. PD (each enemy engaged with it *and* one nearby enemy)—22 damage
Miss: Half damage.

AC	22	
PD	21	**HP 88**
MD	17	

BIG FLUX ELEMENTAL

7th level troop [ELEMENTAL]
Initiative: +12 (probably irrelevant)

Roll 1d4 when the flux elemental rolls initiative and when it shifts to determine its new form, a benefit, and its current attack

1. *Shift to air:* When the big flux elemental shifts to air, it gains flight until it shifts to a different form, and it also gains a +1 attack bonus (cumulative) until the end of the battle!

Wind touch +12 vs. PD—20 damage
Miss: 7 damage.

2. *Shift to earth:* When the big flux elemental shifts to earth, it gains a +1 AC bonus (cumulative) until the end of the battle!

Rocky fist +12 vs. AC—26 damage.

3. *Shift to fire:* When the big flux elemental shifts to fire, it gains a +1d8 damage bonus when it hits with an attack (cumulative) until the end of the battle!

Scorching hands +12 vs. PD—15 fire damage, and 10 ongoing fire damage
Miss: 8 fire damage.

4. *Shift to water:* When the big flux elemental shifts to water, it gains 2d10 additional hp (cumulative) until the end of the battle!

Whoosh and a slam +12 vs. PD—15 damage
Natural even hit: If the target is staggered, it is dazed until the end of its next turn.

Shift: Unless the escalation die is 6+, roll a d6 at the start of the flux elemental's turn. On a 4+, the flux elemental shifts.

AC	21	
PD	21	**HP 100**
MD	18	

LIGHTNING ELEMENTAL

Webs of lightning repeatedly streak in all directions, outlining the form of the creature and then dissipating. Each flash happens so fast, it leaves the thing's image burned into your eyes.

7th level spoiler [ELEMENTAL]
Initiative: +14

Lightning zap +12 vs. AC—20 lightning damage
Natural odd hit: The target is dazed until the end of its next turn
Metal affinity: The attack gains a +1 bonus against an enemy wearing metal armor or wielding a metal weapon.

R: Lightning strike +12 vs. PD (one nearby enemy or a far away enemy at −2 attack)—24 lightning damage
Metal affinity: The attack gains a +1 bonus against an enemy wearing metal armor or wielding a metal weapon.

Flight: Lightning elementals zip from place to place about half-as-quick as lightning, hovering above the ground to avoid being grounded.

Lightning storm transformation: Roll a d8 at the start of each of the lightning elemental's turns. If you roll less than or equal to the escalation die, it shifts into lightning storm form until the end of the battle. While in this form, it gains the following improved attack (and you stop rolling *lightning storm transformation* checks):
C: Storm strike +12 vs. PD (up to 2 nearby enemies)—20 lightning damage
Natural even roll: The elemental can include an additional target in the attack (requires attack roll) that hasn't been hit by *storm strike* this turn, but the attack only deals half damage.
Metal affinity: The attack gains a +1 bonus against an enemy wearing metal armor or wielding a metal weapon.

Resist lightning and thunder 16+: When a lightning or thunder attack targets this creature, the attacker must roll a natural 16+ on the attack roll or it only deals half damage.

AC	22	
PD	22	**HP 100**
MD	15	

EPIC AIR ELEMENTAL

9th level wrecker [ELEMENTAL]

Initiative: +16

Slam +15 vs. AC—40 damage

C: Swirling winds +15 vs. PD (1d3 random conscious nearby enemies)—28 damage
Natural even hit: The target pops free from the elemental.

Flight: It's quick and forceful.

Resist non-spell damage 16+: When a non-spell attack targets this creature, the attacker must roll a natural 16+ on the attack roll or it only deals half damage.

Whirlwind transformation: Roll a d6 at the start of each of the air elemental's turns. If you roll less than or equal to the escalation die, it shifts into whirlwind form until the end of the battle. While in this form, it gains the following improved attack (and you stop rolling *whirlwind transformation* checks):
Elemental whirlwind +17 vs. PD (each enemy engaged with it *and* one nearby enemy)—40 damage
Miss: Half damage.

Nastier Specials

R: Gale force jets +15 vs. PD (one nearby or far away enemy)—40 damage
Natural even hit: The target is dazed until the end of its next turn
Natural even miss: Half damage.

AC	24	
PD	23	**HP 140**
MD	19	

GREATER FLUX ELEMENTAL

9th level troop [ELEMENTAL]

Initiative: +15

Roll 1d4 when the flux elemental rolls initiative and when it shifts to determine its new form, a benefit, and its current attack

1. *Shift to air:* When the greater flux elemental shifts to air, it gains flight until it shifts to a different form, and it also gains a +1 attack bonus (cumulative) until the end of the battle!

Wind touch +14 vs. PD—35 damage
Miss: 15 damage.

2. *Shift to earth:* When the greater flux elemental shifts to earth, it gains a +1 AC bonus (cumulative) until the end of the battle!

Rocky fist +14 vs. AC—44 damage.

3. *Shift to fire:* When the greater flux elemental shifts to fire, it gains a +1d12 damage bonus when it hits with an attack (cumulative) until the end of the battle!

Scorching hands +14 vs. PD—25 fire damage, and 15 ongoing fire damage
Miss: 10 fire damage.

4. *Shift to water:* When the greater flux elemental shifts to water, it gains 6d6 additional hp (cumulative) until the end of the battle!

Whoosh and a slam +14 vs. PD—30 damage
Natural even hit: If the target is staggered, it is dazed until the end of its next turn.

Shift: Unless the escalation die is 6+, roll a d6 at the start of the flux elemental's turn. On a 4+, the flux elemental shifts.

AC	23	
PD	23	**HP 165**
MD	20	

ENTRANCES TO THE GRAND SPIKE

The Grand Spike's purpose was to focus the magic that kept Vantage in the air and undetectable. Waves of colored light flare from its surface, vaporizing the *glitterfall* as it descends; characters who wish to explore it must watch carefully for a gap in the waves of colored light, then rush toward the ruin's base. Once there, they must climb over the jagged metal structure to find an entrance before the magical colored light returns.

In other words, they must get to the exterior [Z], then find a hole to crawl inside [*to A, E, I, O, or U*]. Characters who want to search for an entrance higher up the structure might find it: the hole that enters Area U. However, climbing higher is considerably more dangerous.

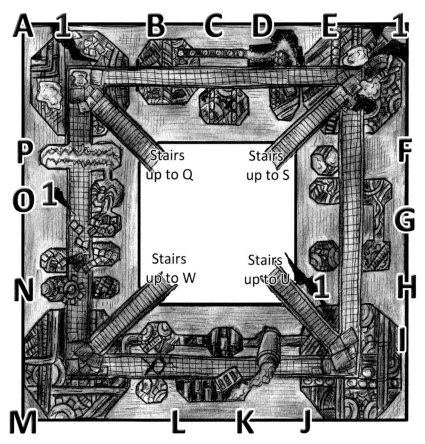

1 : Crack in metal exterior (leads to area Z)

AREAS OF THE GRAND SPIKE

We start with Area Z because it's the outside of the pyramid that the characters must deal with in one way or another as they make their way inside.

Z: THE ZIGGURAT

First impressions: A twisted metal landscape, alternately smooth and jagged.
Second glance: Waves of color wash across the metal, destroying everything they touch.
Joins to areas: A, E, I, O, and U (via holes in the Spike's exterior). U is the hole nearest the top, and it's partially closed off by a dark, crystal growth.

The surface of the Grand Spike is a dangerous place to be. Waves of color wash over it, vaporizing the *glitterfall*; characters who decide to climb up the ziggurat face a similar challenge. The magical waves seem to get stronger higher up the pyramid.

Entering lower: Accessing the lowest level is comparatively easy. If the characters climb (or fly) to the lower-level entrances [*leads to A, E, I, or O*], they must each make an easy save (6+) to enter. Failure means the color waves attack the character. **Color

DUNGEON GOAL

The goal of this dungeon is to get to the top of the spike. The crystal at the top of the spike is insanely valuable to whichever icon the party is friendly with (and highly desired by whichever icon the party opposes).

wave +20 vs. PD** 10 negative energy damage. *Miss:* 5 force damage.

Attempting to enter higher: If the characters climb (or fly) higher, searching for the more difficult entrance [*leads to U*], they must each make a hard save (16+). On a failure, a much more powerful wave attacks the character. **Vicious color wave +20 vs. PD (three attacks)**—15 negative energy damage, and this character cannot roll a skill check to search for the entrance to area U. *Miss:* 5 force damage.

Each character who can still search for a higher entrance may make a DC 25 skill check to find the hole that leads into area U. Only one character must succeed to allow the group to enter without being attacked again; however, if no one succeeds and the group searches high again, handle the saves and attacks as before.

A: ALEMBIC

First impressions: Lots of broken glass, strange fluids everywhere.
Second sniff: There are strange fumes here.
Joins to areas: B, P, Q, and Z

The catwalk through this area is wreathed in fumes. The characters find the devices and great mechanisms that fill the spike rather obscure—they look like an arcane collection of cogs, crystals, and chains. It's also obvious some sort of glass tubing previously ran out from the walls.

A strange liquid drips onto the catwalk (and the characters) from above; it takes a DC 25 skill check to avoid getting splashed by the liquid; failure means the liquid attacks. **Caustic splash +10 vs. AC**—2d10 acid damage.

The catwalk turns a corner here and heads deeper into the gloom [*leads to B and P*], away from the outside light that shines through the hole in the wall [*leads to Z*]. There are also stairs that lead up from the catwalk toward smells of heated metal and something burning [*leads to Q*].

B: BILTONG

First impressions: Strange red cloth dangles between the larger cogs.
Second sniff: That looks like skin, not cloth. There are smells of blood.
Joins to areas: A, and C

As the characters enter this area, they hear a dripping sound. The acolytes who were in this area when Vantage fell were sucked into the mechanism; the crystals absorbed their souls (and most of their bodies).

Long strips of torn skin dangle between the cogs, and the characters realize the dripping sound is blood. Looting the bodies yields one crystal item (see page 189 for details on crystal items).

The catwalk stretches back toward light [*leads to A*] and onward into an even more dimly lit area [*leads to C*].

C: CANTICLE

First impressions: A regular chiming sound, like a distant gong.
Second glance: Runes cover the cogs here.
Joins to areas: B, and D

Magic users who enter this area feel enervated—the runes on the cogs are draining their magic. Those with daily or recharge spells must make a successful DC 20 skill check or the runes suck one expendable ability away from them (they choose what they lose; they regain it at their next full rest).

The crystals in this area are dim, providing highlights to the darkness rather than actual illumination; the crystals brighten with every spell they suck away from the characters.

The catwalk leads forward [*to B*] and back [*to D*].

D: DIRGE

First impressions: A droning sound emanates from somewhere nearby, but it's hard to locate.
Second impression: The sound is slowly rising in pitch.
Joins to areas: C, and E

As the characters explore this area, they notice the crystals in the mechanism getting steadily brighter. It takes a DC 25 skill check to get through this area safely before the crystals discharge. Those who fail their roll might be hit by magical lightning. **Crystal discharge +15 vs. PD**—2d8 + 10 lightning damage.

The catwalk leads toward darkness and chiming sounds [*leads to C*] and toward light and the sounds of a muffled voice [*leads to E*].

E: ELEGY

First impressions: A muffled voice repeats the same words over and over.
Second impression: *"Avant! This chamber harbors dangers! Avant! This chamber harbors dangers!"*
Joins to areas: D, F, S, and Z

This area has a tear in the wall, which lets in light from outside [*leads to Z*]. The catwalk turns the corner here [*leads to D and F*]; and a stairway leads upward [*to S*]. The illumination from the hole in the outer wall lights the room, but it doesn't stretch very far down the catwalk.

A body is caught in the catwalk's rails; it takes a DC 25 skill check to haul it up to the catwalk. The body is that of a dead acolyte. Looting the body yields a crystal magic item (see page 189).

F: FORMIC

First impressions: There's a strong smell of acid.
Second glance: Something dark moves over the cogs above the adventurers.
Joins to areas: E, and G

The smell of acid is very strong here, and something is moving about in the dark. Unless the characters are already fighting a wandering monster battle, hit them with an attack by several lesser black puddings (page 30).

If the characters attacked Rynth instead of defending it, consider adding an oozefolk from page 146 as an extra complication—with no extra credit for the tougher battle!

The catwalk stretches onward toward a darkened tunnel [*leads to G*], and toward a well-lit area with the sounds of a muffled voice [*leads to E*].

G: GOSSAMER

First impressions: Tendrils of light illuminate this area, stretching from floor to ceiling.
Second glance: It looks like the tendrils are weaving together into a web.
Joins to areas: F, and H

The mechanism is attempting to repair itself here. As the characters move through the area, the tendrils of light attempt to grab and crush them to fit their bodies into gaps that remain in the cog work. It is a DC 30 skill check to avoid the tendrils, otherwise they grab hold and try to crush the character. **Tendrils +15 vs. PD (two attacks on each character who failed the roll)—3d4 damage.**

The catwalk here is in almost complete darkness and stretches out both forward and back *[leads to F and H]*.

H: HALCYON

First impressions: The cogs here spin freely, but they don't seem to be connected to the rest of the great mechanism.
Second glance: The cogs are spinning faster and faster.
Joins to areas: G, and I

The mechanism fully repaired itself in this area, but it seems to be missing links to other areas. The cogs spin freely, getting faster and faster as they spin. It doesn't *seem* dangerous. . .
The catwalk here is in almost complete darkness. The characters can head one direction into faint light *[leads to I]* or head the other into darkness *[leads to G]*.

I: INOSCULATE

First impressions: The cogs in this area fit together so finely, they are almost like tiles.
Second sniff: The cogs have glowing writing on them.
Joins to areas: H, J, U, and Z

This area is full of tight-fitting cogs that line the walls like tiles. Upon further inspection, the characters realize the cogs have writing on them, and the writing is glowing. It seems the mechanism fully repaired itself here, but it is missing links to other areas. The glowing writing can mean as much as you want it to mean. If you have odd information to impart that seems appropriate, this could be a good place for cryptic clues.

There is a fissure in the wall that lets in a bit of light from the outside *[leads to Z]*. A stairway leads up into more faint light *[leads to U]* and the catwalk turns a corner here, into an area with a strange smell *[leads to J]* or into darkness *[leads to H]*.

J: JORUM

First impressions: A vat came free from its moorings and crashed through this area, wrecking everything—including the catwalk.
Second sniff: There's a strange smell, like sour milk and salt.
Joins to areas: I, and K

The whole area is soaked with a strange fluid that crawls and moves on its own; it attempts to coat every surface of any object with which it comes into contact. Unfortunately, characters *need* some of their surfaces (such as eyes and lungs). It takes a DC 25 skill check to dodge the moving liquid; failure means it starts to envelop the character. **Suffocating oil +15 vs. PD—2d8+10 damage**

The characters must climb or fly over the vat to continue forward. (DC 20 check to maneuver over the vat without falling; a fall into the nearby crystals forces the usual DC 40 skill check to climb back on the catwalks. The PC automatically climbs back up, but they take a point of damage for each point by which their climbing check result is lower than 40). The catwalk continues toward a dimly lit area *[I]* or into darkness *[leads to K]*.

K: KEN

First impressions: Lots of levers on the underside of the now upside-down platform
Second glance: There are pistons recessed into the walls that thunder to life when the characters approach.
Joins to areas: J, and L

The pistons begin to operate when the characters approach the area. The characters can use the levers on the underside of the catwalk to try to turn off the pistons (DC 20 check; failure increases the pistons' attack roll by +5). **Crushing pistons +15 vs. AC (all creatures in area)—4d8 damage.**

The catwalk stretches onward toward an area with a strange smell *[leads to J]* or toward darkness *[leads to L]*.

L: LACUNA

First impressions: The cogs broke free here; piled in heaps, their spindles judder.
Second glance: The catwalk is unsteady; walking on it will cause it to fall. Time to get down and walk among the cogs!
Joins to areas: M, and K

The catwalk is unsteady here; it will fall if the characters continue to walk along it. If they climb down to walk among the cogs, the cogs unexpectedly start to move while the characters are walking through. It takes a DC 25 skill check to dodge the cogs; failure means the cogs catch at the characters' feet or sever their fingers.

Cogs +15 vs. PD—14 ongoing damage, and target is stuck (save ends both).

The catwalk regains stability after this area and leads into darkness *[to K]* or a darkened area with faint, almost musical sounds *[leads to M]*.

M: MADRIGAL

> **First impressions:** Cogs spinning fast and producing a high-pitched whirring sound.
> **Second glance:** Cogs speed up and slow down, their whirring is almost musical.
> **Joins to areas:** L, N, and W

The cogs in this area spin so fast they produce high-pitched, almost musical whirring sounds. The sounds can lull unwary adventurers to sleep. It takes a DC 30 skill check to shake off the effect in time to avoid the attack.

Cog lullaby +20 vs. MD—Target must start making last gasp saves to avoid falling asleep; once they fail their final save, the target falls into the machinery below and takes 3d20 + 10 damage. They wake up at that point, unless they are unconscious from loss of hit points.

Characters can help their allies avoid falling asleep, which grants a +5 bonus to the target's last gasp saves.

The catwalk turns a corner here and leads toward a random clanging sound *[to N]* or into silent darkness *[leads to L]*. A stairway leads upward *[to W]*.

N: NAVICULAR

> **First impressions:** A single cog falls onto the catwalk.
> **Second glance:** It sounds like more cogs are coming loose.
> **Joins to areas:** M, and O

As the characters enter this area, a single cog falls onto the catwalk from above. If the characters look up, they can see more cogs that appear ready to drop at any moment. Anybody who passes through this area must do so quickly. It takes a DC 20 skill check to effectively dodge the falling cogs; otherwise, they attack.

Falling Cogs +10 vs. AC (two attacks)—2d8 damage.

The catwalk leads onward toward almost musical sounds in one direction *[leads to M]* and a faint light in the other *[leads to O]*.

O: ORDINAL

> **First impressions:** This section doesn't have many mechanisms.
> **Second glance:** Books are scattered about, jamming some of the cogs.
> **Joins to areas:** N, P, and Z

This area is safe (or at least safe from the machines). A crack in the outer wall allows light in from the outside *[leads to Z]*, which makes it easy to see all the books lying around the area—some of which are jamming the cogs.

Investigating the books grants the characters +5 to all rolls in one Grand Spike area of their choosing (*"Hey—I saw the diagram for this mechanism in that book earlier!"*). The players may communally choose to which area the bonus applies when it becomes relevant.

The catwalk leads onward toward clanging sounds in one direction *[leads to N]* or flashes of bright light in the other *[leads to P]*.

P: PANACEA

> **First impressions:** Energy arcs from crystal to crystal.
> **Second glance:** There are mechanical spiders and crystal crabs scurrying about overhead.
> **Joins to areas:** A, and O

The energy arcs here are harmless, but the spider-like constructs that move about high above repairing the cog work are potential threats.

The catwalk continues toward a faint light in one direction *[leads to O]* or an odd smell in the other *[leads to A]*.

If the characters don't try to attract the servitors' attention—or get into other trouble thanks to the tension table—they can probably get by here without a fight. Still, you should ask the unluckiest PC to roll an easy save! With a success, the characters can pass through without a fight; with a failure, use the monster stats in the *Grand Spike Constructs* section on page 152 for the following battle.

#/Level of PCs	Glass Spider	Crystal Crab
3 x 6th level	6	2
4 x 6th level	7	3
5 x 6th level	8	4
6 x 6th level	9	5
7 x 6th level	12	6
3 x 7th level	6	3
4 x 7th level	8	4
5 x7th level	8	6
6 x 7th level	10	8
7 x 7th level	12	10

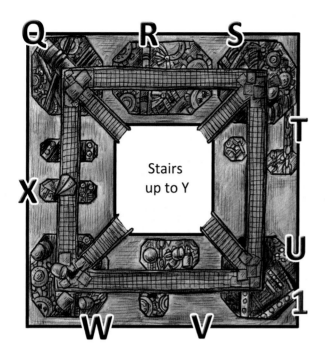

Q: Quoin

First impressions: Two large shafts. Warm jets of air.
Second sniff: There's a burning smell.
Joins to areas: A, R, X, and Y

Two of the great mechanism's large shafts meet here in a complicated joint. Warm jets of air blast from between the cogs. There are several quartz quadrupeds in among the cog work here, welding the joints of the great mechanism.

The catwalk turns a corner here and leads toward sawing sounds in one direction *[leads to R]* and complete darkness in the other *[leads to X]*. One stairway leads upward *[to Y]*, another leads downward *[to A]*.

If the characters pass through without making too much sound (DC 20 to sneak through quietly) the creatures leave them alone; otherwise they attack. You should use a whole mess of quartz quadrupeds from the *Grand Spike Constructs* section on page 151 for this fight.

R: Rictus

First impressions: The mechanism is completely frozen here.
Second glance: There's a grinding sound coming from above.
Joins to areas: Q, and S

A strange mechanical animal is hard at work trying to saw free a cog that is jamming up everything. The creature resembles a bird, but has a reciprocating saw for a beak. It is not alone.

The catwalk continues onward—a faint burning smell in one direction *[leads to Q]* and darkness in the other *[leads to S]*. If the characters pass through without making too much sound (DC 20 check to sneak through quietly) the creatures leave them alone; otherwise they attack. Throw a flight of drill-birds from the *Grand Spike Constructs* section on page 151 at the characters.

S: Sepulture

First impressions: Dead acolytes jam up the mechanism.
Second glance: Some of them are still twitching.
Joins to areas: E, R, T and Y

This area is "safe," though making too much noise runs the risk of attracting mechanical animals' attention (DC 15 check to sneak through quietly).

The catwalk turns a corner here and leads toward a grinding sound *[leads to R]* or the sound of chains rattling *[leads to T]*. One stairway leads upward *[leads to Y]* another leads downward *[to F]*.

If the characters make too much noise, they attract the attention of whatever undefeated enemies lurk in areas Q, R, and T. Use a mix of constructs (but no machine acolytes) from the *Grand Spike Constructs* section for this battle.

T: Terret

First impressions: There are chains everywhere—they loop around and through things, disappearing into the darkness.
Second glance: Mechanical spiders crawl about the chains, spinning metal to replace broken links.
Joins to areas: S, and U

Many chains run through this area, passing through metal hoops and disappearing into the darkness or looping around shafts to drive them. This area is "safe," though making too much noise runs the risk of attracting the attention of the spiders above (DC 15 check to sneak through quietly). If the characters make too much noise, use the same battle as in Area P above.

The catwalk leads toward darkness in either direction *[leads to S and U]*.

U: UMBRAL

> **First impressions:** This area is in near-darkness, no crystals shine here. A small hole leads to the outside.
> **Second glance:** Sounds of crystals crunching. The hole that leads outside is lined with dark crystals.
> **Joins to areas:** I, T, V, Y, and Z

Quartz quadrupeds consume the crystals here and regurgitate them over the hole to the outside to "repair" it *[leads to Z]*.

Characters who enter this area from the outside or exit here to the outside automatically attract the creatures' attention; otherwise, it takes a DC 20 skill check to sneak by without provoking them to attack. If the characters fail their checks, use enough quartz quadrupeds from page 151 to create a normal battle. If the characters first enter the pyramid here, add a machine acolyte or two – but don't make the battle count for extra toward gaining a full heal-up.

The catwalk turns a corner toward the sounds of chains clanking *[leads to T]* or toward darkness *[leads to V]*. One stairway leads upward *[leads to Y]*, another leads downward *[leads to I]*.

V: VOLITION

> **First impressions:** A team of mechanical creatures are trying to unjam some gears.
> **Second glance:** More creatures approach from deeper within the cog work.
> **Joins to areas:** U, and W

If the adventurers entered the pyramid through the hole to the outside in area U, the mechanical creatures are on high alert; they attack, following up on the battle with quartz quadrupeds. Run a battle with mixed creatures from the *Grand Spike Constructs* on page 151.

If the adventurers entered the pyramid on the bottom level, the creatures in this area are only interested in repairing the gears; if the characters don't attack, the creatures ignore them. If the characters do decide to start a fight, deal 2d6 damage to each and wave your hand at the battle. It's not a big deal for heroes who have already fought their way this far.

The catwalk leads toward darkness in either direction *[leads to U and W]*.

W: WEIGHT

> **First impressions:** It looks like counterweights on chains smashed through the cogs--possibly when Vantage fell.
> **Second sniff:** The metal here is hot.
> **Joins to areas:** M, V, X, and Y

Something is broken here: quite broken indeed. The catwalk gets very hot as the characters walk through this area. In addition, the gravity here is "off" somehow; the catwalk seems increasingly steep the higher the characters progress. **Hot metal and strange gravity +15 vs. AC (three attacks per adventurer)—2d6 fire**

damage, and if all three attacks hit, the target hurtles off the catwalk *[to M]*. *Miss:* 5 fire damage.

The catwalk turns a corner here: both directions lead toward darkness *[leads to V and X]*. One stairway leads upward *[to Y]*, another leads downward *[to M]*.

X: XENO

> **First impressions:** An area full of crystals.
> **Second impression:** Everybody can feel a strange presence here—some sort of trapped entity.
> **Joins to areas:** Q, and W

A huge crystal shard is lodged in this area; characters must carefully maneuver around it to get to the other side of the catwalk (DC 20 to maneuver safely; failure drops you into the cogs and crystals below). If you like, this crystal shard could relate to the Great Prism plotline (see *The Great Prism* on page 116 for more details).

The catwalk continues toward a dark area with warm gusts of air coming from it *[leads to Q]* or silent darkness in the other direction *[leads to W]*.

Y: YIELD

> **First impressions:** A single, pure crystal floats in the center of the room.
> **Second glance:** Something lurks in the shadows.
> **Joins to areas:** Q, S, U, and W

The pure crystal in this area is the focus of this great machine—the most vital component to whatever kept Vantage flying.

Depending on what the players deem most important, the crystal might also control the Great Prism, power most of Vantage's defenses, or be the lynchpin of the wards—possibly all three.

Unfortunately, the characters are not alone here—whichever crystal-interested adversary group the characters hate and fear most also made it this far, and they want the crystal for themselves!

Four stairways lead downward *[to Q, S, U, and W]*.

Follow-ups: If the characters lose this fight, their enemies should gain some great advantage for their iconic patron. It's up to you whether you want to extend that type of generosity if the characters win. The crystal may not be all that useful, at first; but, perhaps it comes in handy in the future for something like an ultra-powerful icon relationship advantage.

TOMB OF THE SERPENT ARCHONS

Level range: 6th and 7th

A long line of Archmages captured living dungeons and hid them below Redfield Valley. The Tomb of the Serpent Archons could be part of that grand tradition, or it could be something more. . . The serpent archons were former rulers in an era before the time of the Wizard King, so they're not mere dungeon-threats (unless you want them to be!). That the wards of Vantage contained them for so long is either a sign of their weakness or a testimony to the fact that they can only ever be contained, never eliminated. Vantage's fall, and the subsequent weakening of the wards, could have terrible consequences—unless the PCs decide to enter the dungeon and do what is necessary to keep the serpent archons entombed.

Ancient history: The age of the serpent archons was a terrible time for everyone; but it was especially bad for non-serpentine humanoids. Great dragon-gods ruled the cosmos, and the serpent archons were their chief servants and priests. Their preferred sacrifices/meals (it was hard to tell the difference) were humans, elves, and gnomes. Many of these meals—along with an awful lot of power—got stuck in the serpent archons' maws instead of flowing up to their gods. In the end, it became hard to tell which were the gods and which were the servants.

FRONT-LOADING THE SERPENT ARCHONS

It can be fun to just drop this dungeon on your players, but it tends to work best if you front-load it. If you introduce rumors and legends about the serpent archons prior to the tomb's reveal, it'll be a much bigger thrill/scare for them.

A minstrel might tell the tale of Bran the hero; when she gets to the part of the story about the serpent archons, the elders by the fire shudder and turn away. Who was Bran? It doesn't matter—what matters is that eons later, the mere mention of the serpent archons still elicits fear.

Or, perhaps the adventurers find a magic item from the age of the serpent archons in a previous adventure. They learn that owning such an item is banned in the Dragon Empire, and the usual penalty is ten years' service on the Sea Wall. Later, they come across an evil cult whose altar has snakes carved into it. When they touch the altar, they feel the presence of a slumbering, ancient evil. They now know what kept the evil asleep for so long. . . .

ADVENTURING IN THE TOMB OF THE SERPENT ARCHONS

The tomb's upper level just pushed through the surface—possibly right in front of the adventurers. It's a snake-carved step pyramid with stairs leading to the top. The *glitterfall* begins to form a vortex around it as the ancient evil within starts to wake.

You don't need a tension table for this fully mapped, trapped, and populated dungeon.

Book of Ages offers another approach to this dungeon: the pyramid is the final vestige of the power of the Tyrant Lizard, the terrible queen of the Age of Wild Woods (Book of Ages, page 83). Even if bringing in the Tyrant Lizard doesn't interest you, her lizardman impaler shock troop on Book of Ages page 87 would make a fine addition to these serpent archon battles.

ENTRANCES TO THE TOMB OF THE SERPENT ARCHONS

The characters must access the tomb via stairs up the pyramid's side that lead up to an altar and a complex at the very top. Once there, they find a stairway that descends into the tomb.

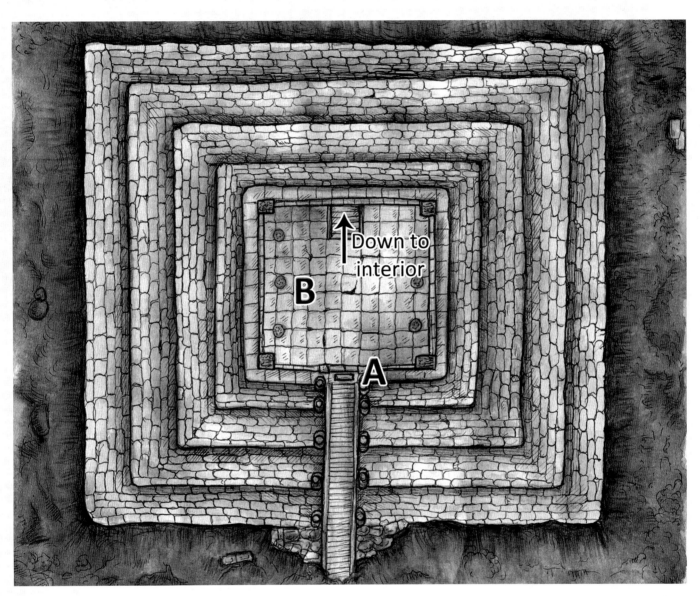

AREAS OF THE TOMB OF THE SERPENT ARCHONS

A: THE SACRIFICIAL ALTAR

The journey up the step pyramid to the altar allows the characters to view the very detailed carvings of the snake kings and get a clearer picture of what they might find here. A sacrificial altar sits at the top of the step pyramid *[Area A]*. The altar is blood-stained, even after centuries.

A set of double doors reveals the inner temple *[leads to B]*.

B: THE INNER TEMPLE

The temple doors lead into a large, square chamber. There are several clay pots here, with jade stone serpents—the temple's guardians—inside. If the characters open a pot, there is a 50% chance they find a jade serpent (DC 15 check to avoid waking it). If the characters smash a pot or cast any spells in this area, the jade serpents awaken. Use the enemies below for this battle; this isn't meant to be a sophisticated fight, merely an attrition challenge.

Stairs in the floor of the temple lead downward, deep into the temple *[leads to C]*.

#/Level of PCs	Jade Cobra	Jade Serpent
3 x 6th level	2	7
4 x 6th level	3	8
5 x 6th level	4	10
6 x 6th level	6	6
7 x 6th level	7	10
3 x 7th level	3	6
4 x 7th level	5	5
5 x7th level	6	10
6 x 7th level	7	15
7 x 7th level	8	20

JADE COBRA

It slept for centuries, dreaming of poisssssson.

7th level spoiler [CONSTRUCT]
Initiative: +11

Jade fangs +12 vs. AC—24 damage, and target is vulnerable to poison (save ends).

R: Poison spit +12 vs. PD (one nearby enemy that is vulnerable to poison)—30 poison damage.

AC	24	
PD	21	**HP 100**
MD	16	

JADE SERPENT

So many snakessssssss.

7th level mook [CONSTRUCT]
Initiative: +9

Jade fangs +12 vs. AC—8 damage
Natural even hit: Target is vulnerable to poison (save ends).

R: Poison spit +12 vs. PD (one nearby enemy that is vulnerable to poison)—20 poison damage.

Spitting mad: Whenever one or more jade serpent mooks are destroyed, roll a hard save (16+) and add the number of jade serpents that were just destroyed. If the save succeeds, make a poison spit attack against a random enemy as a free action.

AC	24	
PD	21	**HP 30 (mook)**
MD	16	

Mook: Kill one jade serpent mook for every 30 damage you deal to the mob.

C: THE WINDING STAIRS

There are regular alcoves in the wall along the stairs that lead down into the tomb. Each alcove contains a fist-sized stone egg, which glows whenever a creature is nearby . . . like, say, the characters!

The eggs are worth 20 gp apiece if the characters take them back to civilization to sell them. Each character can carry one egg per point of strength they have (the eggs are large and heavy). As a light source, the eggs provide the same light as a bright lantern.

The eggs do pose a hidden danger—if they touch each other, their light intensifies; they become painfully bright to look at once five are together. If the characters put six together, the eggs heat up; and if they put seven together, flames erupt. Unwary characters who place seven or more eggs in their pack and continue adventuring take 3d6 fire damage, as their pack smolders and then bursts into flames (they also lose anything else in their pack).

Clever adventurers can doubtless find unconventional ways to use the eggs, though the fire starts slowly enough that throwing flaming eggs at enemies is not a valid tactic (the eggs do the same damage as a thrown rock). Smashing the eggs is not an easy task and destroys their properties.

There are easily over two hundred eggs along the stairway, and hundreds more throughout the dungeon. Smart adventurers pay attention when distant eggs light up (a sure sign an enemy is approaching).

If the adventurers did not fight the jade snakes in the inner temple *[Area B]* they face them here; the stone eggs lighting up awakens them in their pots above. Use the battle from area B, set here amidst the glowing eggs.

The stairs lead to a large, square room at the bottom *[lead to D]*.

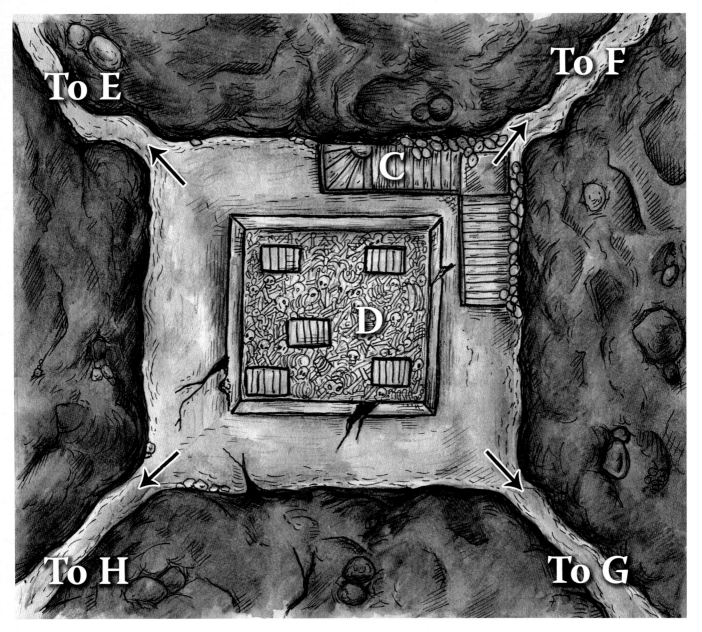

165

D: THE BONE PIT

This large, square room contains a pit of bones at its center. Chains in the ceiling suspend iron cages above the pit. Stairs lead upward *[to C]* and four winding corridors lead out from each corner of the room *[leads to E, F, G, and H]*.

DANGER?

The bones in the pit are from humanoid slaves the serpent archons killed centuries ago. Over the eons, the foul magic of this place seeped into the bones. If at any point you feel that the characters are not having a difficult enough time in this dungeon, these bones rise and form a draconic shape. If the adventurers flee (and remind them that they can do so) before they kill the last of the serpent archons, then the dungeon rumbles to the surface and the armies of the serpent archons march!

You could also use this fight as a surprise, last-gasp strike from the serpent archons after the characters fight the big battle in the Throne Room and are headed out of the pyramid, confident of their victory.

The weird creatures in this fight deliberately skip the undead's usual vulnerability to holy energy.

#/Level of PCs	Shard Dragon	Skeletal Shard
3 x 6th level	1	0
4 x 6th level	1	2
5 x 6th level	1	3
6 x 6th level	1	7
7 x 6th level	2	2
3 x 7th level	1	2
4 x 7th level	1	5
5 x 7th level	1	10
6 x 7th level	2	3
7 x 7th level	2	7

SHARD DRAGON

It's not actually a dragon, but the magic that pulls it together from the sacrificial bones knows the shape of the true masters.

Huge 8th level troop [UNDEAD]
Initiative: +15

Jaws and claws +15 vs. AC (3 attacks)—35 damage
Miss: 15 damage.

Lethal shards: Each time the shard dragon is hit by an attack, place a new skeletal shard mook beside the shard dragon. It acts along with the rest of the skeletal shards in the battle, or immediately after the dragon if all other skeletal shards are destroyed.

Only bones: When the shard dragon would receive a harmful condition, cancel that condition and instead deal 2d20 damage to the shard dragon.

Resist weapons 16+: When a weapon attack targets this creature, the attacker must roll a natural 16+ on the attack roll or it only deals half damage.

Nastier Specials
Escalator: The shard dragon adds the escalation die to its attacks, like a proper dragon.

AC	22	
PD	20	**HP 410**
MD	19	

SKELETAL SHARDS

The bones whirl into shifting towers of spikes and ancient magic.

9th level mook [UNDEAD]
Initiative: +17

Impaling shard +15 vs. AC—30 damage

Resist weapons 16+: When a weapon attack targets this creature, the attacker must roll a natural 16+ on the attack roll or it only deals half damage.

AC	23	
PD	21	**HP 40 (mook)**
MD	17	

Mook: Kill one skeletal shard mook for every 40 damage you deal to the mob.

E: THE SOLDIER EGG

A huge, brass egg sits in the center of this circular room. It's easily 20 feet tall. As the characters enter, hundreds of stone eggs (*see C*) beneath the brass egg begin to glow, then ignite.

It takes a DC 20 skill check to realize the danger and shut their eyes in time; failure means the flame attacks. **Green flame +5 vs. PD**—12 fire damage, and the character is partially blinded (*–4 to attack, save ends*). *Miss:* The character must roll a normal save or be blinded (*–4 to attack, save ends*).

Droplets of metal begin to fall from the brass egg's surface. These cool quickly on the chamber floor, where they become humanoid serpents and attack! Roll initiative.

#/Level of PCs	Scaled Soldier	Jade Serpent (page 164)
3 x 6th level	3	5
4 x 6th level	5	5
5 x 6th level	6	6
6 x 6th level	7	10
7 x 6th level	8	12
3 x 7th level	4	6
4 x 7th level	5	8
5 x 7th level	7*	6
6 x 7th level	8*	10
7 x 7th level	9*	12

*Use a d10 for the scaled soldiers' increasing damage ability instead of a d4.

SCALED SOLDIER

The cursed troops of the serpent archons. Some return to human form when slain, others do not.

6th *level archer* [HUMANOID]
Initiative: +12

Twin two-ended swords +11 vs. AC (two attacks)—8 damage
   Miss: 4 damage.

R: Iron bow +12 vs. AC (one nearby or far away enemy)—18 damage.

Increasing damage: Each time after the first a target is hit by an *iron bow* attack, it takes a cumulative +1d4 poison damage—up to a maximum of +4d4 poison damage.

AC 22	
PD 20	**HP 90**
MD 16	

F: THE OPHIDIAN SLAVES

This area is a network of catacombs filled with plain, stone boxes. Each box contains a hibernating ophidian curled up in straw (see page 188 for a PC-version illustration).

These are the serpent archons' unarmed slaves. Killing them is easy—they are in a deep sleep and cannot defend themselves. Still, if the party decides to slay these creatures, they may face eventual payback for killing unarmed, helpless, and more-or-less innocent slaves.

If characters feel the need to wake slaves and fight them, here are their stats.

If the PCs already defeated the serpent archons in room H, this room shouldn't be a fight. Instead, play it as a triumphant celebration. The ophidian slaves wake free of the archons' control and know that they have the PCs to thank for it.

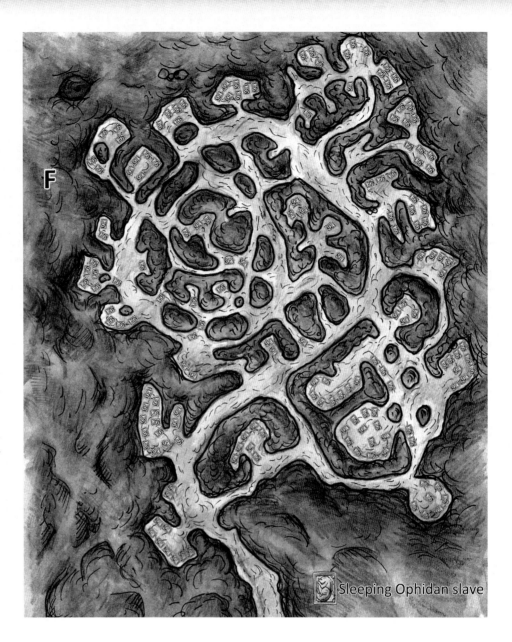

 Sleeping Ophidan slave

OPHIDIAN SLAVE

Each ophidian slave is unique—some have serpent heads, others have multiple arms, some have snake tails instead of legs; however, all look downtrodden.

4th level troop [HUMANOID]
Initiative: +6

Club +8 vs. AC—14 damage.

R: Stone +8 vs. AC—10 damage.

Pick at least one
Multiple arms: Once per fight, reroll a missed attack.
Serpent tail instead of legs: Once per fight, move as a quick action.
Serpent head: Add +1d4 poison damage on an even hit with a club attack.

Creatures asleep in stone boxes frequently wake to become a problem for adventurers! For the PCs to understand that the ophidians are helpless slaves who won't wake to attack, they'd probably need to receive advice to that effect earlier in the adventure—possibly when they learn about the tomb in the first place.

Or maybe this is a good time to take advantage of the new ophidian stats on page 188 and introduce a late-arriving PC who argues for the lives of her sisters.

AC 20
PD 18   **HP 54**
MD 14

G: The Temple of Dragons

This area contains several broken dragon-god statues. When a past Archmage imprisoned the serpent archons here, he wiped the land clean of their dangerous religion and sealed their idols in with them. It's possible he had no choice but to do so; the serpent archons' magic may have forced the less-than-optimal containment measures.

In any case, if the characters explore this area, they uncover treasures from the lost age of the serpent archons. There is a lot of loot here! We list a couple possibilities for magic weapons below, but also acknowledge that this is the perfect place to find one or two cursed items.

Weapons

Default bonus: Attacks and damage when using the weapon: +1 (adventurer); +2 (champion); +3 (epic).

Constricting (any melee weapon): When you hit a target with an attack using this weapon, they receive a −2 penalty to disengage from you until the end of the battle. Quirk: Admires snakes.

Venomous (any weapon): Your attacks with this weapon deal poison damage. When you crit with this weapon, the target takes 5 ongoing poison damage (champion: 10; epic: 20). Quirk: Ridiculously sharp-tongued.

H: THE THRONE ROOM

The serpent archons slumber on carved thrones in this vast, unlit chamber. They look like giant, tentacled snake-people—barely humanoid enough to sit naturally on a throne (refer to the building battles table for the number of serpent archons and already-active warrior servants here).

Unless your campaign is Priestess-centered, with diplomatic or oracular solutions to nearly any problem, the characters likely realize that unless they kill the serpent archons, they'll awaken soon. After sitting motionless for eons, a twitching tentacle or sudden flicker of a forked tongue are the first movements in what could become an unstoppable wave.

The good news is, after time's long assault, the characters can accomplish with a sharp axe what the Archmage and all his magic could not, back when the serpent archons were well-remembered and strong. Killing the first serpent archon is easy, if the characters use a *coup de grace* action (*13th Age* core rules, page 172) and succeed with a DC 20 skill check. However, each successive coup de grace against another serpent archon becomes a cumulative +2 DC harder. A failure merely staggers the serpent archon instead of slaying it; in addition, it wakes and allows all other slumbering serpent archons to attempt a normal save—now and at the start of each turn. If a serpent archon's save succeeds, it wakes. Roll initiative for each serpent archon separately as it wakes; it's more entertaining to let them feed into the battle one or two at a time.

The battle: To further complicate this brutal method of execution, the characters must fight the serpent archons' defenders while they attempt to slay the serpent archons the easy way! The defenders appear from behind the pillars and altar after the characters enter the room and roll initiative. This is probably at least a double-strength battle. . . however, the variety of outcomes possible with the slumbering archons complicates the analysis!

A staggered minor serpent demon or scaled soldier—or one that feels ignored by the characters—may attempt to wake one of the sleeping archons. It takes a standard action and a successful hard save (16+) for one of these creatures to wake an archon.

We imagine icon relationship advantages might become significant in this situation.

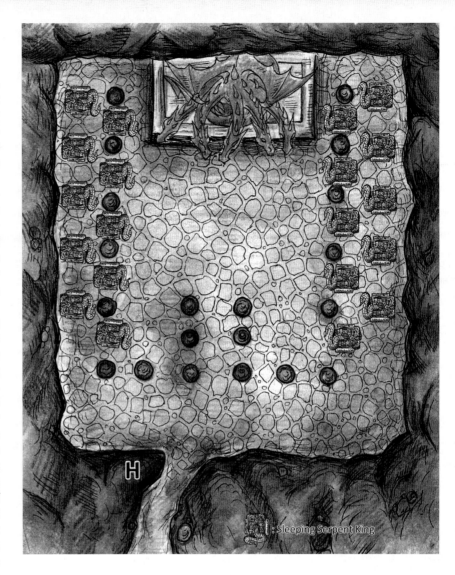

: Sleeping Serpent King

#/Level of PCs	Scaled Soldier	Minor Serpent Demon	Serpent Archon
3 x 6th level	3	2	3
4 x 6th level	3	3	3
5 x 6th level	4	3	4
6 x 6th level	5	4	4
7 x 6th level	6	5	5
3 x 7th level	4	3	3
4 x 7th level	5	4	4
5 x7th level	6	4	5
6 x 7th level	7	5	6
7 x 7th level	7	7	7

SCALED SOLDIER

The cursed troops of the serpent archons. Some revert to human form when slain, others do not.

6th level archer [HUMANOID]
Initiative: +12

Twin two-ended swords +11 vs. AC (two attacks)—8 damage
  Miss: 4 damage.

R: Iron bow +12 vs. AC (one nearby or far away enemy)—18 damage.

Increasing damage: Each time after the first a target is hit by an *iron bow* attack, it takes a cumulative +1d4 poison damage—up to a maximum of +4d4 poison damage.

Transformed soldiers
Most scaled soldiers are born from magical eggs, but the serpent archons can also turn humanoids that are in their presence into scaled soldiers. A magical ritual might restore a transformed soldier long enough to have a conversation, but only the death of the serpent archon who transformed the soldier or very powerful magic found after a quest offers a permanent solution.

AC	22	
PD	20	**HP 90**
MD	16	

MINOR SERPENT DEMON

Progressing sword by sword and death by death toward a full marilith.

7th level troop [DEMON]
Initiative: +13

Four whirling swords +12 vs. AC (4 attacks)—7 damage
  Miss: 2 damage.

C: Beguiling gaze +12 vs. MD (one nearby or far away unengaged enemy)—As a free action, the target immediately moves toward the minor serpent demon, attempting to engage it or get as close as possible to it
  Quick use: 1/round, as a quick action.

Terrible swords: When the escalation die is even, the minor serpent demon's crit range for melee attacks expands by a number equal to the escalation die.

AC	23	
PD	16	**HP 98**
MD	20	

SERPENT ARCHON

Half-asleep, not yet tapped-in to its reservoir of unique, divine power—still terrifying.

Huge weakling 8th level spoiler [GIANT]
Initiative: +10

Scaled touch +13 vs. AC—50 damage
  Natural even hit: Target takes 30 ongoing poison damage
  Natural even miss: The serpent archon can use its *primal word* attack as a quick action.

C: Primal word +13 vs. MD (1d3 nearby or far away enemies)—Target is confused (save ends). Each target can only become confused by a *primal word* attack once per fight.
  Third failed save: The target becomes helpless (save ends). If the target fails to save against the helpless condition, it is transformed into a scaled soldier that obeys the serpent archon's will. Transformed characters turn back upon death or upon the death of the one who transformed them, though you could also quest for powerful iconic magic to reverse the transformation.

Fear Aura: While engaged with the serpent archon, enemies with 48 hp or fewer are dazed (−4 attack) and do not add the escalation die to their attacks.

AC	24	
PD	18	**HP 210**
MD	22	

LESSER GODS

The stats we present here are for serpent archons in their weak and just-awakened state. This battle in the tomb, still blanketed by what's left of the Archmage's ancient suppression spells, is the only place they're likely to register as 8th level creatures. Calling them weaklings and treating them as having only half the strength of other huge 8th level creatures is a bit of sleight of hand—it allows us to make them scary without killing every last PCs if they screw up their chance to coup de grace the archons early.

How powerful would these "living gods" be if they could slither to the surface? Probably at least as powerful as the fomori tyrant and fomori torturer on pages 85 and 86 of *Bestiary 2*. . . perhaps even more. Thankfully, the source of their power is in buried dungeons where adventurers can cut away at it, scale by scale, until the serpent archons can once again be defeated as epic-tier threats.

CHAPTER 9:
CROWNING SPELL

AN ADVENTURE FOR EPIC LEVEL CHARACTERS

This epic-level dungeon should not come as a surprise to your players. If you intend to use it, provide ample clues for how they should approach and deal with it during your campaign.

The Tomb of the First Emperor is ideal for groups that have a grudge against the Archmage or Emperor. If the adventurers work for evil icons (especially the Lich King), this is an ideal target: it is a simple smash-and-grab tomb with some desecration and looting.

Most of *Shards of the Broken Sky* assumes the adventurers are in league with good or ambiguous icons. If neither the current Archmage nor the Emperor have gone bad in your campaign, smashing into the First Emperor's tomb as written may be an odd way to apply the player characters' epic-tier heroics.

It's possible to rephrase the adventure so that PCs aligned with good icons need to plunder the tomb, but it requires some thought. Perhaps they're seeking lost treasures they need to save the world, or perhaps the line between good and evil isn't as clear as it was at the start of the campaign. See the *Iconic Angles* section for more possibilities.

THE TOMB OF THE FIRST EMPEROR

A popular folktale in Appleton and Crownhill says the legendary First Emperor died during a battle in a nearby valley. The folktale gets the story about half-right; however, the fatal battle was closer than "nearby"—it was *in* Redfield Valley (see *Redfield Rising* on page 101).

The Archmage suppressed this hidden tomb's existence. The First Emperor's *official* burial place is in Axis—the imperial capital—but that tomb (though well-guarded and warded) is empty. Official records even obfuscate the battle in which the Emperor fell—stating it took place occurred far from Redfield Valley.

ICONIC ANGLES

Epic-tier PCs tend to have strong relationships with several icons. The First Emperor's tomb is the type of target to bring those relationships into play. It may also involve adversary groups other than those we've relied on so far in this campaign.

The Emperor: The Archmage went to a lot of trouble to hide the First Emperor's body. It is doubtful the current Emperor even knows the official tomb is a fake. Once the "lost" tomb is uncovered, the Emperor wants to know its secrets and prevent others from exploiting the tomb. If the PCs aren't already working for him, the Emperor likely sends agents to recover what belongs to him.

The Diabolist: The Diabolist wants the First Emperor's heart so she can cast a love spell—the First Emperor's heart to win the current (and possibly last?) Emperor's heart.

The Lich King: The man who became the First Emperor led the forces that destroyed the Lich King; though, ultimately, the Orc Lord was the one who decided the war. The Lich King is willing to give much and risk even more to gain possession of the First Emperor's body—either as a source of power or to mock him by raising him as an undead servant. The tomb might also contain some important treasures close to the Lich King's withered, undying heart—but that's for you to decide, if it suits your campaign.

The Three: The Blue may want to marry the Emperor, uniting the Dragon Emperors' dynasty with the bloodline of one of the mightiest dragons ever to live (and placing her in a position of power at the heart of the Empire). What better way to woo her intended and become the Blue Empress than to present him with the First Emperor's lost crown? We hadn't planned to place that treasure in this dungeon; but if your PCs care about it enough, make it happen!

YOUR PENULTIMATE ADVENTURE?

We don't see this as the final adventure of a campaign. As you'll see, successfully pushing through this dungeon doesn't necessarily provide the climactic action and drama we prefer when ending many campaigns.

Instead, consider using this dungeon as the next-to-last adventure in your campaign. You know what the PCs confronted during adventurer-tier and champion-tier. Play off the events of your campaign. Use the shadowy figure of the First Emperor's spirit as the final quest-giver or the source of the magic artifact that enables the PCs to embark upon their true final quest.

Adventuring in the Tomb

The First Emperor's tomb is an old-school dungeon, full of traps and tricks. We encourage you to come up with even more, especially while the adventurers are in the Maze of Death.

The adventurers can access the tomb through a secret door in *Area E: The Hall of Flame*, in the Lost Tomb adventure from Chapter 6. The hidden doorway is not visible to adventurer-tier characters; only after the adventurers become epic-tier do they realize the room holds additional secrets.

If the adventurers did not previously visit the Lost Tomb, use a traveling montage scene to get them to the door. However, now that they are epic-tier characters, they don't need to go through the motions in a 1st level dungeon.

So many traps: The former Archmage's plan with this trap-filled tomb was to slow down intruders until he could respond to a magical alarm and deal with them himself. Unfortunately, he didn't plan for Vantage to fall on the tomb. Maybe Vantage's magical "radiation" interferes with the alarm, or maybe Vantage's fall created more pressing weaknesses that preoccupy the current Archmage—especially because he knows there are additional safety features in place (see below). Either way, neither the Archmage nor forces from Horizon show up to help. . . unless the PCs count as such forces!

Another past Archmage put an emergency system in place to protect the tomb—the dungeon of Rynth. Once adventurers make it past the Great Door (Area E in the Maze of Death section below) they encounter oozefolk warriors teleported in from Rynth to repel intruders. We discuss the mechanics for these teleported oozefolk warrior squads on page 176, after the Great Door (yes, you have further options if the PCs already killed or dealt with the living dungeon of Rynth).

Old-School Warning

Though I toned down or revised many of what ASH refers to as "old-school" traps and tricks in Shards of the Broken Sky, *I was more hands-off in the* Tomb of the First Emperor. *If an old-school ending for one or more epic-tier characters' careers isn't something you want in your campaign, you may need to temper many of the tricks that follow or use icon relationship advantages to create new-school paths to survival.*

The Maze of Death

This magical maze was designed to slow down, trap, and kill intruders. The maze itself shifts, so we don't provide a map; the only certainty is that the party enters through Area A: The Entrance.

Thereafter, each time the party leaves a room, their best dungeoneer must roll a DC 30 skill check to navigate the maze.

Successful navigation skill checks: If the skill check is successful, the party manages to dodge the random traps in the various dead-end corridors and ends up in a random room (*B, C, or D*) of the maze they have not yet visited. After the PCs survive Areas A through D, a successful skill check gets them into Area E: the exit from this maze of death.

Failed navigation skill checks: If the dungeoneer fails a skill check, the party stumbles through a shifting magical maze of traps, dead-ends, illusions, and exploding runes. Randomly choose one to three PCs, invent amusing traps, and roll a **+20 vs. AC/PD/MD (as appropriate) vs. each PC**. If an attack hits, deal 3d20 damage to the target. This isn't likely to kill them, and they may have time for a quick rest before they find the next room in the maze of death; however, it does whittle them down recovery by recovery.

Afterward, the maze leads the PCs back into a room they already visited—and they must choose whether to give up or push onward.

A: The Entrance

The characters access this area through a secret door in the Hall of Flame (see Area K from *The Lost Tomb* on page 79).

The room itself is a simple, circular chamber with doors around the outside. No door can open while another (including the door to the *Hall of Flame*) is open. If all the doors are closed and there is weight on the room's floor, the room's exterior rotates while jets of flame spew forth from gargoyle faces set between the doors. The adventurers must make a DC 25 skill check to dodge the flames and avoid being barbequed, while also trying to determine which door they want to go through. **Flame jets +15 vs. PD**—4d8 fire damage.

The flames can't hit the characters if they stand in the center of the room, but that position means the fire obscures the doors. To further confuse matters, the center of the room randomly spins clockwise and counter-clockwise, making it difficult to track which door is which. The mechanism eventually winds down in about an hour or so, but by then the fire has burnt up the oxygen in the room. If the characters don't need to breathe, this is a valid strategy; otherwise, they must brave the fire and enter a door into the maze. Clever players will find a way to mark which doors they already opened. There are 12 identical-looking doors; 10 of them open to walls with explosive runes. **Explosive runes +15 vs. PD (the first time a door is opened)**—4d8 force damage. *Subsequent openings:* 2d8 force damage.

There is a silver key hidden under a flagstone in this area (DC 22 check to spot the loose flagstone).

B: THE HALL OF MIRRORS

This area resembles a classic hall of mirrors, except the mirrors are made from a strange, silvery metal, which appears to be priceless platinum. The characters need to make a DC 35 skill check to know enough alchemy to realize the metal is really sodium, which reacts explosively with water and produces a caustic spray.

The only pathway through the hall of mirrors is a trough of water about an inch deep. The ceiling is carved with lightning bolt insignias and copper rods dangle throughout the area. The copper rods are a diversion—the real danger lies in splashing water on the mirrors and causing an alchemical reaction.

The characters must make a DC 35 skill check to dodge the reaction if they choose to run through the area, or a DC 25 skill check if they take things more slowly. **Chemical burns +15 vs. AC**—4d8 fire and acid damage.

A plinth holding a platinum key stands at the center of the hall.

C: THE INFINITY POOL

This circular room contains a pool so deep that the characters cannot see to the bottom. There is a door on the far side of the pool, and the ceiling above is a shimmering field of stars—an obvious illusion. Characters who can pierce illusions naturally (or magic users who succeed on a DC 25 skill check) see beyond the illusion to a shaft that stretches up as high as they can see. The imperial golem wedged high up in the shaft is not visible from the ground.

It takes a DC 20 skill check to jump over the water to the other side; if successful, the characters avoid the trap. However, if they fail, they fall into the water. The water is enchanted, and it sucks wayward adventurers down into its depths. The bottom of the pool contains a portal to the top of the shaft, from where the hapless character falls for 100 feet while being magically accelerated. . . before they slam once more into the water. The whole incident deals 15 damage, and the character needs a DC 25 skill check to swim out of the water before it happens again.

The imperial golem drops down out of the shaft as soon as the first character either successfully crosses the pool or falls into it. Assuming the characters survive the golem, they notice it wears a golden key on a chain link around its "neck."

You don't need to use a fully-built battle here—have the PCs fight just the one golem. If this doesn't qualify as a serious fight for your PCs, don't give them credit toward their next full heal-up.

IMPERIAL GOLEM

Thankfully, few of these four-armed giants exist. Each was constructed from smelted magic items, bones of holy and unholy warriors, and stone from deep below the Iron Sea.

Huge 11th level wrecker [CONSTRUCT]
Initiative: +15

Swinging fists +16 vs. AC (four attacks, each deals a different damage type: cold, fire, lightning, or holy)—50 damage, and 25 ongoing damage of the same type as the fist
Natural even miss: 25 damage of the same type as the fist.

C: Enervating eye beams +16 vs. PD (2d3 nearby or far away enemies in a group)—110 negative energy damage
Natural 16+: The imperial golem heals 20 hp, using up one of the target's recoveries. If the target has no remaining recoveries, the imperial guardian cannot heal.

Seeker: The imperial golem can track anybody or anything, unless extreme magical measures are taken to prevent it. Even if it loses the trail, it may still turn up years later—it never stops searching for its enemy.

Flight: The golem can hover and fly on jets of flame. Whenever it disengages from or engages with an enemy, that enemy takes 25 fire damage.

Golem immunity: Non-organic golems are immune to effects. They can't be dazed, weakened, confused, made vulnerable, or touched by ongoing damage. You can damage a golem, but that's about it.

AC	27	
PD	24	**HP 600**
MD	20	

D: THE CRUSHER

This is another circular chamber, with a dais in the center. The dais has fifteen puzzle tiles on it, which the characters can slide about in a square. The room's ceiling looks like a series of circular rings that radiate outward from the center. There is no obvious second door in the room.

Unless the characters wedge open the door they enter through, it magically slides shut and locks once the last character is inside (DC 25 check to reopen). When the characters move the puzzle pieces, one of several things happens (roll a d4):

1. Nothing obvious happens, but there is a slight rumbling sound.
2. The circular rings slam down from the ceiling, in sequence, until the room is reduced to a cylinder around the dais. It takes a DC 25 skill check to dodge the falling rings, unless the character is standing at the dais. Characters caught under a falling ring take 24 damage and can only free themselves by moving toward the dais.
3. The rings rise back up to the ceiling.
4. The room rotates slightly (which causes the door they entered through to open into solid stone, if they manage to unlock it).

It's a DC 25 skill check to solve the puzzle by moving the tiles; each failure causes one of the above consequences, and lightning shoots from between the puzzle pieces to zap the hands of the character trying to solve it. Realizing the lightning is going to strike and dodging it requires a DC 20 skill check. **Puzzling lightning +15 vs. PD (whoever is trying to solve the puzzle)—** 4d6 lightning damage.

Solving the puzzle causes the room to rotate completely, revealing a door. It also "gifts" the characters a steel key, which teleports in and clatters on the tiles.

E: The Great Door

This area is a hallway. There is an imposing set of double-doors at the far end, with four fearsome dragons in steel, silver, gold, and platinum prominently displayed across them.

The doors have a single keyhole; the characters must insert and turn all four keys found elsewhere in this level of the dungeon in the correct order (Steel, Silver, Gold, Platinum) to unlock the doors. However, if they insert the keys in the wrong order or attempt to pick the lock, a wave of magical energy slams into them (DC 25 check to dodge). **Locked door trap 15 vs. PD (each adventurer present)—** 2d12 force damage.

A *knock* spell allows the characters to make do with three of the four keys. The characters cannot pick the "lock" mechanism— it mystically responds to the presence of the metals themselves (yes, sticking other steel, silver, gold, and platinum objects into the lock works). The door, once open, leads into next area of the dungeon.

With a DC 20 skill check, the characters can spot a hidden room just off this area that contains a bed, a wardrobe, a wash-basin, etc. Nobody has been here for centuries—the wood is dry and crumbly, and everything is covered in dust. Cleaning supplies such as a mop, a bucket, a broom, brushes, etc. stand in the corner.

Treasure: There are two epic-tier healing potions on a high dusty shelf among empty bottles, and a third potion that has gone bad (drinking it costs a recovery but grants no healing).

The Tomb

Actually, this is the *fake* tomb. We didn't use that as the header in case players are peeking.

This is an epic-tier environment and the fake "true tomb" of the First Emperor. That's right—the PCs made it through the Maze of Death to access a tomb that secretly isn't real. Maybe they'll notice, but it's not likely because of the quality of the security arrangements! The Archmage saved his most devious traps and some tough guardians to keep this false tomb safe.

Elite Oozefolk Squads

Speaking of tough guardians, the "wandering" monsters in this dungeon aren't really wanderers. They're oozefolk warriors the Archmage trained (and possibly even created) as a last line of defense if the rest of Vantage's systems went down.

Story alternatives: What if the PCs befriended the oozefolk of Rynth? What if one or more PCs are oozefolk?

The first option is that these oozefolk squads are teleporting in from somewhere that's not quite Rynth. Perhaps Rynth was the creche for the oozefolk legions, but the toughest of them were somewhere else. This could crank up the melodrama—after a few violent interactions, the oozefolk defenders come to realize the PCs aren't necessarily enemies.

Alternatively, you can replace these battles with desperate fights against nasty adversary groups. That might make more sense for your story.

Oozefolk encounters: If you decide to go forward with oozefolk defenders, we suggest hitting the PCs with battles against the oozefolk elite at least twice during the rest of this dungeon exploration. The table lists two battles per level, both worth about a normal battle, with the understanding that groups with many characters need slightly bigger challenges.

Groups accustomed to dazing and stunning and otherwise controlling their enemies may be unpleasantly surprised when they fight the high-level rainbow puddings, since oozes are, by definition, immune to conditions.

Oozefolk Battle Wizard

Save vs. amazement.

9th level caster [HUMANOID]
Initiative: +15

Lightning staff +14 vs. PD—45 lightning damage
  Miss: 15 damage.

R: Acid arrow spell +14 vs. PD (one nearby or faraway enemy)—50 acid damage, and 15 ongoing acid damage.

C: Skullzfyre zap +14 vs. PD (one nearby enemy that misses with an attack with a natural 1-5)—15 lightning damage, and the target loses all bonuses and powers from one random true magic item until the end of the battle.
  Limited use: 2/battle, as an interrupt action.

C: Counter-magic +14 vs. MD (1 nearby enemy casting a spell)—The enemy's spell is canceled and has no effect.
  Natural even hit: The spell is expended as though the target had cast it (not a problem for at-will spells, but a big problem for others.)
  Limited use: 1/battle, as an interrupt action.

AC	24	
PD	19	**HP 180**
MD	23	

#/Level of PCs	Oozefolk Battlewizard	Rainbow Pudding	Oozefolk High Priest	Oozefolk Fanatic	Oozefolk Champion
3 x 8th level	1	0	0	4	1
3 x 8th level	1	1	1	0	0
4 x 8th level	1	0	1	4	1
4 x 8th level	2	1	0	3	0
5 x 8th level	1	1	1	4	1
5 x 8th level	0	0	2	2	2
6 x 8th level	1	2	1	4	1
6 x 8th level	0	0	2	8	2
7 x 8th level	1	2	1	4	2
7 x 8th level	0	0	2	8	3
3 x 9th level	3	0	0	4	1
3 x 9th level	1	1	2	0	0
4 x 9th level	3	0	0	5	2
4 x 9th level	2	2	2	0	0
5 x 9th level	3	0	0	7	3
5 x 9th level	5	2	2	0	0
6 x 9th level	3	0	2	7	3
6 x 9th level	5	2	4	0	0
7 x 9th level	3	0	2	8	4
7 x 9th level	4	4	3	0	0
3 x 10th level	4	2	0	0	0
3 x 10th level	0	0	2	6	2
4 x 10th level	4	3	0	0	1
4 x 10th level	0	0	3	6	3
5 x 10th level	4	3	1	0	2
5 x 10th level	1	0	3	8	4
6 x 10th level	4	3	2	0	3
6 x 10th level	2	0	3	8	5
7 x 10th level	4	3	3	0	4
7 x 10th level	2	1	3	12	5

RAINBOW PUDDING

Cyan, coral, striped pink, golden, or blue and green: anything but black for the pudding oozes of Rynth.

Large 9th level wrecker [OOZE]
Initiative: +9

C: Acid-drenched pseudopod +14 vs. PD (up to 3 attacks, each against a different nearby enemy)—60 damage, and 15 ongoing acid damage
Miss: 15 acid damage.

Climber: A rainbow pudding sticks to ceilings and walls when it wishes, sliding along as easily as on the floor.

Slippery: The pudding has *resist weapons 12+*.

AC	23	
PD	20	**HP 320**
MD	19	

OOZEFOLK HIGH PRIEST

Closer, our Archmage, to You.

10th level leader [HUMANOID]
Initiative: +16

Sacrificial spiked hammer +15 vs. AC—40 damage
Natural even miss: 20 holy damage.

R: Word of dissolution +13 vs. MD (one nearby or far away enemy)— 50 psychic damage, and 14 ongoing acid damage.

C: Bolstering word +15 vs. MD (1d3 nearby or far away enemies in a group)—40 holy and acid damage
Natural even hit: One oozefolk heals 25 hit points
Limited use: Only when the escalation die is odd.

Oozefolk form-shifting tricks: Once per round, when intercepted or about to suffer an opportunity attack, the priest can ignore the interception or attack, but has a −2 attack penalty until the end of its next turn.

AC	26	
PD	24	**HP 220**
MD	20	

OOZEFOLK FANATIC

Years of training ends in seven seconds of mayhem.

11th level mook [HUMANOID]
Initiative: +18

Acid-channeling spear +18 vs. AC—30 damage
Natural even hit or miss: 10 ongoing acid damage.

Surprising reach +18 vs. AC (1 nearby enemy)—15 damage
Natural even hit or miss: 10 ongoing acid damage.

Acidly defiant: An enemy taking ongoing acid damage can slay one oozefolk fanatic mook at most with an attack. Stop dealing damage to the mob at the point that another mook would be slain.

AC	26	
PD	25	**HP 68 (mook)**
MD	21	

Mook: Kill one oozefolk fanatic mook for every 68 damage you deal to the mob.

OOZEFOLK CHAMPION

She's a whole war of trouble in one quickly flowing warrior.

11th level blocker [HUMANOID]
Initiative: +18

Wicked blade +16 vs. AC—70 damage
Miss: 35 damage.

Engulf +16 vs. PD (2 attacks)—35 damage
Natural 16+: Target is engulfed if oozefolk champion wishes.

R: Acid arrow spell +16 vs. PD (one nearby or faraway enemy)—55 acid damage, and 15 ongoing acid damage.

Engulfed: An engulfed creature is grabbed, moves with the oozefolk champion, and takes half damage from each attack that hits the oozefolk. Ending the grab ends the engulfed condition. The oozefolk may only have one enemy engulfed at a time.

Desperate reach: When the oozefolk champion is staggered, it can make melee attacks against all nearby enemies as though it were engaged with them.

Ooze-fu: The oozefolk champion is immune to opportunity attacks, effects, and conditions.

Ooze-slinging: Provided there is a solid surface nearby, the legendary oozefolk champion can elongate its body to reach it; the oozefolk champion can move along any solid surface, sticking to it like glue.

AC	27	
PD	25	**HP 240**
MD	22	

AREAS IN THE TOMB

Now that the characters have met the major defenders, it's time to find out exactly what they're defending.

F: THE CORRIDOR OF AIR

This 200-foot long corridor is more than it seems. Anybody can see that it's a circular metal tube, inscribed with designs of warriors on horses fighting undead creatures. Once inside the corridor, the tube shifts back and forth slightly, and winding mechanisms fire darts through cunningly concealed holes. It takes a DC 25 skill check for each character to dodge.

One thousand darts +15 vs. AC—6d6 damage.

Once the characters reach the halfway point of the corridor, it reveals its true nature and pivots to become a vertical shaft. It is a DC 30 skill check for the most perceptive adventurer to figure out what's up before it all goes down, allowing the characters to grab hold and avoid falling. **Sudden drop +20 vs. AC (each adventurer present, unless they were warned in time)**—4d10 damage.

But wait, that's not all. When the shaft becomes vertical, it begins to fill with hot acid from the bottom, up (DC 30 check to get above the acid). **Acid pool +20 vs. PD (each adventurer present)**—3d6 + 20 acid damage.

There's more! A horrid word in a long-forgotten, abyssal language is written in shimmering letters on the ceiling at the top of the shaft. It requires a DC 30 skill check for each character to realize that's not a place they should look. **Worm words +20 vs. MD (each adventurer who looks at the word on the ceiling)**—30 psychic damage.

There's a small, recessed lever at the very top of the vertical shaft, which resets the corridor (provided everybody is at the upper part of the shaft) and takes everybody back to the beginning of the corridor once more.

The only way to avoid these traps is to float down the corridor without touching it at all, or to jam the mechanism before entering the corridor in the first place (DC 30 skill check). The corridor exits into the Glass Hall.

G: THE GLASS HALL

This floor in this large, square room is made from square panes of glass. There are doorways in the four corners of the room *[leads to F, H, I, and J]*. Under the floor is a pool of boiling hot acid, in which magical acid-proof lava sharks swim.

It is a DC 25 skill check to crawl slowly across the floor, while evenly distributing weight to avoid breaking the glass and falling in to the boiling acid. The panes magically levitate—just because one character falls, doesn't mean the others do. There's a message etched in tiny letters on each floor tile:

"You are obviously intent on finding what is hidden here. That is why I, the Archmage, etched this glass floor with explosive runes. Farewell forever!"

Reading the message causes that floor tile to explode (3d20 force damage) and the surrounding tiles to shatter, dumping the character straight into the acid. The acid does 10 points of acid and fire damage each round; climbing out of the acid onto the glass floor just breaks additional floor tiles. The only way to get out of the acid is to swim to the edge, shatter the glass tiles, and climb up to a door (takes 2d4 move actions). Unfortunately, the lava sharks attack anybody who falls into the acid. Use as many lava sharks as you feel are dramatically necessary.

LAVA SHARK

It either survived a world where the oceans were full of lava, or it's a wizard's idea of a joke.

Huge 8th level troop [BEAST]
Initiative: +16

Maw +13 vs. AC (3 attacks)—35 damage
   Natural even roll: 10 fire damage
   Natural odd roll: The lava shark may pop free if it wishes.

Resist acid and fire 18+: When an acid or fire attack targets this creature, the attacker must roll a natural 18+ on the attack roll or it only deals half damage.

Swim: Lava sharks can swim in boiling acidic pools; however, though they can survive in regular water, their body-chemistry tends to kill all other plants and animals in that water after a couple of days.

AC	24	
PD	22	**HP 432**
MD	18	

SHARK ATTACK

The Archmage made these lava sharks immortal. . . and they're hungry. There is a chance they just start leaping up through the glass even if the PCs manage to avoid breaking the floor themselves. By the way, if you end up running a full oozefolk battle in this room, the oozefolk have no problem sliding over the glass without breaking it.

H: THE TOMB OF WOLVES

The well-carved door to this tomb depicts wolves paying homage to a figure that looks like the First Emperor's profile on ancient coins. The tomb is chock-full of gold coins, magical treasures, and forgotten artifacts from a lost time. Yes, this is great loot! Pick four to six true magic items and scatter them throughout the tomb. Some may only be champion-tier; still, frolic in the loot.

The sarcophagus: The stone sarcophagus at the end of the room does not contain the Emperor's corpse or anyone else, living or dead. However, opening the sarcophagus triggers a preset teleport that ushers in a squad of constructs. Use a battle from the *Golem* adversary group (page 207). If you're tired of golem battles, splice in a few oozefolk.

Make it abundantly clear that this is not the tomb the characters were hoping to find.

I: THE TOMB OF DRAGONS

This tomb is laid out in the same way as the Tomb of Wolves [*area H*], but the carving on its door depicts a crowned human female commanding an army of dragon-riders. The sarcophagus here contains a mummified human woman, dressed in golden armor blazoned with the Emperor's symbol. (Note that we didn't say an undead mummy. She's merely dead. She's Lich King-proof.)

This incredibly rich sarcophagus, the treasure it contains, and the lack of guardians found in all the false tombs, are designed to satisfy looters' desires.

But there's more. . . Under the mummified body, the sarcophagus has a false bottom (DC 30 check to spot it). If the characters open the false bottom, it reveals a set of steps that leads downward [*leads to K*].

Loot: There's more great loot here—as many as four true magic items scattered among the treasure in the room and another four to six in the sarcophagus. These should be items the PCs really want. Maybe even an artifact.

J: THE TOMB OF STALLIONS

This tomb is identical to the Tomb of Wolves [*area H*], except the door depicts a crowned man riding a stallion, dressed in full plate as though ready for battle. The sarcophagus contains a living statue of one of the First Emperor's lieutenants. And by living statue, we mean *"a creature that looks like a living statue and fights a lot like an Imperial Golem."* We provide slightly variant stats below. Roll initiative.

We don't see this as a fight that has to be balanced, but if there are too many PCs for a fight against a single golem to be interesting, add a somewhat damaged imperial golem (page 175) to the mix; possibly the somewhat self-repaired golem the characters thought they eliminated earlier.

Loot: Scatter 2 to 5 true magic items in this room. Choose these randomly; they do not necessarily need to be items the PCs have at the top of their wish lists.

GOLEM LIEUTENANT

That's Lieutenant Golem to you.

Triple-strength 12th level wrecker [CONSTRUCT]
Initiative: +17

Fist and shockwave +17 vs. PD (three attacks, each against a different nearby target)—80 damage, plus 20 damage for each fist and shockwave attack that hit earlier this round
Miss: 25 damage.

Seeker: When a nearby enemy casts a spell, the golem lieutenant rolls a hard save as a free action. If the save succeeds, the golem can add an extra target to its next *fist and shockwave* attack.

Golem immunity: Non-organic golems are immune to effects. They can't be dazed, weakened, confused, made vulnerable, or touched by ongoing damage. You can damage a golem, but that's about it.

AC	28	
PD	22	**HP 1100**
MD	26	

THE SECRET THRONE

This is truly (well, more or less!) the First Emperor's final resting place; and the Archmage prepared traps here that could kill anything short of a demigod. If the characters have made it this far, they should be prepared for the worst.

Defenders: Oozefolk and golems sporadically teleport into the dungeon. Every time the characters explore a new area, have the least lucky PC roll a normal save. If the save fails, a fresh bunch of oozefolk and/or golem defenders teleport into the dungeon somewhere near the Radiant Pool [*Area K*] and come for the PCs as quickly as they can. If the PCs make the save too often, you have our permission to fake a glance at a tension table and rule that the save DC went up an increment.

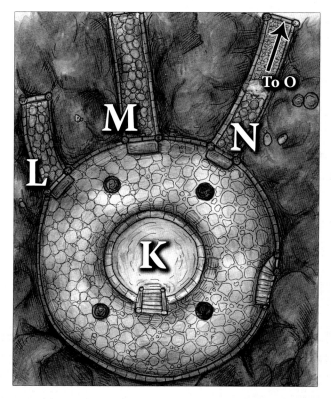

K: THE RADIANT POOL

This wide, domed room has three doors in the far wall *[leads to L, M, and N]*, and a set of steps that lead up to a hidden door at the bottom of a sarcophagus *[leads to I]*.

There's a reflecting pool full of a super-healing potion in the center of the room. It takes a DC 35 skill check to realize the healing potion has another enchantment on it.

Anybody who drinks the potion instantly heals to full hit-points. . . and then teleports, naked, to a point high above the dungeon's exterior (4d10 + 40 falling damage). Their equipment and clothing remain in the pool.

Anybody who steps into the pool (to say, fish out their friend's stuff) or accidentally falls in during a fight against oozefolk also teleports naked into the sky.

Characters who watch their colleagues disappear have little reason to believe the pool did not just evaporate their friends. An hour-long ritual (DC 30 skill check) turns 1d10 doses of the drops-you-out-of-the-sky potion into half as many regular epic-tier healing potions.

Clothed Alternatives

I said I kept ASH's old-school dungeon old-school and look—that's some old-school naked teleportation right there! Still, this feels like the type of PC removal that we work to avoid in 13th Age.

If your group contains players who are interested in finding out what happens to a naked, epic-tier character who drops from a height on top of the trap-filled dungeon that was tough to navigate as a full party. . . well, you know your group. Perhaps high-level magic or icon relationship advantages can offer a quick solution. Or maybe people who drink out of glowing pools in a dungeon that just went to ridiculous lengths to kill them deserve to sit out awhile!

Alternatively, if you'd rather not GM or wave your hand at a PC who is suddenly cut off from the group, use this effect instead: the pool powers-up all true magic items—to the point that they take over the character until after at least the next battle. See page 285 of the 13th Age core rulebook for a reminder of what the PC is in for with this effect. Have the PC roll a hard save at the end of each battle to attempt to shake off the effect.

L: THE HALL OF DOOM

This empty hallway seems to have only the one door through which the characters entered *[leads to K]*. As soon as a character steps through it, a magical projection of an oozefolk wizard in the garb of the Archmage appears and berates the intruder.

> *"Halt. Go no further. You are brave, and bravery should be rewarded; but what lies within this place is not for you. Turn back, and I shall richly reward you. Proceed and face my wrath."*

If the adventurers can convince the Archooze-projection that they need to find the First Emperor's body (a DC 40 skill check, or some very clever role-playing and a DC 30 skill check) it directs them back to the third door *[leads to N]* in the Radiant Pool *[Area K]* and offers to provide magical aid. It can enchant up to three items, making them epic-level magic items (this is also what it offers for the characters to turn back). It also disarms the Hall

of Destruction *[Area N]* for them and calls off the teleporting squads of oozefolk and golem defenders. At this stage, the Archooze-simulacrum has limited knowledge. It knows nothing of The Starry Stair *[Area O]* or what lies beyond; and it knows only about this dungeon, not anything the Archmage created before or since.

If the characters cannot convince it to help, the Archooze smiles (?) sadly (?) and disappears in a burst of magic (see *Ooze & Consequences*).

OOZE & CONSEQUENCES

As discussed earlier, this dungeon probably shouldn't be the last adventure of your campaign. The Archooze influences our judgement! If the PCs fail to convince the Archooze of their good intentions, it opposes them for the rest of their epic-tier lives, or until they somehow manage to convince it that they truly are on the Archmage's side (even if they're not!).

Here's one example of how the Archooze might resurface: keep track of every time a character rolls a 1 for any icon relationship. Each instance becomes a moment that the Archooze simulacrum flickers into existence to mess with the PCs' lives. The Archooze might summon a new monster to a battle, force a reroll of a crucial save, or make a fumble with a spell into a truly embarrassing fiasco.

Alternatively, if the PCs end up in the Archooze's good graces, you could allow the Archooze to flicker in occasionally to help, perhaps as a feature of an Archmage icon relationship advantage or perhaps as its own thing.

M: THE ILLUSIONARY HALLWAY

This long hallway is cloaked in illusion (DC 30 check to spot the illusion), which hides an identical hallway—the hallway is disguised as itself and overlays an illusion of the characters onto themselves.

As soon as a character steps fully into the hallway, it teleports them back to the Glass Hall *[Area G]*, but their illusion continues to walk forward. Those watching believe their companion stepped safely into the hallway (DC 35 check to spot the deception).

This empty hallway has only one door, through which the characters entered *[leads to K]*.

N: THE HALL OF DESTRUCTION

This long hallway appears to be empty, just like the other two *[Areas L and M]*; however, once a character steps inside, they immediately see through the illusion.

There's a huge pile of gold (over 20,000 gp) at the end of the corridor, hidden from the outside by the illusion. The gold is mostly in the form of coins, but there are a few bars, bags of gold dust, and jewelry. Glittering gems, huge pearls, and platinum are mixed in with the gold. It's genuine treasure, just waiting for somebody to claim it.

The treasure, however, is cursed. The instant more than one character touches the loot, the curse activates—causing all characters in the area to become confused (hard save ends) and start to fight over the gold.

It takes a day-long ritual and a DC 35 skill check to remove the curse from the loot. Behind the huge pile of loot is a door *[leads to O]*; however, the characters cannot access the door until they move the gold out of the way.

O: THE STARRY STAIR

Through the door are stepping stones that lead up through several dimensions, suspended in a celestial void.

Stepping from one stone to the next is easy at first but becomes increasingly difficult. It takes a DC 15 skill check for the first stone, then a DC 20 skill check, and so on—until the last check requires a DC 35 skill check. Failure at any point means the character falls into the celestial void.

Characters who tumble through the celestial void must make last gasp saves or be lost in time and space (if they save, they land on a lower stepping stone). Another character may attempt to grab a falling character (DC 30 check to grab hold of a floating friend); but, if they fail, they must roll a normal save (11+) or fall into the void themselves.

Being lost in time and space isn't the same as dying, but whether the character can return is up to GM fiat or the remaining characters carrying out a very cunning metaphysical rescue plan.

Double doors sit at the top of the stepping stones *[leads to F]*.

If you lose a character to the celestial void, well. . . the end of the 10th level and the campaign are near. It sounds like you are about to start a new campaign.

A hero who falls out of the sky into an unfamiliar situation could be a great start to a new campaign (see Evil Dead 3: Army of Darkness, Wizard of Oz, Superman, etc.). You can even "reset" the character to a lower level if the campaign is starting at adventurer-tier or epic-tier.

Sure, we would not typically drop a character's level, but this provides a way to bring an epic-tier character back to adventurer-tier so they can go adventuring all over again. You could even let the player re-stat the character "Hey, that journey through the cosmic void weakened me but gave me magical powers. I guess I'm not a barbarian anymore; instead, I'm a wizard!"

P: THE FINAL THRONE

Through the double doors, the characters step into a paradise: the sky is blue, with a permanent rainbow; the grass is green, and fluffy bunnies hop among the dandelions while butterflies flutter just over their heads; a brook bubbles musically; and everywhere they look, there are fruits and berries to pick and eat.

Some of the fruit has magical properties that act as epic-tier healing potions. A feeling of peace and tranquility settles over the characters. The weather is perfect—the artificial sun is not too hot and, if they stick around long enough, the characters find that the diamond-lit nights are never too cold.

The area is quite large—about a two-day walk across at its widest point—and thousands of shimmering portals to various parts of the Dragon Empire sit around its edge. The portals are huge, and they allow anybody in this realm to step through to almost anywhere in the Dragon Empire (or at least within sight of their destination). Any character who steps through a portal finds themselves somewhere else in the Dragon Empire; however, they cannot return to the paradise—the portals don't work that way). An earlier Archmage might have used this as his personal transportation hub.

A small hill in the center of the area holds a giant, golden throne, flanked by ten imperial golems (page 175). This is the First Emperor's final resting place—a golden throne that looks out on portals to the empire.

QUESTIONS FOR YOUR CAMPAIGN

As mentioned earlier, we won't tell you precisely how to end an epic-tier adventure that's so close to the end of your campaign. It seems likely that PCs with good reasons for fighting their way through to the First Emperor's spirit may have worthwhile questions or requests. . . or missions created by the iconic angles discussed on page 40. Unless you're using one of those iconic angle plotlines, or the PCs are out to destroy the Empire, it seems entirely possible that the spirit of the First Emperor might look favorably upon heroes who've been so determined to win an audience.

Or maybe your campaign's unique events have set things up so that the Empire is hopelessly corrupt and the First Emperor needs to come back to start over? Epic-tier campaigns usually have their own list of ongoing questions and earth-shaking potential answers. In case you're reading this in search of such questions, here are a few we might ask in our campaigns:

- Is this the end of your campaign, or a springboard toward the end?
- Do the imperial golems allow the characters to approach the throne? (Probably not, if they're enemies.)
- Can the characters win a fight against ten imperial golems if it comes to that? (Possibly not.)
- Does the First Emperor's spirit want to speak with the PCs?
- Does the spirit possess artifacts or wisdom the PCs need to save the Empire? Or, for some reason known only to your campaign, to destroy it?
- Is the First Emperor really a fan of fluffy bunnies and eternal rainbows, or is there another, more imperial layer of reality that becomes apparent as soon as the PCs are in his or her presence?
- Is the First Emperor's spirit here, or did it already go on ahead to where the PCs must now quest to aid it?

CHAPTER 10:

NEWCOMERS

The fall of Vantage and Redfield Valley's failing wards could add three new player character races to your campaign. It's your call whether you'd like to make these races part of the standard player character pool or treat them as great *uniques*.

The **lava dwarves** of Magaheim may or may not be the same as the azers, which the PCs may have encountered before. It's up to you. If so, adventurers occasionally encounter them in deep places under volcanoes, but a whole city of them appearing on the surface could change the politics of the Dragon Empire.

It's possible nobody has ever seen **oozefolk** before, but just as likely they are a long-forgotten race that has returned.

Most everyone in the current Dragon Empire who knows about the **ophidians** believes they are mythical or long-extinct . . . for what that's worth! Surely magicians other than the PCs have noticed that everything dead eventually lives again!

PLAYER CHARACTERS ARE DIFFERENT

The lava dwarves, oozefolk, and ophidian heroes who qualify as PCs aren't like the others of their kind! Some of the abilities for the player characters that follow exceed or vary greatly from the abilities of similar creatures we created as monsters. That's how PCs roll; but, if you're feeling ambitious and want to complicate life for your PCs instead of helping them out, feel free to fold some of these new abilities into recurring villains, as well.

Feat mechanics: Unless specified, the feats linked to these racial powers and talents aren't progressive. Characters must take a feat that corresponds to their tier.

LAVA DWARF

+2 Con OR +2 Wis

BLISTERING HEAT (RACIAL POWER)

Once per battle, after you are hit by an enemy attack, you may make a basic or at-will attack as a free action with the attacking enemy as the only target. Your attack deals fire damage instead of any other type; if that requires rephrasing a spell, it's your fiery supernatural power that takes precedence!

Adventurer Feat: Gain *resist fire 16+*. When you successfully resist a fire damage attack, you gain temporary hit points equal to your Constitution modifier (champion: double your Constitution modifier; epic: triple).

Adventurer Feat: You can cast the wizard cantrip *spark* at-will as a quick action.

Adventurer Feat: Once per day, when you suffer a critical hit, heal using a free recovery (unless you are dead).

Adventurer Feat: When attacking an enemy that deals cold damage, roll an additional die and take the higher result. If at least two of your attack rolls would hit, the attack is a critical hit (if three attack rolls would hit, the critical hit does triple damage, and so on).

Champion Feat: On an even attack roll, your *blistering heat* attack does ongoing fire damage equal to three times your level.

Champion Feat: Gain a +1 bonus to AC.

Champion Feat: This feat requires the first adventurer feat listed above. Your *resist fire* ability from the adventurer feat improves to 18+, and temporary hit points gained increase to triple your Constitution modifier (epic: quadruple).

Lava dwarf feats: Unlike other races, you don't have to take the lava dwarf feats in any specific order. If you wish, you can skip all the adventurer feats and choose only a champion feat.

FLAME BORN (RACIAL TALENT)

Special: A lava dwarf may take this racial talent in place of one of their class talents.

Gain two adventurer-tier lava dwarf feats.

LAVA DWARF STORIES

In *Shards of the Broken Sky*, the lava dwarf race is a result of the Old Tusk dwarves interbreeding with demons and living in a city bathed in volcanic energies. They might resemble dwarves with magma-like skin or miniature fire giants.

In your campaign, lava-dwarves might only originate in the city of Magaheim, or they might be the Dwarf King's secret, or this may be how you want to introduce azers as player characters.

LAVA DWARVES AND THE ICONS

Lava dwarves should shake up the status quo. To start, they may not acknowledge the supremacy of the Dwarf King and might fight against his attempts to bring them under his control.

Their affinity for fire and volcanoes, together with their demonic heritage, could see them working for the Diabolist.

The Red (of The Three) might also find eager followers in the pyromantic dwarves.

Lava dwarves may also end up serving The Crusader, if they are keen to express centuries of pent-up frustration at their more respectable, "demonic" neighbors in Magaheim.

OOZEFOLK

+2 Dex OR +2 Con

Acidic blood: Your melee attacks do acid damage while you are staggered.

OOZY (RACIAL POWER)

Once per battle, when you are subjected to a condition (dazed, hampered, ongoing damage, etc.), you can either pop free as a move action OR roll a save as a free action to end it, even if the condition does not normally end on a save (such as being dazed until the end of your next turn).

Adventurer Feat: You have a +5 bonus to checks that involve squeezing through narrow spaces, escaping restraints, and similar checks that are just easier if you're oozy.

Champion Feat: You can use both *oozy* effects once each per battle (so, you can both pop free AND make a free save against a condition).

Epic Feat: Once per day, when you are stunned or helpless in a battle (including when making death or last gasp saves), you can use a standard action on your turn to make a basic or at-will attack against the closest nearby enemy (determine randomly if there's more than one), OR you may use a move action to move closer to an enemy. (These are the only actions possible using this feat—you're using your ooziness instinctively, not trying to figure out how best to use a standard action while helpless.)

ACIDIC TOUCH (RACIAL TALENT)

Special: Oozefolk may take this racial talent in place of one of their class talents.

On an even hit, your melee and weapon attacks do extra acid damage equal to twice your level.

When you are grabbed (or swallowed, etc.) the creature grabbing you takes acid damage equal to twice your level at the start of your turn.

OOZEFOLK STORIES

If you follow the plot from the dungeon of Rynth, oozefolk start the game trapped in a living dungeon; therefore, they're probably extremely rare. Then again, in your campaign, oozefolk may live in a lot of living dungeons—as well as in the underworld. They may not be as hidden as the Archmage intended.

If oozefolk are truly unaware of the outside world beyond the half-remembered legends of their god, the Archmage, their heroes' interactions with the Dragon Empire are perfect for the fish/ooze out of water/dungeon roleplaying some players love.

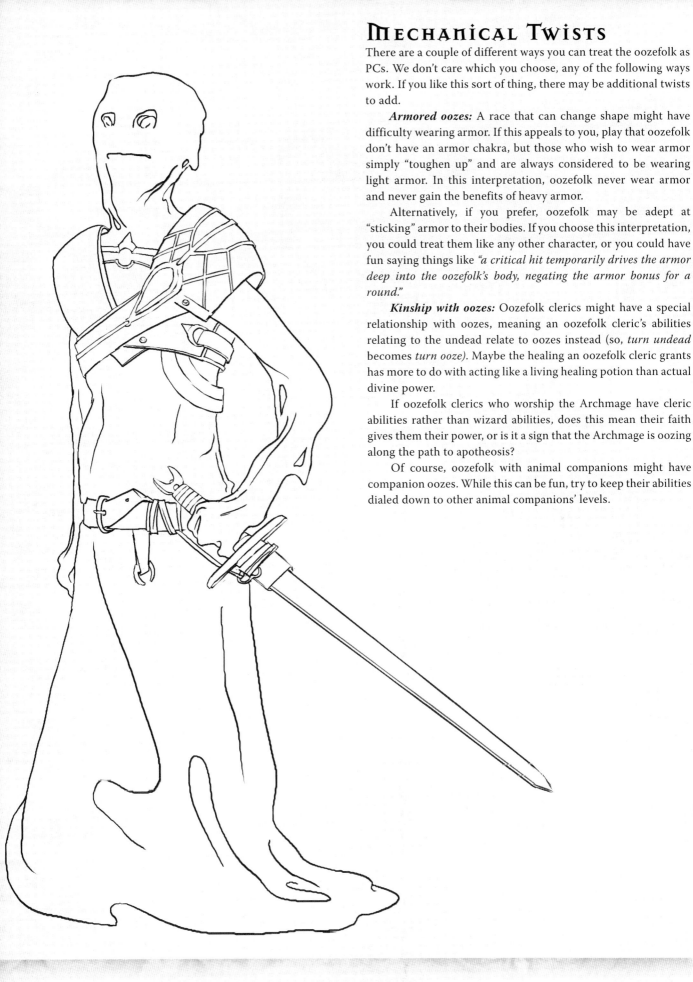

MECHANICAL TWISTS

There are a couple of different ways you can treat the oozefolk as PCs. We don't care which you choose, any of the following ways work. If you like this sort of thing, there may be additional twists to add.

Armored oozes: A race that can change shape might have difficulty wearing armor. If this appeals to you, play that oozefolk don't have an armor chakra, but those who wish to wear armor simply "toughen up" and are always considered to be wearing light armor. In this interpretation, oozefolk never wear armor and never gain the benefits of heavy armor.

Alternatively, if you prefer, oozefolk may be adept at "sticking" armor to their bodies. If you choose this interpretation, you could treat them like any other character, or you could have fun saying things like *"a critical hit temporarily drives the armor deep into the oozefolk's body, negating the armor bonus for a round."*

Kinship with oozes: Oozefolk clerics might have a special relationship with oozes, meaning an oozefolk cleric's abilities relating to the undead relate to oozes instead (so, *turn undead* becomes *turn ooze*). Maybe the healing an oozefolk cleric grants has more to do with acting like a living healing potion than actual divine power.

If oozefolk clerics who worship the Archmage have cleric abilities rather than wizard abilities, does this mean their faith gives them their power, or is it a sign that the Archmage is oozing along the path to apotheosis?

Of course, oozefolk with animal companions might have companion oozes. While this can be fun, try to keep their abilities dialed down to other animal companions' levels.

Ophidian

+2 Int OR +2 Wis

Poison Fangs (Racial Power)

Once per battle, when an enemy makes a melee attack against you or becomes engaged with you, make an attack against them as an interrupt action. Instead of your usual attack bonus, the attack bonus is equal to your level +4 vs. AC (champion tier: level +6; epic tier: level +8). A hit deals 1d6 x your level damage, and an even hit adds half that much ongoing poison damage.

> *Adventurer Feat:* When you roll a natural, even hit for the first attack on your turn, you may use a move action as a quick action once before the end of your turn.

> *Champion Feat:* You may use *poison fangs* a second time each battle; however, the second attack only does ongoing poison damage on a natural 18+.

> *Epic Feat:* When you roll a natural even miss for the first attack on your turn, you may make an at-will or basic attack as a quick action before the end of your turn.

Ophidian Stories

These snake-like, possibly legless and many-armed humanoids were the serpent archons' (probably) unwilling servants. If the adventurers allow the serpent archons' tomb to rise to the surface, there are soon a lot of ophidians in the world—not just those who awaken from the tomb, but also those who were hibernating elsewhere. Even if the adventurers kill the serpent archons and all the hibernating ophidians, they might still miss a few slaves who make their way out of Redfield Valley.

Conceptually, the ophidians are close to dragonics; so, if you like one but not the other, you could substitute them throughout your campaign. Maybe ophidians and dragonic are two branches of the same race (like high elves and drow), or perhaps they are ancient enemies that predate the coming of the warm-blooded races.

Ophidians might be very rare, or they might emerge from hibernation all over the Dragon Empire. Maybe they *already* emerged and helped bring Vantage down to free their trapped masters.

In fact, that scenario seems especially likely if you want to introduce ophidian PCs during your first run through Redfield Valley! If you wait until epic-tier player characters get around to climbing the serpent archons' pyramid, you pretty much guarantee there won't be any ophidians in the earlier tiers. Maybe an ophidian PC drawn to Redfield Valley foreshadows the threat of the serpent archons. The PC's epic destiny is to confront the monsters that enslaved their people.

Serpents' Praise

Ophidians once worshiped dragon gods, but those gods are long gone. . . or are they? Might the dragon gods reawaken? Perhaps the draconic icons (The Three and the Great Gold Wyrm) *are* the last of the dragon gods.

APPENDIX A:
MAGICAL TREASURES

Adventurers can find the following magical items in the ruins of Vantage.

FADING ITEMS

Fading items have some sort of external, mystical power source—when separated by distance or time from that source, their magic fades. Vantage's magic empowered these items. Some were not originally weapons at all, they were just part of Vantage. There may be a way to recharge some of these items, but that probably requires a quest and that charge is more than likely to fade, as well.

FADING WEAPONS

Twist of Glowing Metal (light two-handed melee weapon): Ignore the normal default bonus for weapons. The first session you have this weapon, it has a +4 to hit and damage; the next session, it has a +2 to hit and damage; the session after that, the glow fades and it is just a piece of sharp metal. Quirk: Insists on picking up and trying to fix broken things.

Glowing Lump of Rock (heavy two-handed melee weapon): Ignore the normal default bonus for weapons. The first session you have this weapon, it has a +1 attack bonus and deals +2d8 damage; the next session, it has no attack bonus and deals +1d8 damage; the session after that, it is just a big rock with –2 to hit. Quirk: Wants to get as high as possible.

Shard of Frozen Lightning (any thrown weapon — recharge 11+): Ignore the normal default bonus for weapons. The first session you have this weapon, you may teleport as a quick action after a natural even hit; the next session, you may teleport as a move action after a natural even hit; the session after that, the lightning fades away and the item is a large piece of glass. Quirk: Risky behavior around heights and magic.

Energy Bow (shortbow or longbow—recharge 11+): Ignore the normal default bonus for weapons. The first session you have this weapon, when you hit a target, you may include a second nearby target in the attack using the same attack roll; the next session, when you hit a target, you may include a second nearby target in the attack, but must make a new attack roll for the second target; the session after that, it's just a regular bow. Quirk: Eyes on the skies to the point of missing things on the ground.

FADING WONDROUS ITEM

Glowing Rune-Carved Pebble (recharge 11+): The first session you have this item, you may heal a nearby ally to full hp as a quick action by spending a recovery; the next session, you may heal a nearby staggered ally to half hp as a quick action by spending 2 recoveries; the session after that, the glow fades and it is just a rock. Quirk: Hyperactive concern for the safety of others.

CRYSTAL ITEMS

A vast number of magical crystals were worked into Vantage's lattices, towers, and defenses. Some crystals can still function as magical treasure now that their original purpose was eliminated.

CRYSTAL SHARDS

These shards grow larger as the character to whom they are attuned rises in tier. Crystal shards begin as wands in adventurer tier, transitioning from wand to staff at either champion or epic tier.

Default bonus: Attack and damage with arcane spells or attacks: +1 (adventurer); +2 (champion); +3 (epic).

Prismatic Shard: You deal +2d6 damage of a random type with your *second* attack each battle (champion: +2d12; epic: +2d20) Roll for the random type after you roll to attack.

1. Acid, 2. Cold, 3. Fire, 4. Force, 5. Holy, 6. Lightning, 7. Negative Energy, 8. Poison, 9. Psychic, 10. Thunder. Quirk: Obsessed with rainbows.

Dark Crystal: When you miss all targets with a daily attack spell, you may forgo any miss effect and spend a recovery to heal as a free action. Quirk: Unhealthy obsession with torture; either delivered or received.

Verdant Gem (recharge 11+): The first time an enemy takes a move action to engage you in battle, it must make an easy save (6+) or it becomes weakened until it is no longer engaged with you. Quirk: Megalomania.

CRYSTAL WEAPONS

Default bonus: Attacks and damage when using the weapon: +1 (adventurer); +2 (champion); +3 (epic).

Crystal Blade (any bladed melee weapon): You may make basic ranged attacks with this weapon. Quirk: Sketches and paints landscapes. Constantly.

Gem Weapon (any weapon): When you roll a critical hit with this weapon, the target becomes vulnerable to your attacks (save ends). Quirk: Squints in bright light.

Rainbow Knife (any heavy thrown weapon): Increase the damage dice for this weapon by 1 step (d6=d8, d8=d10, etc.). Can also be used as a light, two-handed melee weapon. Quirk: Fascinated by refracted light and prisms.

CRYSTAL WONDROUS ITEMS

These crystals still hold some of Vantage's power. So far, it hasn't faded.

Default bonus: None.

Crystal Cutter: You can coax a ray of coherent light from this gemstone. While not suitable for combat, it can be focused and used to swiftly cut through any non-magical material. Cutting through a lock on a door takes 1 full round; cutting through iron manacles takes 2 rounds, cutting a hole in a steel cage large enough to climb through takes 3 rounds. The crystal has 1d3 charges per day. Quirk: Cuts through things that maybe shouldn't be destroyed when there's nothing available that needs to be cut through.

Crystal Lantern (recharge 11+): Create "solid light" objects that appear to be made of rainbow light and fade away quickly. As a quick action, you may give an ally +3 to their AC, MD, or PD until the end of their next turn (champion: +4; epic +5). Quirk: Must speak a rhyme at the start of each battle.

Glowshard (recharge 6+): The crystal sheds bright light. As a quick action, you may intensify the light, revealing any undead in your presence for what they are. Disguised undead become obvious, invisible undead become visible, and those with strong links to the Lich King are revealed. Revealed undead take −1 to all defenses until the start of your next turn. Quirk: Fear of darkness.

Higher Level Items

Sometimes, your PCs might get ahold of a higher-level item. The 13th Age core rulebook says they may attune to such an item, but it counts as 2 or 3 items-worth of attunement. For example, if an adventurer-tier character attunes to a champion-tier item, they fill up 2 "slots" (or chakras); if they attune to an epic-tier item, they fill up 3 chakras. If a champion-tier character attunes to an epic-tier item, they fill up 2 chakras. Attuning to an item of the same tier (or lower) costs 1 chakra.

I do things a bit differently in my home game. I say items that appear at different levels (such as a sword that has a +1, +2, and +3 version) are always the same tier as the person wielding them. Basically, more powerful characters have more powerful souls and can bond more deeply with their magic items; lower-tier items have hidden powers that require time to unlock; and items that only appear at champion or epic tiers simply reject characters of a lower tier as unworthy to wield them.

I'm stingier with magic items, but I allow the items that do show up to remain with a character for the rest of their adventuring career. Choose what works best for your campaign, of course!

ADVERSARY GROUPS

Building battles is part of the fun of planning sessions of your campaign, but it's a drag to buy a book that doesn't help set up at least *some* of the battles for you. This *Adversary Groups* section splits the difference. We provide one or two interesting battles per tier for several adversary groups, as well all the monster stats for those fights. For other groups, we provide harvesting guidelines for grabbing monsters from other books.

Remember that fights don't always have to be fair, but these tables provide multiple options for what a fair fight should look like. Some of them are built slightly tougher than the exact number of PCs, especially when there are 5 to 7 heroes. If a fight is tougher than you planned, enemies don't *have* to fight to the death and might leave to heal and return later . . . or be driven off by the adventurers' ferocity. If a fight is easier than you intended, it could be because the enemies are stalling for time until reinforcements can come. Generally, adventurers should face four fair fights before getting a full heal-up, or two tough double-strength skin-of-the-teeth fights.

Reprints: This section includes reprints of monsters from a variety of *13th Age* books. Some of the "reprints" are actually level-ups—for example, the 6th level devoted blue sorcerer on page 198 is an update of the original 3rd level blue sorcerer (**13B**: 21).

New monsters: For a list of all the new monsters we introduce in this book, see the New Monster table on page 221.

ADVERSARY GROUP SUMMARIES

Here's a quick summary of what's in this appendix.

Agents of the Prince of Shadows: Special abilities for double-agents devoted to the Prince of Shadows, who is too cool to do anything as crass as send squadrons and warriors of mages.

Agents of the Three: Prebuilt battles for adventurer-tier and champion-tier, including two or three new monsters.

Demons of the Prism: Prebuilt battles for adventurer-tier and champion-tier, as well as four or five all-new monsters.

Golems: A note on adventurer-tier battles, followed by three new golems and battles for champion-tier.

Lava demons: Prebuilt battles for adventurer-tier and champion tier, along with four new demons.

Orcs of the Orc Lord: Notes on building battles, a variant rule for Orc Lord battles, and three new monsters.

Orcwell: Notes on building battles and two new monsters.

Raptors: A couple new monsters and battles built with them for 4th through 7th levels.

Undead: Notes about recruiting monsters from other books, accompanied by two new monsters.

Wizards & Spellcasters: Our list of adventurer-tier and champion-tier creatures includes six or seven new spellcasters and bodyguards, depending on how you count.

AGENTS OF THE PRINCE OF SHADOWS

There isn't an adversary group for the Prince of Shadows. Squads of warriors and magical cadres are too blunt for the Prince. Instead, pick some creatures from another icon's agents—they are actually working for the Prince of Shadows. *Shhh!*

The Prince of Shadows has probably just co-opted humanoids as double-agents... but you can never tell. Perhaps he convinced dragons to join him or slipped an agent into Rynth to bring the ultra-loyal oozefolk to his side.

Here's a list of abilities that creatures who work for the Prince of Shadows might possess. Using such abilities might risk betraying the creature's true allegiance too early, but in a world with all types of magical power, the Prince's agents know how to use misdirection.

Shadow-walking: Once per fight as a standard action the creature can "walk into the shadow" and is removed from play. At the start of its next turn, it returns to play at a point on the battlefield of its choosing. Its next attack deals double damage.

Surprise attack: Once per fight on an enemy's turn after the enemy makes an attack roll, the creature interrupts the attack before it is resolved and makes an attack against the enemy whose attack was interrupted. After the attack against the enemy is resolved; the enemy must roll a save (11+) or their attack roll counts as a miss.

Filching: Once per fight, at the end of its turn as a free action; the creature may roll an attack (**+14 vs MD**) against an enemy with which it is engaged. On a success, the creature steals a magic item from the enemy.

Vanish: Once per fight, the creature may attempt to vanish (via a smoke bomb, teleportation spell, or other low-down trickery) and leave the fight. The creature makes an attack against the nearest enemy (**+14 vs MD**), on "hit" the creature vanishes and leaves the battle. On a crit it may attempt to use *filching* as it vanishes, even if it does not normally have the ability (or has already used it in this fight). On a failure, the creature's attempt at trickery fizzles at its feet, making it look rather foolish.

AGENTS OF THE THREE

The Three are likely villains, possessing the mix of brute force and magical savagery that seems required to take down a fortress like Vantage. The Three also suit plotlines in which the villains work at cross-purposes with each other. For example, the Black might have engineered the fall of Vantage while the Blue and Red scramble to catch up!

ADVENTURER-TIER AGENTS OF THE THREE

You're most likely to use this adversary group while adventuring in the *glitterfall*, Shattered Spine, Lightning Spires, and perhaps the adventures in Redfield Valley and the Orcwell. To expand the roster, consider Rezlorkis the dragonic wizard (page 13, and also appropriate for champion-tier), and the rest of the kobolds from *13th Age Bestiary* (page 124) and *13th Age Bestiary 2*. We left out many of our favorites that would fit right in as part of either main grouping presented in the Building Battle tables.

#/Level of PCs	Kobold Grand-Wizard	Kobold Warrior	Half-Dragon Warrior	Kobold Hero	Black Dragon Marauder	Greenscale Wild Stalker	Kobold Bravescale	Kobold Shadow-Warrior
3 x 1st level	4	1	0	1	0	0	0	0
4 x 1st level	4	2	0	1	0	0	0	0
5 x 1st level	6	1	0	2	0	0	0	0
6 x 1st level	4	4	0	1	0	0	0	0
7 x 1st level	4	2	1	1	0	0	0	0
3 x 2nd level	6	2	0	1	0	0	0	0
3 x 2nd level	3	1	1	0	0	0	0	0
4 x 2nd level	0	1	0	2	1	0	0	0
4 x 2nd level	6	2	1	0	0	0	0	0
5 x 2nd level	1	2	0	2	1	0	0	0
5 x 2nd level	8	1	1	0	1	0	0	0
6 x 2nd level	4	3	0	2	1	0	0	0
6 x 2nd level	4	3	1	0	1	0	0	0
7 x 2nd level	1	2	1	2	1	0	0	0
7 x 2nd level	8	1	2	0	1	0	0	0
3 x 3rd level	0	0	0	0	2	1	0	0
3 x 3rd level	0	1	1	2	0	0	0	0
4 x 3rd level	0	0	0	0	2	2	0	0
4 x 3rd level	4	2	1	2	0	0	0	0

(continued)

#/Level of PCs	Kobold Grand-Wizard	Kobold Warrior	Half-Dragon Warrior	Kobold Hero	Black Dragon Marauder	Greenscale Wild Stalker	Kobold Bravescale	Kobold Shadow-Warrior
5 x 3rd level	0	0	0	0	2	1	0	4
5 x 3rd level	0	2	1	1	2	0	0	0
6 x 3rd level	2	0	1	0	2	1	0	5
6 x 3rd level	0	1	1	1	2	0	1	0
7 x 3rd level	2	0	1	0	2	1	0	5
7 x 3rd level	0	1	1	1	2	0	1	0
3 x 4th level	0	0	2	0	0	1	0	2
3 x 4th level	0	0	0	0	0	2	2	3
4 x 4th level	0	0	2	0	1	1	0	3
4 x 4th level	0	0	0	0	1	2	2	5
5 x 4th level	0	1	2	1	0	2	1	0
5 x 4th level	0	0	0	0	1	3	2	6
6 x 4th level	0	0	2	2	0	3	1	0
6 x 4th level	0	1	0	0	1	3	2	10
7 x 4th level	0	0	2	1	2	3	1	0
7 x 4th level	0	0	0	0	0	2	1	4

KOBOLD GRAND-WIZARD

"Beware my mighty power! Mighty power!"

0 level mook [HUMANOID]
Initiative: +8

Static jolt +5 vs. AC—2 lightning damage

R: Painful liver inversion hex +4 vs. PD—4 poison damage, or 6 poison damage against dwarves

Evasive: Kobolds take no damage from missed attacks.

AC 15
PD 13   **HP 5 (mook)**
MD 9

Mook: Kill one kobold grand-wizard mook for every 5 damage you deal to the mob.

KOBOLD WARRIOR

Not expected to survive long, but oh so glad to be stomping on the ruins of a fallen sky city.

1st level troop [HUMANOID]
Initiative: +4

Spear +8 vs. AC—4 damage
   Natural even roll: The kobold warrior can pop free from the target.

Evasive: Kobolds take no damage from missed attacks.

Not brave: Kobold warriors with single digit hit points will run away the first chance they get.

AC 18
PD 115   **HP 22**
MD 12

HALF-DRAGON WARRIOR

The ways of dragons are strange and dangerous. They don't get any simpler when they walk on two legs.

Double-strength 2nd level wrecker [HUMANOID]

Initiative: +5

Double-ended axe +8 vs. AC (2 attacks)—5 damage
Natural even hit: As a free action, make a *breath weapon* attack that must include the target of the *double-ended axe* attack.

R: Javelin +8 vs. AC (one nearby or faraway enemy)—10 damage

C: Breath weapon +8 vs. PD (1d3 nearby enemies in a group)—3 acid, lightning, or fire damage*

*Dragon's breath: Choose the damage type of the *breath weapon* at the start of the battle; the half-dragon warrior paints its scales black, blue, or red to reflect its heritage.

Nastier Special
Natural scale armor: Once per battle, the half-dragon warrior can force an enemy to roll a hit against its AC or PD, but not a critical hit.

AC	17	
PD	17	**HP 70**
MD	15	

KOBOLD HERO

2nd level leader [HUMANOID]

Initiative: +3

Shortsword +7 vs. AC—6 damage, and each nearby non-leader kobold deals +3 damage with its next attack that hits this battle
Natural even miss: 3 damage.

Evasive: Kobolds take no damage from missed attacks.

AC 18	
PD 16	**HP 34**
MD 12	

BLACK DRAGON MARAUDER

Young, but deadly.

3rd level wrecker [DRAGON]

Initiative: +9
Vulnerability: thunder

Claws and bite +8 vs. AC (2 attacks)—5 damage
Natural 16+: The target also takes 5 ongoing acid damage.

C: Acid breath +9 vs. PD (1d3 nearby enemies)—6 acid damage, and 5 ongoing acid damage
Miss: 3 acid damage.

Draconic grace: At the start of each of the black dragon's turns, roll a d6 to see if it gets an extra standard action. If the roll is equal to or less than the escalation die, the black dragon can take an extra standard action that turn.

After the first success, the grace die bumps up to a d8. After the second success, it's a d10, then a d12 after the third success, and finally a d20 after the fourth one.

Intermittent breath: A black dragon marauder can use *acid breath* 1d3 times per battle, but never two turns in a row.

Water-breathing: Black dragons swim well and can breathe underwater.

Resist acid 12+: When an acid attack targets this creature, the attacker must roll a natural 12+ on the attack roll or it only deals half damage.

AC 19	
PD 17	**HP 40**
MD 15	

GREENSCALE WILD STALKER

Suddenly, reptilian eyes open and the vegetation erupts as a green-scaled dragonic hidden among the foliage lunges for you.

3rd level archer [HUMANOID]
Initiative: +6

Poisoned claws +8 vs. AC—4 damage, and 3 ongoing poison damage
First failed save: The ongoing poison damage increases by 2.
Second failed save: The target is also weakened (save ends both).

R: Poisonous spit +8 vs. PD—8 poison damage
Natural even hit: The target is partially blinded and takes a −2 penalty to attacks and defenses until the end of its next turn.

Superior camouflage: The wild stalker's scales naturally change to blend with its surroundings, allowing it to hide in plain sight and making checks to detect it take a −5 penalty. When it attacks from concealment without being seen first, the target is vulnerable to its attack. It can regain its camouflage by moving out of direct sight and hiding (hard DC check to spot).

Resist poison 14+: When a poison attack targets this creature, the attacker must roll a natural 14+ on the attack roll or it only deals half damage.

AC	19	
PD	16	**HP 42**
MD	12	

KOBOLD BRAVESCALE

These iron-clad woad-painted kobolds don't run away from danger!

4th level blocker [HUMANOID]
Initiative: +9

Spear +9 vs. AC—13 damage
   Natural roll is above target's Wisdom (trapster): The kobold pushes or trips the target into a trap. (See **Trapster** at the end of the kobold entry in *13th Age Bestiary*, page 128. If you don't have the book, deal 5 ongoing damage until the player buys it for you. Oh, alright—normal save ends.)

Disciplined maneuver: If the escalation die is 3+ and this creature has at least two bravescale allies in the battle, whenever an enemy moves to engage the bravescale, it can make a *spear porcupine* attack against that enemy as a free action.
   Spear porcupine +11 vs. AC—10 damage

Lock shields: For each other kobold bravescale next to the bravescale or engaged with a creature that this bravescale is engaged with, the bravescale gains a +2 bonus to AC (maximum of +4), and each enemy engaged with the bravescale takes a –2 penalty (maximum of –4) to disengage checks.

AC	20	
PD	18	**HP 55**
MD	14	

KOBOLD SHADOW-WARRIOR

Stealthy kobolds with color-changing skin, they climb the walls like lizards and strike from the shadows.

4th level mook [HUMANOID]
Initiative: +9

C: Throwing star +9 vs. AC (one nearby enemy)—7 damage

C: Stinging dust +6 vs. PD (up to 2 nearby enemies in a group)—5 damage, and the target takes a –1 penalty to attacks until the end of its next turn

Elusive: If a shadow-warrior hasn't been attacked since the end of its last turn, it can spend all of its actions on its turn to disappear from sight (remove it from play as it gets into position). At the start of its next turn, it reappears (dropping down from the ceiling or springing out of cover and re-entering play) and can make an *elusive strike* attack as a standard action.
   C: Elusive strike +13 vs. AC (one nearby creature)—18 damage

Evasive: Kobolds take no damage from missed attacks.

Wall-crawler: A kobold shadow-warrior can climb on ceilings and walls as easily as it moves on the ground.

AC	20	
PD	13	**HP 14 (mook)**
MD	17	

Mook: Kill one kobold shadow-warrior mook for every 14 damage you deal to the mob. Apply damage to shadow-warriors using the elusive ability last (or ignore that damage).

CHAMPION-TIER AGENTS OF THE THREE

The champion-tier representatives of the Three include more spellcasters, more dragons, and fewer mooks.

#/Level of PCs	Dragonic Black Sorcerer	Blackscale Shadow Dancer	Devoted Blue Sorcerer	Redscale Fiery Vanquisher	Dragonic Scaleshield	Medium Red Dragon	Huge Black Dragon	Blackscale Light-Killer
3 x 5th level	0	0	0	2	0	1	0	0
3 x 5th level	1	1	2	0	0	0	0	0
4 x 5th level	0	0	0	1	1	1	0	0
4 x 5th level	1	2	2	0	0	0	0	0
5 x 5th level	0	2	0	1	1	1	0	0
5 x 5th level	1	2	2	0	0	1	0	0
6 x 5th level	1	0	0	1	1	0	1	0
6 x 5th level	1	2	1	1	1	0	0	0
7 x 5th level	0	4	0	0	0	1	1	0
7 x 5th level	1	3	1	1	1	0	0	0
3 x 6th level	1	0	1	1	1	1	0	0
3 x 6th level	1	3	2	0	0	0	0	0
4 x 6th level	1	0	1	1	0	1	1	0
4 x 6th level	1	0	1	1	2	1	0	0
5 x 6th level	1	2	1	1	0	0	1	0
5 x 6th level	1	0	1	2	2	1	0	0
6 x 6th level	1	0	2	1	2	0	1	0
6 x 6th level	0	3	0	0	2	0	0	1
7 x 6th level	0	2	0	2	0	0	1	1
7 x 6th level	1	0	2	2	2	0	1	0
3 x 7th level	1	0	1	1	1	0	1	0
3 x 7th level	0	2	0	0	0	2	0	1

(continued)

#/Level of PCs	Dragonic Black Sorcerer	Blackscale Shadow Dancer	Devoted Blue Sorcerer	Redscale Fiery Vanquisher	Dragonic Scaleshield	Medium Red Dragon	Huge Black Dragon	Blackscale Light-Killer
4 x 7th level	2	0	2	2	0	0	1	0
4 x 7th level	1	2	0	0	2	0	0	1
5 x 7th level	2	0	2	2	3	1	0	0
5 x 7th level	0	4	1	0	0	0	1	1
6 x 7th level	2	0	2	2	2	1	1	0
6 x 7th level	0	2	0	0	3	0	0	2
7 x 7th level	2	0	2	2	2	0	2	0
7 x 7th level	0	3	0	0	3	1	0	2

DRAGONIC BLACK SORCERER

The wyrm-fervor is strong in this one.

6th level caster [HUMANOID]
Initiative: +8

Sharpened claws +10 vs. AC—17 damage

R: Acidic spit +11 vs. PD—8 acid damage, 5 ongoing acid damage, and the sorcerer can't use this attack again this battle except when it recharges (see below)
Quickened recharge: After the black sorcerer uses this attack, it rolls a save at the start of each of its turns. On a success, it can use *acidic spit* once that turn as a quick action. The save gains a bonus equal to the escalation die.

R: Chaotic forcebolt +11 vs. PD (1d2 nearby or far away enemies)—18 force damage against a single enemy, or 9 force damage if the bolt splits and hits two enemies
Natural 16+: The target pops free from all enemies and is pushed away from its current location (no opportunity attacks). The target must roll a save to avoid falling if it's in a precarious position (like on a ledge).

AC 22
PD 17   **HP 85**
MD 18

BLACKSCALE SHADOW DANCER

The only thing you notice before it strikes is a slight wavering of the shadows.

6th level spoiler [HUMANOID]
Initiative: +12

Scale blade +11 vs. AC—18 damage, and the shadow dancer can pop free from the target

C: Shadow vapors +11 vs. PD (1d3 nearby enemies)—10 acid damage
Shadows everywhere: Hit or miss, the nearby area around the shadow dancer is filled with shadowy vapors until the end of the battle that make it difficult to see. Other creatures besides shadow dancers in the vapors take a −2 penalty to attacks and defenses.
Quick use: 1/battle, as a quick action.

R: Hand crossbow +11 vs. AC—20 damage

Step into the shadows: Twice per battle as a move action, a shadow dancer can step in heavy shadows, or shadows created by its *shadow vapors,* and step back out of nearby or far away shadows. It often uses this ability to move next to a target. When it attacks an enemy after stepping out of the shadows, it gains a +2 bonus for that attack.

Resist acid 14+: When an acid attack targets this creature, the attacker must roll a natural 14+ on the attack roll or it only deals half damage.

AC 21
PD 21   **HP 80**
MD 16

DEVOTED BLUE SORCERER

In retrospect, signing a treaty that allowed the world's elder evil sorcerer to establish a city where she trains cadres of fanatical reptilian spellcasters may not have been one of the Empire's shining moments.

6th level caster [HUMANOID]
Initiative: +13

Nasty dagger or short spear +11 vs. AC—17 damage

Minor Spell

R: Lightning fork +11 vs. PD—13 lightning damage
Natural even hit or miss: The sorcerer can target a different nearby enemy with the attack.

Major Spells

C: Breath of the Blue +11 vs. PD (one nearby enemy)—20 lightning damage, and at the start of the target's next turn, 1d6 nearby allies of the target take 10 lightning damage

C: Chaos orb +11 vs. MD (1d3 nearby enemies)—16 lightning damage
Natural even hit: The sorcerer gains one use of the target's racial power, if any. It must use that power by the end of the battle or lose it, and it can't use the power this turn.

Power-monger: When the blue sorcerer starts its turn and it didn't *gather power* the previous turn, choose whether it will gather power or cast a spell this turn. When it chooses to cast a spell, roll a d20 to see if it uses a minor spell or a major spell: **1–10:** minor spell; **11–20:** major spell.

Gather power: Like a PC sorcerer, a blue sorcerer can use its standard action to gather power in order to cast a double-strength and double-damage spell with its next standard action. When it gathers power, the sorcerer rolls a d6 and gains one of the following chaotic benefits.

1–2: The sorcerer gains a +2 bonus to AC until the start of its next turn.

3–4: One nearby enemy of the sorcerer's choice takes damage equal to sorcerer's level (6).

5–6: Each nearby enemy engaged with the sorcerer's allies takes damage equal to sorcerer's level (6); OR grant one nearby dragon with *intermittent breath* an additional use of its breath weapon this battle.

Nastier Specials

Escalating caster: Add the escalation die to the sorcerer's *power-monger* rolls and attack rolls.

Sorcerous evasion (kobold sorcerers only): Once per battle when an attack misses the sorcerer, the attacker takes the miss damage from that attack, if any, and the sorcerer takes no damage.

AC	21	
PD	17	**HP 100**
MD	20	

REDSCALE FIERY VANQUISHER

This thick-bodied, red-scaled dragonic brute tries to slash you in half with a mighty axe stroke, then gives you a blast of fiery breath when it gets in close.

7th level wrecker [HUMANOID]
Initiative: +9

Heavy axe +12 vs. AC—26 damage
Natural even hit or miss: The fiery vanquisher can make a *burning breath* attack against the target as a free action.

[Special trigger] **C: Burning breath +11 vs. PD (one nearby enemy)**—3 fire damage, and 5 ongoing fire damage

Red rage: When the escalation die is odd, the fiery vanquisher can roll two d20s for its *heavy axe* attack and use the best result.

Resist fire 14+: When a fire attack targets this creature, the attacker must roll a natural 14+ on the attack roll or it only deals half damage.

AC	23	
PD	21	**HP 110**
MD	15	

DRAGONIC SCALESHIELD

Their black dragon scale shields look as dangerous as the swords they bear.

7th level blocker [HUMANOID]
Initiative: +9

Longsword +12 vs. AC—14 damage

Shield slam +9 vs. PD—8 damage
Natural even hit or miss: The scaleshield can choose one: the target is dazed until the end of its next turn; OR the scaleshield can try to force the target to move a short distance. When it tries to move a target, the target can make a DC 23 Strength or Dexterity check to resist. On a failure, the target gets shoved out of engagement (and possibly falls off the shelf or ramp) where the scaleshield wants it to go.

Slash & slam: As a standard action, the scaleshield can make both a *longsword* attack and a *shield slam* attack.

Resist acid 14+: When an acid attack targets this creature, the attacker must roll a natural 14+ on the attack roll or it only deals half damage.

AC	24	
PD	22	**HP 110**
MD	17	

Medium Red Dragon

Breathing fire makes a red dragon hungry. Eating makes a red dragon bloodthirsty. Bloodthirstiness gets a red dragon into fights, where it likes to use its fiery breath.

6th level wrecker [DRAGON]
Initiative: +11
Vulnerability: cold

Fangs, claws, and tail +11 vs. AC (2 attacks)—8 damage
 First natural even hit or miss each turn: Roll another *fangs, claws, and tail* attack.

C: Fiery breath+11 vs. PD (2d3 nearby enemies)—10 fire damage
 Miss: Half damage.

Intermittent breath: A medium red dragon can use *fiery breath* 1d3 times per battle, but never two turns in a row.

Resist fire 12+: When a fire attack targets this creature, the attacker must roll a natural 12+ on the attack roll or it only deals half damage.

AC 21	
PD 20	**HP 90**
MD 16	

Huge Black Dragon

Huge 9th level wrecker [DRAGON]
Initiative: +17

Claws and bite +14 vs. AC (3 attacks)—30 damage
 Natural 16+: The target also takes 15 ongoing acid damage.
 Miss: 20 damage.

C: Acid breath +14 vs. PD (1d3 nearby or far away enemies)—50 acid damage, and 15 ongoing acid damage
 Miss: 4d12 acid damage.

Draconic grace: At the start of each of the huge black dragon's turns, roll a d4 to see if it gets an extra standard action. If the roll is equal to or less than the escalation die, the black dragon can take an extra standard action that turn.

 After the first success, the grace die bumps up to a d6. After the second success, it's a d8, then a d10 after the third success. The fourth success is a d12, and finally a d20 after the fifth one.

Intermittent breath: A huge black dragon can use *acid breath* 2d3 times per battle, but never two turns in a row.

Water-breathing: Black dragons swim well and can breathe underwater.

Resist acid 18+: When an acid attack targets this creature, the attacker must roll a natural 18+ on the attack roll or it only deals half damage.

AC 25	
PD 23	**HP 510**
MD 21	

Blackscale Light-Killer

It blends into the shadows, the gleam from its eyes the only clue that you are being stalked.

10th level archer [HUMANOID]
Initiative: +15

Blackened blade +14 vs. AC—40 damage
 Natural even hit: 10 ongoing acid damage.
 Natural even miss: The blackscale light-killer gains a darkness token (see below).

R: Acidic breath +16 vs. PD (1d3 nearby enemies)—25 acid damage
 Natural even hit: 12 ongoing acid damage.
 First natural even miss each turn: The blackscale light-killer gains a darkness token (see below).

Darkness spreads: The light-killer can expend a darkness token as a quick action to make a nearby enemy weakened until the end of its next turn. Enemies that don't need to see to fight or who can pierce magical darkness ignore this effect.

Resist acid 16+: When an acid attack targets this creature, the attacker must roll a natural 16+ on the attack roll or it only deals half damage.

Nastier Specials
Darkling maw: The blackscale light-killer gains a darkness token on odd misses too.

Speed of dark: Instead of a quick action to use darkness spreads, it's a free action. Wait and use it just before a PC attacks.

Tail whip: The dragonic deals 2d8 extra damage to a target it misses with a melee attack.

AC	25	
PD	25	**HP 206**
MD	19	

DEMONS OF THE PRISM

If these demons are one of your principal adversary groups, see *Book of Demons* for many demon stats we don't reprint here, for the improved list of random demonic abilities (page 43), and for a few strange hellholes that could be secreted around Redfield Valley as problems the Archmage was keeping hidden. To balance the scales, the PCs might recruit a player character demonologist character from *Book of Demons*!

ADVENTURER-TIER DEMONS OF THE PRISM

#/Level of PCs	Bone Imp Mage-Eater	Lesser Envy Demon	Ghostly Cultist	Claw Demon	Chaos Demon	Hopping Imp	Imprismed Despoiler	Otherness Pod
3 x 1st level	0	2	0	0	0	0	0	0
4 x 1st level	4	1	1	0	0	0	0	0
5 x 1st level	0	2	0	1	0	0	0	0
6 x 1st level	4	1	1	1	0	0	0	0
7 x 1st level	0	2	1	1	0	0	0	0
3 x 2nd level	5	1	1	0	0	0	0	0
3 x 2nd level	0	0	0	2	0	0	0	0
4 x 2nd level	5	0	1	0	0	0	1	0
4 x 2nd level	5	0	0	1	1	0	0	0
5 x 2nd level	0	3	0	0	0	1	0	0
5 x 2nd level	0	0	0	2	0	0	1	0
6 x 2nd level	5	0	1	0	1	1	0	0
6 x 2nd level	5	0	0	1	0	1	1	0
7 x 2nd level	5	0	1	2	0	0	1	0
7 x 2nd level	0	1	0	2	0	0	0	1
3 x 3rd level	0	2	0	0	0	0	1	0
3 x 3rd level	0	0	1	2	0	0	0	0
4 x 3rd level	4	1	0	0	0	1	1	0
4 x 3rd level	0	0	1	0	1	1	0	0
5 x 3rd level	0	0	1	2	0	0	0	1

(continued)

#/Level of PCs	Bone Imp Mage-Eater	Lesser Envy Demon	Ghostly Cultist	Claw Demon	Chaos Demon	Hopping Imp	Imprismed Despoiler	Otherness Pod
5 x 3rd level	0	1	0	0	1	1	1	0
6 x 3rd level	7	0	0	2	1	0	0	1
6 x 3rd level	0	0	0	0	1	1	2	0
7 x 3rd level	0	0	2	1	0	0	0	2
7 x 3rd level	0	0	0	1	1	1	2	0
3 x 4th level	0	0	0	0	1	1	1	0
3 x 4th level	0	2	1	0	0	0	0	1
4 x 4th level	0	2	0	0	1	1	1	0
4 x 4th level	0	1	1	2	0	0	0	1
5 x 4th level	0	0	0	0	2	1	2	0
5 x 4th level	0	0	1	2	0	0	0	2
6 x 4th level	0	0	0	0	2	2	2	0
6 x 4th level	0	2	1	2	0	0	0	2
7 x 4th level	0	2	0	0	2	2	2	0
7 x 4th level	0	2	2	2	0	0	0	2

BONE IMP MAGE-EATER

A nasty little surprise for wizards, and a swift cure for magical hubris.

Weakling 2nd level mook [DEMON]
Initiative: +10

Frenzied teeth +6 vs. AC—4 damage

Freakish speed: On rounds when the escalation die is odd, the imp may move as a quick action once on its turn, flapping its wings madly as it dashes about.

Resist magic 13+: This creature has *resist damage 13+* to all damage from magic sources (even magic weapons). When a magic attack targets this creature, the attacker must roll a natural 13+ on the attack roll or it only deals half damage.

Weakling: When building battles using this monster, it counts as half a normal monster. And that's half a normal mook!

Nastier Special

Magic eater: When this imp resists magic while the escalation die is odd, it takes no damage instead of half damage, and the crit range for all bone imp mage-eaters' attacks expand by 1 (to a maximum of 6+) until the end of the battle.

AC	18	
PD	12	**HP 4 (mook)**
MD	16	

Mook: Kill one bone imp mage-eater mook for every 4 damage you deal to the mob. Because these mooks are half-strength, you can use twice as many of them.

Lesser Envy Demon

Body of a blister-covered toad, head of the worst "person" you'll 'meet'.

2nd level spoiler [DEMON]
Initiative: +7

Needle claws +7 vs. AC—4 damage
  Natural odd hit: The envy demon can make a *gaze of envy* attack as a free action this turn.

[Special attack] **C: Gaze of envy +7 vs. MD (one nearby enemy)**—The target is filled with envy and makes an immediate basic or at-will attack against a nearby ally as a free action—a sudden, strong desire for something that creature owns (like a precious magic item) overcomes them and they lash out.

Resist fire 18+: When a fire attack targets this creature, the attacker must roll a natural 18+ on the attack roll or it only deals half damage.

AC	17	
PD	13	**HP 44**
MD	15	

Ghostly Cultist

A few of the demons' cultists survived imprisment with their masters. Well, sort of survived.

Weakling 3rd level spoiler [UNDEAD]
Initiative: +6

Ghostly dagger +8 vs. PD—5 damage
  Natural odd hit: Ghostly cultist can use its *half-remembered chant* attack on its next turn.

R: Half-remembered chant +8 vs. MD (1d3 nearby enemies)—5 psychic damage, +1d6 psychic damage if target is engaged with one or more demons.

Ghostly: This creature has *resist damage 14+* to all damage except holy damage. A ghost can move through solid objects, but can't end its turn inside them.

AC	19	
PD	13	**HP 20**
MD	17	

Claw Demon

Technically it's a claw-claw-claw-claw demon, but you don't get time to say that.

3rd level troop [DEMON]
Initiative: +8

Hooking claws +8 vs. AC (1d4 attacks)—5 damage

Nastier Specials
Finding the range: Third and fourth *hooking claws* attacks each turn, if any, also deal 3 ongoing damage.

AC	20	
PD	17	**HP 40**
MD	14	

Chaos Demon

A whirling ball of tentacles or claws or fangs that reshapes itself every time it blinks out. You assume it's still the same demon when it comes back because the place you hit it with your sword is still bleeding. . . .

4th level wrecker [DEMON]
Initiative: +10

Shredding tentacles/claws/fangs +9 vs. PD—16 damage
  Natural 16+: The target is dazed (save ends).

Blink out: At the start of each round in which the escalation die is odd, remove the chaos demon from the battle. At the start of the next round, when the escalation die is even, the chaos demon returns to the battle in a more or less random location near where it blinked away. No time passes for the demon while it is gone; it isn't taking a turn or taking ongoing damage or rolling saves while it is "away."

AC	22	
PD	17	**HP 64**
MD	15	

HOPPING IMP

When an imp is too fat to fly, it gets tougher or dies. (Well, it probably dies anyway, but noisily.)

4th level spoiler [DEMON]
Initiative: +8

Festering claws +8 vs. AC—10 damage, and 5 ongoing damage

R: Blight jet +8 vs. PD—10 damage, and the target is dazed (save ends)
First natural 16+ each turn: The imp can choose one: the target is weakened instead of dazed; OR the imp can make a *blight jet* attack against a different target as a free action.

Curse aura: Whenever a creature attacks the imp and rolls a natural 1–5, that creature takes 1d12 psychic damage.

AC 21	
PD 15	**HP 50**
MD 17	

IMPRISMED DESPOILER

Despoilers seek to use their enemy's strengths against them. Even when defeated, their taunts may sting. . .

4th level caster [DEMON]
Initiative: +9

Horns and daggers +8 vs. AC (2 attacks)—7 damage
Natural 16+: Imprismed despoiler can pop free from the target after finishing both attacks.

R: Abyssal whispers +9 vs. MD (one nearby or far away enemy)—15 psychic damage, and the target is confused (save ends); OR the target can choose to avoid the confusion effect by taking 6d6 psychic damage to clear their head.

C: Sow discord +9 vs. MD (2 nearby enemies engaged with the same creature or with each other)—one target makes an at-will melee attack against this power's other target
Quick use: 1/day, as a quick action.

Furiously determined: The imprismed despoiler adds the escalation die to its saves.

AC	19	
PD	14	**HP 58**
MD	18	

OTHERNESS POD

A vaguely oval bag of terrifying magical gases from a reality that has nothing in common with our own. Covered in strange eyes, but they rarely open.

5th level spoiler [DEMON]
Initiative: +9

R: Otherness blorp +10 vs. PD (one or two random nearby enemies)—10 damage
Natural odd hit: Also roll on the *otherness effect table* for an additional effect on the target.

Otherness Effect Table (roll a d6):
1–2: 5 ongoing negative energy damage
3–4: 4 lightning damage
5: 8 negative energy damage
6: Teleport target a short distance in a random direction (complications may ensue)

Flight: The otherness pod bumps along mid-air as if uncertain where it wants to go.

Lost opportunity: This creature can't make opportunity attacks.

Problematic presence: Enemies engaged with the otherness pod are hampered.

Otherness feedback: When the otherness pod is hit by a natural odd attack roll, the attacker must roll a normal save. If the save fails, the attacker suffers one of the following two consequences, depending on their natural save roll:
Natural odd save: after this attack, attacker is dazed (save ends)
Natural even save: 10 negative energy damage.

AC 19	
PD 16	**HP 80**
MD 18	

CHAMPION-TIER DEMONS OF THE PRISM

By the time the PCs face champion-tier adversaries, cultists and crazies alienated from the Diabolists' service have had time to follow the trail of blood to the new demonic force in play. For at least a time, the demons of the Prism must accept all the help they can find.

#/Level of PCs	Bone Imp Skullbiter	Giggling Demon	Greater Claw Demon	Cultist Bloodhunter	Wilder Chaos Demon	Greater Frenzy Demon	Imprismed Despoiler Mage
3 x 5th level	2	5	2	0	0	0	0
3 x 5th level	2	0	0	1	1	0	0
4 x 5th level	2	0	2	0	0	1	0
4 x 5th level	0	0	0	1	1	1	0
5 x 5th level	2	5	2	0	0	1	0
5 x 5th level	0	0	0	2	2	0	0
6 x 5th level	0	0	2	0	0	1	1
6 x 5th level	1	0	0	1	2	1	0
7 x 5th level	0	5	2	0	0	1	1
7 x 5th level	1	0	1	1	2	1	0
3 x 6th level	0	4	2	0	0	0	1
3 x 6th level	2	0	0	1	1	1	0
4 x 6th level	0	4	2	0	1	0	1
4 x 6th level	2	0	0	2	1	1	0
5 x 6th level	0	2	1	0	1	0	2
5 x 6th level	2	0	0	2	2	1	0
6 x 6th level	0	4	2	0	1	0	2
6 x 6th level	0	0	0	2	2	2	0
7 x 6th level	0	4	2	0	2	0	2
7 x 6th level	0	7	0	2	2	2	0
3 x 7th level	0	5	1	0	0	0	2
3 x 7th level	0	0	0	2	1	2	0
4 x 7th level	0	6	0	0	2	0	2

(continued)

#/Level of PCs	Bone Imp Skullbiter	Giggling Demon	Greater Claw Demon	Cultist Bloodhunter	Wilder Chaos Demon	Greater Frenzy Demon	Imprismed Despoiler Mage
4 x 7th level	2	0	0	2	2	2	0
5 x 7th level	0	10	1	0	2	0	2
5 x 7th level	0	0	2	1	2	3	0
6 x 7th level	0	10	0	0	2	0	3
6 x 7th level	2	0	2	2	2	3	0
7 x 7th level	0	10	1	0	3	0	3
7 x 7th level	0	0	3	3	2	3	0

Bone Imp Skullbiter

No one is as good at exploiting weakness as the perpetually trod upon.

4th level troop [DEMON]
Initiative: +11

Marrow-seeking tongue +9 vs. AC—14 damage, or 20 damage vs. a staggered target

C: Bone splinters +8 vs. AC (1d3 nearby or far away enemies in a group)—10 damage

Freakish speed: On rounds when the escalation die is odd, the imp may move as a quick action once on its turn, flapping its wings madly as it dashes about.

Nastier Special
Resist magic 13+: This creature has *resist damage 13+* to all damage from magic sources (even magic weapons). When a magic attack targets this creature, the attacker must roll a natural 13+ on the attack roll or it only deals half damage.

```
AC  18
PD  15          HP 60
MD  18
```

Giggling Demon

6th level mook [DEMON]
Initiative: +10

Sharp little teeth +11 vs. AC—6 damage

Pinned down: These demons torment with their tickling tails. Enemies that disengage from them suffer a cumulative −1 penalty on all checks and attacks until the end of the character's turn (no maximum penalty).

Weakling: When building battles with this monster, it only counts a half a normal mook.

```
AC 19
PD 13          HP 11 (mook)
MD 17
```

Mook: Kill one giggling demon mook for every 11 damage you deal to the mob.

Greater Claw Demon

Worse of the same.

6th level troop [DEMON]
Initiative: +11

Hooking claws +11 vs. AC (1d4 attacks)—10 damage

Nastier Specials
Finding the range: Third and fourth *hooking claws* attacks each turn, if any, also deal 5 ongoing damage.

```
AC  23
PD  20          HP 80
MD  17
```

CULTIST BLOODHUNTER

This human wears blood-stained furs and has ritualistically scarred much of her flesh. She raises her scimitar and grins at you with filed teeth.

7th level troop [HUMANOID]
Initiative: +11

Bloody scimitar +13 vs. AC—24 damage
Bloody escalator: The target and the bloodhunter take extra damage when this attack hits equal to 2 x the escalation die.

Demon ally: Demons and demonic beasts will work with this humanoid without immediately slaying it. In addition, while a demon is engaged with the same enemy as the bloodhunter, the bloodhunter gains a +1 bonus to all defenses and saves.

AC	22 (23)	
PD	20 (21)	**HP 110**
MD	17 (18)	

WILDER CHAOS DEMON

A whirling ball of tentacles or claws or fangs that reconfigures itself every time it blinks out.

7th level wrecker [DEMON]
Initiative: +14

Shredding tentacles/claws/fangs +12 vs. PD (2 attacks)—32 damage
Natural 16+: The target is dazed (save ends).

Blink out: At the start of each round in which the escalation die is odd, remove the chaos demon from the battle. At the start of the next round, when the escalation die is even, the chaos demon returns to the battle in a more or less random location near where it blinked away. No time passes for the demon while it is gone; it isn't taking a turn or taking ongoing damage or rolling saves while it is "away."

AC	25	
PD	23	**HP 128**
MD	21	

GREATER FRENZY DEMON

Their chunky bodies and claws are red, but not quite blood-red. That's your clue to where the frenzy demon's skin ends and the bloodstains begin.

8th level wrecker [DEMON]
Initiative: +13

Claw +12 vs. AC (2 attacks)—20 damage

Raging frenzy: Whenever the frenzy demon misses with a melee attack, it gains a +1 attack bonus and deals +1d10 damage until the end of the battle (maximum bonus +4, +4d10).

AC	24	
PD	20	**HP 140**
MD	20	

IMPRISMED DESPOILER MAGE

Finally free; fully furious.

9th level caster [DEMON]
Initiative: +14

Horns and swords +13 vs. AC (2 attacks)—20 damage
Natural 16+: The despoiler mage can pop free from the target.

R: Abyssal whispers +14 vs. MD (one nearby or far away enemy)—45 psychic damage, and the target is confused (save ends); OR the target can choose to avoid the confusion effect by taking 10d10 psychic damage to clear their head. . .

R: Magic missile (one nearby or far away enemy)—10 automatic force damage
Quick use: 1/round, as a quick action.

C: Sow discord +14 vs. MD (2 nearby enemies engaged with the same creature or with each other)—one target makes an at-will melee attack against this power's other target
Quick use: 1/battle, as quick action.

Aura of betrayal: At the start of each of the despoiler mage's turns, choose a random nearby enemy. Until the start of the despoiler mage's next turn, that creature's allies no longer consider it an ally, though its enemies' powers can still target it as an enemy. The creature isn't compelled to attack its former friends, but the effect tends to screw up all sorts of spells, bardic songs, and the Diabolist knows what else. But at least the betrayal effect is likely to target someone else next round.

Furiously determined: The imprismed despoiler adds the escalation die to its saves.

AC	24	
PD	19	**HP 170**
MD	23	

GOLEMS

Many sections in *Shards of the Broken Sky* feature golems. Generally, they are ageless guardians the Archmage set to watch the valley or servants and defenders of Vantage. Under normal circumstances, golems don't tend to cluster in bunches, but Vantage was never normal.

Most of these golems act as defenders or avengers. Their internal goals might be tangentially related to the Archmage's original interests, but they're likely out-of-control automatons whose programming is damaged.

That's why we've left out the spell golems from *13th Age Bestiary 2* (page 251). The 6th level spell golem warder and the 9th level spell golem mage hunter look more like golems somebody would use in an attack on Vantage than as part of its defenses. Add them to other adversary groups that need anti-magic backup!

ADVENTURER-TIER GOLEMS

For golem fights at 1st through 4th level, see the battles against Shattered Spine constructs on page 58. We don't reprint stats for the wicker golem, clockwork automaton, and the two primal golems here.

Additional golem battles for 4th level PCs appear at the start of the champion-tier Building Battles table below.

CHAMPION-TIER GOLEMS

If you have the first bestiary, consider replacing a stone golem with a marble golem. The fight will be a bit harder—hooray! Note also that you can treat stone lion golems and obsidian golems as interchangeable, mix and match them as you like; we put them in a single column below.

#/Level of PCs	Reshaped Clay Golem	Stone Lion Golem OR Obsidian Golem	Griffon Golem	Bronze Golem	Stone Golem
3 x 4th level	3	0	0	0	0
3 x 4th level	0	1	0	0	0
4 x 4th level	1	1	0	0	0
4 x 4th level	3	0	0	0	0
5 x 4th level	4	0	0	0	0
5 x 4th level	1	1	0	0	0
6 x 4th level	0	0	0	1	0
6 x 4th level	0	0	1	0	0
7 x 4th level	1	0	0	1	0
7 x 4th level	1	0	1	0	0
3 x 5th level	0	0	1	0	0
3 x 5th level	0	0	0	1	0
4 x 5th level	0	1	0	1	0
4 x 5th level	0	1	1	0	0
4 x 5th level	0	0	0	0	1

#/Level of PCs	Reshaped Clay Golem	Stone Lion Golem OR Obsidian Golem	Griffon Golem	Bronze Golem	Stone Golem
5 x 5th level	0	1	0	1	1
6 x 5th level	0	2	1	0	0
6 x 5th level	0	2	0	1	0
7 x 5th level	0	0	1	0	1
7 x 5th level	0	0	0	1	1
3 x 6th level	0	0	0	0	1
4 x 6th level	0	0	0	2	0
4 x 6th level	0	0	2	0	0
5 x 6th level	0	0	0	1	1
5 x 6th level	0	0	1	0	1
6 x 6th level	0	0	0	0	2
6 x 6th level	0	0	0	3	0
6 x 6th level	0	0	3	0	0
7 x 6th level	0	0	0	2	1
7 x 6th level	0	0	2	0	1
3 x 7th level	0	0	0	1	1
3 x 7th level	0	0	1	0	1
4 x 7th level	0	0	0	3	0
4 x 7th level	0	0	0	0	2
5 x7th level	0	0	0	1	2
5 x7th level	0	0	2	2	0
6 x 7th level	0	0	0	0	3
6 x 7th level	0	0	1	2	2
7 x 7th level	0	0	2	2	2
7 x 7th level	0	0	4	0	1

Reshaped Clay Golem

It's possible to mold a clay golem to resist everyone's magic but yours, if you're the Archmage! But the clay gets stretched out and is never quite as strong.

Large 3rd level troop [CONSTRUCT]
Initiative: +3

Brutal fists +7 vs. AC—18 damage
Cursed wound: A non-dwarf creature damaged by a clay golem can't be healed to above half its maximum hit points until after the battle.

Weakened golem immunity: This golem can't be dazed, weakened, confused, made vulnerable, or touched by ongoing damage . . . *except by* an enemy with a positive or conflicted icon relationship with the Archmage or the NPC equivalent!

Ignore attacks 11+: When an attack hits this creature, the attacker must roll a natural 11+ on the attack roll or it misses instead. That's *all* attacks.

AC 17	
PD 15	**HP 66**
MD 11	

Stone Lion Golem

Wizards with an aesthetic eye employ golems that can double as statuary.

Huge 4th level wrecker [CONSTRUCT]
Initiative: +8

Mighty jaws +12 vs. AC—30 damage

Ponderous claws +9 vs. AC (1d3 attacks)—32 damage

R: Roar and pounce +9 vs. AC (one nearby or far away enemy)—42 damage and the stone lion golem engages the enemy.
Miss: The stone lion golem engages the target, which may immediately make a basic attack against the golem as a free action.

Golem immunity: Non-organic golems are immune to effects. They can't be dazed, weakened, confused, made vulnerable, or touched by ongoing damage. You can damage a golem, but that's about it.

AC 20	
PD 18	**HP 162**
MD 14	

Obsidian Golem

INTRUDER ALERT! INTRUDER ALERT!

Large 5th level blocker [CONSTRUCT]
Initiative: +9

Hard fist of the law +10 vs. AC—30 damage
Natural 12+: The target is also dazed (save ends). If the target is already dazed, the target becomes stunned (again, save ends).
Natural 18+: The target is stunned (save ends)

R: Imprison +10 vs. PD (one adjacent stunned target)—The golem flows to imprison the stunned victim within its body. While imprisoned, the victim cannot act except to try to break free (hard save, 16+). The victim is automatically freed if the golem is destroyed; however, any damage above that needed to destroy the golem gets transferred to the trapped victim. An obsidian golem can only imprison one victim at a time.

Relentless pursuit: As an interrupt action when a nearby enemy takes a move action, the obsidian golem can move. This move must be a response to the enemy's move—the golem could, for example, move to engage with that foe, or move to block an exit, or chase after the foe, but could not use this move action to move to engage an unrelated adversary.

Golem immunity: Golems are immune to effects, and cannot be stunned, dazed, weakened, confused, made vulnerable, or touched by ongoing damage. You can damage a golem, but that's about it.

AC 21	
PD 19	**HP 133**
MD 15	

Griffon Golem

This stone and verdigris bronze golem is modeled after a griffon. An unusually attractive griffon, it must be confessed, since the golem serves ornamental purposes until its true purposes surface in a hail of spikes.

Triple-strength 6th level wrecker [CONSTRUCT]
Initiative: +12

Claw, claw, bite +11 vs. AC (3 attacks)—22 damage, and if all three attacks hit the same target the target is stuck (save ends, or the griffon attacking a new target or moving away ends).

R: Hail of spikes +11 vs. AC (2d3 nearby or far away enemy enemies)—40 damage as the griffon opens concealed hatches and fires out dozens of spikes.

Golem immunity: Non-organic golems are immune to effects. They can't be dazed, weakened, confused, made vulnerable, or touched by ongoing damage. You can damage a golem, but that's about it.

Flight: This golem can fly, and fly fast. It isn't too great at turning tight circles, though.

Nastier Specials

Cunning warrior: The golem is smart. If it uses a full round (standard, move, and quick actions) to attack and attacks the same target, it does half damage on a miss.

AC 22
PD 20   **HP 270**
MD 16

BROOZE GOLEM

The golem's overly ornate construction hides severe design flaws. Fail to locate those flaws and its fists will drum on your armor and ring you like a bell.

Large 7th level blocker [CONSTRUCT]
Initiative: +11

Gong-like fists of bronze +12 vs. AC (2 attacks)—20 damage
  Natural even hit against a target in heavy armor: The target is dazed (save ends).
  Natural odd hit against a target in light armor or no armor: The target takes 10 extra damage.
  Miss: 4d6 damage.

Golem immunity: Non-organic golems are immune to effects. They can't be dazed, weakened, confused, made vulnerable, or touched by ongoing damage. You can damage a golem, but that's about it.

Hidden flaw: An enemy who hits the bronze golem with a natural 18+ attack roll can roll a DC 25 skill check using Intelligence or Wisdom to notice the bronze golem's hidden flaw! On a success, until the end of the battle, the golem loses its damage resistance and becomes vulnerable to all attacks (against each enemy informed of the flaw).

Resist damage 18+: When an attack targets this creature, the attacker must roll a natural 18+ on the attack roll or it only deals half damage.

Nastier Specials

Percussion resonance: When the escalation die reaches 3+, the bronze golem gains a bonus to its first *gong-like fists of bronze* attack roll each turn equal to the number of attacks made against it so far that turn. (Each turn is separate, not cumulative.)

Spiky: When an enemy engaged with the bronze golem misses it with a melee attack, that enemy takes 2d12 damage.

AC 22
PD 21   **HP 190**
MD 17

STONE GOLEM

Ages ago, stone golems were idols brought to life by worship. Some of these godlike golems still wait patiently in hidden places. In more recent ages, the worship rituals have been refined into spells of binding, and they work just as well or better.

Large 8th level blocker [CONSTRUCT]
Initiative: +11

Massive stone fists +12 vs. AC (2 attacks)—35 damage
  Miss: 15 damage.

Finishing smash +14 vs. AC (one staggered enemy)—80 damage, and the target pops free and moves a short distance away (the golem chooses where)
  Natural even hit: +20 damage, and the target is hampered (save ends).
  Natural even miss: The target is hampered (save ends)
  Natural odd miss: 20 damage, and the target is dazed (save ends).

Golem immunity: Non-organic golems are immune to effects. They can't be dazed, weakened, confused, made vulnerable, or touched by ongoing damage. You can damage a golem, but that's about it.

AC 25
PD 23   **HP 280**
MD 18

LAVA DEMONS

If you opt to turn Old Tusk into an erupting hellhole (page 118), this adversary group probably leads the eruption. It could also be useful if things go badly for Magaheim (page 120).

Used as one of the groups that helped destroy Vantage, they could be creatures who weakened the Archmage's wards so that other villains could destroy the flying city. Or perhaps the opening salvo was a massive wedge of demonically-charged lava blasting out of Old Tusk, setting Vantage on fire and offloading a horde of demonic attackers?

ADVENTURER-TIER LAVA DEMONS

Now that we've provided a few adversary groups with fully built battles, we're leaving the battle building to you.

BURNER

A demonically animate fireball. Remind it that it's awful weak for a fireball.

1st level archer [DEMON]
Initiative: +7

Flickers of flame +7 vs. AC—3 fire damage

R: Flickers of flame +7 vs. AC—5 fire damage
  Miss: Deal 3 fire damage to a random nearby creature (yes, could be enemy or ally!).

Quick flicking fire: Adds the escalation die to its disengage checks.

Flight: Bobs along low to the ground; if it gets higher than 6 feet, it drops, as if tethered to the earth.

AC	18	
PD	16	HP 24
MD	14	

SMALL EARTH ELEMENTAL

3rd level troop [ELEMENTAL]
Initiative: +5

Rocky fists +7 vs. AC (2 attacks)—7 damage
  Miss: 2 damage.

Repair damage 10 and below: When the earth elemental is targeted by a natural attack roll of 10 or less, the elemental heals 1d6 damage before taking any damage from the attack.

AC	19	
PD	18	HP 40
MD	13	

SMALL FIRE ELEMENTAL

3rd level troop [ELEMENTAL]
Initiative: +8

Whipping flames +8 vs. PD—8 fire damage, and 4 ongoing fire damage to a random nearby enemy (including an unconscious one)

Melee burn: When an enemy makes a natural odd melee attack roll against the fire elemental, that attacker takes 1d8 fire damage.

Resist fire 18+: When a fire attack targets this creature, the attacker must roll a natural 18+ on the attack roll or it only deals half damage.

AC	19	
PD	18	HP 42
MD	15	

MAGMA ELEMENTAL

Fire elementals weren't meant to spend centuries trapped in a demonic volcano.

4th level archer [ELEMENTAL]
Initiative: +7

Fiery smash +8 vs. AC—10 damage
  Natural even hit: 5 ongoing fire damage.

R: Flying magma +8 vs. PD (one nearby or faraway enemy)—8 damage, or 12 damage to a nearby target
  Natural even hit: 5 ongoing fire damage.

C: Local eruption +8 vs. PD (1d4 + 1 nearby enemies)—15 fire damage
  Limited use: 1/battle when the escalation die is even. The magma elemental deals 4d6 damage to itself when it uses this ability, and it won't hesitate to blow itself up!

Conditional escalator: The magma elemental adds the escalation die to its attacks when it attacks an enemy that did not move on its previous turn or is delaying or holding a readied action.

Resist fire 16+: When a fire attack targets this creature, the attacker must roll a natural 16+ on the attack roll or it only deals half damage.

AC	21	
PD	17	HP 50
MD	14	

CHAMPION-TIER LAVA DEMONS

If you opt against making this a true adversary group, draft its demons into Magaheim or as creatures controlled by the *Wizards & Spellcasters* adversary group.

BIG BURNER

A serious demonically animate fireball.

5th level archer [DEMON]
Initiative: +11

Flickers of flame +11 vs. AC—10 fire damage

R: Flickers of flame +11 vs. AC—18 fire damage
  Miss: Deal 10 fire damage to a random nearby creature (yes, could be enemy or ally!).

Quick flicking fire: Adds the escalation die to its disengage checks.

Flight: Bobs along low to the ground; if it gets higher than 6 feet, it drops, as if tethered to the earth.

AC	22	
PD	20	**HP 66**
MD	18	

EARTH ELEMENTAL

5th level blocker [ELEMENTAL]
Initiative: +7

Rocky fists +9 vs. AC (2 attacks)—11 damage
  Miss: 4 damage.

Boulder up: Roll a d10 at the start of each of the earth elemental's turns. If you roll less than or equal to the escalation die, it shifts into boulder guardian form until the end of the battle. While in this form, it gains a +2 bonus to AC and the *relentless pursuit* ability (and you stop rolling *boulder up* checks).

Relentless pursuit: The elemental must be in boulder guardian form to use this ability. Staggered enemies can't disengage from the earth elemental. (They can pop free, but they can't roll disengage checks.)

Repair damage 10 and below: When the earth elemental is targeted by a natural attack roll of 10 or less, the elemental heals 1d12 damage before taking any damage from the attack.

AC	21	
PD	20	**HP 66**
MD	15	

FIRE ELEMENTAL

5th level wrecker [ELEMENTAL]
Initiative: +10

Whipping flames +10 vs. PD—14 fire damage, and 7 ongoing fire damage to a random nearby enemy (including an unconscious one)

Melee burn: When an enemy makes a natural odd melee attack roll against the fire elemental, that attacker takes 1d12 fire damage.

Resist fire 18+: When a fire attack targets this creature, the attacker must roll a natural 18+ on the attack roll or it only deals half damage.

Wildfire transformation: Roll a d10 at the start of each of the fire elemental's turns. If you roll less than or equal to the escalation die, it shifts into wildfire form until the end of the battle. While in this form, it gains the following improved attack (and you stop rolling *wildfire transformation* checks):
  C: Elemental wildfire +10 vs. PD (one nearby enemy OR each nearby enemy taking ongoing fire damage)—20 fire damage, and 7 ongoing fire damage
  Miss: 7 ongoing fire damage.

AC	21	
PD	20	**HP 66**
MD	17	

OLD TUSK LAVA DEMON

Casting a holy spell in the caldera is like casting finger of death in the Priestess' Cathedral.

6th level blocker [DEMON]
Initiative: +10

Lava-oozing smash +11 vs. AC—18 damage
 Natural even hit: 5 ongoing fire damage, and target is stuck (save ends both).

Unholy hatred: The first time each round that a nearby enemy deals holy damage, the lava demon must roll a normal save. If the save fails, the lava demon must use its attack action on its next turn to attack that enemy OR take a –5 attack penalty.

The slowest shall fall: The lava demon adds the escalation die to its attacks when it attacks an enemy that did not move on its previous turn or is delaying or holding a readied action.

Resist fire 16+: When a fire attack targets this creature, the attacker must roll a natural 16+ on the attack roll or it only deals half damage.

AC	20	
PD	19	**HP 110**
MD	17	

FIRE DEMON

If fire wasn't already perfect, the demons would have tried to invent it.

7th level troop [DEMON]
Initiative: +14
Vulnerability: cold

Claws of flame +13 vs. AC—20 fire damage
 Natural even hit: Target is vulnerable to fire and any resistance to fire is canceled (save ends both).
 Miss: Make a *flowing flame* attack against a different nearby enemy as a free action.

C: Flowing flame +13 vs. PD (one nearby enemy)—20 fire damage

Fiery hatred: The fire demon adds the escalation die to its attacks against any creature that has used a cold attack this battle.

Resist fire 18+: When a fire attack targets this creature, the attacker must roll a natural 18+ on the attack roll or it only deals half damage.

AC	23	
PD	19	**HP 108**
MD	19	

TWISTED MAGMA ELEMENTAL

Its half-life is taking yours with it.

7th level archer [ELEMENTAL]
Initiative: +10

Fiery smash +11 vs. AC—20 damage
 Natural even hit: 10 ongoing fire damage.

R: Flying magma +11 vs. PD (one nearby or faraway enemy)—16 damage, or 24 damage to a nearby target
 Natural even hit: 10 ongoing fire damage.

C: Local eruption +11 vs. PD (1d4 + 1 nearby enemies)—30 fire damage
 Limited use: 2/battle when the escalation die is even. The magma elemental deals 4d12 damage to itself when it uses this ability, and it won't hesitate to blow itself up!

Conditional escalator: The magma elemental adds the escalation die to its attacks when it attacks an enemy that did not move on its previous turn or is delaying or holding a readied action.

Resist fire 16+: When a fire attack targets this creature, the attacker must roll a natural 16+ on the attack roll or it only deals half damage.

AC	24	
PD	20	**HP 100**
MD	17	

VOLCANO IMP

Batwinged party crasher. Also: on fire.

Weakling 8th level spoiler [DEMON]
Initiative: +10

Scrappy claws +13 vs. AC—15 damage

Pin-wheeling calamity +13 vs. PD—20 fire damage, and target is hampered until the end of its next turn.
 Miss: 10 damage.
 Limited use: Only when the volcano imp starts its turn unengaged and flies to engage an enemy.

Curse aura: When a creature attacks the fire imp and rolls a natural 1-5, the fire imp deals 10 psychic damage to the attacker.

Flight: Reckless and out of control.

Resist fire 16+: When a fire attack targets this creature, the attacker must roll a natural 16+ on the attack roll or it only deals half damage.

AC	25	
PD	18	**HP 66**
MD	21	

ORCS OF THE ORC LORD

We're handling the *Orcs of the Orc Lord* adversary group differently than the others. The *13th Age* core rulebook and the *13th Age Bestiary* provide an excellent assortment of dangerous orcs, as well as miscellaneous trolls and hobgoblins and hags and dire animals. Throw in the slightly more specialized orc warriors on pages 95-99 *of High Magic & Low Cunning* and you'll have several orc warbands.

We aren't reprinting all the stat blocks from *13th Age Bestiary*. If you don't own the book, focus on other icons until you find it in the wreckage of a burning caravan.

Onslaught and survival: Instead of specific pre-built battles with creatures of the Orc Lord, we suggest using a chaotic variant that plays up the Orc Lord's aggressive stance. Don't worry about building a battle precisely. Use orcs and warriors from roughly the right levels and throw them at the PCs in higher numbers that force the PCs to be on the defensive for a change.

Start the escalation die at 0 as normal, but raise it by 2 points at the start of each subsequent round. When the escalation die reaches 6, orc morale begins to break. Trolls and the like fight to the death, but regular orcs realize that they have not won the battle according to plan. At the start of each orc's turn, it rolls a normal save. If it fails, the orc seeks to disengage and flee the battle. If the orc is already staggered, the save is a hard save.

Holding on until the escalation die reaches 6 is a different tactical problem than eliminating enemies as quickly as possible. If some fights against the Orc Lord follow this trajectory, but other fights against the orcs are more like standard battles, you'll keep the PCs guessing about what's going to hit them next.

New creatures: We added a couple new creatures to this adversary group.

The orc spear grunts are low-level mooks who are just a savage scream away from throwing away their spears and shields and fighting with claws and teeth. Maybe orcs from outside Redfield Valley are feeling the Orcwell's influence, or maybe some of the Orc Lord's followers are always this savage. You could also use these creatures as examples of how hard it would be for the Orc Lord to "train up" creatures from the Orcwell.

The rhinosaur howdah is a glimpse at the Orc Lord's first stab at controlling the great beasts.

ORC SPEAR GRUNT

Even for an orc, this foaming-mouthed frenzy is over the top. Something has to break.

3rd level mook [HUMANOID]
Initiative: +5

Spear +8 vs. AC—7 damage

Mob of seven: The maximum size of an orc spear grunt mob is 7 mooks. When you include more than seven orc spear grunts in a battle, use another mob.

Bestial reversion: When an orc spear grunt's attack drops an enemy to 0 hp or below, or when one or more orc spear grunts drop to 0 hp, roll a single normal save for the orc spear grunt mob, with a bonus equal to the number of remaining mooks in the mob. If the save fails, all remaining mooks in the mob cast away their weapons and shields and become feral grunts until the end of the battle (use that stat block instead).

AC	20	
PD	16	**HP 13 (mook)**
MD	12	

Mook: Kill one orc spear grunt mook for every 13 damage you deal to the mob.

FERAL GRUNT

The shield and spear got in the way.

3rd level mook [HUMANOID]
Initiative: +5

Claws and teeth +6 vs. AC—5 damage

Feral aversion: When a feral grunt is engaged with a non-staggered target at the start of its turn, roll a d20:

Natural even roll: The grunt uses the roll result as a *claws and teeth* attack.

Natural odd roll: The grunt uses the roll result as a disengage check that may or may not succeed. If the grunt disengages, it moves to engage and attack a staggered enemy, if possible. If the grunt doesn't disengage, it stays to fight, rolling a normal *claws and teeth* attack.

AC	17	
PD	16	**HP 13 (mook)**
MD	14	

Mook: Kill one feral grunt mook for every 13 damage you deal to the mob.

Rhinosaur Howdah

So many moving parts it's hard to. . . here it comes!

Huge 5th level troop [BEAST & HUMANOID]
Initiative: +10

Tramply smash +10 vs. PD (1d4 engaged enemies)—15 damage

Orc spears +12 vs. AC (2 attacks)—8 damage
   Quick use: 1/round as a quick action

R: Thrown spears +8 vs. AC (1 or 2 nearby enemies)—8 damage
   Quick use: 1/round as a quick action

Finite orcs: When the rhinosaur howdah is staggered, it becomes vulnerable to magic (like the other great beasts) and can no longer use its *orc spears* or *thrown spears* attacks.

Immune to some mental conditions: The rhinosaur howdah has enough going on in its brain and varied frenzies that it can ignore conditions dealt by many attacks. Effects that daze, stun, weaken, or hamper don't affect the rhinosaur howdah. Ongoing damage does still affect it.

AC	21	
PD	19	HP 220
MD	16	

ORCWELL

The orcs coming out of the Orcwell aren't equipped like the forces of the Orc Lord. They're basically not equipped at all—there's no one handing them just-forged swords when they come out of the well, and if the world is going to stay in one piece, that needs to remain true.

We published the orcs that were originally destined for this Orcwell section in the *13th Age Bestiary*. The pit-spawn orc (2nd), cave orc (3rd), death-plague orc (3rd), and orc tusker (3rd) were originally designed as creatures from the Orcwell. Similarly, the orcish environmental effects described on *Bestiary* page 159 make perfect sense near the Orcwell.

The long delay on *Shards of the Broken Sky* sent the Orcwell orcs charging into the *Bestiary* instead of waiting for a book with uncertain timing. As with the Orc Lords' forces, we don't reprint multiple pages of the *Bestiary* here; instead, we add a couple more Orcwell creatures.

Orclings are fast-moving bestial mooks meant to be used in swarms. They benefit from bonuses based on the number of orcling mook mobs still in the fight, a number that shouldn't be apparent to PCs seeking to wipe out mobs. Orcling mooks from different mobs mix together chaotically. As GM, you should know which mooks belongs to which mob, but the PCs should be in the dark until after their attacks manage to eliminate multiple mooks.

Like the orcling, the thunder orc is a creature the world could do without.

Orcling

Trouble in numbers, lethal alone.

4th level mook [HUMANOID]
Initiative: +20 (yes: 20)

Teeth +8 vs. AC—5 damage
   Natural even hit: The orcling pops free and moves to engage another target as a free action.

Furious death +8 vs. AC—10 damage, and drop the orcling to 0 hp.
   Miss: 5 damage.
   Limited use: Only if the orcling is the last orcling in its mob.

Mobs of four: Use orclings only in mobs of exactly four orclings apiece.

Mob bonus: For each mob still in the battle, the orcling gains a +1 attack and damage bonus (maximum +4).

AC	19	
PD	18	HP 16 (mook)
MD	13	

Mook: Kill one orcling mook for every 16 damage you deal to the mob.

Thunder Orc

In this nightmare called reality, orcs are now giants that crackle and hum with lightning.

Huge 7th level spoiler [HUMANOID]
Initiative: +14

Thundering fists +12 vs. AC (1d4 attacks)—50 thunder damage and target is weakened until the start of its next turn
   Natural even miss: Half damage.

R: Storm roar +12 vs. AC (1d3 nearby or far away enemies in a group)—90 thunder damage, split between the enemies targeted (30/30/30, or 45/45, or 90)

Living storm: When the orc is struck by a metal weapon or a lightning attack, make a *crackling aura* attack as a free action

[Special trigger] C: Crackling aura +12 vs. PD (1d3 nearby or far away enemies, attack must include the enemy that triggered the attack and the other targets must be the enemies nearest that creature)—30 lightning damage

Thunder orc rage: The thunder orc's crit range expands by 1 every time it is hit by a weapon attack

Not that bright: The thunder orc's crit range shrinks by 1 every time it is hit by a spell.

AC	21	
PD	21	HP 320
MD	17	

RAPTORS

The Repository had an annex where failed prototype constructs were kept. The annex was built into a back wall and heavily warded by magic.

In an age when the metallic dragons grew unreliable, an Archmage experimented with flying constructs—these semi-living weapons of war called iron and steel raptors were intended to function as front-line troops that could strike at rear areas when it suited them. It didn't work out. They proved too difficult to control on the battlefield, so the Archmage ended up storing them in an annex of the Repository.

Well, you've seen what a mess the Repository is in the 13th age. The toxic mixtures in the Repository's basement spoiled the wards on the annex, waking the raptors and allowing some to slip out into the valley. Those that can fly, fly free; others take up residence in the deeper parts of the Repository, consuming the tastier artifacts they find there and growing strange. Use the raptors when you want a strange wandering construct battle that doesn't focus on golems.

Iron Raptor

This six-legged living metal creature may be rusted around the beak, but it moves with a feline grace and its claws are sharp enough to cut through stone.

4th level troop [CONSTRUCT]
Initiative: +12

Rend and sunder +8 vs. PD (2 attacks)—6 damage

Pack hunter: The raptor gains a +2 bonus to damage if at least one ally is engaged with the target.

Furnace vision: Not only can the iron raptor see creatures that are invisible, intangible, ghostly, etc., but any creature that uses a spell such as *invisibility* or *blur*, or is phasing, ghostly, or similar takes 2 fire damage at the start of each of its turns until it is fully visible and tangible again.

Flight: Blade-like wings allow the raptor to fly like an eagle.

Nastier Specials
Each iron raptor is unique. If the players are having too easy a time, you can throw an unexpected curveball or two at them mid-flight.

Defensive posture: Twice per battle, as a move action, the iron raptor can roll up into a ball like an armadillo or pangolin. If it doesn't move on its turn, the raptor gains a +4 bonus to all defenses until it takes another action.

Really smart: If both attacks are even hits against the same target, the raptor can weaken the target as a quick action until the end of the target's next turn. Tricks could include swatting a wand out of a wizard's hand, headbutting the cleric as she is about to call upon her deity, etc.

Spikes: Razor-sharp blades and barbed spikes slide out from the beast's armored plates. The iron raptor deals 3 damage on a miss.

AC	22	
PD	18	**HP 40**
MD	14	

Steel Raptor

Maybe these constructs got moth-balled because calling them raptors gave everyone the wrong idea. They're more like insanely powerful six-limbed sword-cats. With beaks.

7th level troop [CONSTRUCT]
Initiative: +15

Sundering bite, rending claws +11 vs. PD (2 attacks)—10 damage

Pack hunter: The raptor gains a +4 bonus to damage if at least one ally is engaged with the target.

Furnace vision: Not only can the iron raptor see creatures that are invisible, intangible, ghostly, etc., but any creature that uses a spell such as *invisibility* or *blur*, or is phasing, ghostly, or similar takes 4 fire damage at the start of each of its turns until it is fully visible and tangible again.

Heavily armored: This creature is more than just steel-plated—even its bones, muscles, and brain are metal. It has *resist damage 16+* to all damage.

Flight: Blade-like wings allow the raptor to fly like an eagle.

Nastier Specials
Each steel raptor is unique. If the players are having too easy a time, you can throw an unexpected curveball or two at them mid-fight.

Acrobat: This steel raptor gains +2 to all defenses against all attacks except melee attacks that target AC, as it twists and leaps with cat-like speed and grace.

Defensive posture: Twice per battle, as a move action, the steel raptor can roll up into a ball like an armadillo or pangolin. If it doesn't move on its turn, the raptor gains a +4 bonus to all defenses until it takes another action.

Really smart: If both attacks are even hits against the same target, the raptor can weaken the target as a quick action until the end of the target's next turn. Tricks could include swatting a wand out of a wizard's hand, headbutting the cleric as she is about to call upon her deity, etc.

Spell eater: When the raptor is targeted by a spell, odd hits become misses as the raptor literally eats the spell!

Spikes: Razor-sharp blades and barbed spikes slide out from the beast's armored plates. The steel raptor deals 5 damage on a miss.

AC	24	
PD	21	**HP 52**
MD	17	

#/Level of PCs	Iron Raptor	Steel Raptor
3 x 4th level	3	0
4 x 4th level	1	1
4 x 4th level	4	0
5 x 4th level	2	1
5 x 4th level	5	0
6 x 4th level	3	1
6 x 4th level	6	0
7 x 4th level	7	0
7 x 4th level	4	1
7 x 4th level	1	2
3 x 5th level	6	0
3 x 5th level	0	2
4 x 5th level	5	1
4 x 5th level	2	2
5 x 5th level	7	1
5 x 5th level	4	2
6 x 5th level	6	2
6 x 5th level	3	3
7 x 5th level	8	2
7 x 5th level	5	3
3 x 6th level	0	3
4 x 6th level	0	4
5 x 6th level	0	5
6 x 6th level	0	6
7 x 6th level	0	7

UNDEAD

We don't provide prebuilt battles for the Lich King's forces. There's room to use most any undead we've published in some versions of the *Shards of the Broken Sky* story, but your key decision is which creatures you'll choose as leaders. Without leadership, mindless undead aren't likely to pull Vantage from the sky or have much luck exploiting its fall.

We've provided a couple new creatures for the Lich King's leader cadre below. A wide variety of necromancers will show up in the upcoming *Icon Followers* book. From our other books, you might consider . . .

- Ghouls, who can be smarter than they look (**13B**: 97)
- Hags, who don't normally get along with the Lich King, but might find common ground in this great victory (**13B**: 104)
- Liches, who want the magic for themselves (**13B**: 134)
- Martuk: death priest wight, or his stats for another creature (**CC**: 138)
- Mummies, who may have schemed to escape Vantage for centuries (**13TW**: 197)
- Specters, just one variant of the non-corporeal undead with enough initiative to mastermind their own plots (**13TW**: 201)

INITIATED DEATH CULTIST

Death cultists have the game fixed. They kill you, they win. You kill them, they "win."

3rd level caster [HUMANOID]
Initiative: +7

Sacrificial dagger +8 vs. AC—8 damage
  Miss: 1d6 damage, if the death cultist deals an identical amount to itself

R: Whispering skull +8 vs MD (one nearby or far away enemy)—8 negative energy damage
  Natural even hit: Target is weakened (save ends) unless it chooses to take 2d6 psychic damage, instead.

AC	19	
PD	13	HP 40
MD	19	

DARK CHAMPION

Blessed is the dark, for it is eternal.

7th level wrecker [HUMANOID]
Initiative: +14

Wicked blade +12 vs. AC (2 attacks)—15 damage
  If both attacks hit the same target: Target becomes vulnerable to negative energy damage until the end of the fight.

C: Evil eye +12 vs. MD (1d3 nearby or far away enemies in a group)—25 negative energy damage
  Limited use: 1/battle when the escalation die is odd

Curse aura: When the dark champion dies, it attempts to place a *death curse* on whomever dealt the killing blow (or cast the killing spell).
  [Special trigger] **C: Death curse +12 vs. MD (the enemy who killed the dark champion)**—When an ally of the target spends a recovery to regain hit points, deal negative energy damage to the target equal to half the number of hit points their ally heals (two hard saves, 16+, end the curse).

AC	23	
PD	17	HP 100
MD	21	

WIZARDS & SPELLCASTERS

This group is a bit of a catch-all. It could represent wizards connected to Vantage, reeling from their world's collapse. It could represent forces devoted to enemy icons who helped bring Vantage down or who served as a distraction while the real attack came from somewhere in the overworld. It could represent opportunistic factions aiming to plunder the wreckage. The strange mix of creatures in the group suggests that it could be part of a story of unlikely allies that can only be fleshed out in your campaign.

The group isn't all spellcasters. We've included a few monsters meant to function as skilled bodyguards.

DARK DRUID

Did you know that blood makes an excellent fertilizer?

1st level spoiler [HUMANOID]
Initiative: +5

Sickle or scythe +6 vs. AC—5 damage
  Natural 16+: All druids gain a cumulative +1 attack and damage bonus to their *briarwood vines* attacks (up to a maximum of +4).

C: Briarwood vines +4 vs. AC (1d3 nearby or far away enemies in a group)—2 damage and the target is stuck until the end of their next turn.

AC 17
PD 13   HP 27
MD 13

GREATER HOMUNCULUS

"Go away. Farther! Farther!"

2nd level troop [CONSTRUCT]
Initiative: +5

Sharp claws +5 vs. AC—7 damage

R: Alchemical blurp +7 vs. PD (1d3 nearby or far away enemies in a group)—6 acid damage

First natural 16+: The next ally to attack the target gains +2 to hit.

AC 18
PD 16   HP 36
MD 12

MERCENARY CASTER

Spells are tattooed over this emaciated figure. It beats carrying spellbooks.

2nd level caster [HUMANOID]
Initiative: +7

Desperate dagger +6 vs. AC—5 damage
  Natural 11+: The mercenary may choose to do no damage and instead, as a free action, disengage and cast a spell with a −2 attack penalty.

C: Lightning orb +7 vs. PD (1d3 nearby or far away enemies in a group)—5 lightning damage
  Natural 11+: Use one of the three triggered spells

Triggered Spells
[*Special trigger*] **Quick and dirty enchantment:** One nearby ally gains a +2 attack bonus to their next attack.
[*Special trigger*] **Time-twist:** One nearby ally may move as a free action.
[*Special trigger*] **Rapid hex:** One nearby enemy becomes stuck (easy save ends).

AC 18
PD 16   HP 36
MD 12

MERCENARY WARRIOR

This thug is only in it for the gold; but that doesn't mean you can buy her off—she can take your gold once you're dead.

3rd level troop [HUMANOID]
Initiative: +7

Spear and shield +8 vs. AC—10 damage

R: Clunky crossbow +8 vs. AC (one nearby or far away enemy)—10 damage
  Natural 16+: This weapon normally takes a move action to reload, on a natural 16+ it is a quick action.

AC 19
PD 17   HP 54
MD 13

BONDED VEIL

What happens when you bond to a magic cloak or robe? This, apparently.

Triple-strength 4th level troop [CONSTRUCT]
Initiative: +10

Fluttering shroud +12 vs. AC—30 damage
  Natural even hit: The bonded pops free and flies until the end of its turn as a free action. It must land at the end of its turn, or take falling damage.
  Natural 20: The target becomes weakened and vulnerable (save ends), and the bonded can fly until the end of its next turn.
  Miss: 15 damage.
  Special, once per battle: The bonded makes this attack as a free action on somebody else's turn.

Cut to ribbons +10 vs. AC (4 attacks)—20 damage
  Natural even hit or miss: The bonded must pop free and as a free action engage a different enemy it has not already attacked this turn; it then continues its *cut to ribbons* attack if it still has any of its four attacks left. If there are no other enemies that can be attacked, the *cut to ribbons* attack ends.
  Special, once per battle: The bonded makes this attack as a free action on somebody else's turn.

Nastier Special
Veiled: Until the bonded is hit, it has a +4 bonus to all defenses.

AC	19	
PD	16	**HP 140**
MD	16	

DARKER DRUID

Sharper sickle, tougher vine.

4th level spoiler [HUMANOID]
Initiative: +7

Sickle or scythe +9 vs. AC—14 damage
  Natural 16+: All druids gains a cumulative +1 to their *briarwood vines* attacks (up to a maximum of +4).

C: Briarwood vines +9 vs. AC (1d3 nearby or far away enemies in a group)—10 damage and the target is stuck until the end of their next turn.

AC	20	
PD	16	**HP 52**
MD	16	

MERCENARY WIZARD

The tattoos fade as the power grows.

5th level caster [HUMANOID]
Initiative: +7

Desperate dagger +9 vs. AC—12 damage
  Natural 11+: The mercenary may choose to do no damage and instead, as a free action, disengage and cast a spell at −2 to hit.

R: Lightning orb +10 vs. PD (1d3 nearby or far away enemies in a group)—12 lightning damage
  Natural 11+: Use one of the three triggered spells

Triggered Spells
[Special trigger] **Quick and dirty enchantment:** One nearby ally gains a +2 attack bonus to their next attack.
[Special trigger] **Time-twist:** One nearby ally may move as a free action.
[Special trigger] **Rapid hex:** One nearby enemy becomes stuck (easy save ends).

AC	20	
PD	15	**HP 76**
MD	19	

OGRE MAGE KNIGHT

If the naginata doesn't get you, the lightning will.

Large 6th level wrecker [GIANT]
Initiative: +13

Naginata +11 vs. AC—The effect depends on the roll.
  Natural even hit: 25 damage, and the ogre mage knight can use *lightning pulse* as a free action.
  Natural odd hit: 20 damage, and the ogre mage knight can use *voice of thunder* as a free action.
  Natural even miss: 10 damage, and the ogre mage knight can teleport to any nearby location it can see before using *magi's lightning chain* as a free action.
  Natural odd miss: The ogre mage knight can use *cone of cold* as a free action.

R: Magi's lightning chain +11 vs. PD—15 lightning damage, and each time this attack has a natural even attack roll, the ogre mage knight can target a different creature with the ability

C: Cone of cold +11 vs. PD (up to 3 nearby enemies in a group, also targets the ogre's allies engaged with the targets)—20 cold damage
  Miss: 10 cold damage.

C: Lightning pulse +11 vs. PD (one random nearby or far away enemy)—20 lightning damage
  Natural even hit: The target is weakened (save ends).

C: Voice of thunder +11 vs. PD (1d3 nearby enemies)—15 thunder damage

Resist exceptional attacks 16+: When a limited attack (not an at-will attack) targets this creature, the attacker must roll a natural 16+ on the attack roll or it only deals half damage.

Trollish regeneration 15: While an ogre mage is damaged, its uncanny flesh heals 15 hit points at the start of the ogre mage's turn. It can regenerate five times per battle. If it heals to its maximum hit points, that use of regeneration doesn't count against the five-use limit.

When the ogre mage is hit by an attack that deals fire or acid damage, it loses one use of its *trollish regeneration* and can't regenerate during its next turn.

Dropping an ogre mage to 0 hp doesn't kill it if it has any uses of *trollish regeneration* left.

Nastier Specials

Ki: Gain 1d4 ki at the start of each battle. Spend a point of ki as a free action, once per round, to change the ogre mage knight's natural attack result by one—a natural 1 could become a 2, a natural 19 could become a natural 20, and so on.

AC	22	
PD	19	**HP 160**
MD	17	

ELITE WIZARD

The best of the near-to-best.

Double-strength 7th level caster [HUMANOID]
Initiative: +13

R: Forked lightning +12 vs. PD—40 lightning damage
Natural even hit: As a free action; make another *forked lightning* attack against a new target nearby the target you just hit. If you keep rolling natural even hits, you can keep making attacks until you run out of enemies you have not already hit.
Natural odd hit: 20 ongoing thunder damage.

Enchanted Staff +12 vs. AC—50 force damage and the target pops free
Natural 16+ hit: Make a *psychic dagger cloud* attack as a free action.
[Special trigger] **C: Psychic dagger cloud +12 vs. MD (1d3 nearby enemies)**—25 ongoing psychic damage
Natural even miss: The target is teleported to a nearby spot the wizard chooses.

Flight: Yes, these wizards fly. Each one flies in a different way (spectral wings, discs of pure force, mental levitation), but fly they do.

AC	24	
PD	21	**HP 160**
MD	21	

APPENDIX C:
NEW MONSTER LIST

This list ignores monsters like the creatures in the *Corpse of Kroon* section (page 31) that make little sense outside their original adventure setting.

Level	Role	Name	Summary	Size	Page
0	mook	lesser homunculus	alchemical construct	normal	22
0	mook	villager	commoner who should be fleeing	normal	9
0	troop	homunculus	questionably sane minor construct servitor	normal	22
0	wrecker	wicker golem	strangely flammable construct	huge	59
1	mook	goblin wretch	better with a bow than most, and a bit tougher	normal	15
1	mook	pie mimic	pie with a bite	normal	18
1	spoiler	dark druid	scythe & vine	normal	218
1	spoiler	prize-winning pie mimic	definitely tastier than other pie mimics	normal	18
1	troop	hungry goblin grunt	will fight for pie	normal	19
1	wrecker	box golem	it's not treasure	triple-strength	73
2	archer	minor living spell	a magic missile with minor sentience	normal	57
2	caster	mercenary caster	slightly skilled magician	normal	218
2	mook	tough villager / Vakefort soldier	NPC just tough enough to die fighting	normal	9
2	spoiler	lesser envy demon	harshes the vibe	normal	202
2	spoiler	tiny lightning elemental	just a spark	normal	84
2	troop	goblin wolfrider	spears, fangs, and desperate speed	normal	15
2	troop	greater homunculus	slightly less-tiny construct servitor	normal	22
2	troop	white wolf	pack member, tougher than most wolves	normal	108
2	wrecker	half-dragon warrior	badass dragon warrior	double-strength	194
2	wrecker	primal golem	arcane mockery of the High Druid's creatures	large	59

Level	Role	Name	Summary	Size	Page
3	archer	spell-warrior	magical spirit	normal	84
3	blocker	Bykki Gritsour	burly dwarf and possible thief	double-strength	14
3	blocker	diamond pup	four-footed engineer construct	normal	78
3	blocker	knightmare	leftover spirit warrior of the Nightmare Prince	normal	23
3	caster	initiated death cultist	spellcaster who forces hard choices	normal	217
3	mook	orc spear grunt	barely trained warrior prone to reverting to savagery	normal	214
3	mook	puck	sharp-toothed fairy prankster	normal	24
3	troop	ghostly cultist	what's left of a demon cultist after centuries of magical imprisment	weakling	202
3	troop	mercenary warrior	spear and crossbow	normal	218
3	troop	reshaped clay golem	modified for Archmage security	large	209
3	wrecker	black dragon marauder	slightly more dangerous version of the core book dragon	normal	194
3	wrecker	tougher box golem	still not treasure	triple-strength	73
4	archer	magma elemental	fiery eruptor who keeps enemies on the move	normal	211
4	caster	imprismed despoiler	slightly improved by its ordeal	normal	203
4	caster	Rezlorkis	dragonic wizard	double-strength	13
4	leader	goblin packmaster	sword and worg tactics	normal	15
4	mook	orcling	fast-moving orc swarmers	normal	215
4	spoiler	best-in-show pie mimic	smells so good, bites so hard	normal	19
4	spoiler	darker druid	slows enemies with vines	normal	219
4	spoiler	hopping imp	too heavy for its wings	normal	203
4	spoiler	Lients Recharche	half-elf bard with a dangerous magic sword	double-strength	10
4	spoiler	lizardman hunter	javelin and net-armed entangler	normal	110
4	troop	Commander Hosard	the Vakefort's half-orc commander	double-strength	10
4	troop	featherback	dino pack-hunter	double-strength	98

Level	Role	Name	Summary	Size	Page
4	troop	Gwyddion	half-elf actor and spy	double-strength	13
4	troop	iron raptor	discarded military construct with unique powers	normal	216
4	troop	ophidian slave	enslaved speed bump	normal	169
4	wrecker	chaos demon	here half the time, elsewhere the other	normal	202
4	wrecker	larger primal golem	like the label says	large	59
4	wrecker	stone lion golem	defensive statuary	huge	209
5	archer	citizen of Rynth	normal ooozefolk	normal	145
5	archer	living spell	magical side-effect that serves various masters	normal	25
5	caster	Magaheim street-mage	dwarven/demonic spellcaster	normal	124
5	caster	mercenary wizard	orb and lightning	normal	219
5	leader	Elder Beck Rashman	human cleric and inspirational leader	double-strength	14
5	spoiler	Magaheim "demonic" citizen	somewhat demonic, very hexy, all Magaheim	normal	124
5	spoiler	mist dragon	mist obscures attacks at distance	large	112
5	spoiler	otherness pod	floating demonic chaos vector	normal	203
5	troop	clubtail	dinosaur with club for brains	huge	100
5	troop	druidic white dragon	spellcasting white dragon	large	109
5	troop	Magaheim dwarf warrior	axes: check; demonic heritage: double-check	normal	124
5	troop	oozefolk warrior	swingy basher	double-strength	145
5	troop	rhinosaur howdah	battle dino with orc riders	huge	215
5	wrecker	Irkma	half-orc bounty hunter and native of Redfield Valley	double-strength	11
5	wrecker	lizardman champion	ripping attacks make your disengage bonuses worthwhile	normal	110
6	archer	scaled soldier	cursed victims/troops of the serpent archons	normal	167
6	blocker	gray ooze	hungry predator	normal	30
6	blocker	Old Tusk lava demon	slow-moving lava-oozing human-consuming	normal	213

Level	Role	Name	Summary	Size	Page
6	blocker	quartz quadruped	weird crystal-breathing construct	large	151
6	caster	devoted blue sorcerer	more powerful version of caster from Bestiary	normal	198
6	mook	catastrophic wibble	errors have been made	normal	129
6	mook	flying monkey	comedy relief or horror-intensifier	normal	114
6	spoiler	drill-bird	monstrous construct tool kit	normal	151
6	spoiler	Magaheim tiefling	net-and-trident armed soldier	normal	125
6	troop	glassteel golem	hardly visible and hard to kill	normal	94
6	wrecker	griffon golem	artsy-fartsy stone-bronze killer	triple-strength	209
6	wrecker	oozefolk templar	holy champion	normal	146
7	archer	twisted magma elemental	demonically twisted eruptor	normal	213
7	blocker	dragonic scaleshield	leveled up and corrected version of blackshield from HM & LC	normal	198
7	caster	elite wizard	powerful and versatile spellcaster	double-strength	220
7	leader	oozefolk priest	powerful spellcaster in oozefolk warbands	normal	146
7	mook	glass spider	mechanomagical servitor	normal	152
7	mook	jade serpent	poisonous construct, but fragile	normal	164
7	spoiler	jade cobra	poisonous construct	normal	164
7	spoiler	thunder orc	magical Orcwell foreshadowing of a horrible future	huge	215
7	troop	fire demon	fiery claws that peel away resistance	normal	213
7	troop	steel raptor	powered-up military construct with surprising powers	normal	216
7	wrecker	crystal crab	well-programmed guardian servitor construct	normal	152
7	wrecker	dark champion	deadly in melee, deadly when dying	normal	217
7	wrecker	fangmaw tyrant	charismatic megapredator dinosaur	huge	100
7	wrecker	wilder chaos demon	unreliable ally and wicked enemy	normal	206
7	wrecker	lesser black pudding	flailing acid-drenched dungeon threat	normal	30

Level	Role	Name	Summary	Size	Page
7	wrecker	octave of terror	disturbing demonic sin-manipulator	normal	125
8	blocker	stone golem ghost rock	spirit-collecting stone golem	large	29
8	spoiler	machine acolyte	telekinetic engineer	normal	152
8	spoiler	serpent archon	demigod that is thankfully still not fully awakened	huge weakling	172
8	spoiler	volcano imp	flaming pest	weakling	213
8	troop	lava shark	lava shark	huge	180
8	troop	shard dragon	magically reassembled bones of hideously sacrificed people	huge	166
8	wrecker	greater frenzy demon	leveled-up from the core rulebook	normal	206
9	caster	imprismed despoiler mage	angrier than the core rulebook version	normal	206
9	caster	oozefolk battle wizard	trained by people the Archmage trained	normal	176
9	mook	Magaheim horde demon	chains and spikiness	normal	125
9	mook	skeletal shards	splinters of sacrificial victims that haven't entirely powered-up	normal	166
9	wrecker	rainbow pudding	like a black pudding, but colorful	large	178
10	leader	oozefolk high priest	spiky magician	normal	178
10	spoiler	thunder stomper	bronto	huge	100
11	blocker	oozefolk champion	she puts the ooze into oozefolk	normal	178
11	mook	oozefolk fanatic	surprisingly dangerous minion	normal	178
11	wrecker	imperial golem	four-armed and overly skilled construct	huge	175
12	wrecker	golem lieutenant	even worse than an imperial guardian	triple-strength	181